PIECES OF A SPIRAL

Volume 8

By Kaimu Tachibana

CONTENTS

CAST OF CHARACTERS

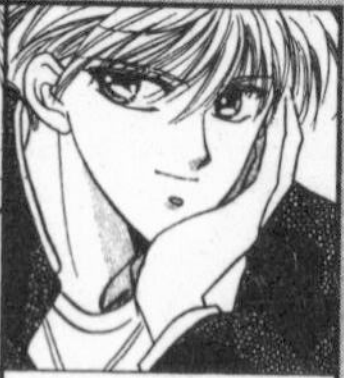

KAZUKI OKINO
SAKUYA'S REINCARNATION. INHERITED BISHU'S APPEARANCE AND VOICE.

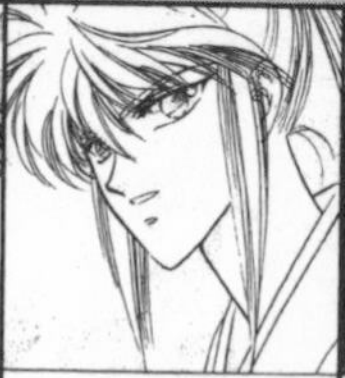

BISHU
BORN OF A DEMON FATHER AND HUMAN MOTHER, POSSESSES TREMENDOUS POWER.

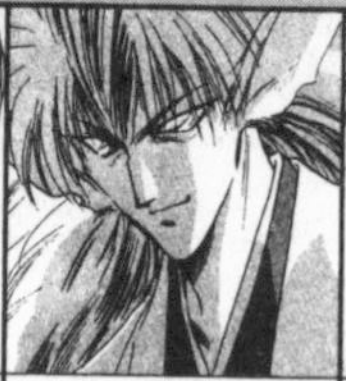

GARAI
BISHU'S FATHER AND LORD OF ALL DEMONS. HAS ESCAPED BONDAGE AND IS FREE.

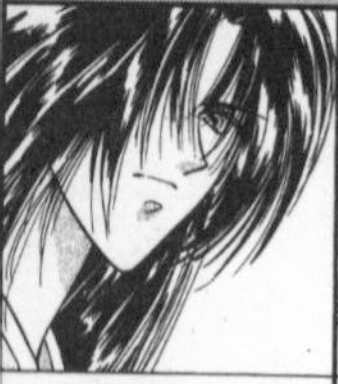

RYOKEI KONO
ONMYOJI. GARAI MURDERED HIS ENTIRE FAMILY. PASSIONATELY HATES DEMONS.

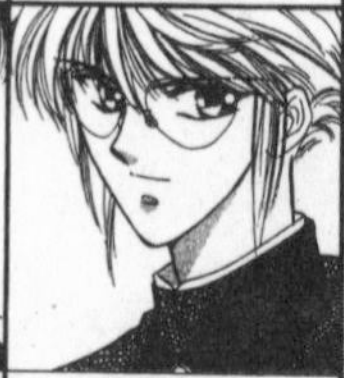

MAKOTO IMAIZUMI
WAKYO'S REINCARNATION. INHERITED BISHU'S APPEARANCE AND VIOLET EYES.

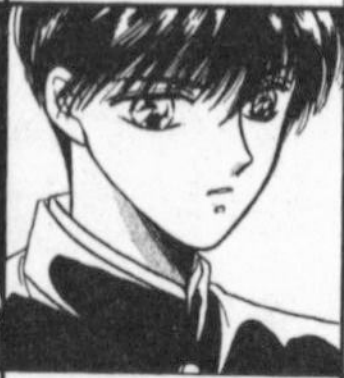

MASAYUKI KAGA
KAZUKI'S BEST FRIEND. BISHU'S REINCARNATION BUT WITH HIS OWN IDENTITY.

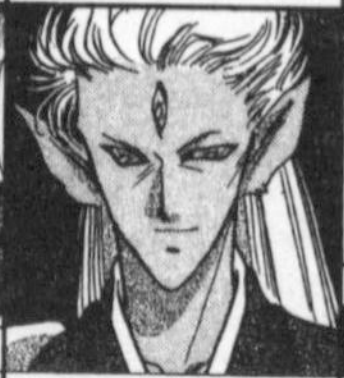

SAJO
LORD OF THE THREE-EYE FACTION. SUBMITS TO GARAI.

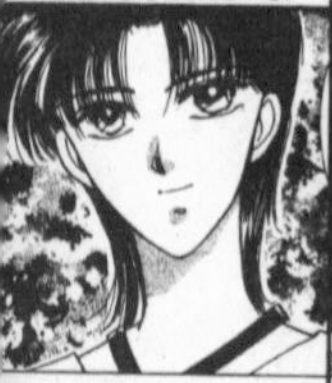

MAYUKO
STUDENT RETURNED FROM AMERICA. RYOKEI'S REINCARNATION.

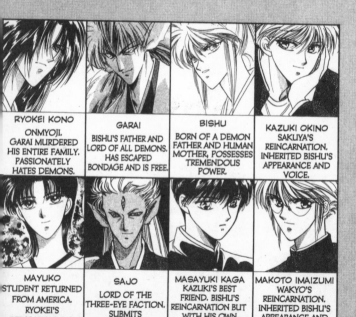

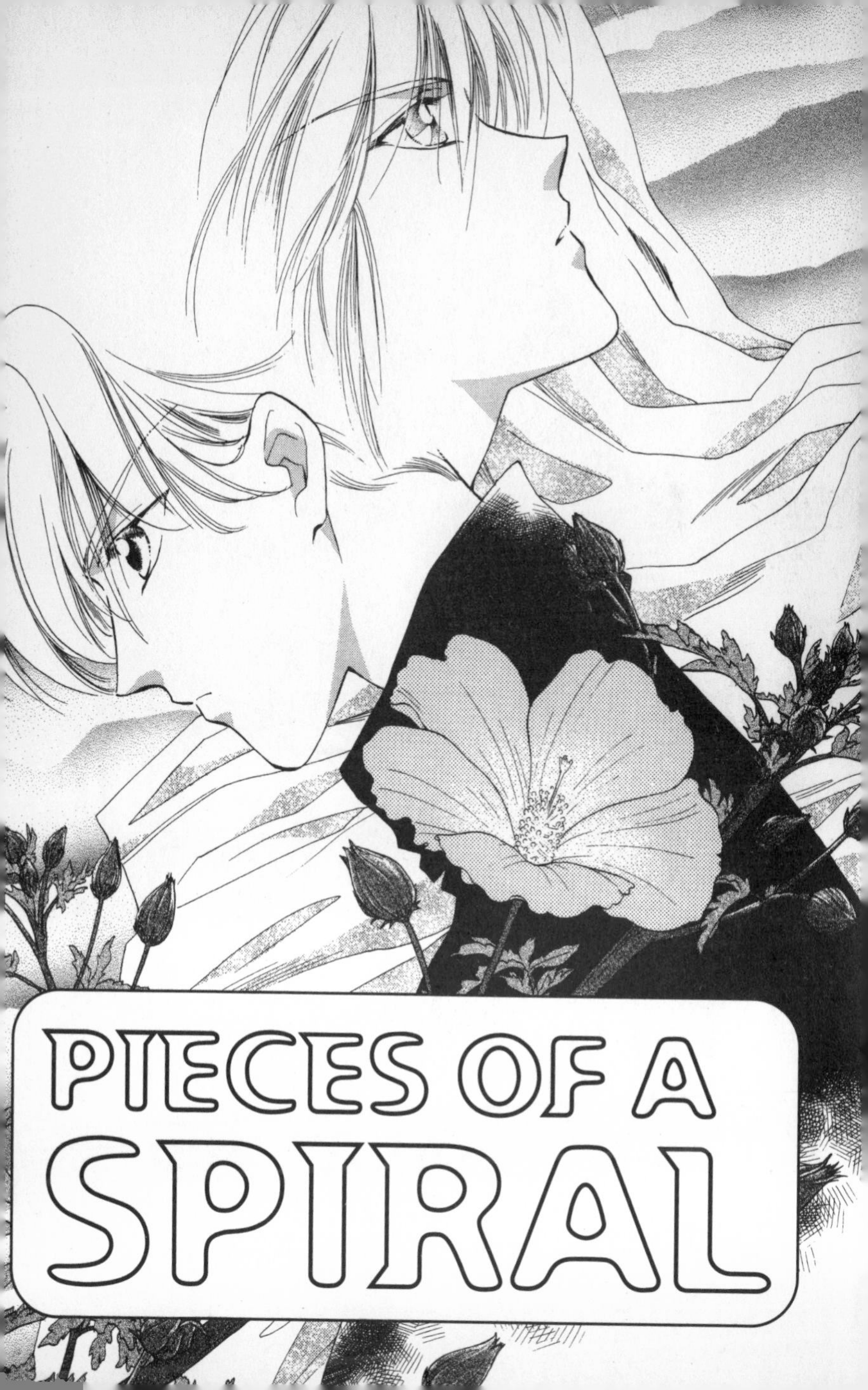
PIECES OF A
SPIRAL

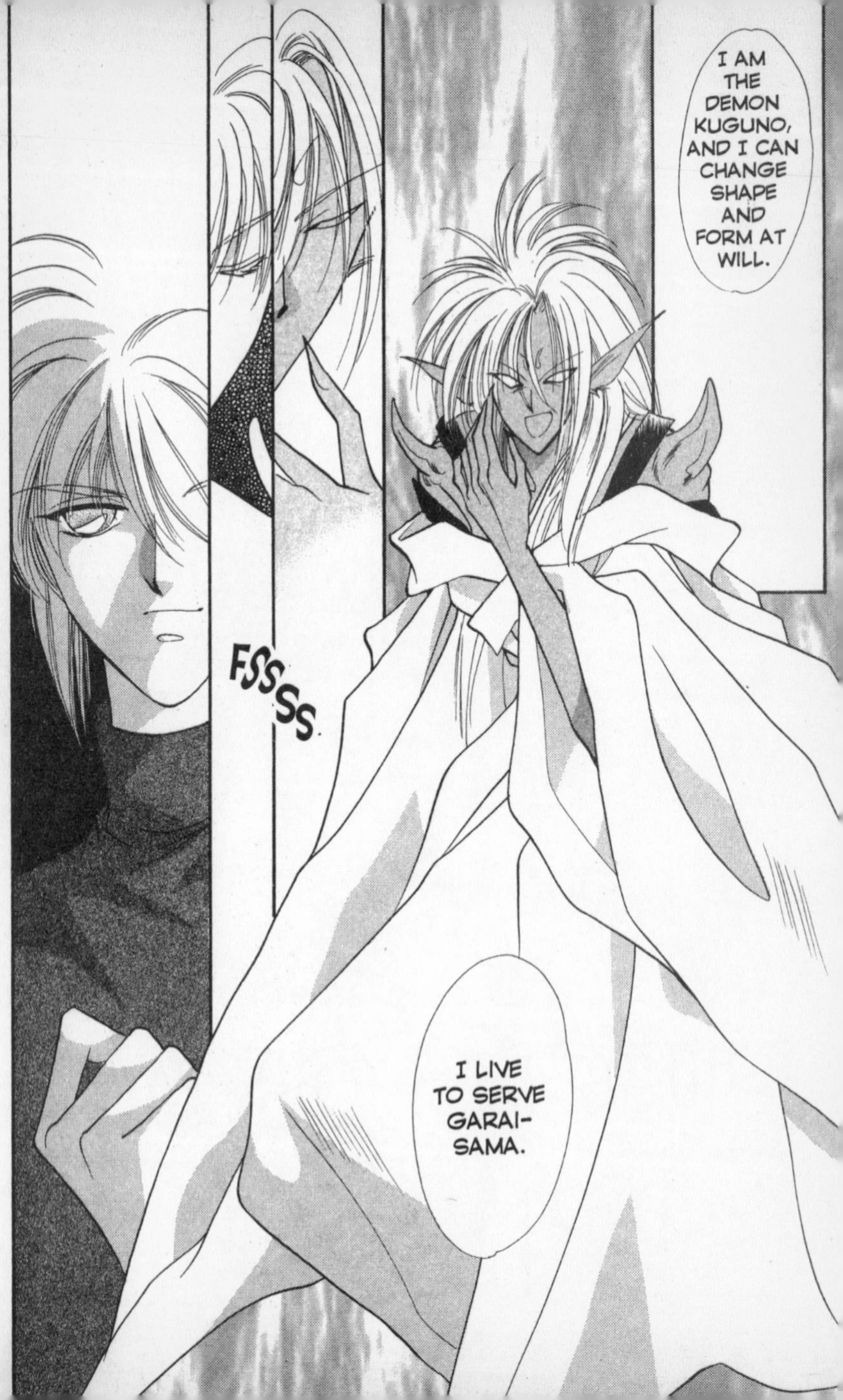
I AM THE DEMON KUGUNO, AND I CAN CHANGE SHAPE AND FORM AT WILL.
FSSSS
I LIVE TO SERVE GARAI-SAMA.

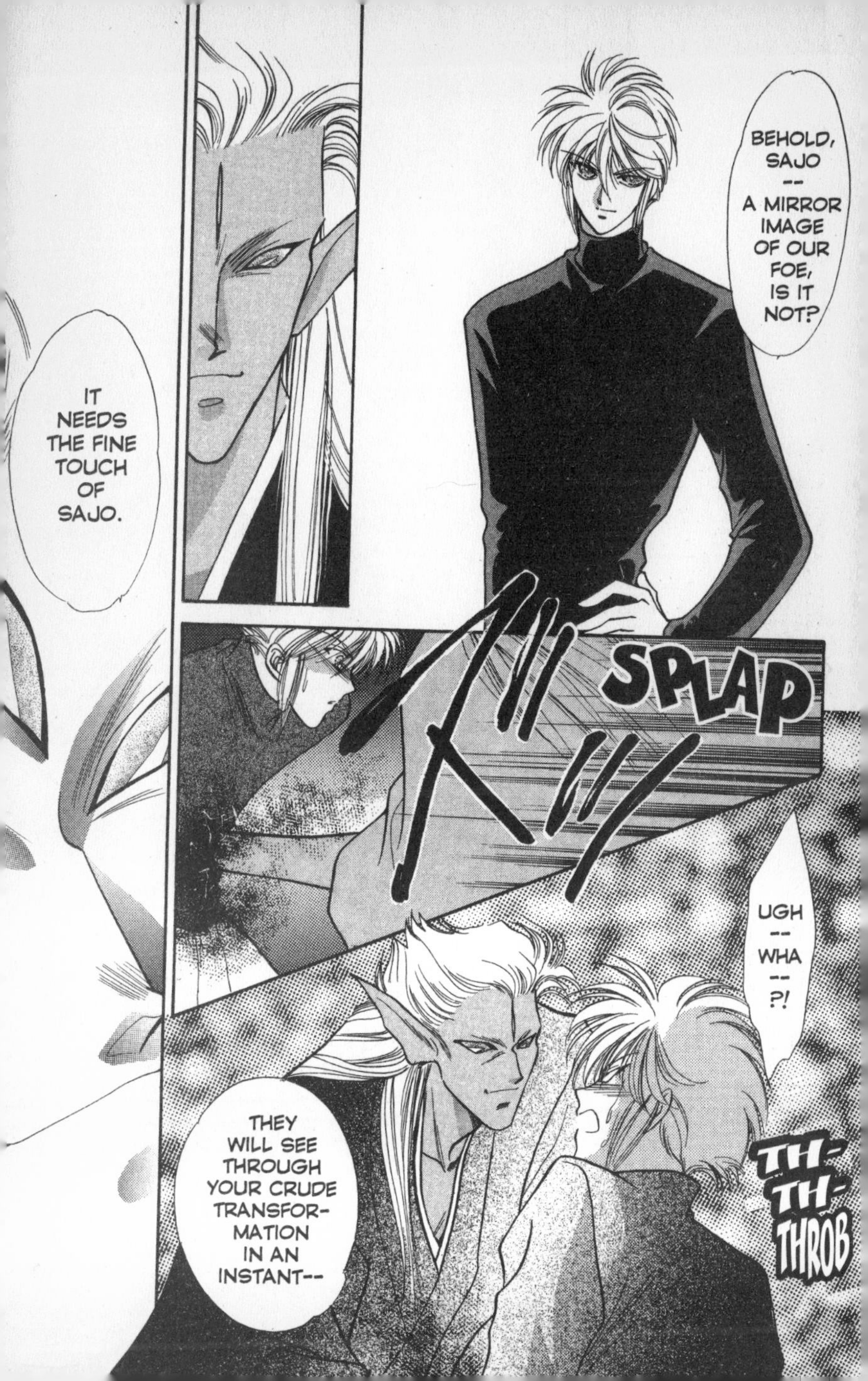
BEHOLD, SAJO -- A MIRROR IMAGE OF OUR FOE, IS IT NOT?
IT NEEDS THE FINE TOUCH OF SAJO.
SPLAP
UGH -- WHA --?!
THEY WILL SEE THROUGH YOUR CRUDE TRANSFOR-MATION IN AN INSTANT--
TH-TH-THROB

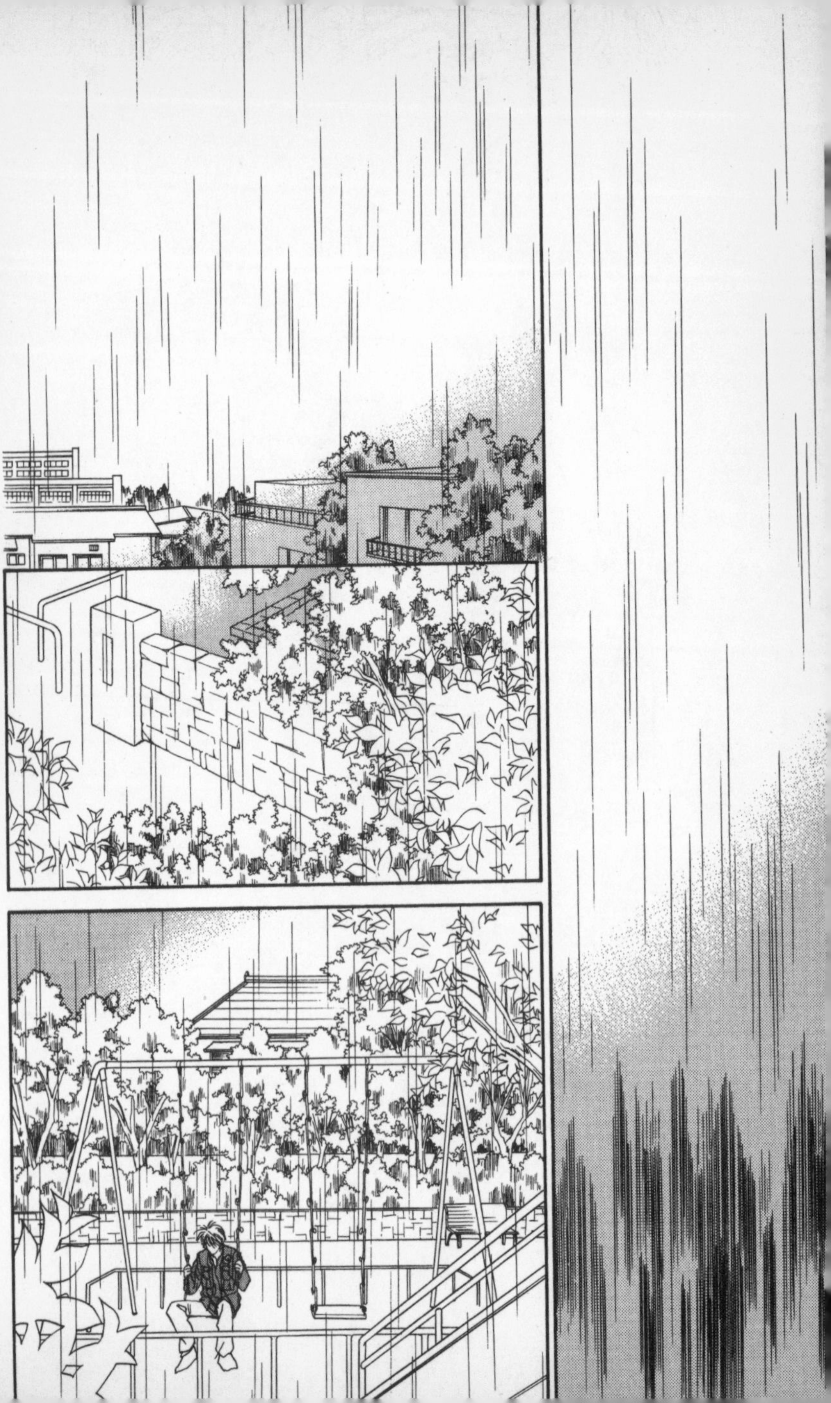

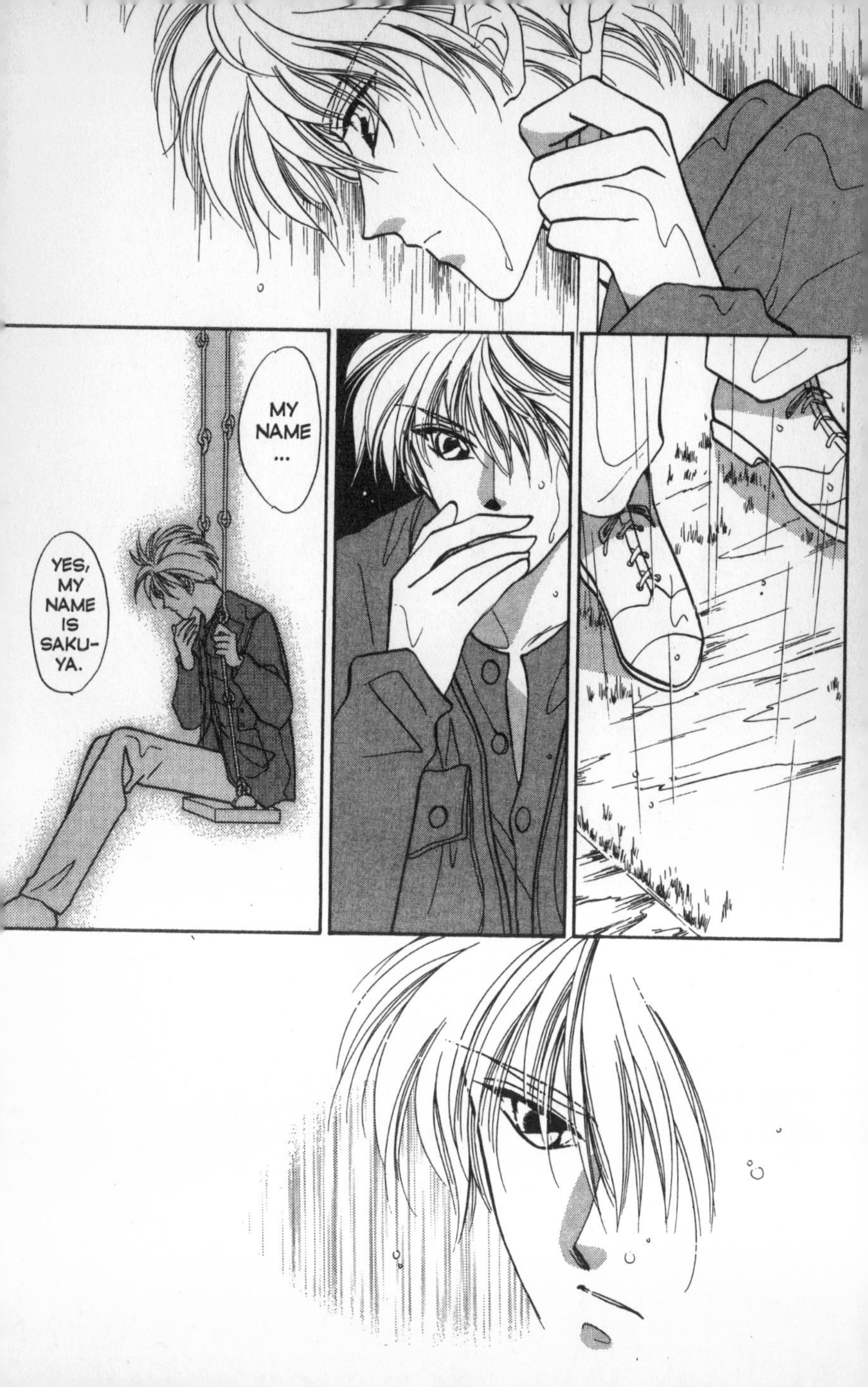
MY NAME ...
YES, MY NAME IS SAKU-YA.

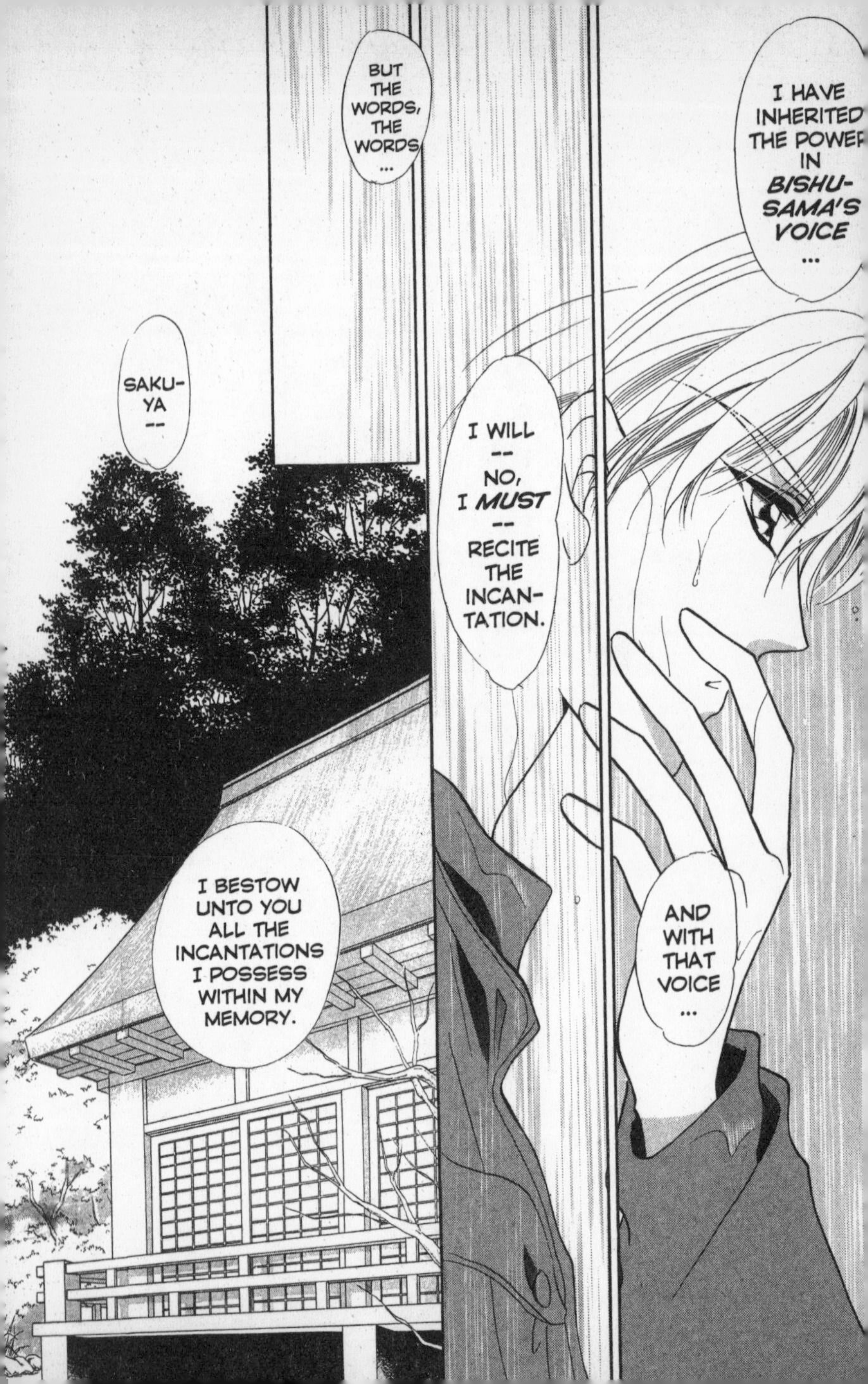
I HAVE INHERITED THE POWER IN *BISHU-SAMA'S* VOICE ...
AND WITH THAT VOICE ...
I WILL -- NO, I *MUST* -- RECITE THE INCANTATION.
BUT THE WORDS, THE WORDS ...
SAKU-YA --
I BESTOW UNTO YOU ALL THE INCANTATIONS I POSSESS WITHIN MY MEMORY.

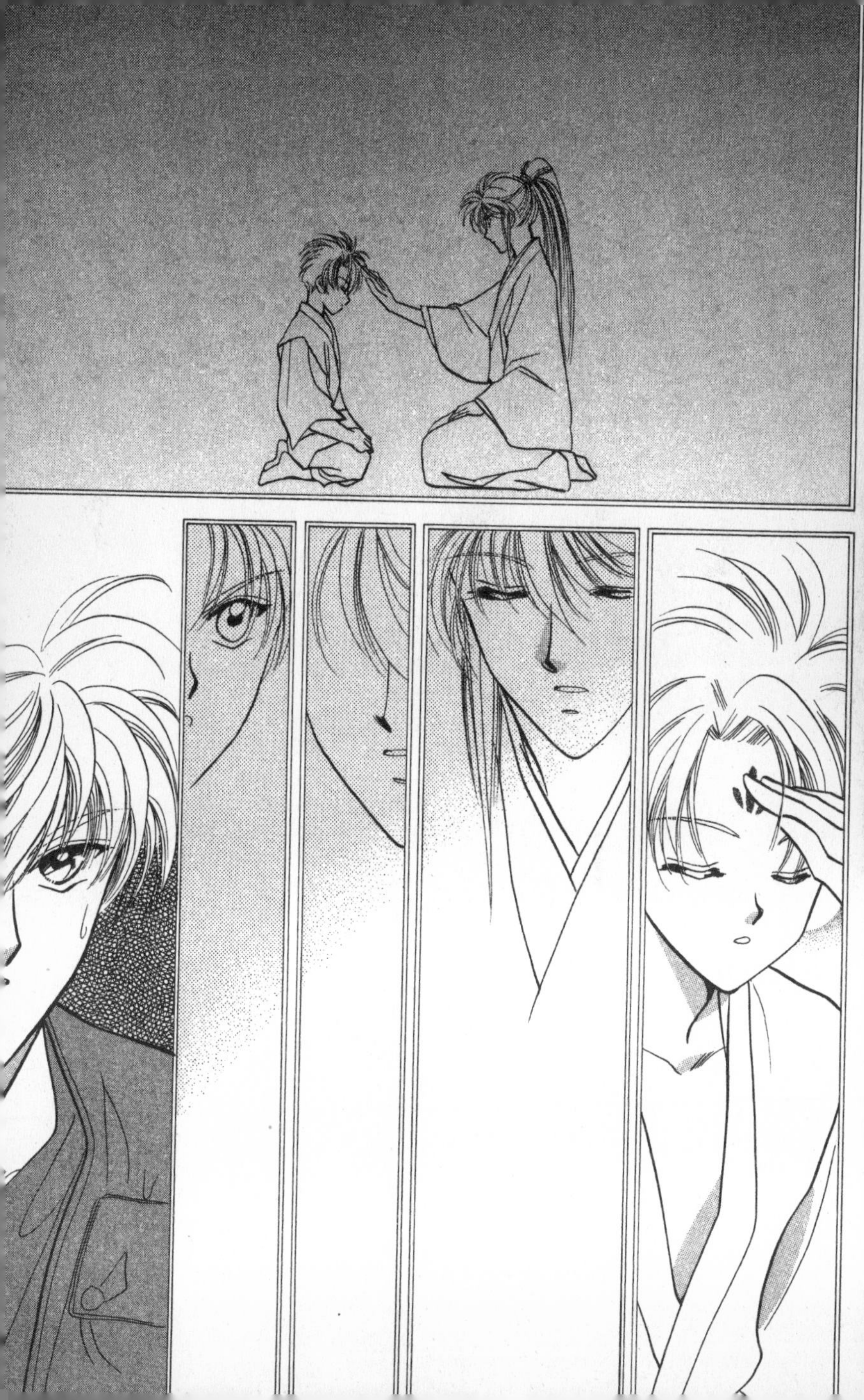

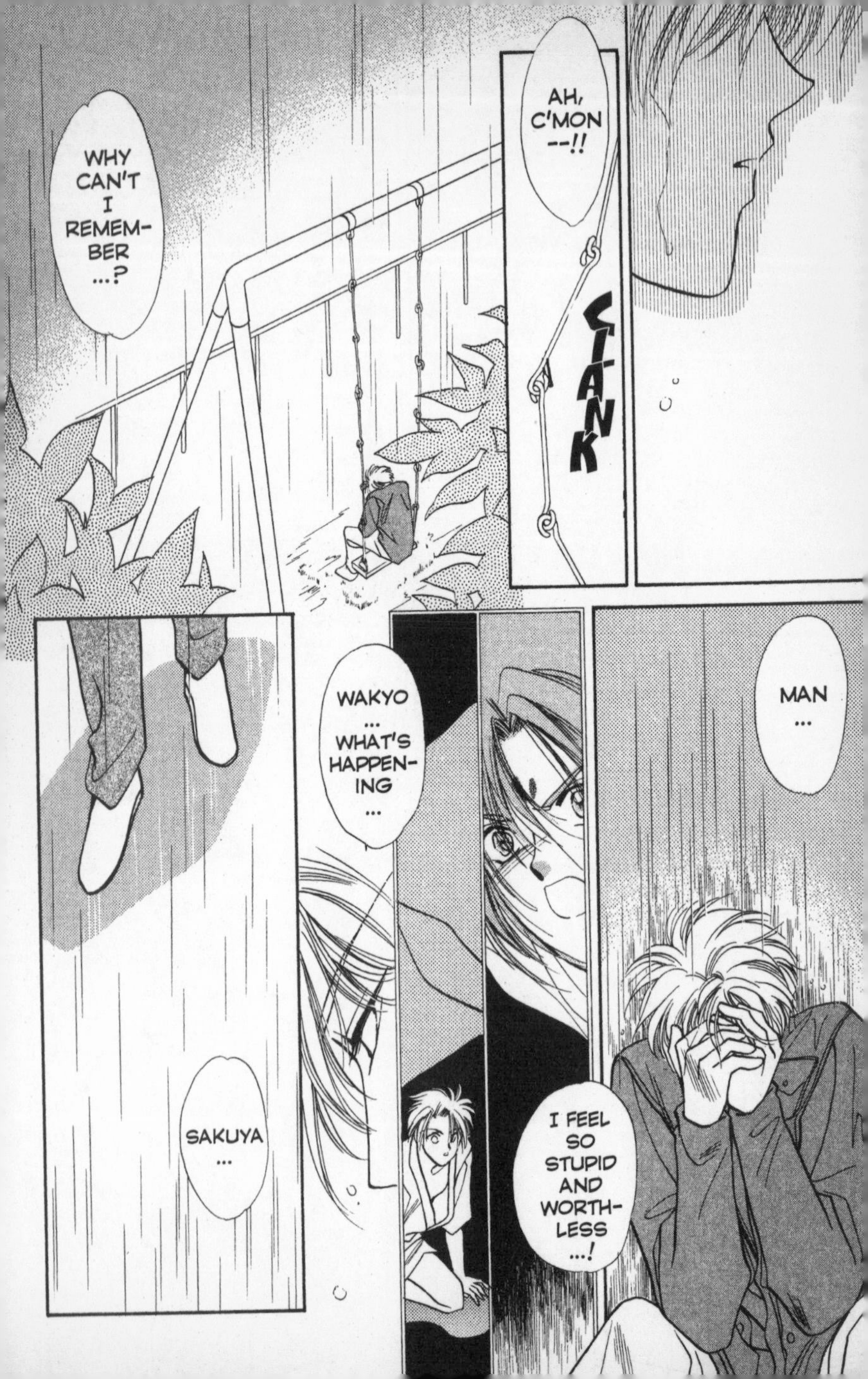
AH, C'MON --!!
CLANK
WHY CAN'T I REMEMBER ...?
MAN ...
I FEEL SO STUPID AND WORTHLESS ...!
WAKYO ... WHAT'S HAPPENING ...
SAKUYA ...

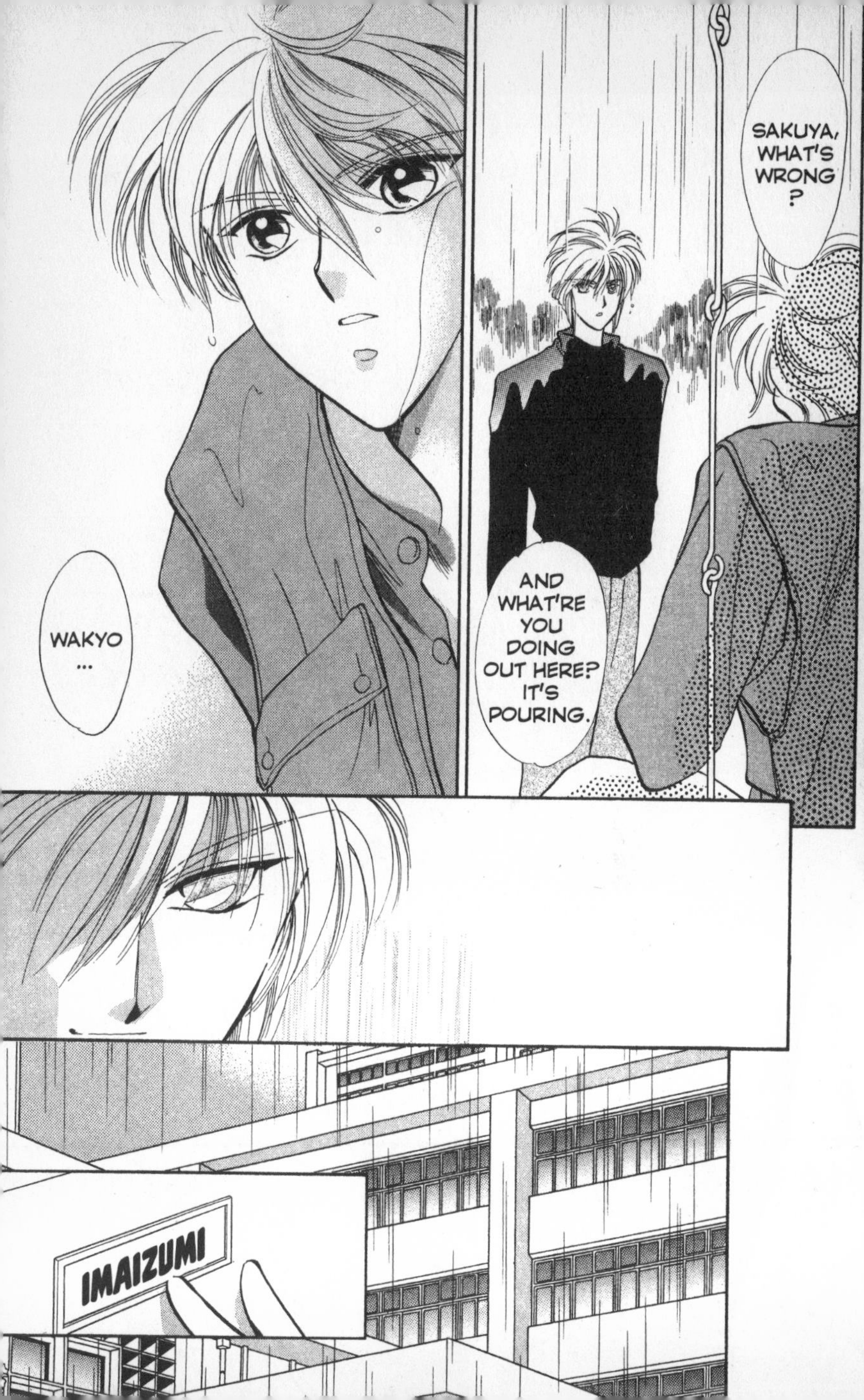
SAKUYA, WHAT'S WRONG?
AND WHAT'RE YOU DOING OUT HERE? IT'S POURING.
WAKYO...
IMAIZUMI

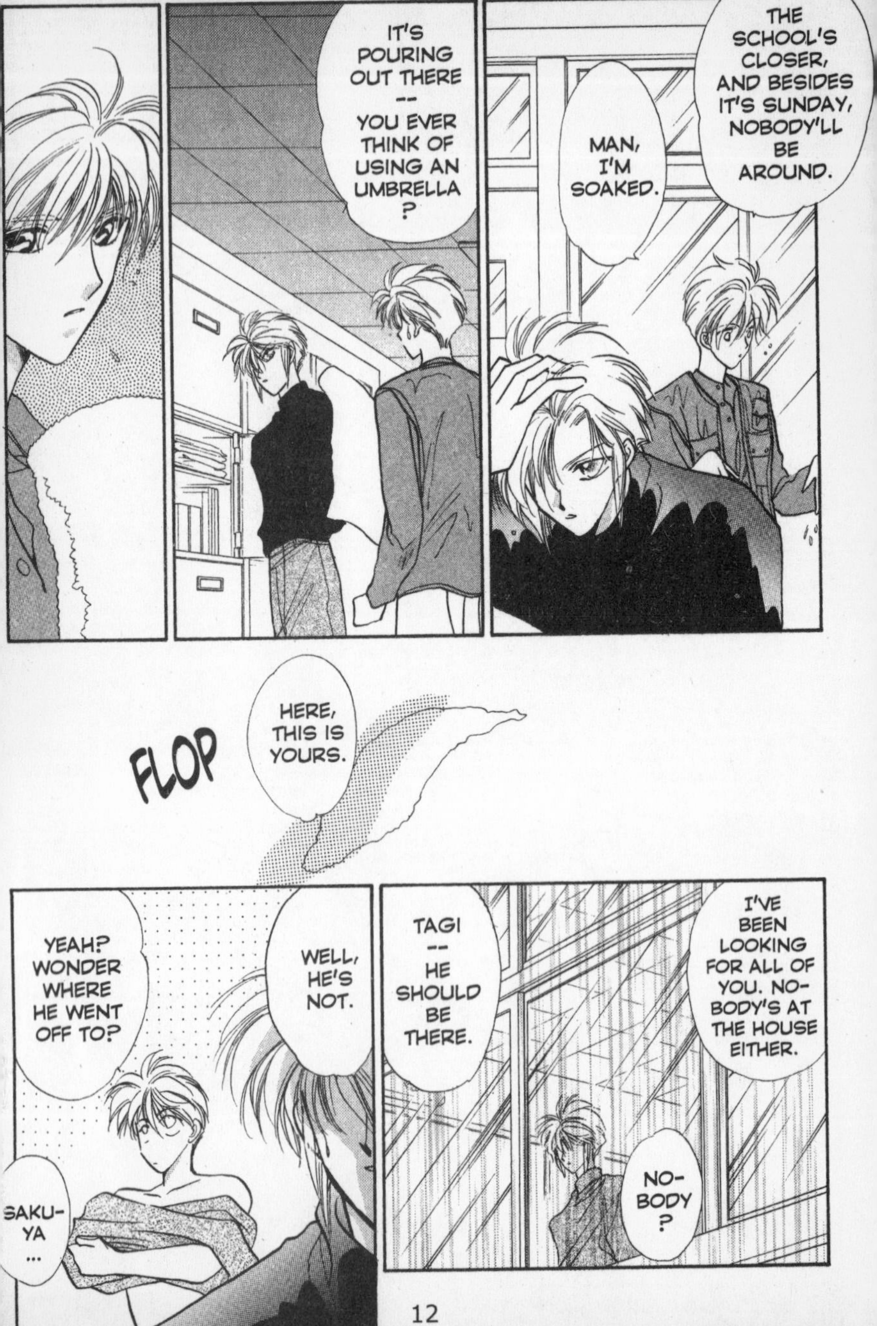
THE SCHOOL'S CLOSER, AND BESIDES IT'S SUNDAY, NOBODY'LL BE AROUND.
MAN, I'M SOAKED.
IT'S POURING OUT THERE -- YOU EVER THINK OF USING AN UMBRELLA?
HERE, THIS IS YOURS.
FLOP
I'VE BEEN LOOKING FOR ALL OF YOU. NO-BODY'S AT THE HOUSE EITHER.
TAGI -- HE SHOULD BE THERE.
NO-BODY?
WELL, HE'S NOT.
YEAH? WONDER WHERE HE WENT OFF TO?
SAKU-YA ...

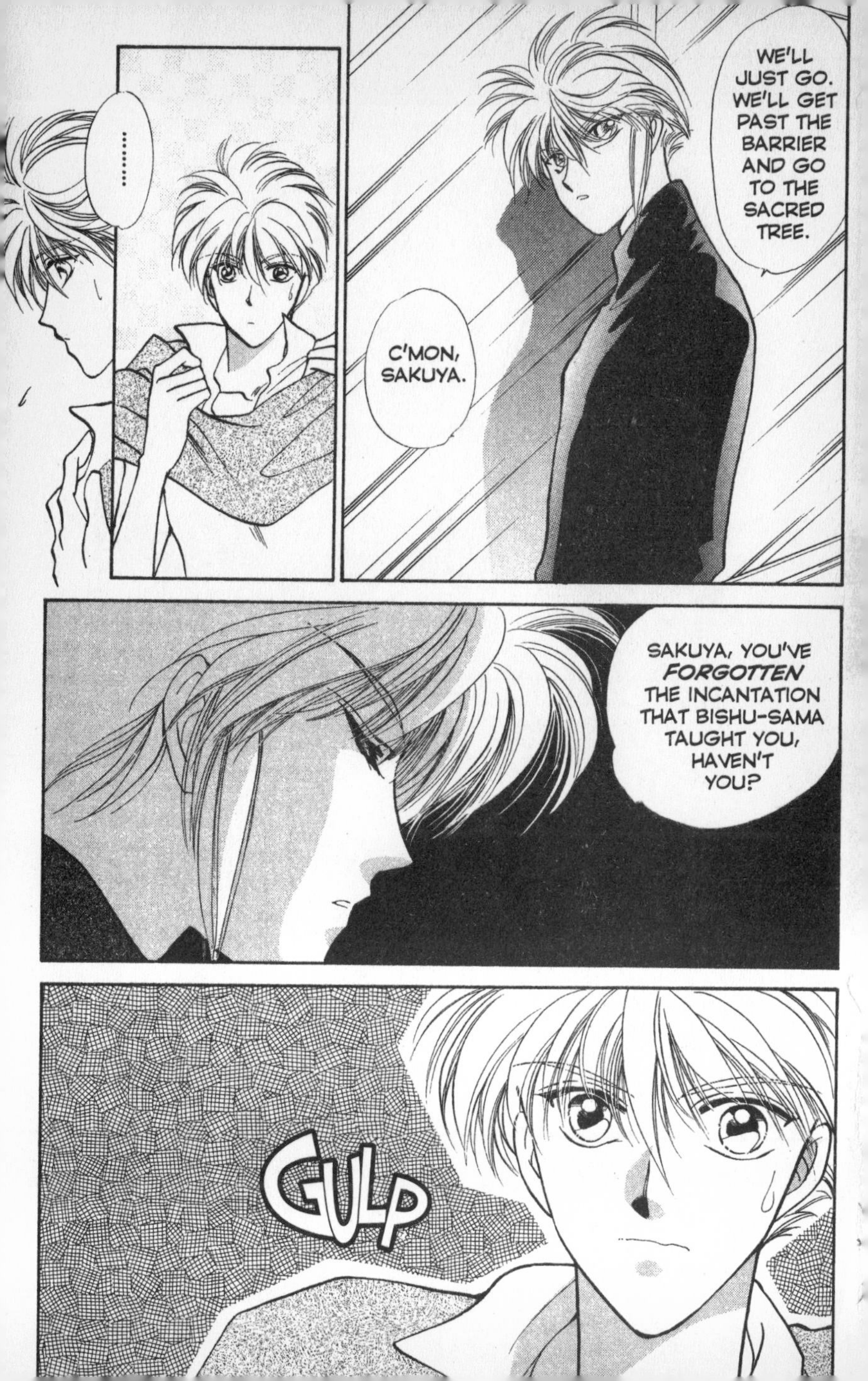
WE'LL JUST GO. WE'LL GET PAST THE BARRIER AND GO TO THE SACRED TREE.
C'MON, SAKUYA.
....
SAKUYA, YOU'VE *FORGOTTEN* THE INCANTATION THAT BISHU-SAMA TAUGHT YOU, HAVEN'T YOU?
GULP

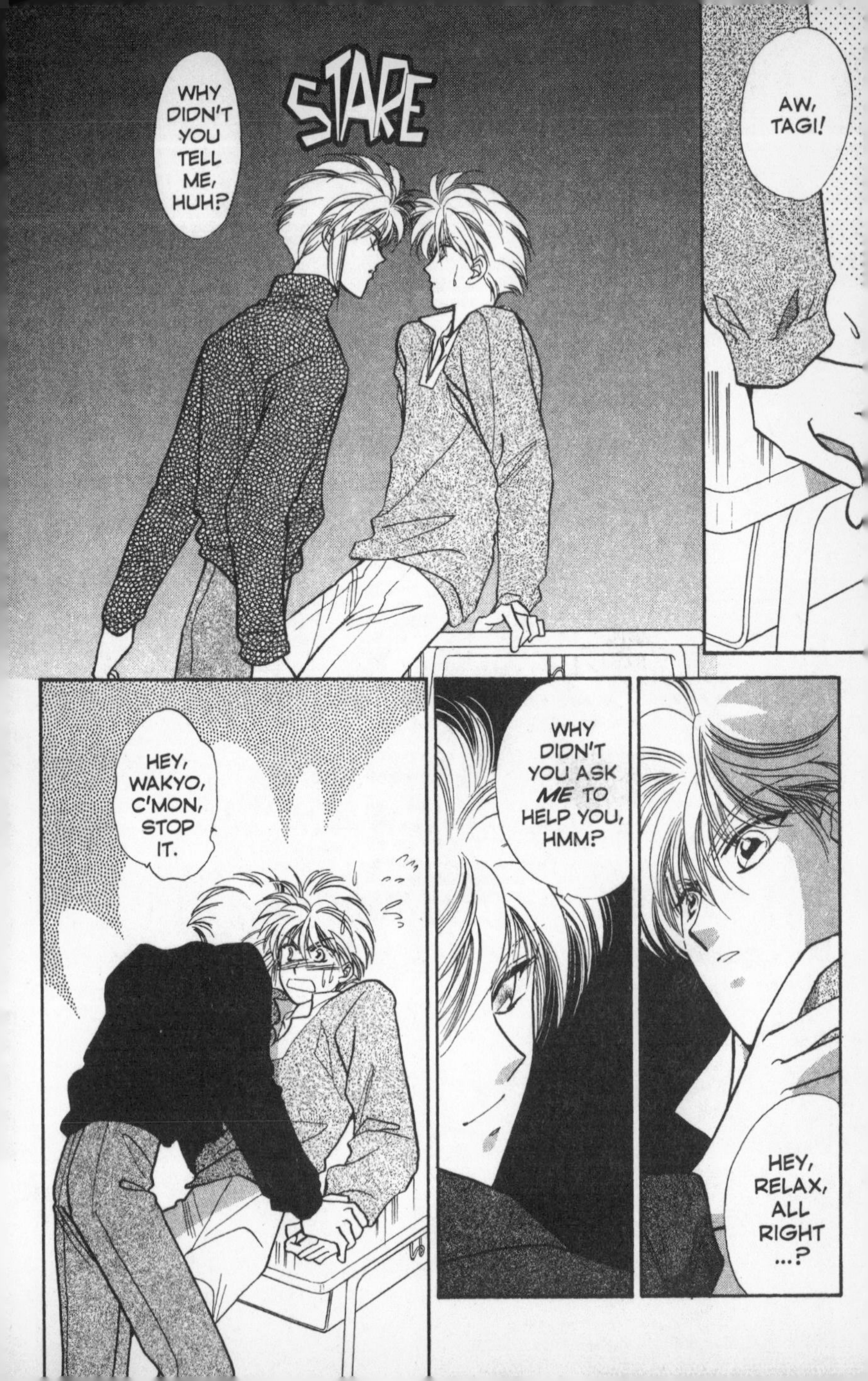
AW, TAGI!
STARE
WHY DIDN'T YOU TELL ME, HUH?
HEY, RELAX, ALL RIGHT ...?
WHY DIDN'T YOU ASK *ME* TO HELP YOU, HMM?
HEY, WAKYO, C'MON, STOP IT.

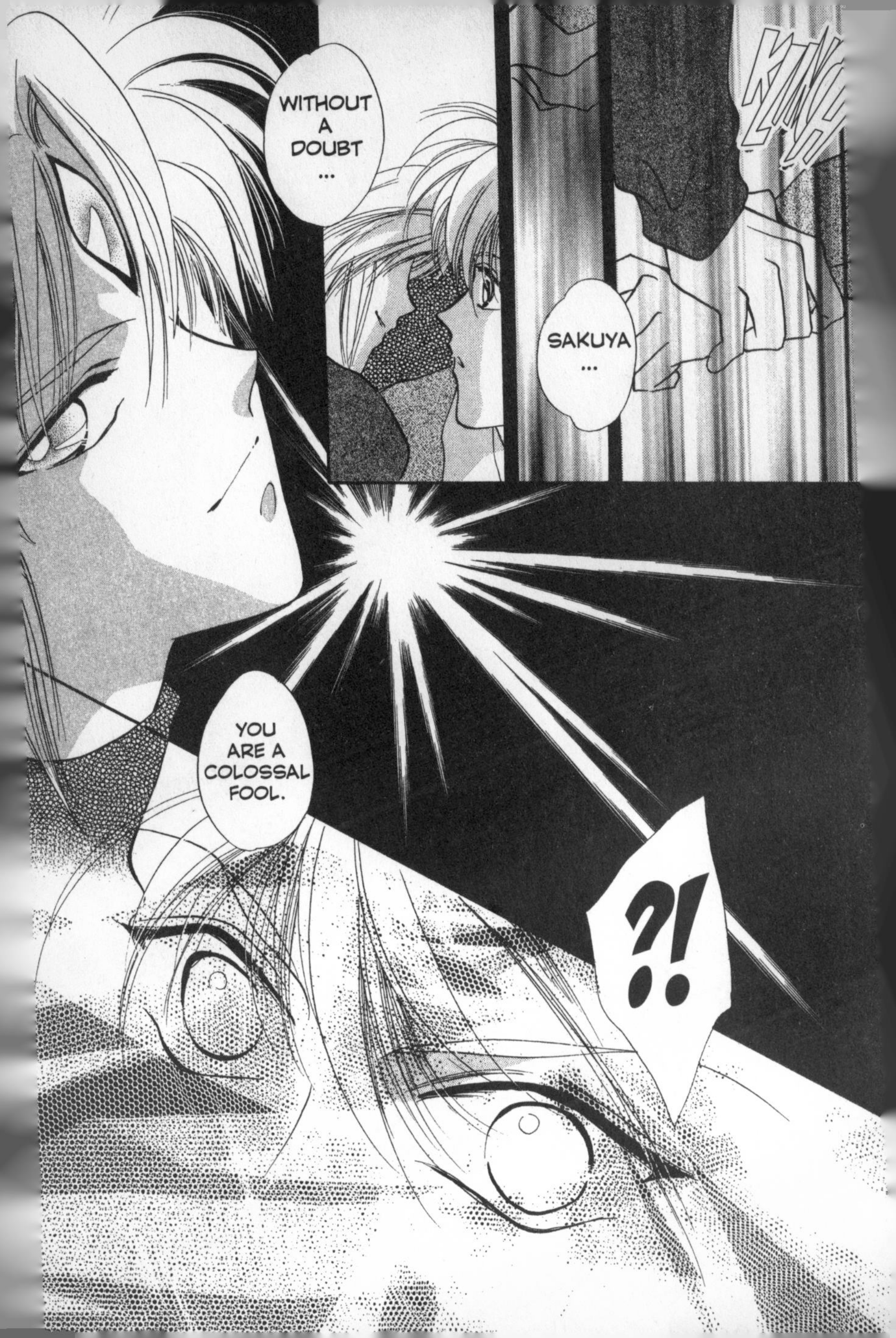
SAKUYA ...
WITHOUT A DOUBT ...
YOU ARE A COLOSSAL FOOL.
?!

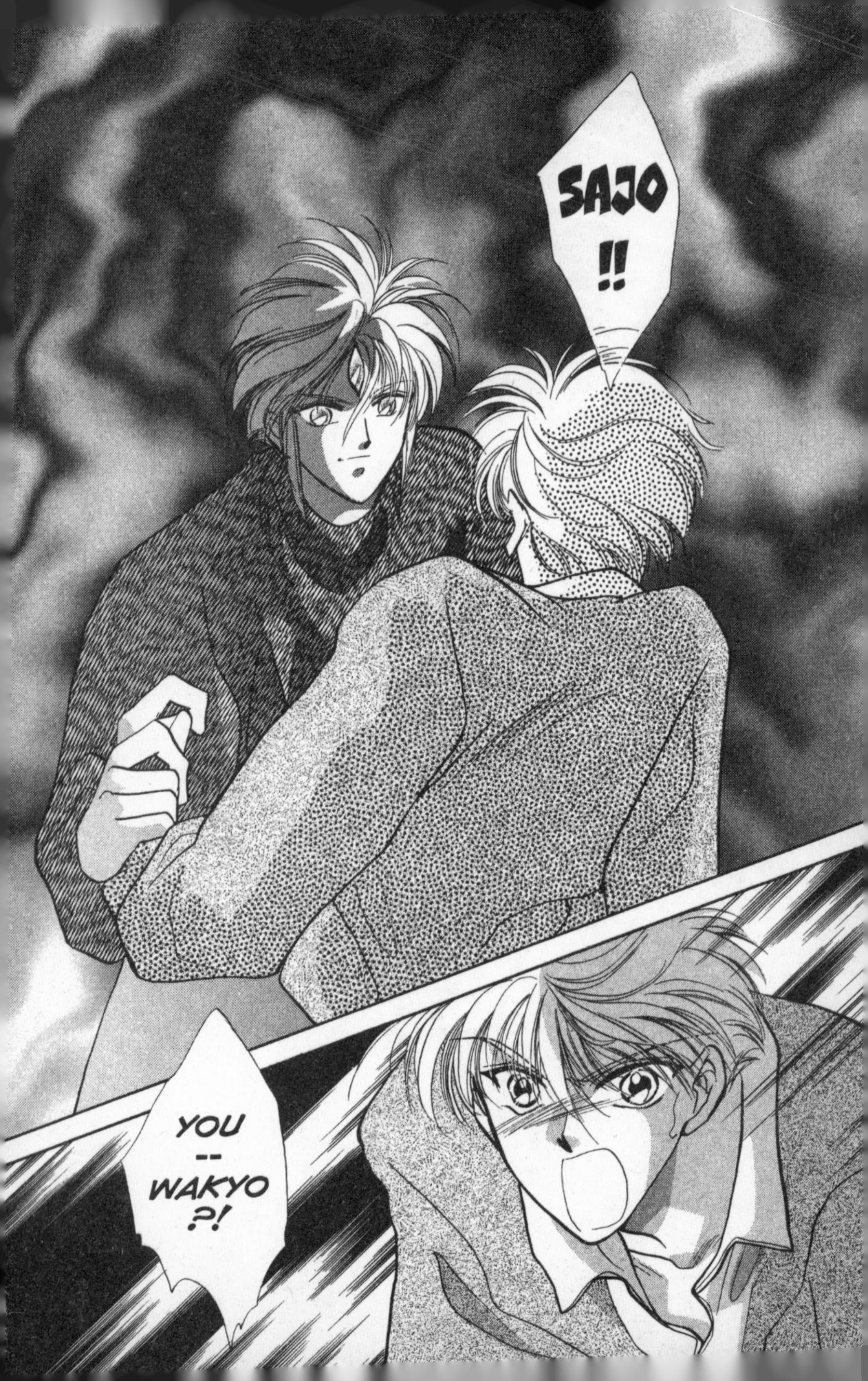
SAJO !!
YOU -- WAKYO ?!

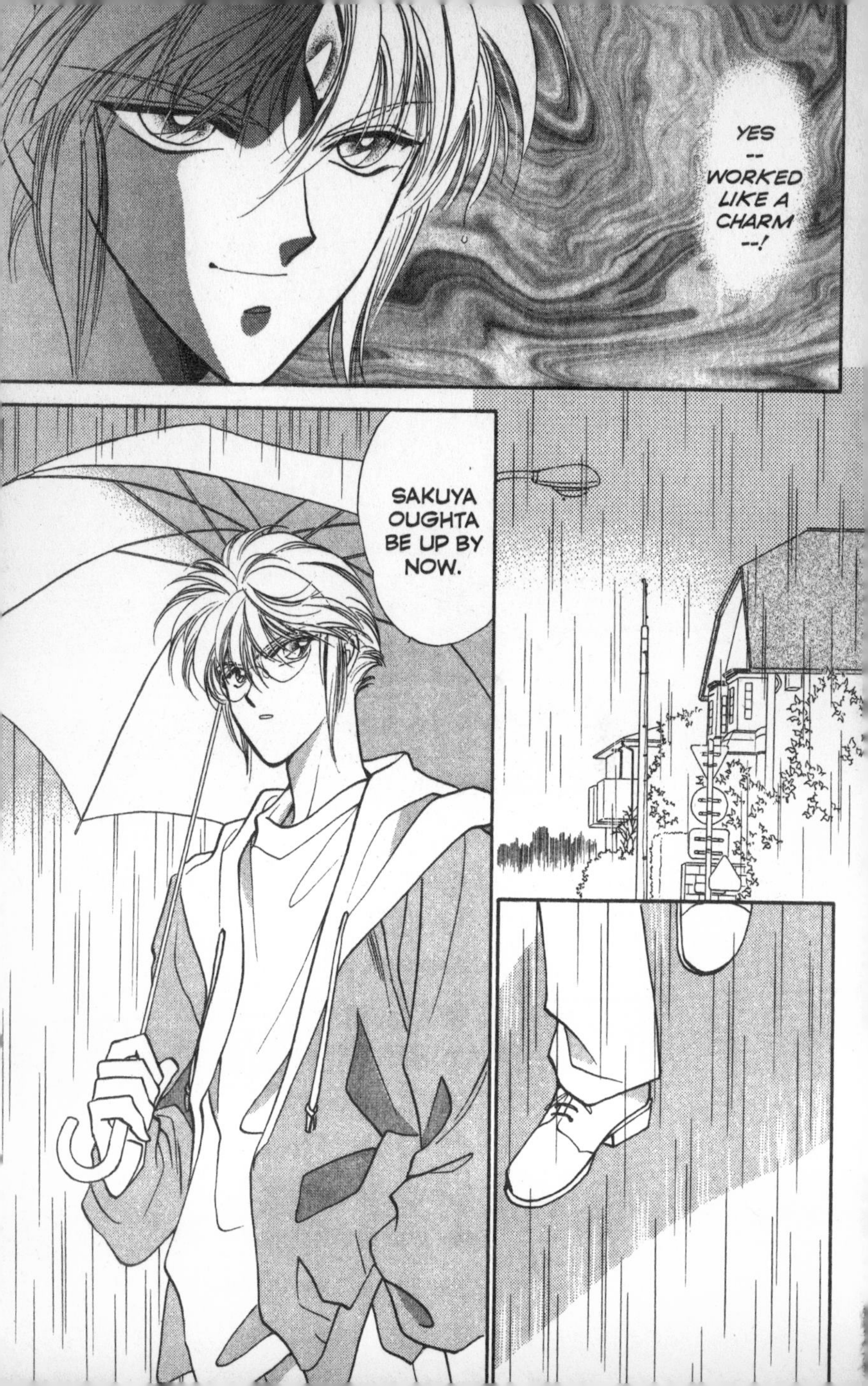
YES -- WORKED LIKE A CHARM --!
SAKUYA OUGHTA BE UP BY NOW.

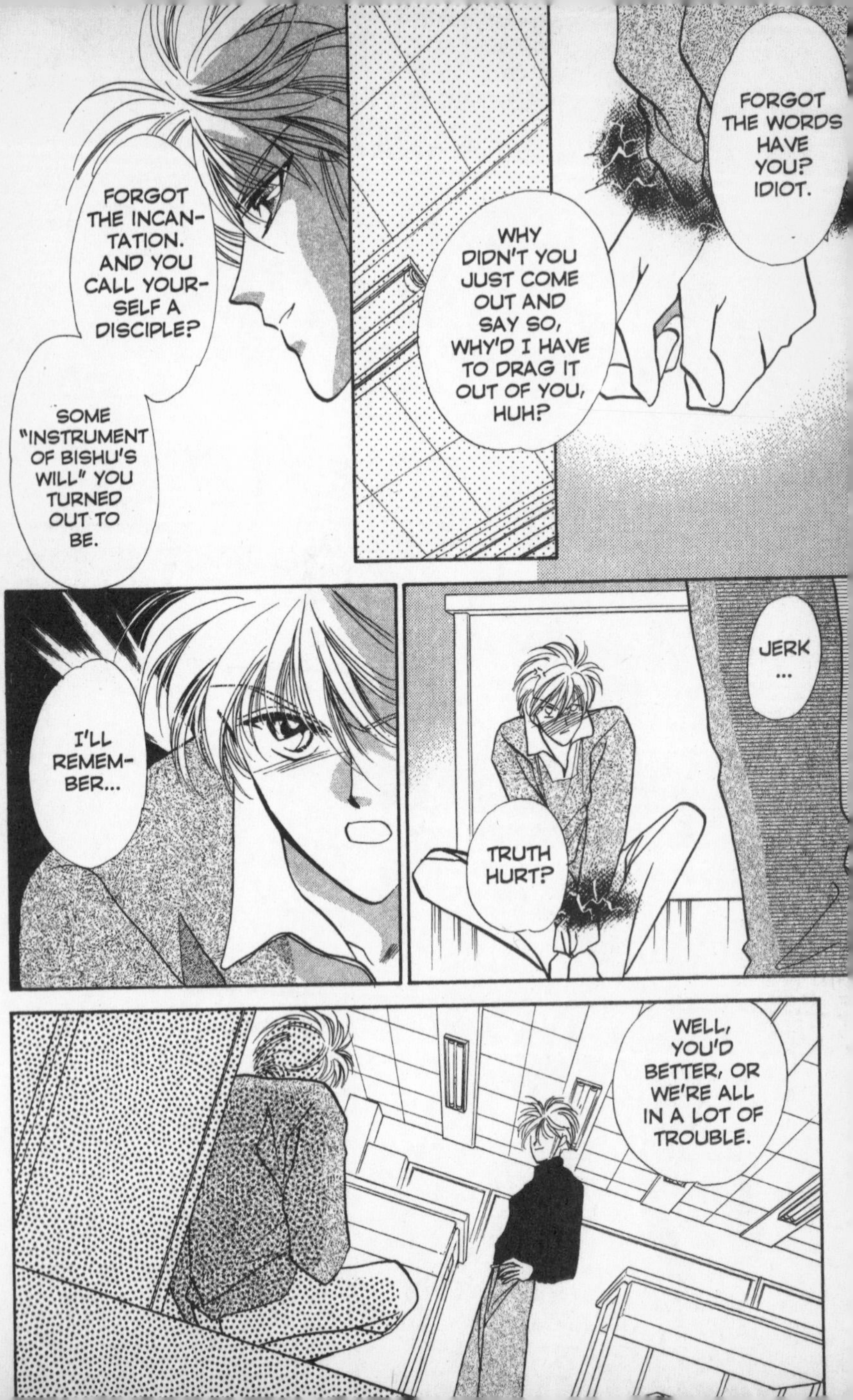
FORGOT THE WORDS HAVE YOU? IDIOT.
WHY DIDN'T YOU JUST COME OUT AND SAY SO, WHY'D I HAVE TO DRAG IT OUT OF YOU, HUH?
FORGOT THE INCAN-TATION. AND YOU CALL YOUR-SELF A DISCIPLE?
SOME "INSTRUMENT OF BISHU'S WILL" YOU TURNED OUT TO BE.
JERK ...
TRUTH HURT?
I'LL REMEM-BER...
WELL, YOU'D BETTER, OR WE'RE ALL IN A LOT OF TROUBLE.

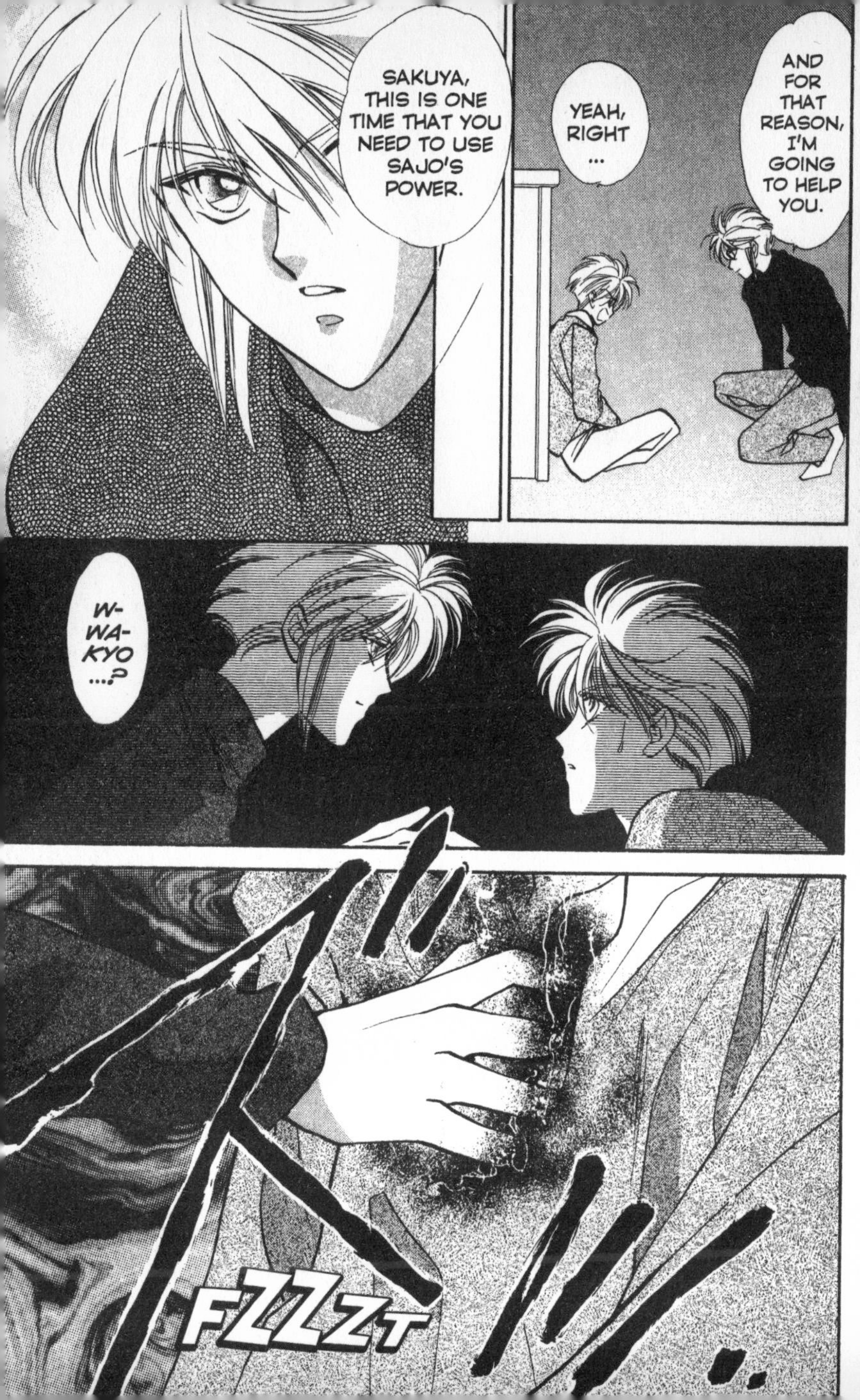
AND FOR THAT REASON, I'M GOING TO HELP YOU.
YEAH, RIGHT ...
SAKUYA, THIS IS ONE TIME THAT YOU NEED TO USE SAJO'S POWER.
W-WAKYO ...?
FZZZT

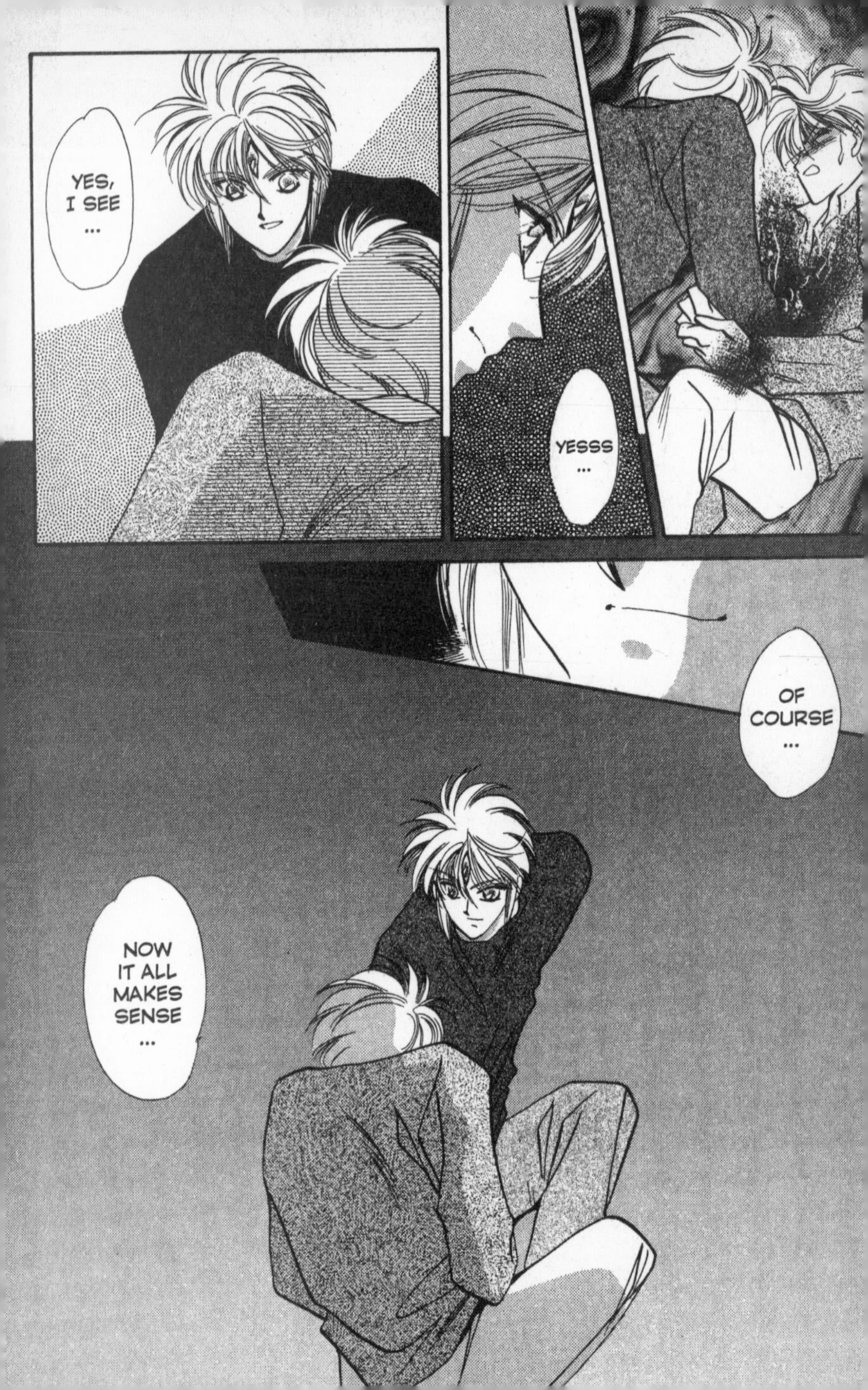
YESSS ...
YES, I SEE ...
OF COURSE ...
NOW IT ALL MAKES SENSE ...

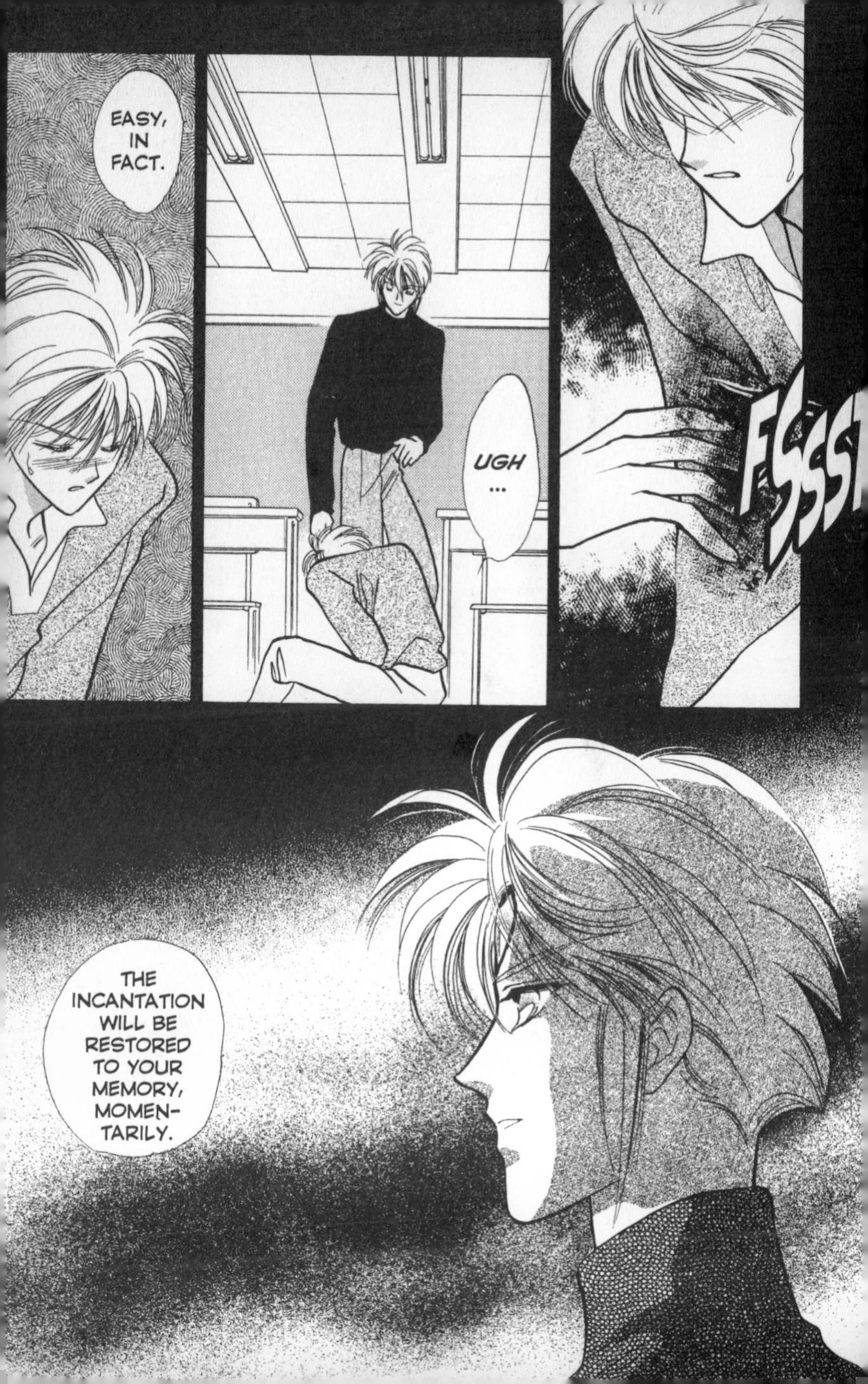
FSSST
UGH ...
EASY, IN FACT.
THE INCANTATION WILL BE RESTORED TO YOUR MEMORY, MOMENTARILY.

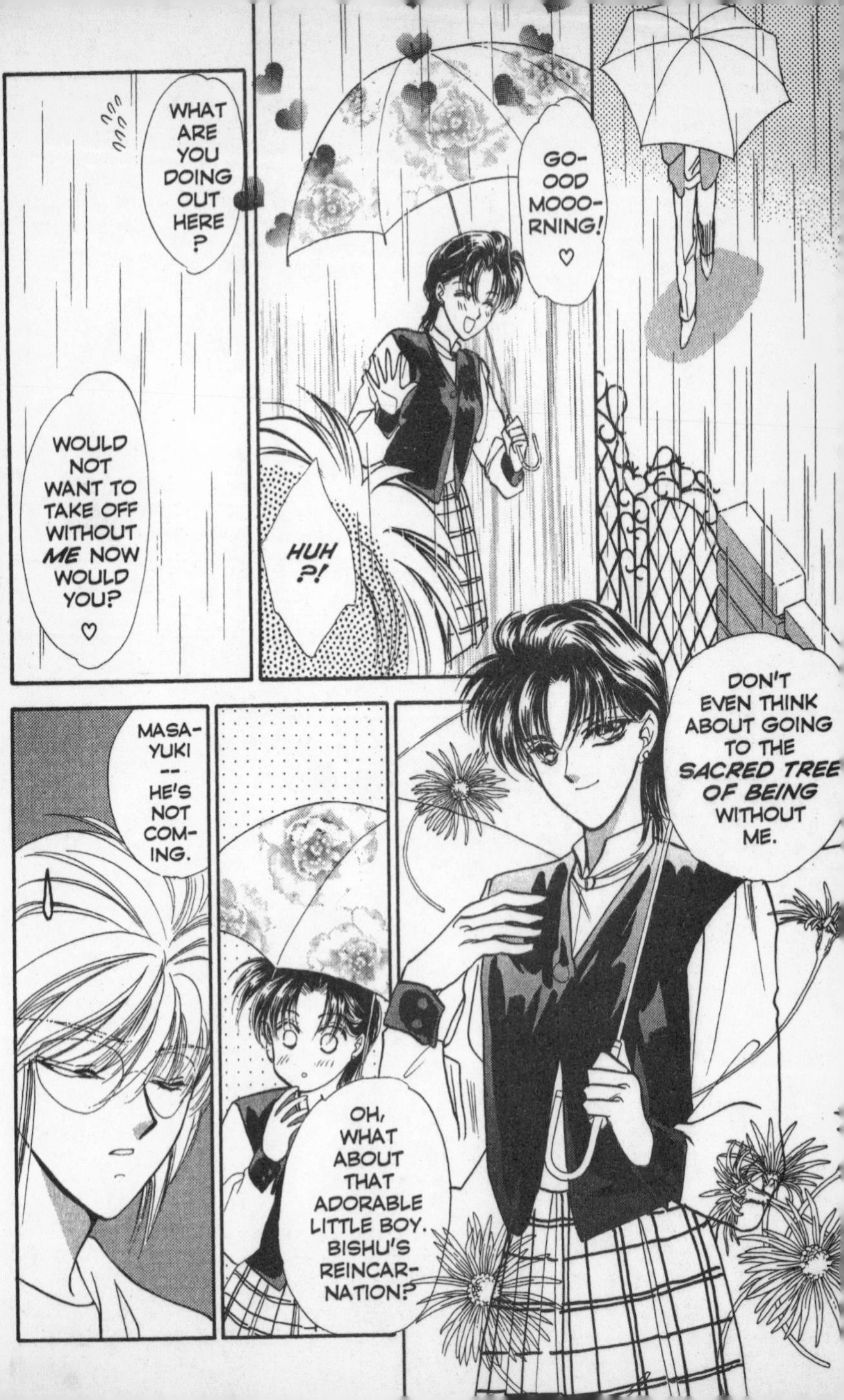
GO-OOD MOOO-RNING! ♡
HUH?!
WHAT ARE YOU DOING OUT HERE?
WOULD NOT WANT TO TAKE OFF WITHOUT *ME* NOW WOULD YOU? ♡
DON'T EVEN THINK ABOUT GOING TO THE *SACRED TREE OF BEING* WITHOUT ME.
OH, WHAT ABOUT THAT ADORABLE LITTLE BOY. BISHU'S REINCAR-NATION?
MASA-YUKI -- HE'S NOT COM-ING.

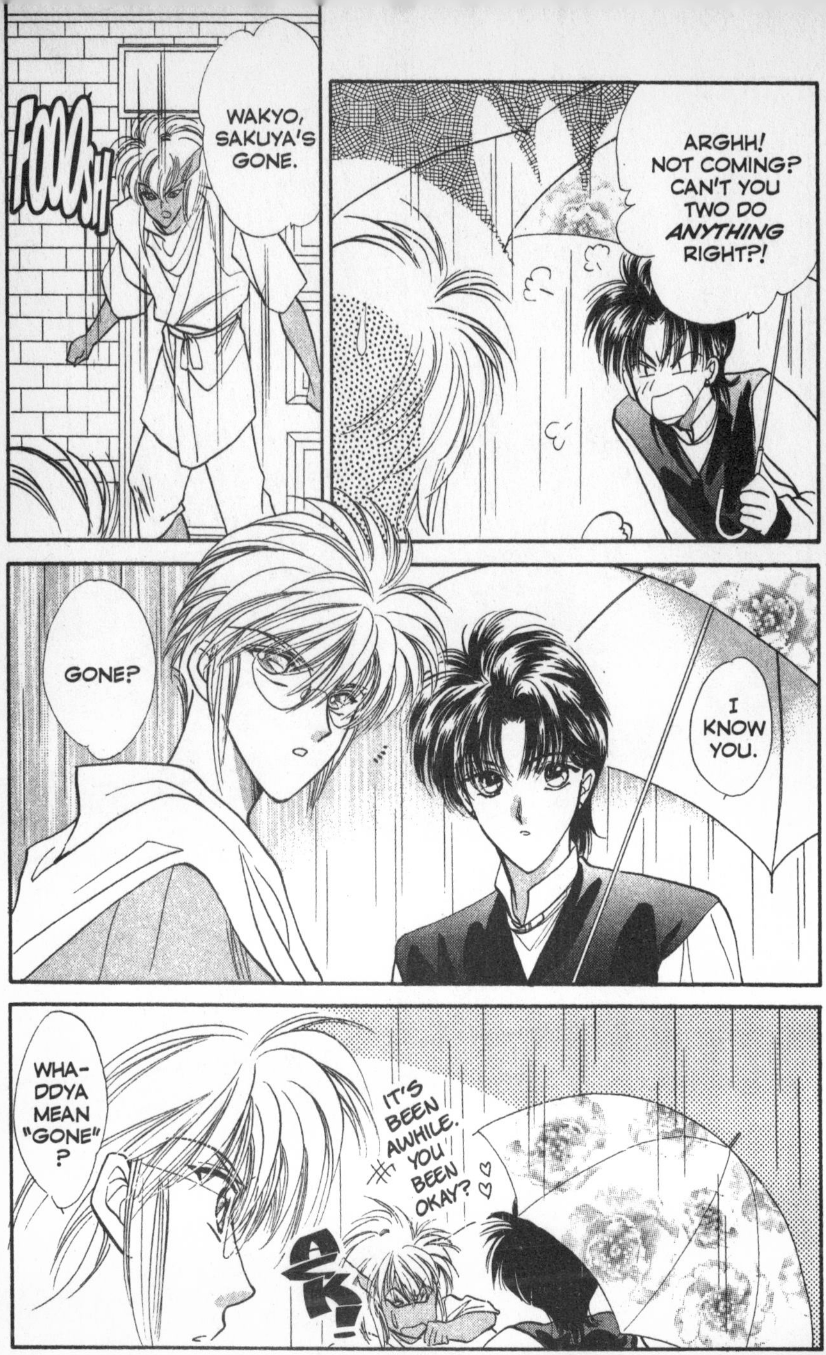
ARGHH! NOT COMING? CAN'T YOU TWO DO *ANYTHING* RIGHT?!
WAKYO, SAKUYA'S GONE.
FOOOSH
I KNOW YOU.
GONE?
IT'S BEEN AWHILE. YOU BEEN OKAY?
EK!
WHADDYA MEAN "GONE"?

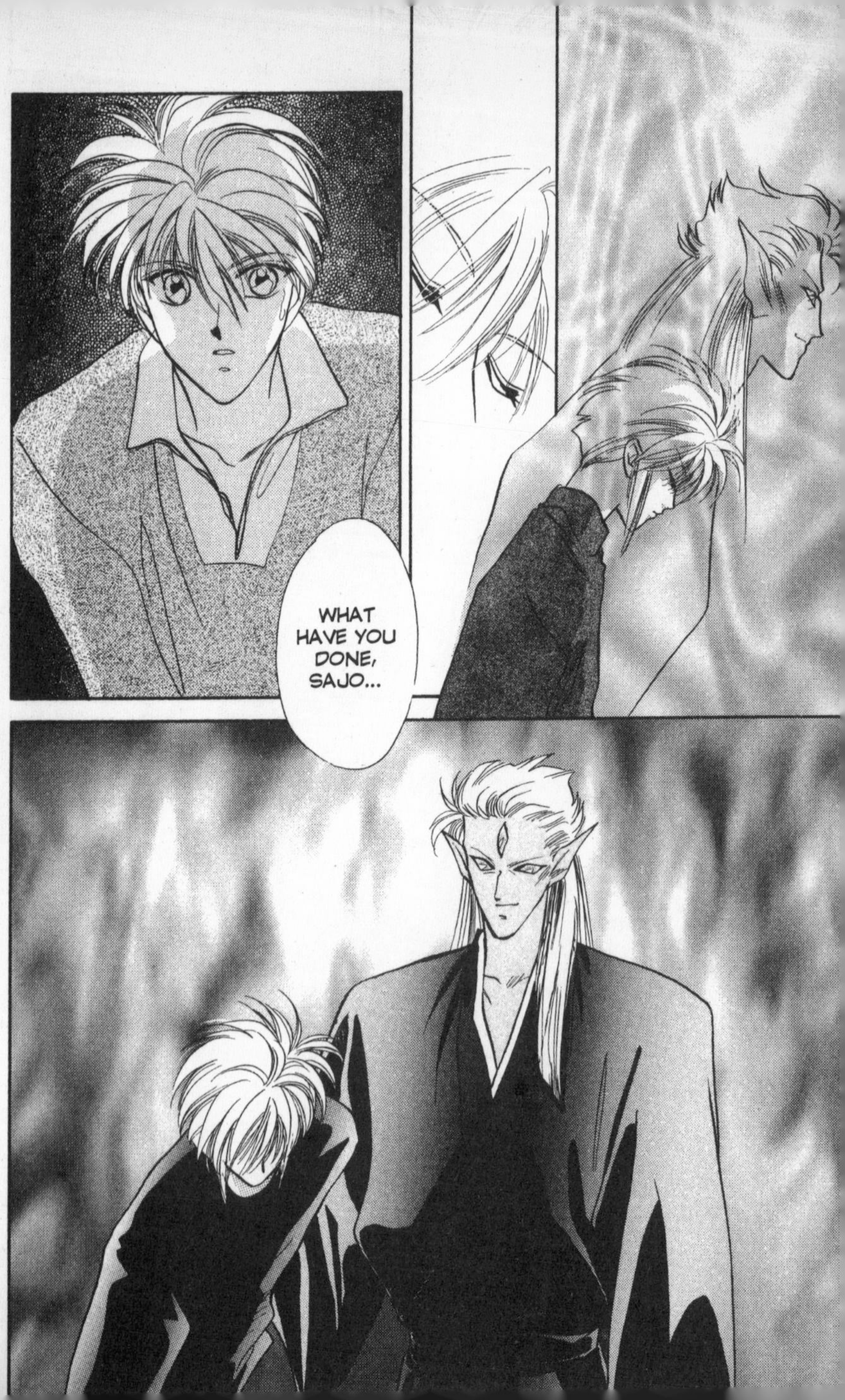
WHAT HAVE YOU DONE, SAJO...

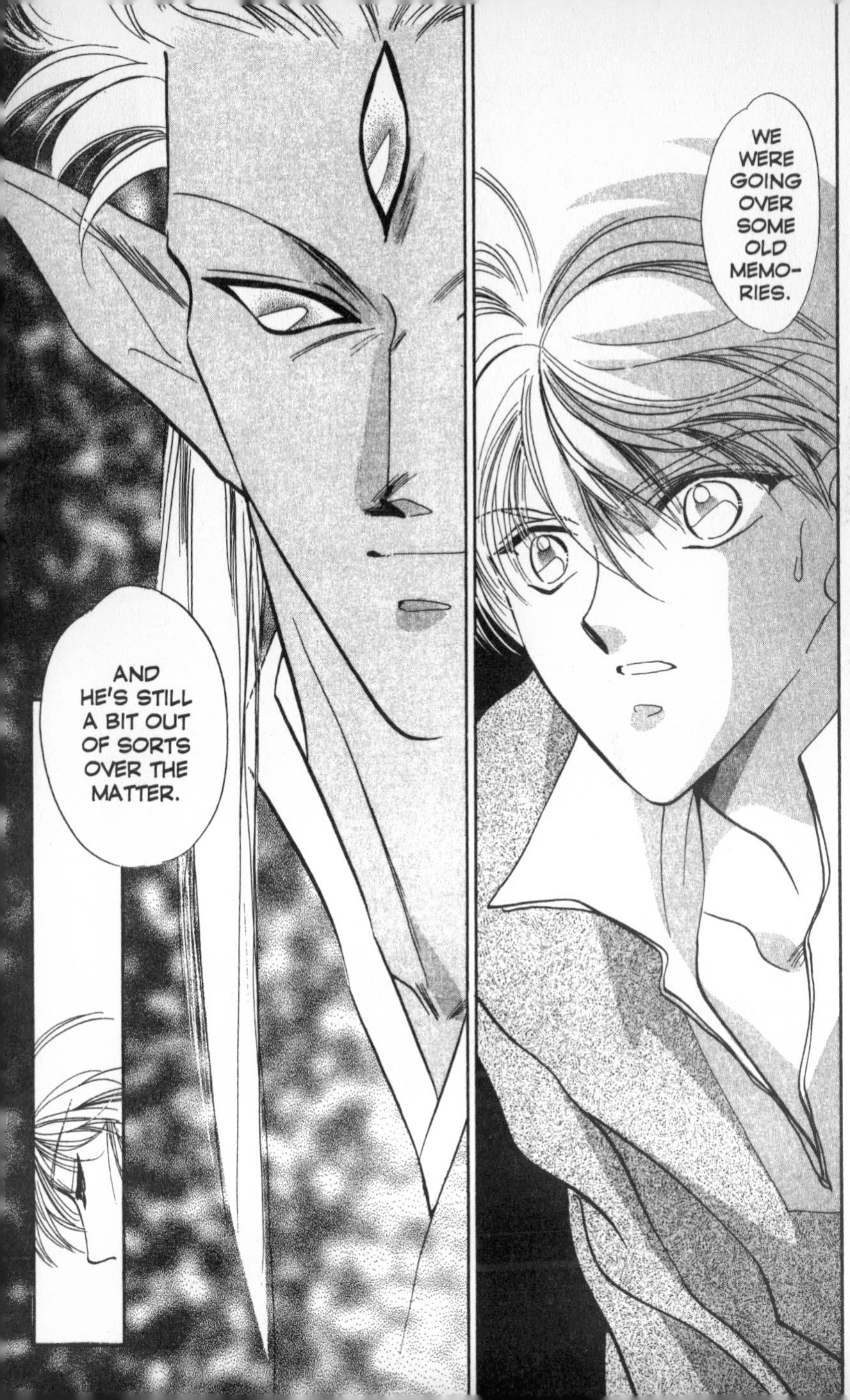
WE WERE GOING OVER SOME OLD MEMORIES.
AND HE'S STILL A BIT OUT OF SORTS OVER THE MATTER.

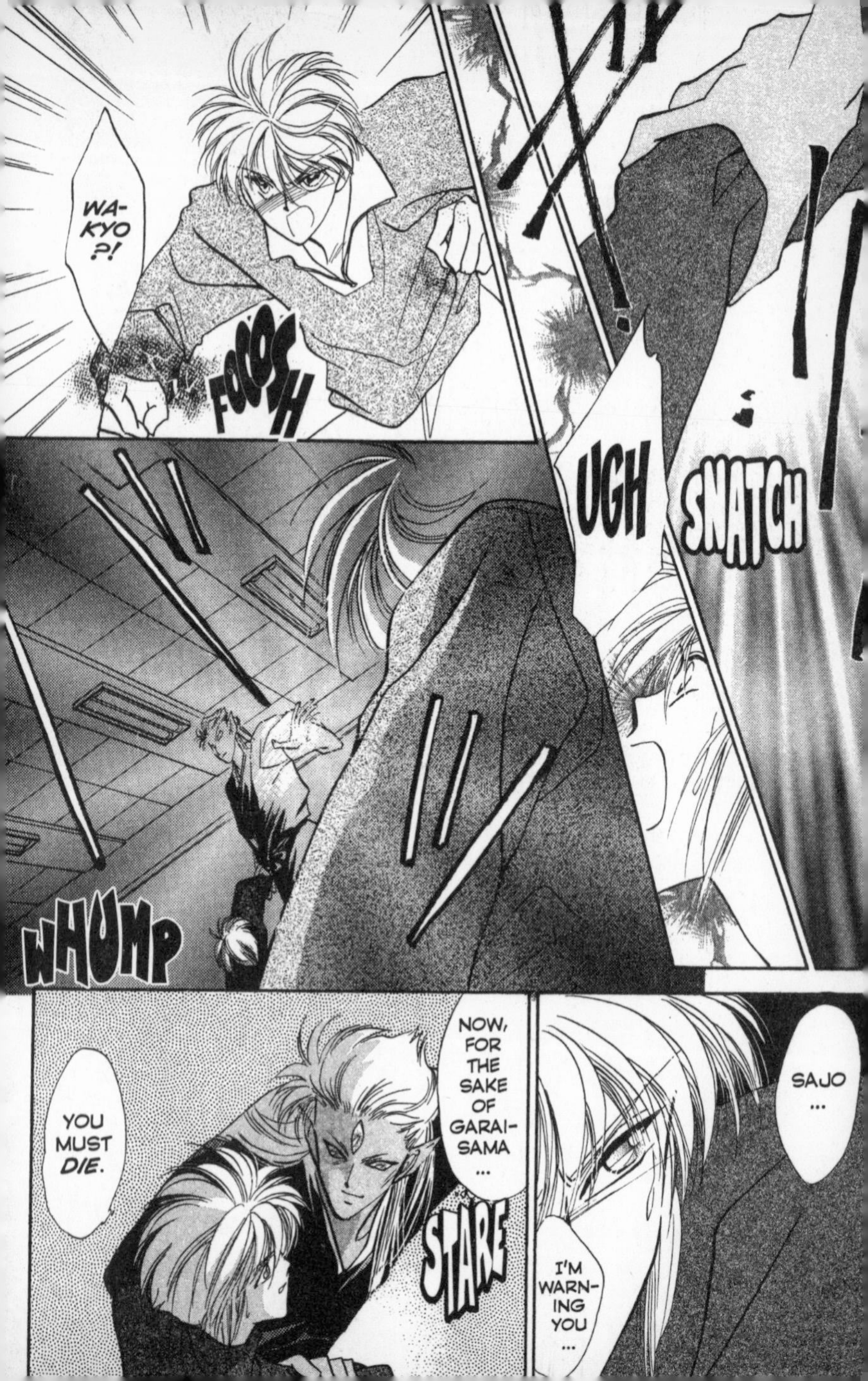
UGH
SNATCH
WA-KYO ?!
FOOOSH
WHUMP
SAJO ...
I'M WARNING YOU ...
NOW, FOR THE SAKE OF GARAI-SAMA ...
STARE
YOU MUST *DIE*.

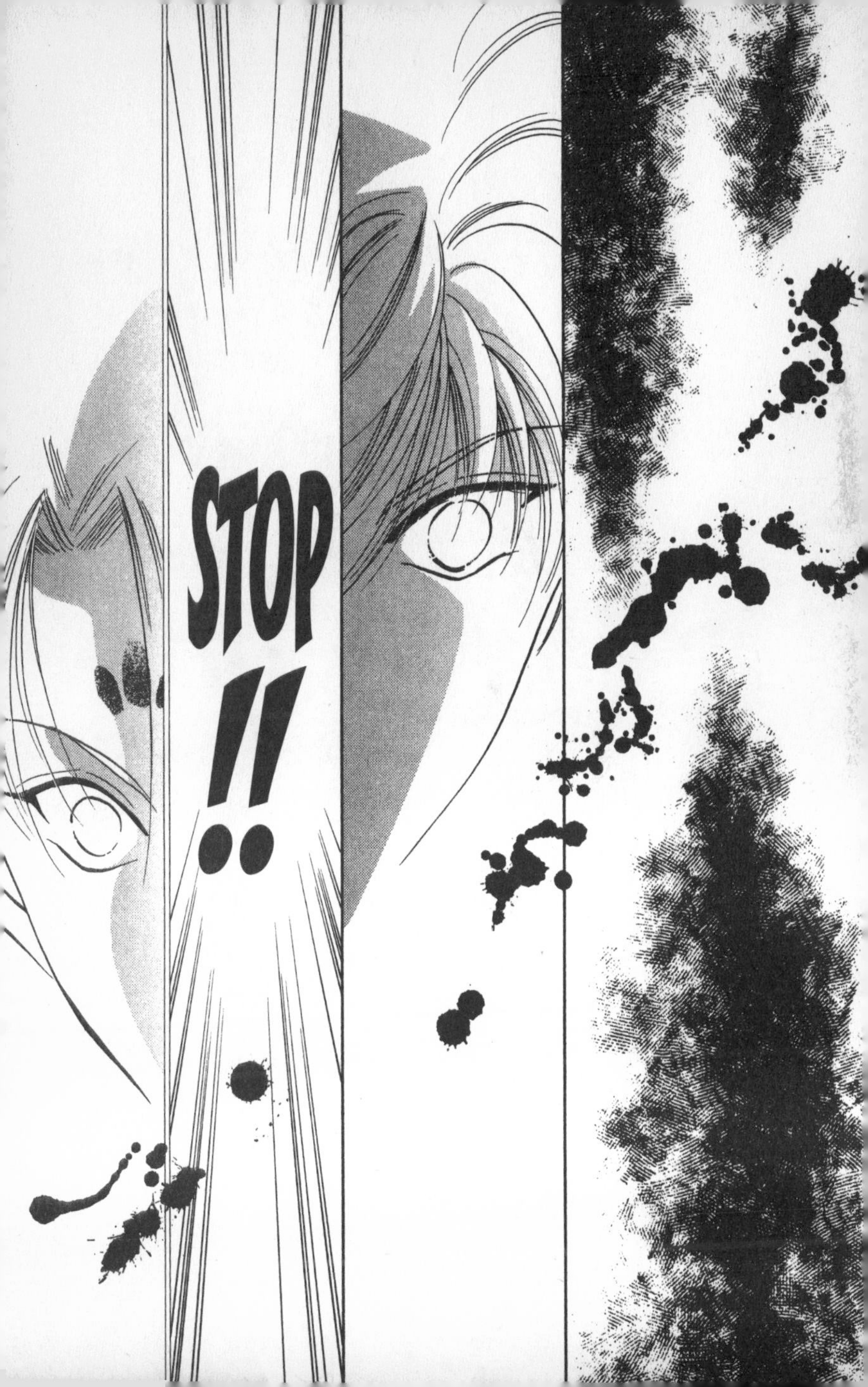
STOP!!

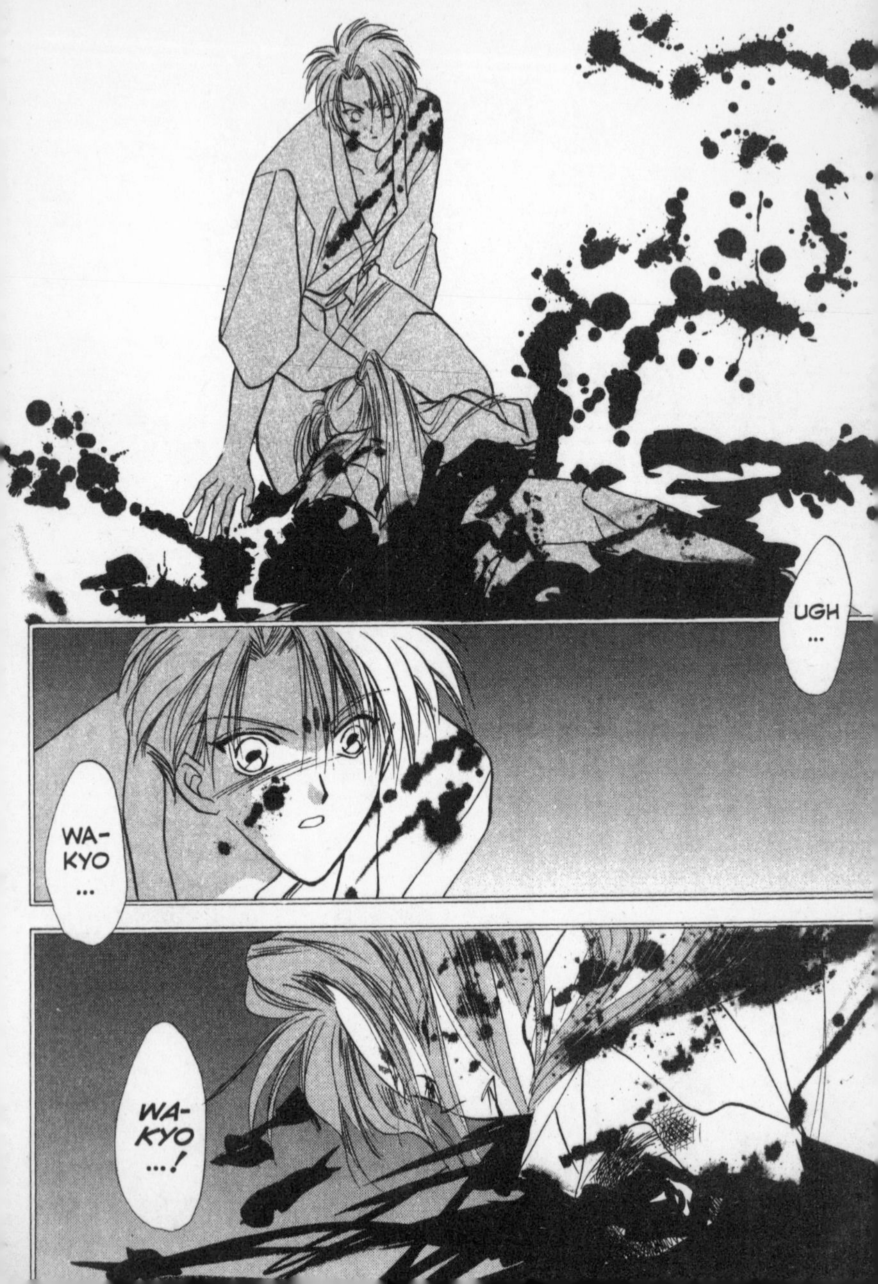
UGH ...
WA-KYO ...
WA-KYO ...!

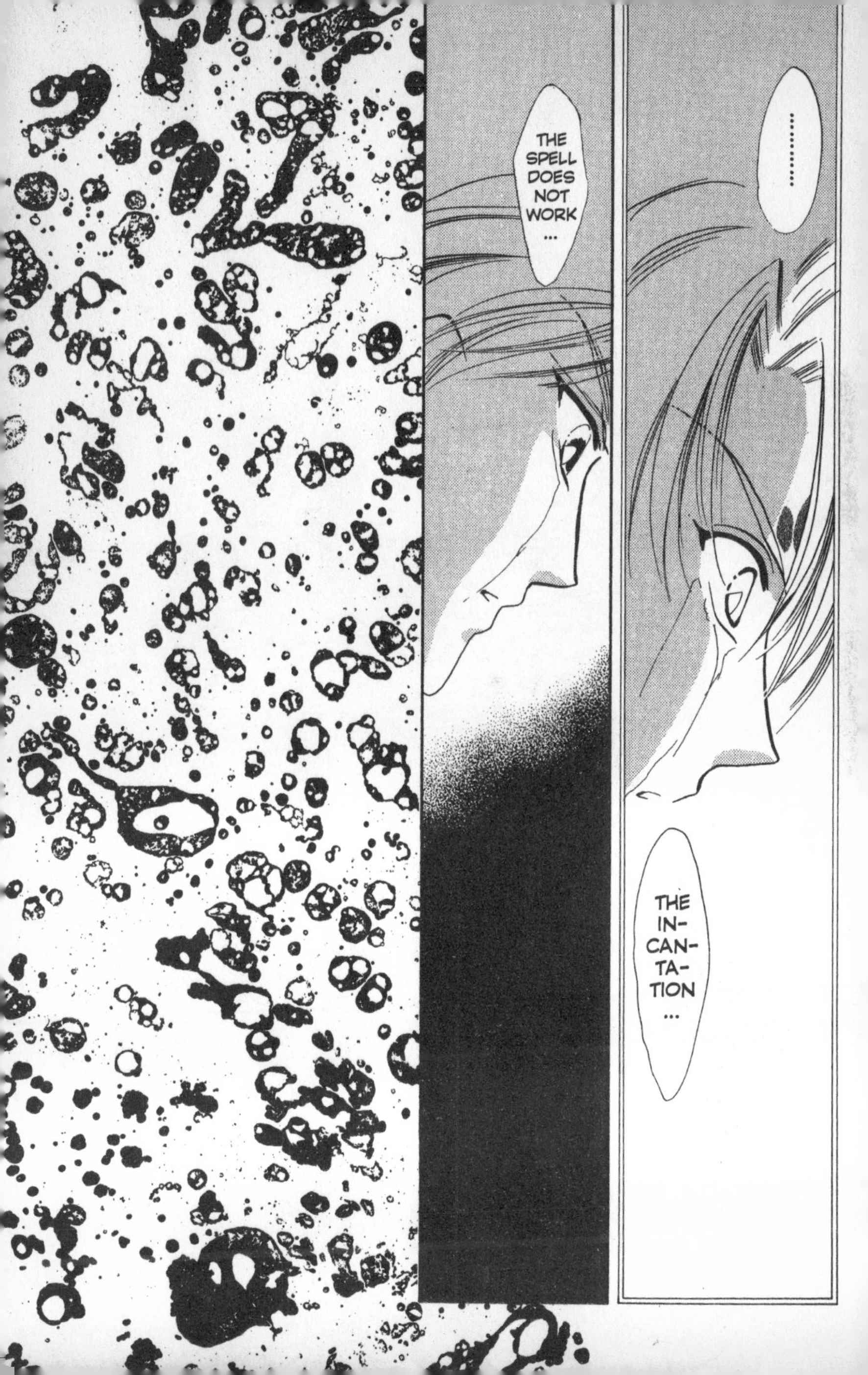
....
THE IN-CAN-TA-TION ...
THE SPELL DOES NOT WORK ...

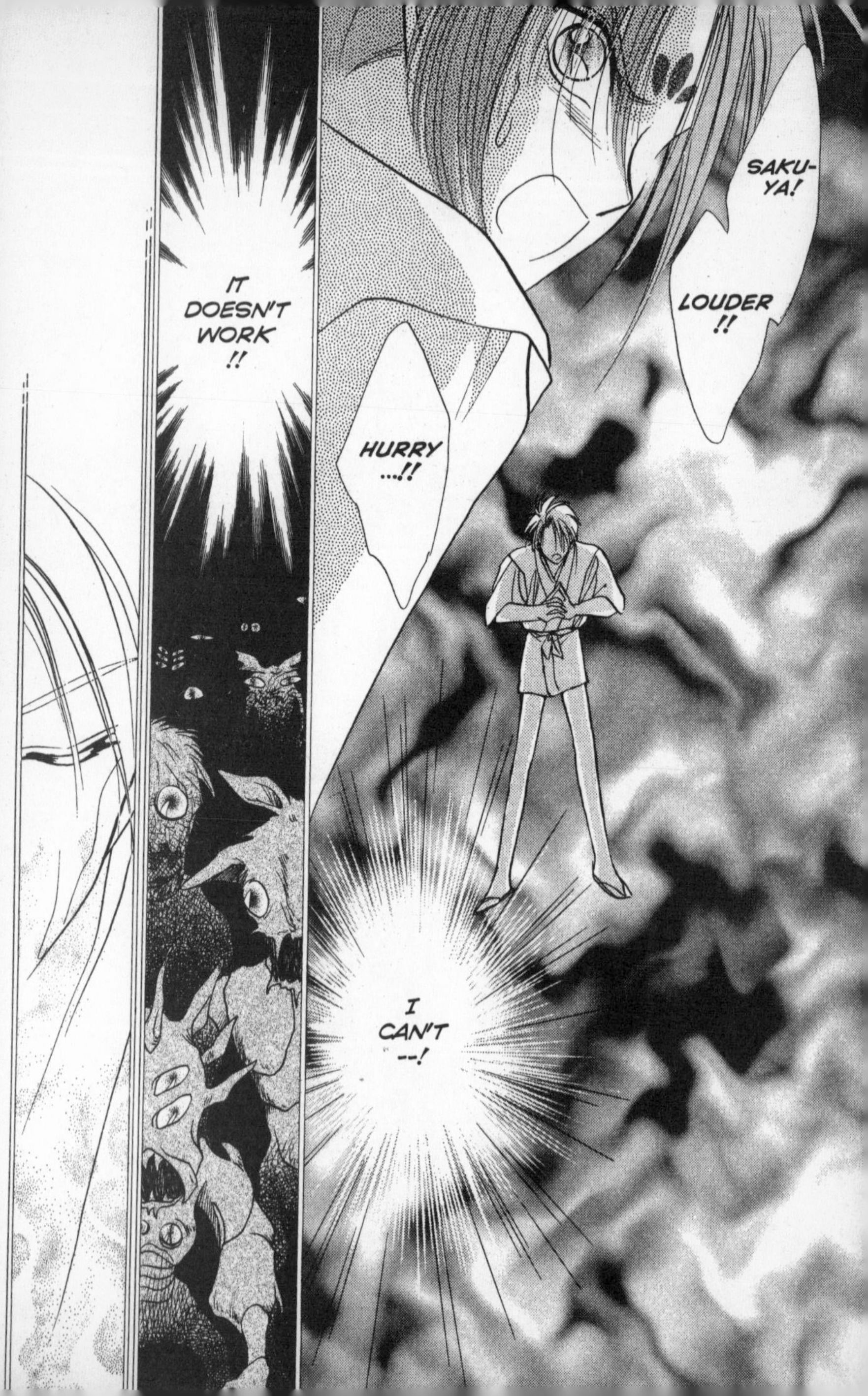
SAKU-YA!
LOUDER !!
HURRY ...!!
I CAN'T --!
IT DOESN'T WORK !!

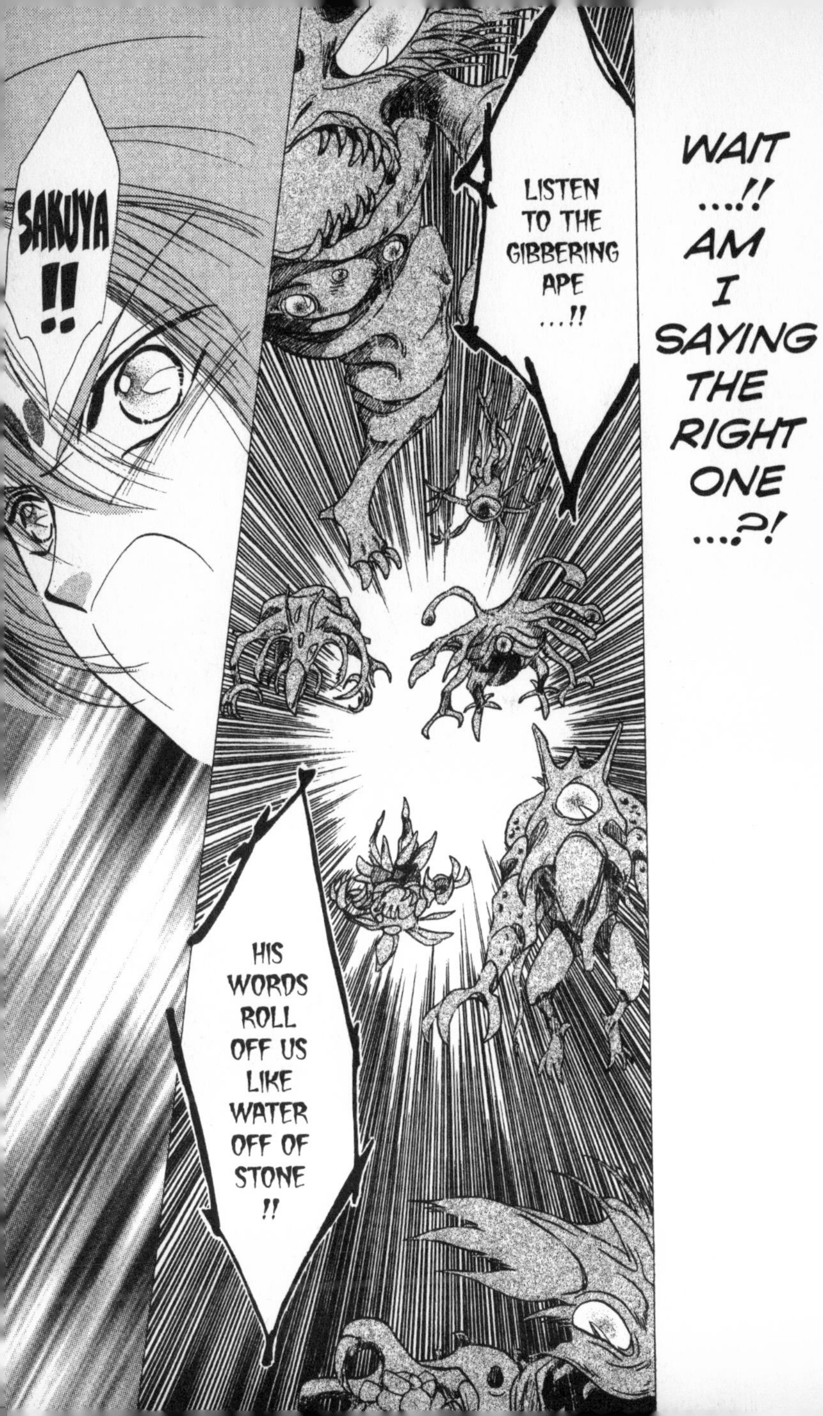
WAIT ...!! AM I SAYING THE RIGHT ONE ...?!
LISTEN TO THE GIBBERING APE ...!!
HIS WORDS ROLL OFF US LIKE WATER OFF OF STONE !!
SAKUYA !!

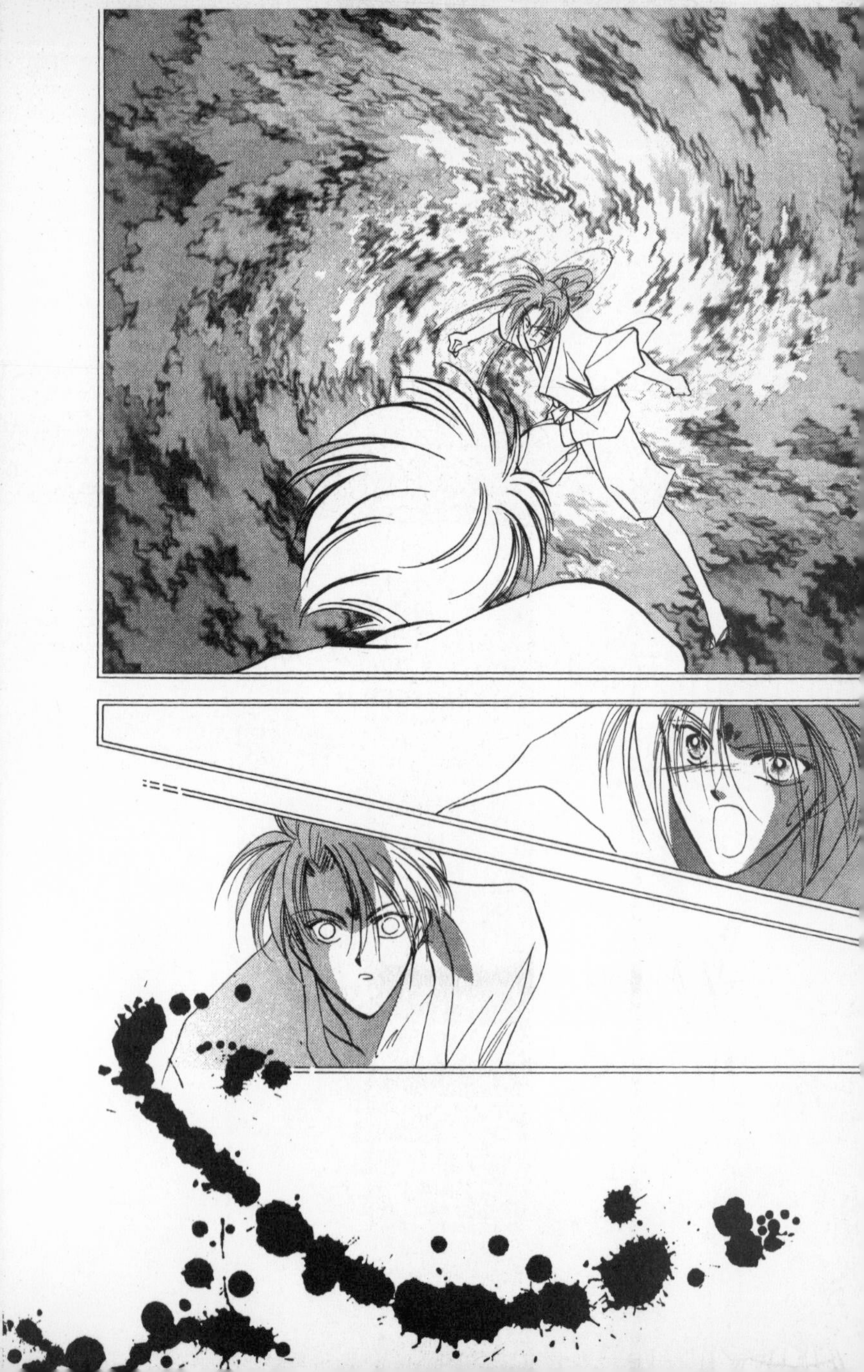

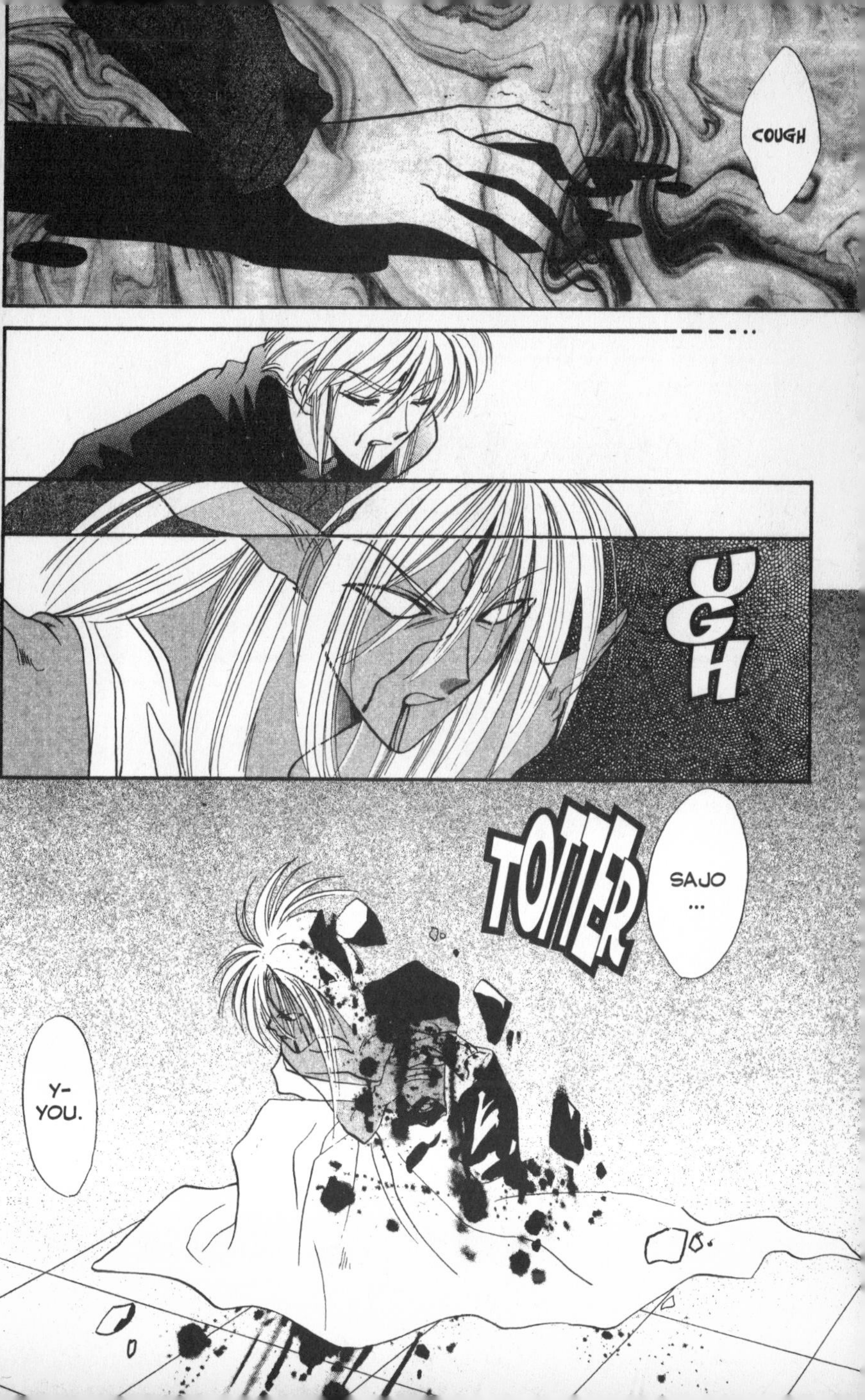
COUGH
UGH
SAJO ...
TOTTER
Y-YOU.

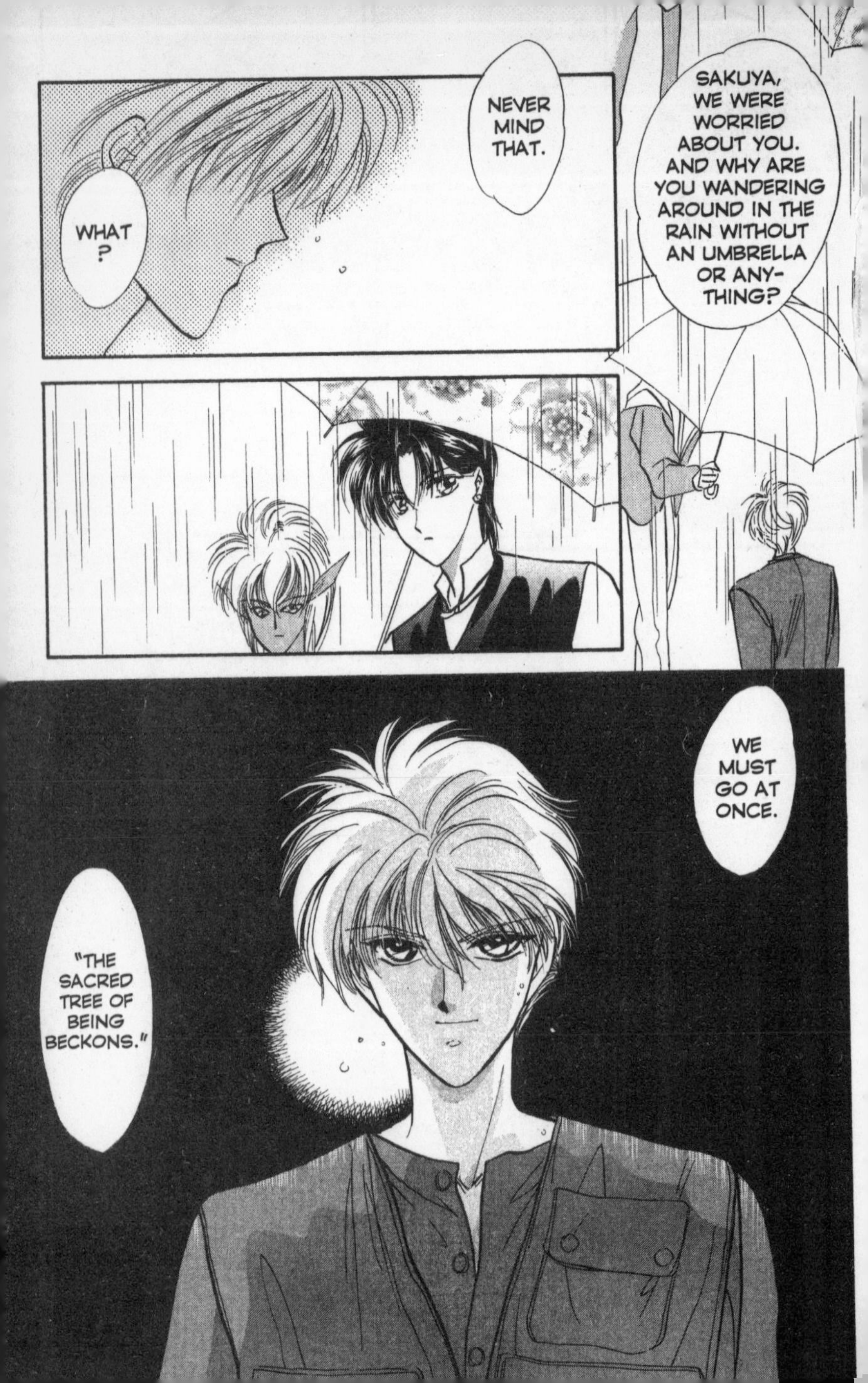
SAKUYA, WE WERE WORRIED ABOUT YOU. AND WHY ARE YOU WANDERING AROUND IN THE RAIN WITHOUT AN UMBRELLA OR ANY-THING?
NEVER MIND THAT.
WHAT?
WE MUST GO AT ONCE.
"THE SACRED TREE OF BEING BECKONS."

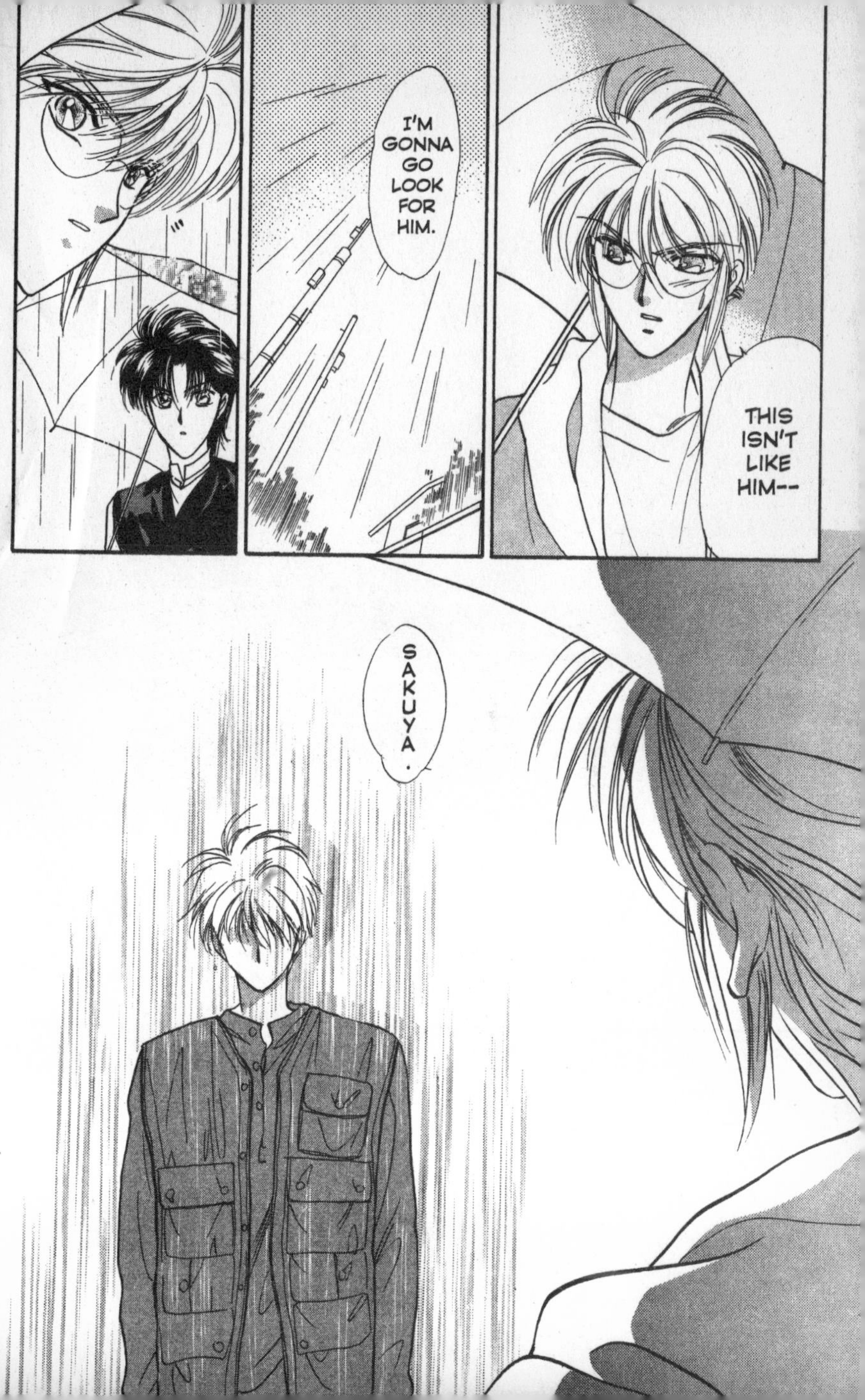
THIS ISN'T LIKE HIM--
I'M GONNA GO LOOK FOR HIM.
SAKUYA.

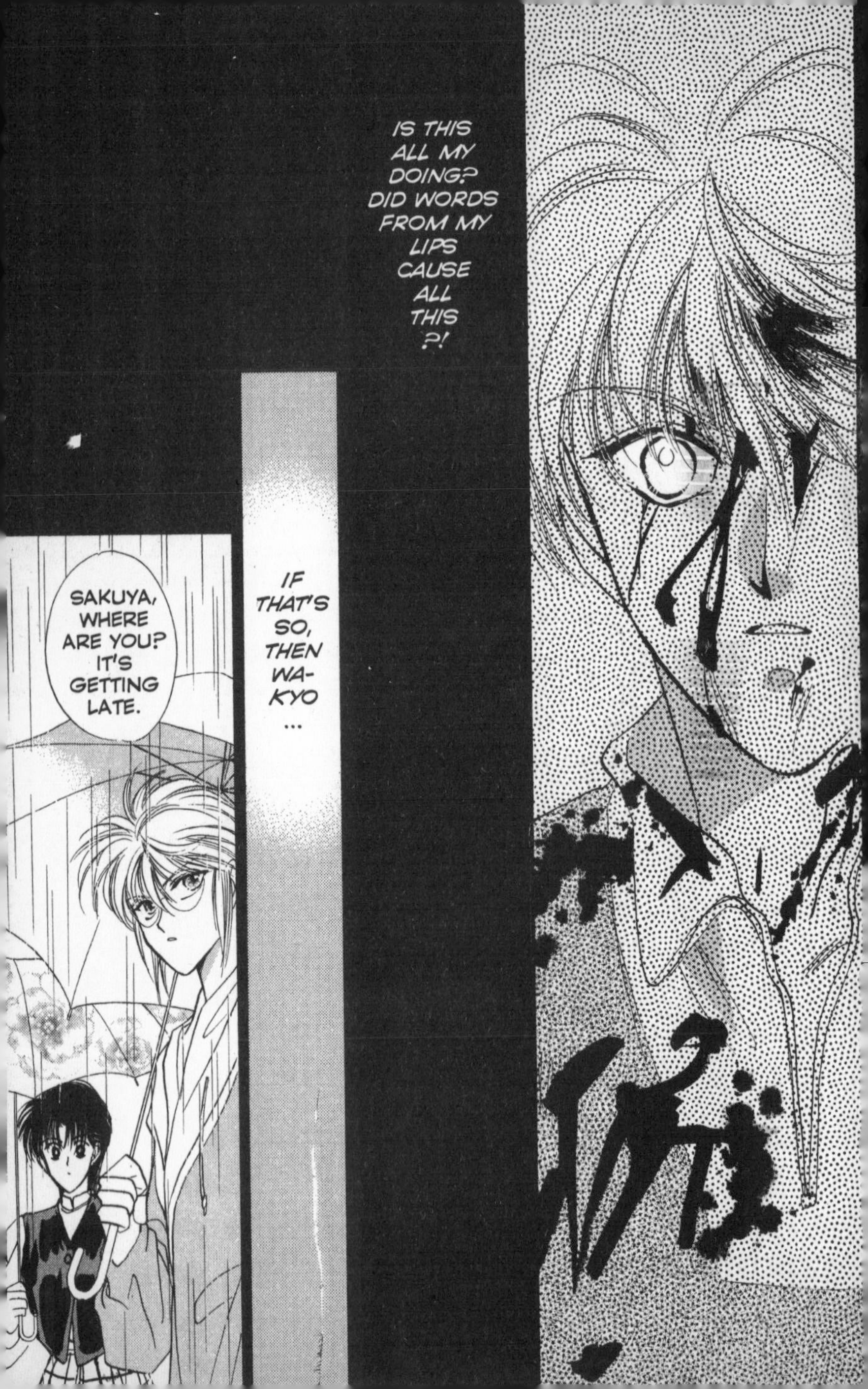
IS THIS ALL MY DOING? DID WORDS FROM MY LIPS CAUSE ALL THIS ?!
IF THAT'S SO, THEN WA-KYO ...
SAKUYA, WHERE ARE YOU? IT'S GETTING LATE.

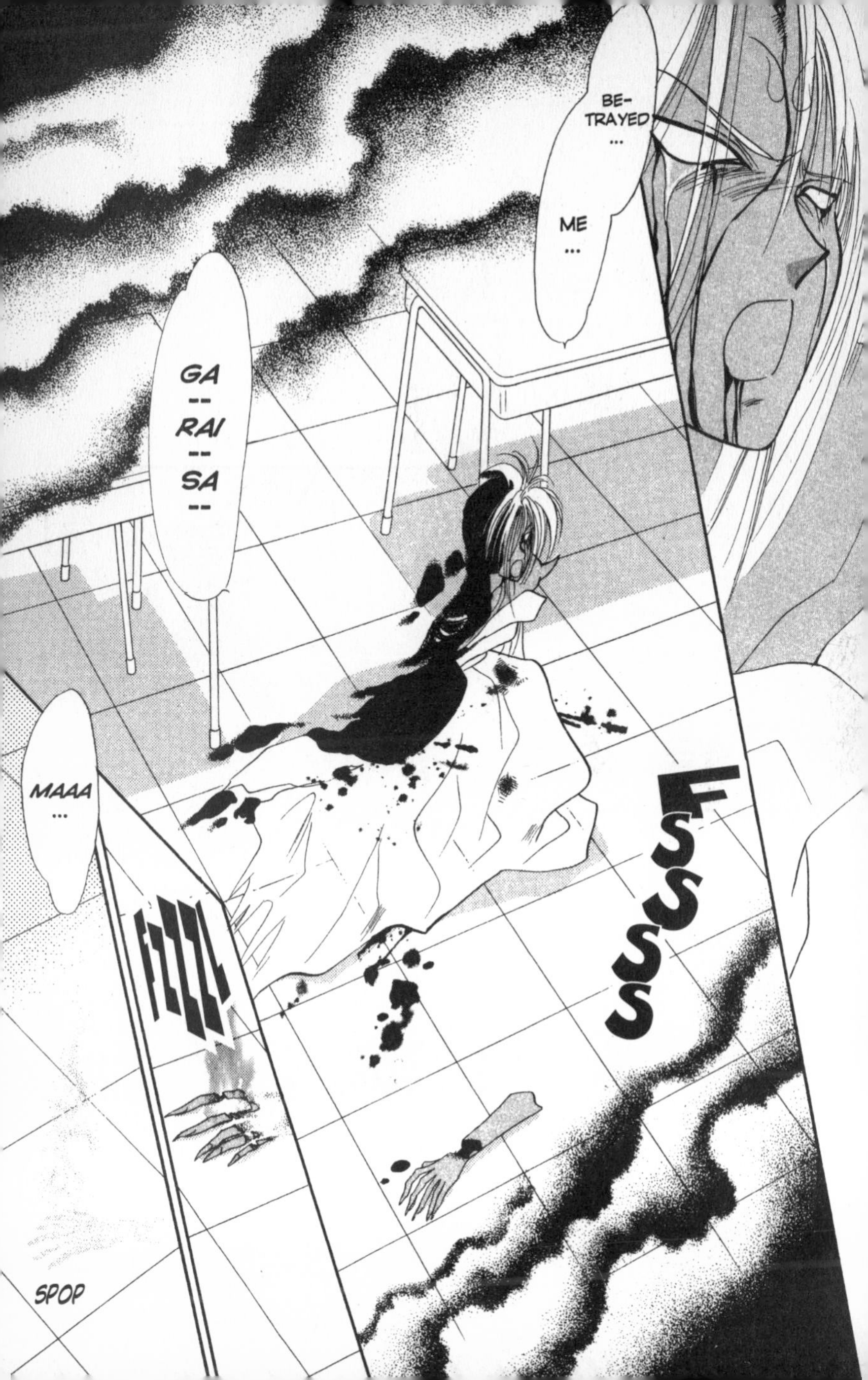

BE-TRAYED ...
ME ...
GA -- RAI -- SA --
FSSSS
MAAA ...
FIZZL
SPOP

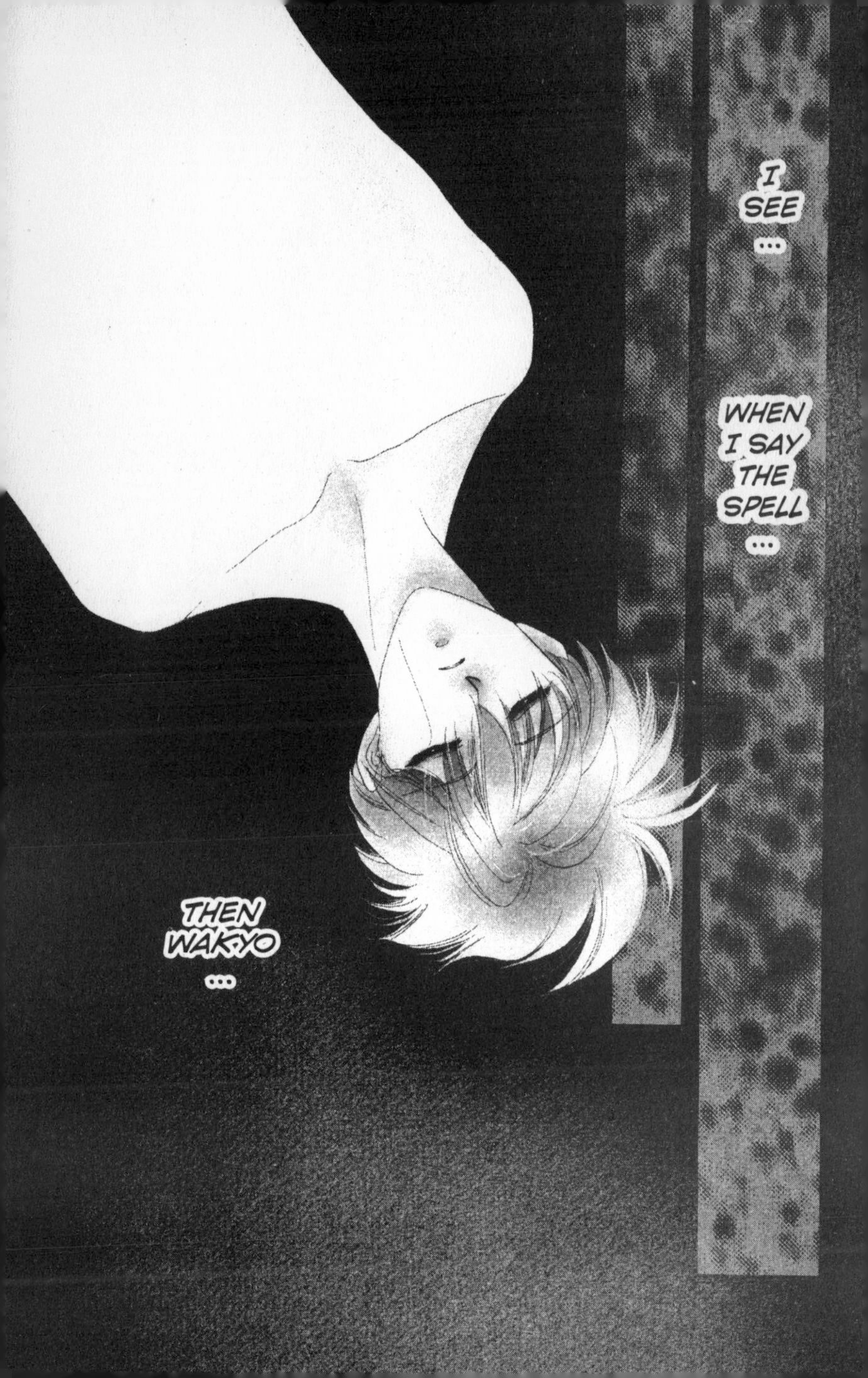
I SEE ...
WHEN I SAY THE SPELL ...
THEN WAKYO ...

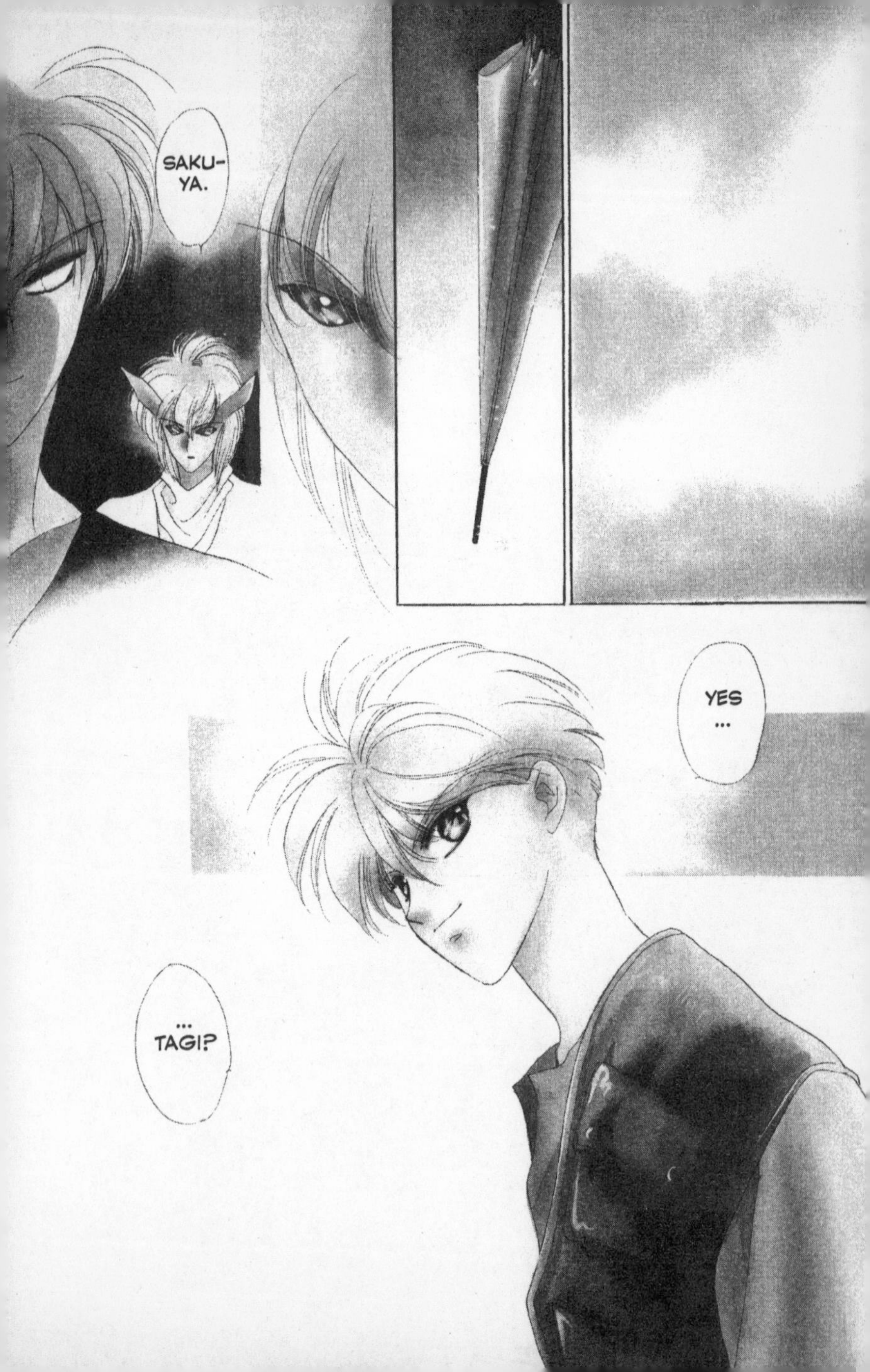
SAKU-YA.
YES ...
... TAGI?

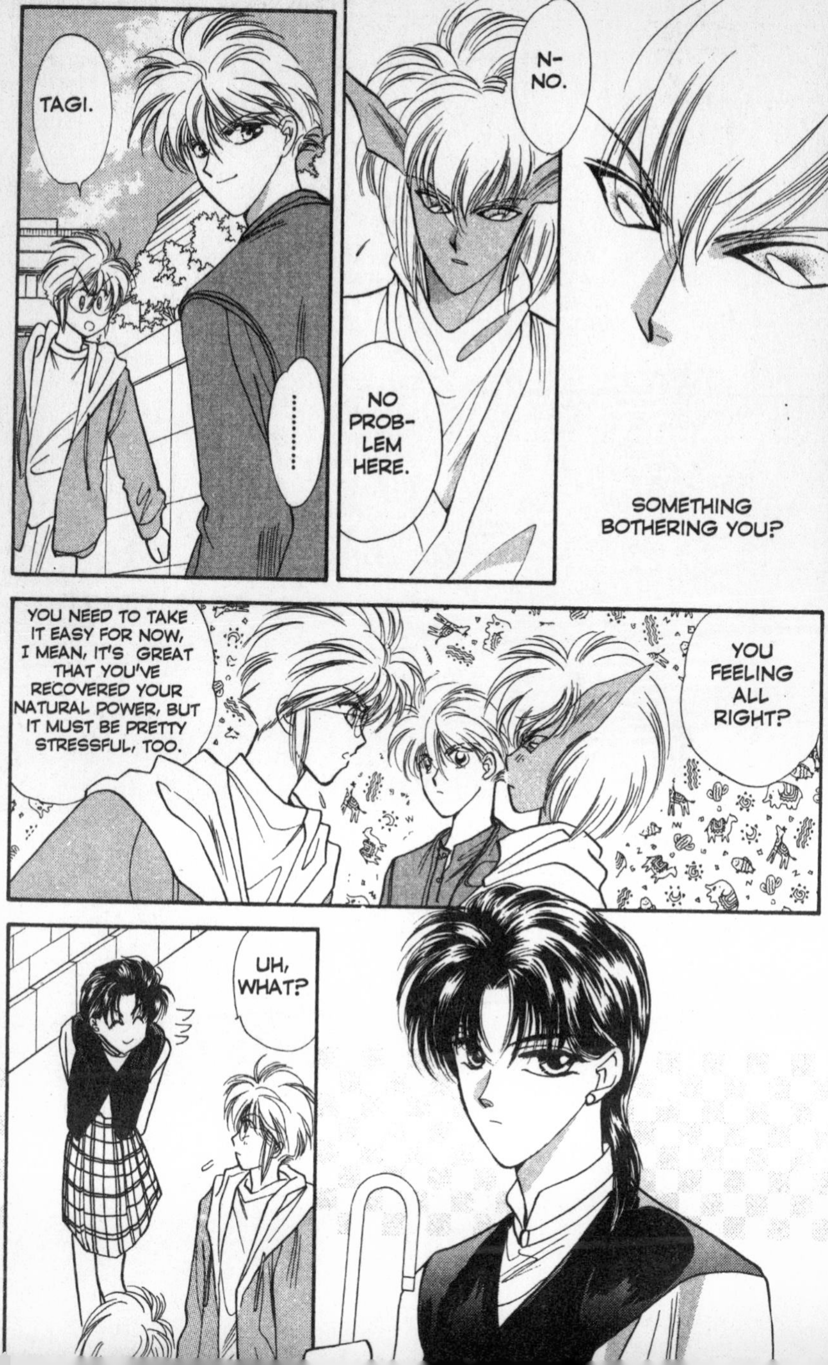
SOMETHING BOTHERING YOU?
N-NO.
NO PROBLEM HERE.
TAGI.
....
YOU FEELING ALL RIGHT?
YOU NEED TO TAKE IT EASY FOR NOW, I MEAN, IT'S GREAT THAT YOU'VE RECOVERED YOUR NATURAL POWER, BUT IT MUST BE PRETTY STRESSFUL, TOO.
UH, WHAT?

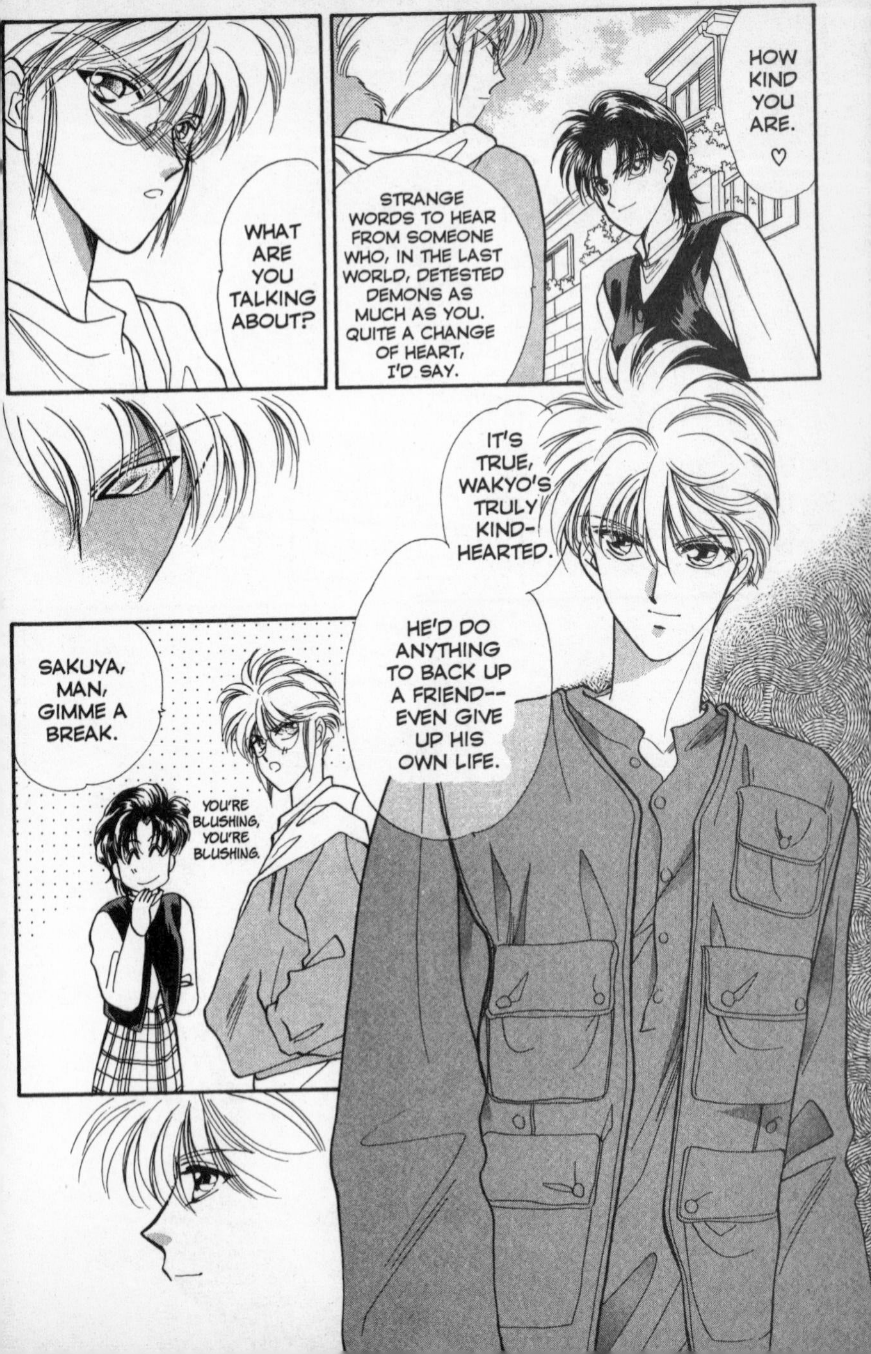
HOW KIND YOU ARE. ♡
STRANGE WORDS TO HEAR FROM SOMEONE WHO, IN THE LAST WORLD, DETESTED DEMONS AS MUCH AS YOU. QUITE A CHANGE OF HEART, I'D SAY.
WHAT ARE YOU TALKING ABOUT?
IT'S TRUE, WAKYO'S TRULY KIND-HEARTED.
HE'D DO ANYTHING TO BACK UP A FRIEND-- EVEN GIVE UP HIS OWN LIFE.
SAKUYA, MAN, GIMME A BREAK.
YOU'RE BLUSHING, YOU'RE BLUSHING.

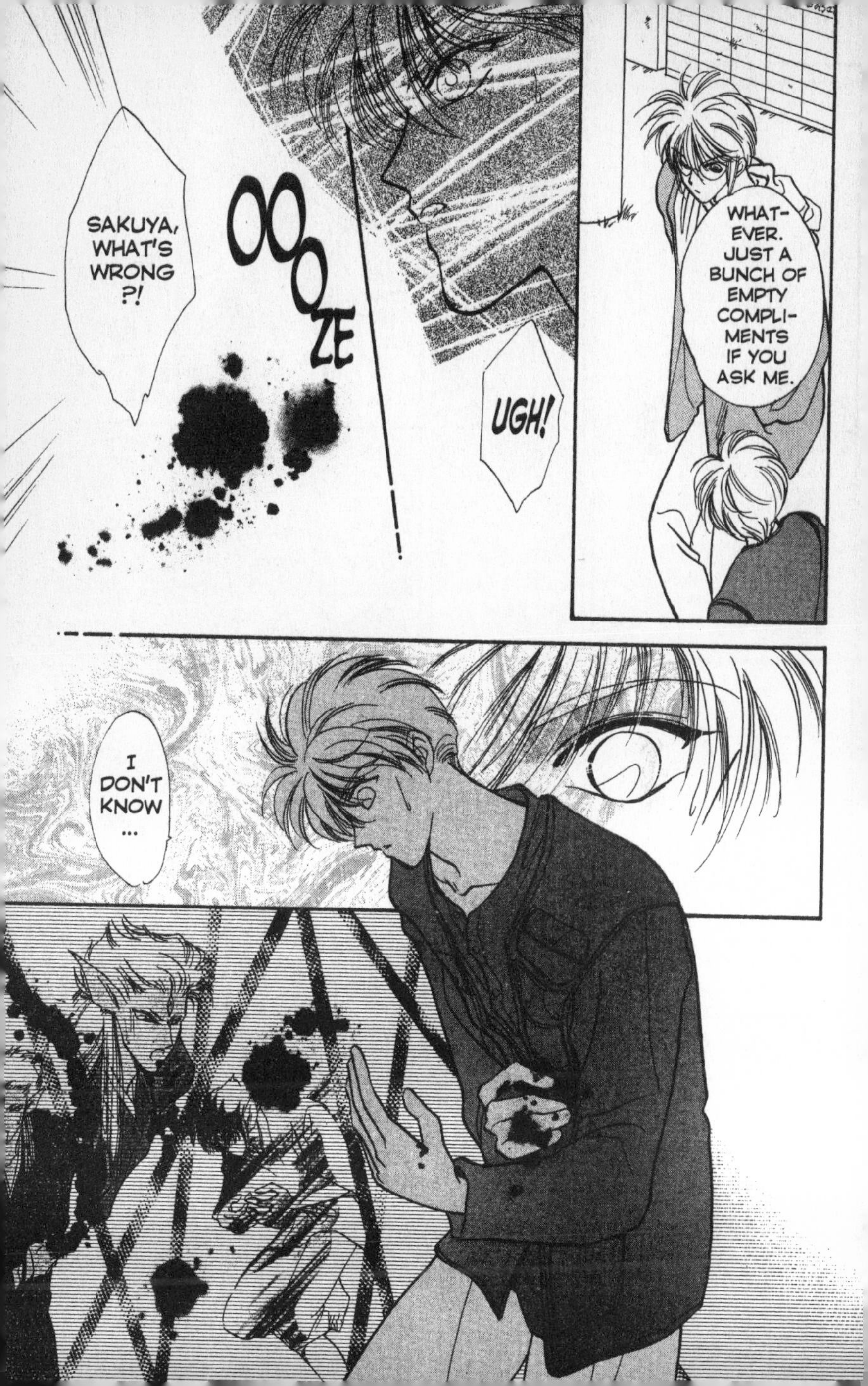
WHAT-EVER. JUST A BUNCH OF EMPTY COMPLI-MENTS IF YOU ASK ME.
UGH!
OOOZE
SAKUYA, WHAT'S WRONG ?!
I DON'T KNOW ...

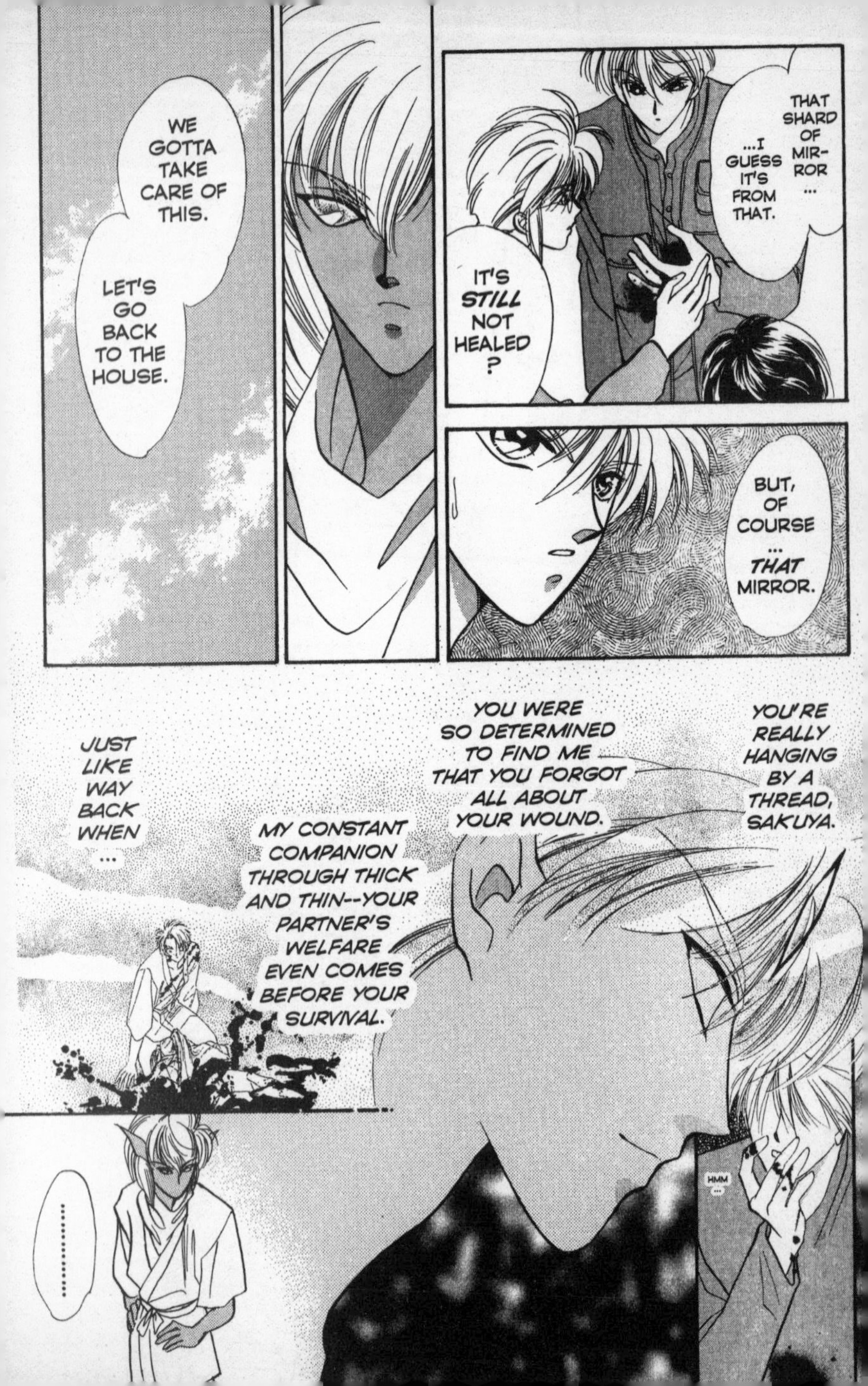
THAT SHARD OF MIRROR ...
...I GUESS IT'S FROM THAT.
IT'S *STILL* NOT HEALED?
BUT, OF COURSE ... *THAT* MIRROR.
WE GOTTA TAKE CARE OF THIS.
LET'S GO BACK TO THE HOUSE.
YOU'RE REALLY HANGING BY A THREAD, SAKUYA.
YOU WERE SO DETERMINED TO FIND ME THAT YOU FORGOT ALL ABOUT YOUR WOUND.
MY CONSTANT COMPANION THROUGH THICK AND THIN--YOUR PARTNER'S WELFARE EVEN COMES BEFORE YOUR SURVIVAL.
JUST LIKE WAY BACK WHEN ...
HMM ...
....

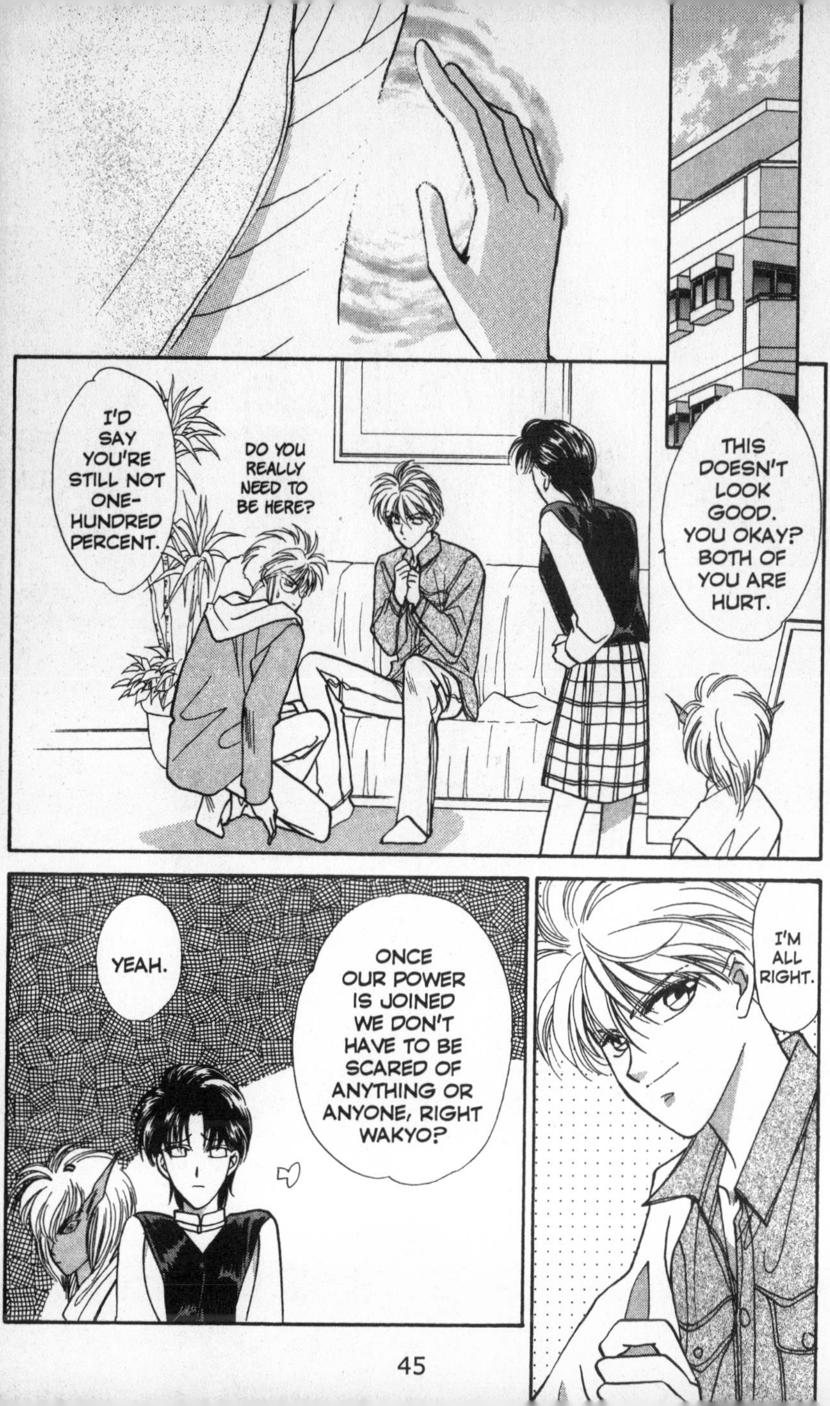
THIS DOESN'T LOOK GOOD. YOU OKAY? BOTH OF YOU ARE HURT.
DO YOU REALLY NEED TO BE HERE?
I'D SAY YOU'RE STILL NOT ONE-HUNDRED PERCENT.
I'M ALL RIGHT.
ONCE OUR POWER IS JOINED WE DON'T HAVE TO BE SCARED OF ANYTHING OR ANYONE, RIGHT WAKYO?
YEAH.

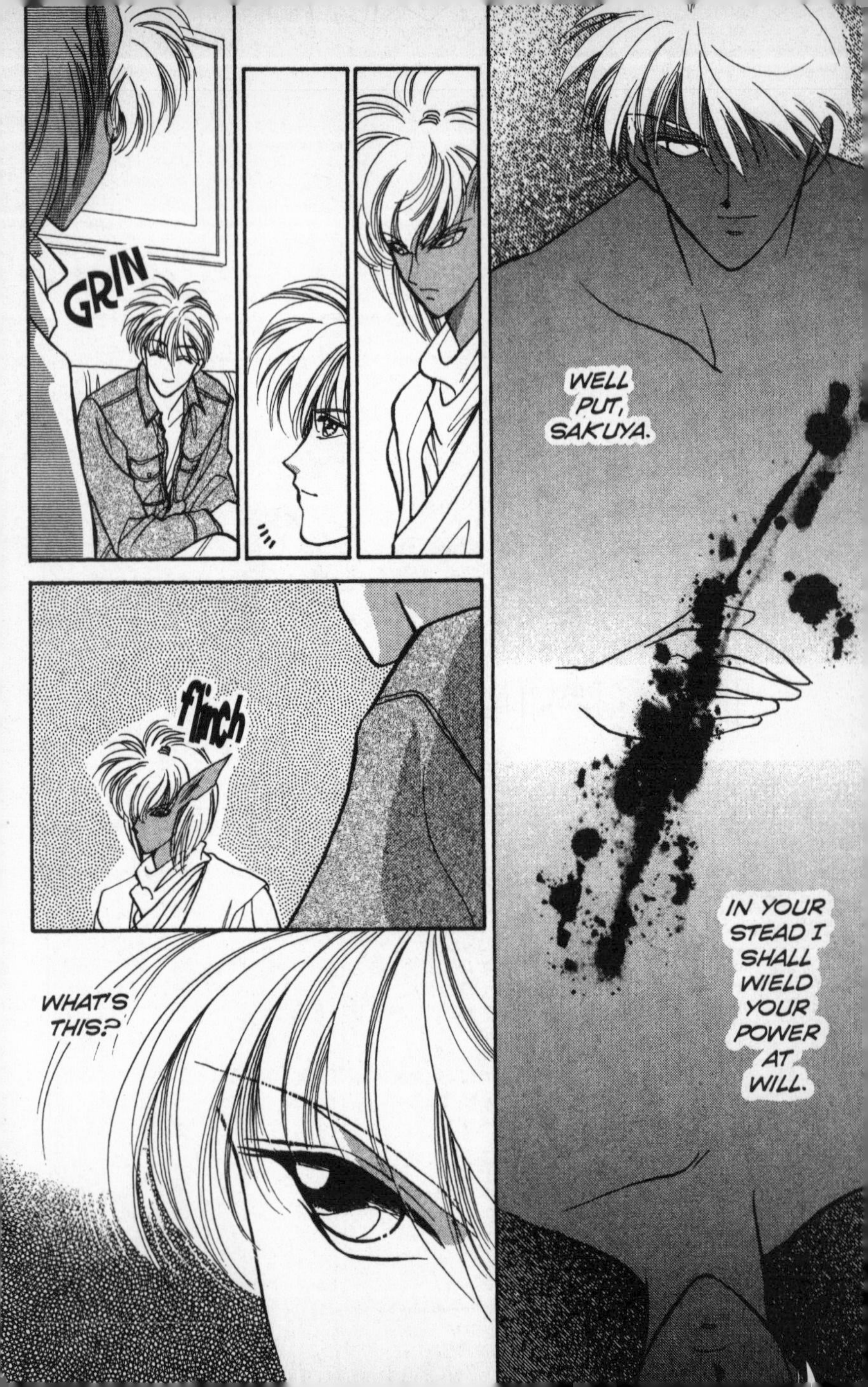
WELL PUT, SAKUYA.
IN YOUR STEAD I SHALL WIELD YOUR POWER AT WILL.
GRIN
flinch
WHAT'S THIS?

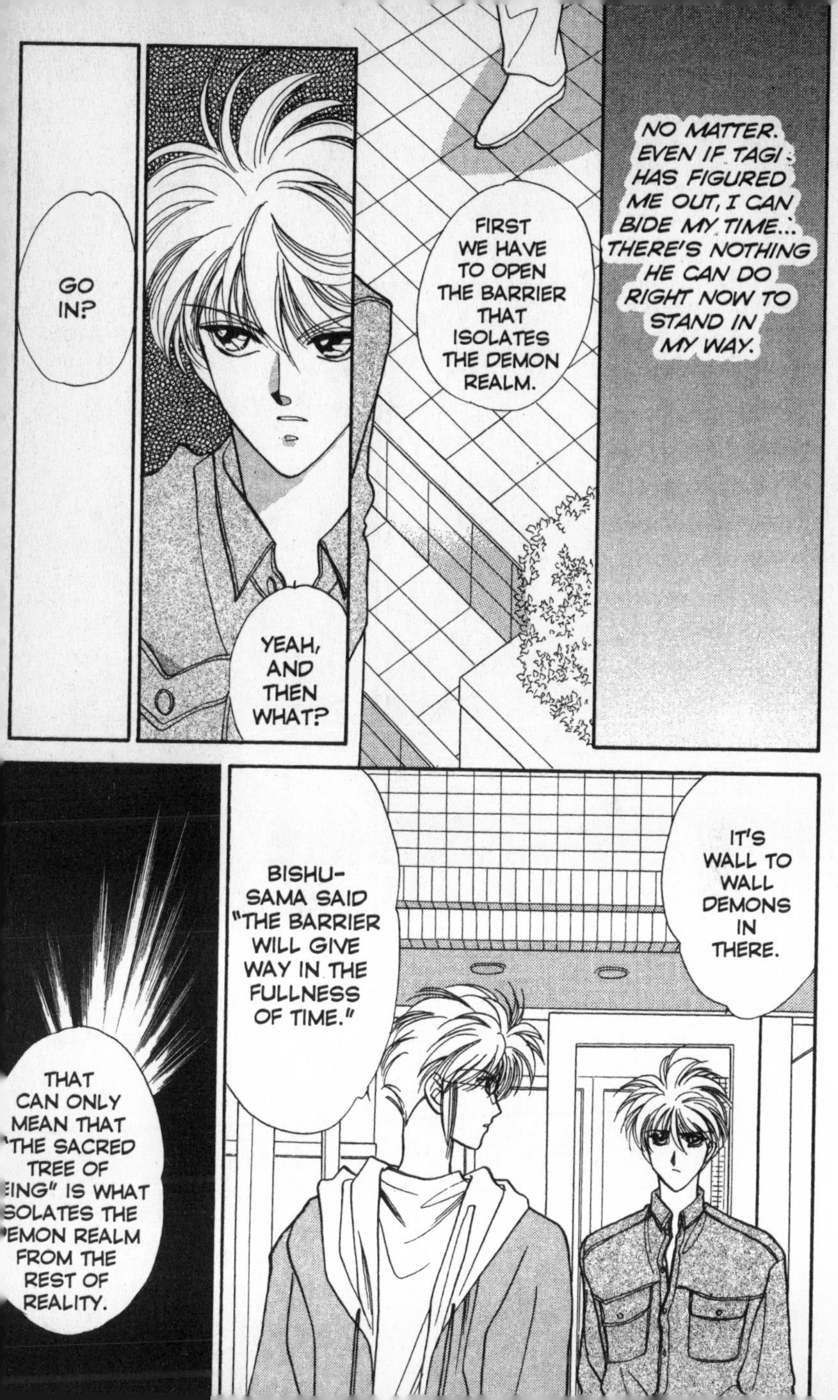
NO MATTER. EVEN IF TAGI HAS FIGURED ME OUT, I CAN BIDE MY TIME... THERE'S NOTHING HE CAN DO RIGHT NOW TO STAND IN MY WAY.
FIRST WE HAVE TO OPEN THE BARRIER THAT ISOLATES THE DEMON REALM.
YEAH, AND THEN WHAT?
GO IN?
IT'S WALL TO WALL DEMONS IN THERE.
BISHU-SAMA SAID "THE BARRIER WILL GIVE WAY IN THE FULLNESS OF TIME."
THAT CAN ONLY MEAN THAT "THE SACRED TREE OF EING" IS WHAT SOLATES THE EMON REALM FROM THE REST OF REALITY.

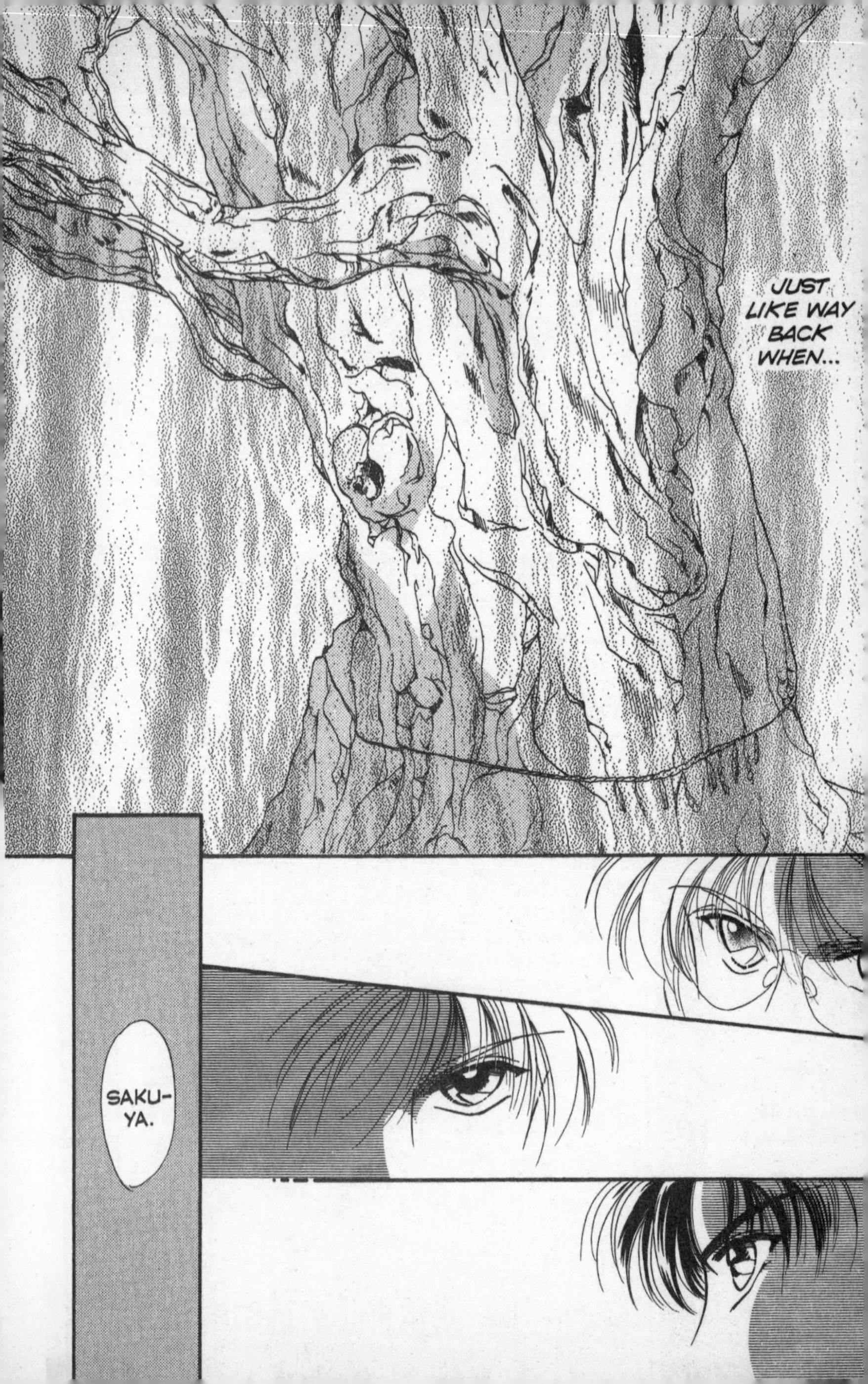
JUST LIKE WAY BACK WHEN...
SAKU-YA.

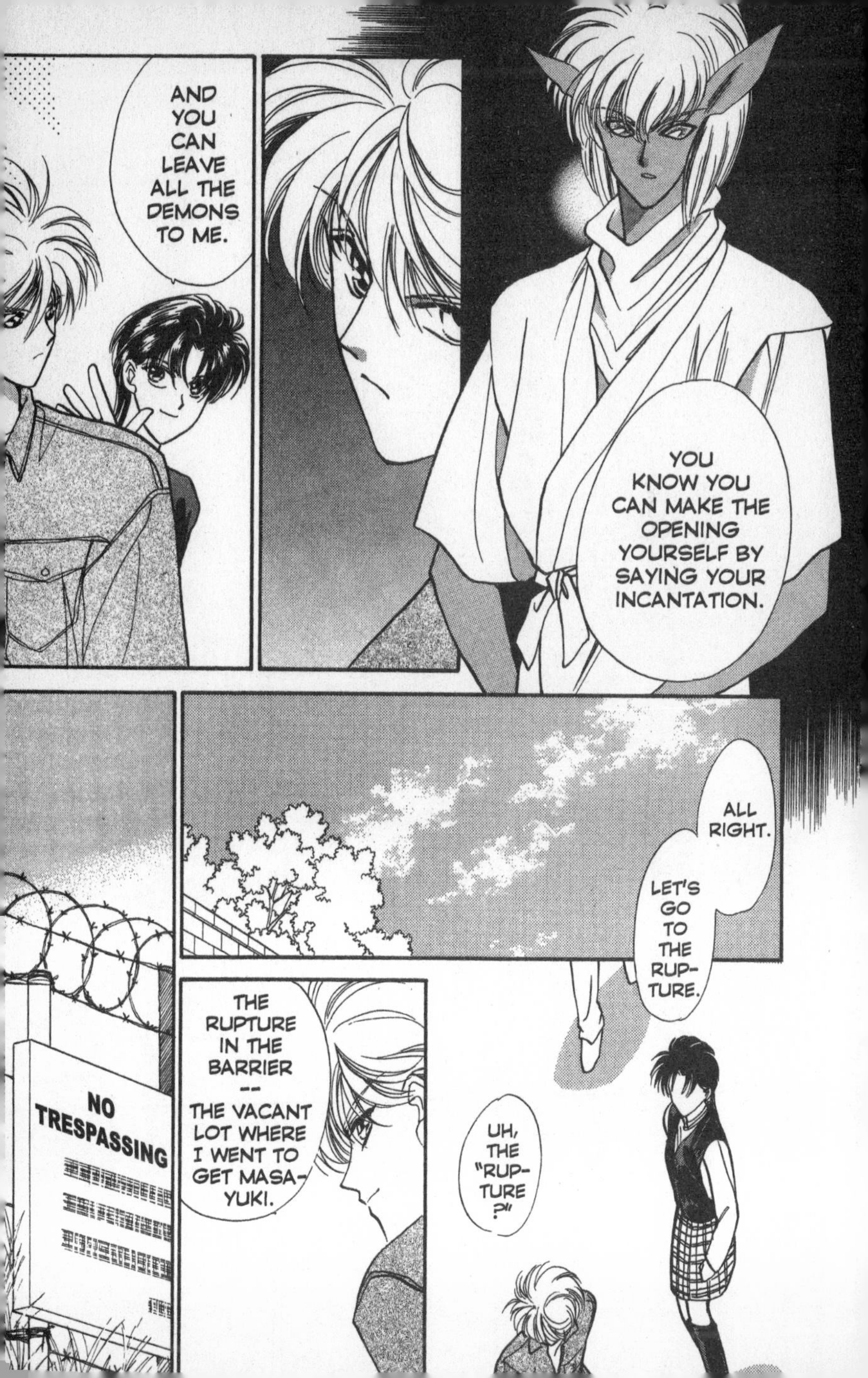
YOU KNOW YOU CAN MAKE THE OPENING YOURSELF BY SAYING YOUR INCANTATION.
AND YOU CAN LEAVE ALL THE DEMONS TO ME.
ALL RIGHT.
LET'S GO TO THE RUP-TURE.
UH, THE "RUP-TURE?"
THE RUPTURE IN THE BARRIER -- THE VACANT LOT WHERE I WENT TO GET MASA-YUKI.
NO TRESPASSING

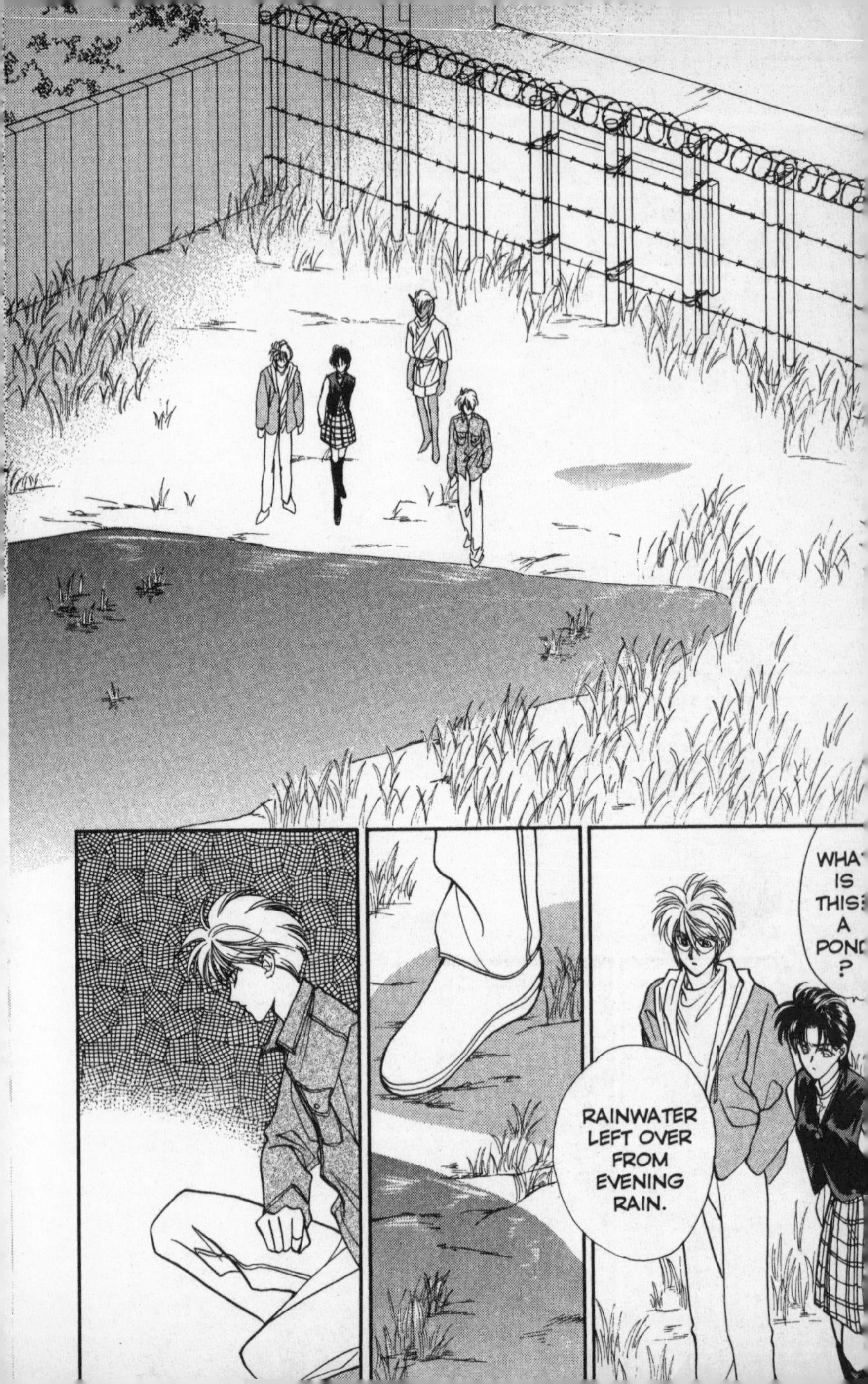
WHAT IS THIS? A POND?
RAINWATER LEFT OVER FROM EVENING RAIN.

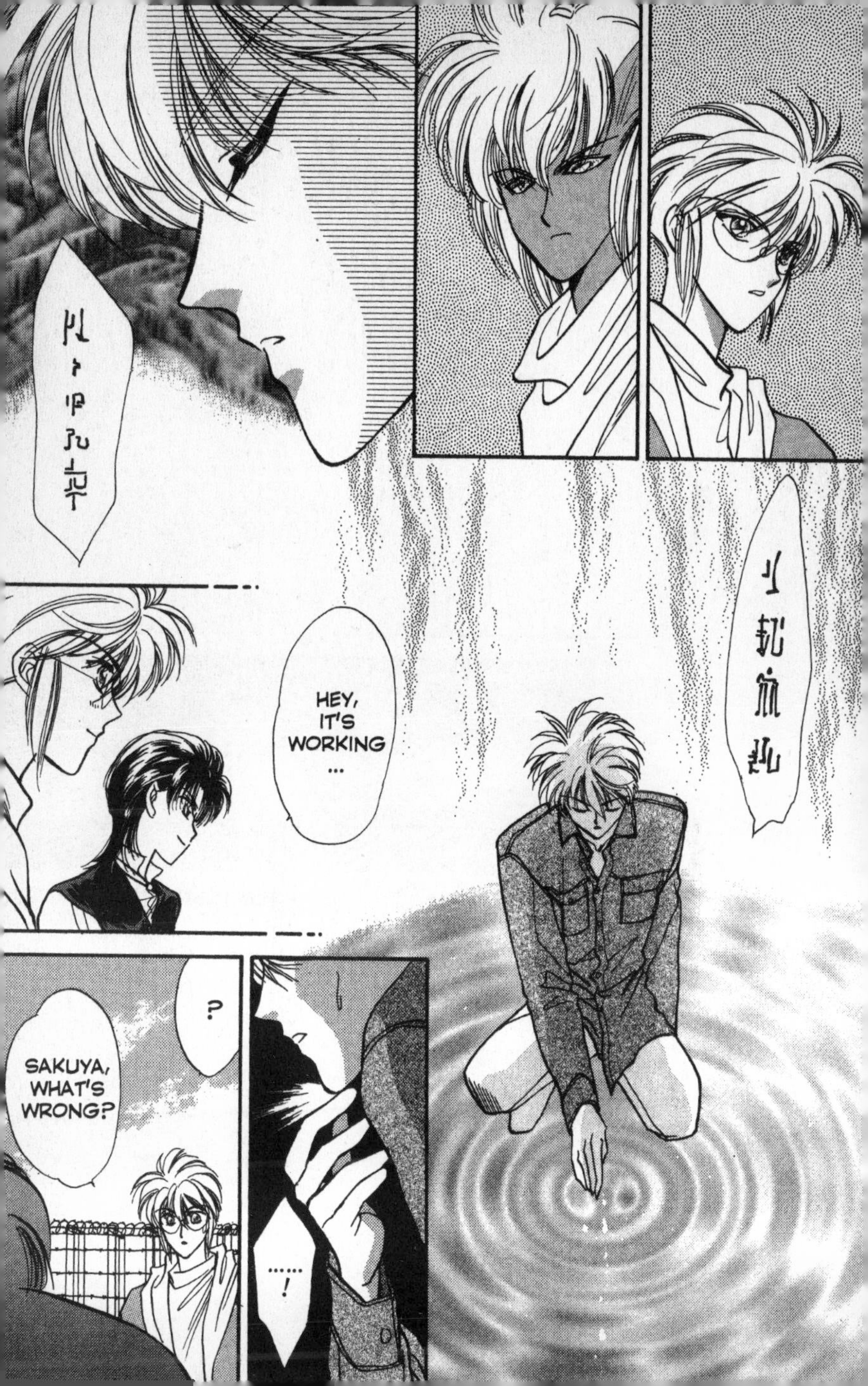
HEY, IT'S WORKING ...
......!
?
SAKUYA, WHAT'S WRONG?

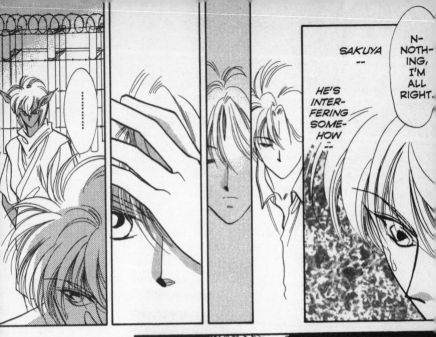

N-NOTHING, I'M ALL RIGHT.
SAKUYA --
HE'S INTERFERING SOMEHOW --
....
TSK, THIS IS A WASTE OF TIME --
THE INCANTATION HAS NO EFFECT.
TING
NO PROBLEM -- I'M SURE YOU WON'T MIND, SAKUYA.

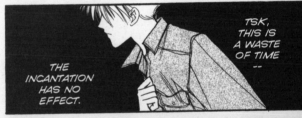

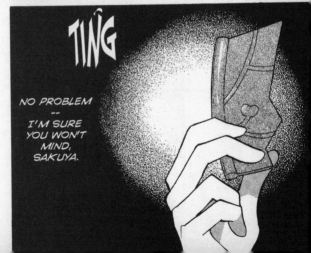

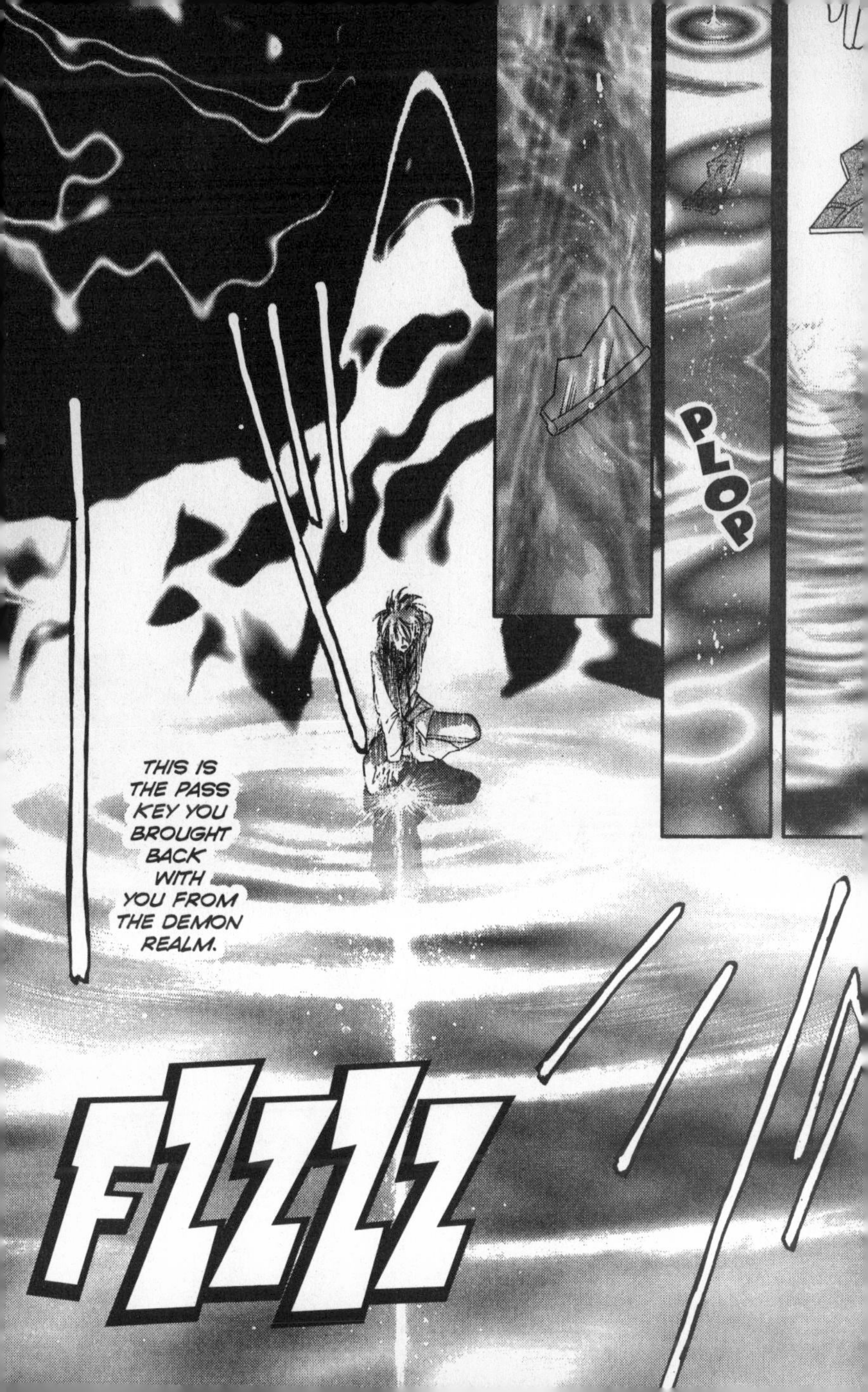
PLOP
THIS IS THE PASS KEY YOU BROUGHT BACK WITH YOU FROM THE DEMON REALM.
FZZZZ

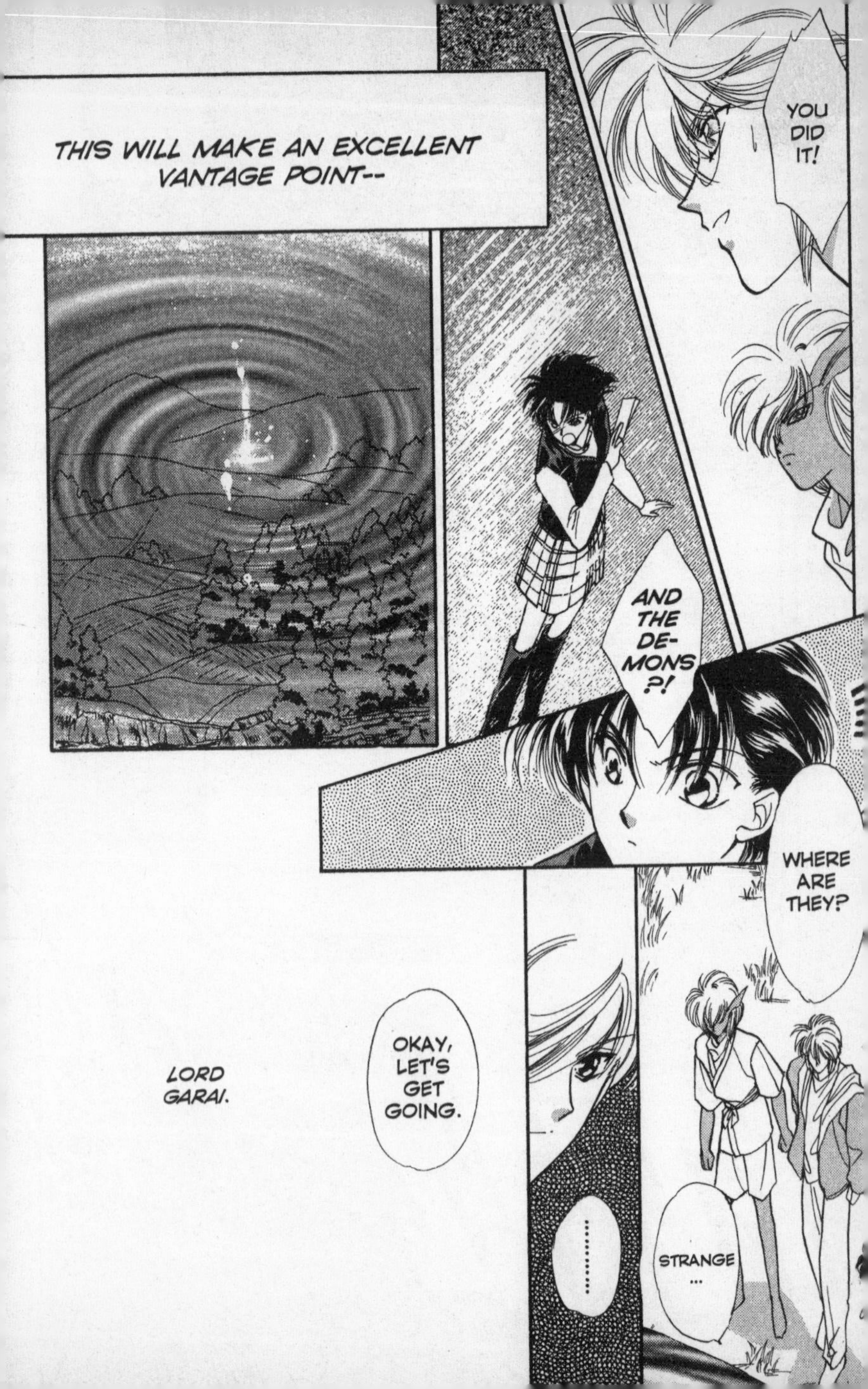
YOU DID IT!
AND THE DE-MONS?!
WHERE ARE THEY?
THIS WILL MAKE AN EXCELLENT VANTAGE POINT--
STRANGE...
....
OKAY, LET'S GET GOING.
LORD GARAI.

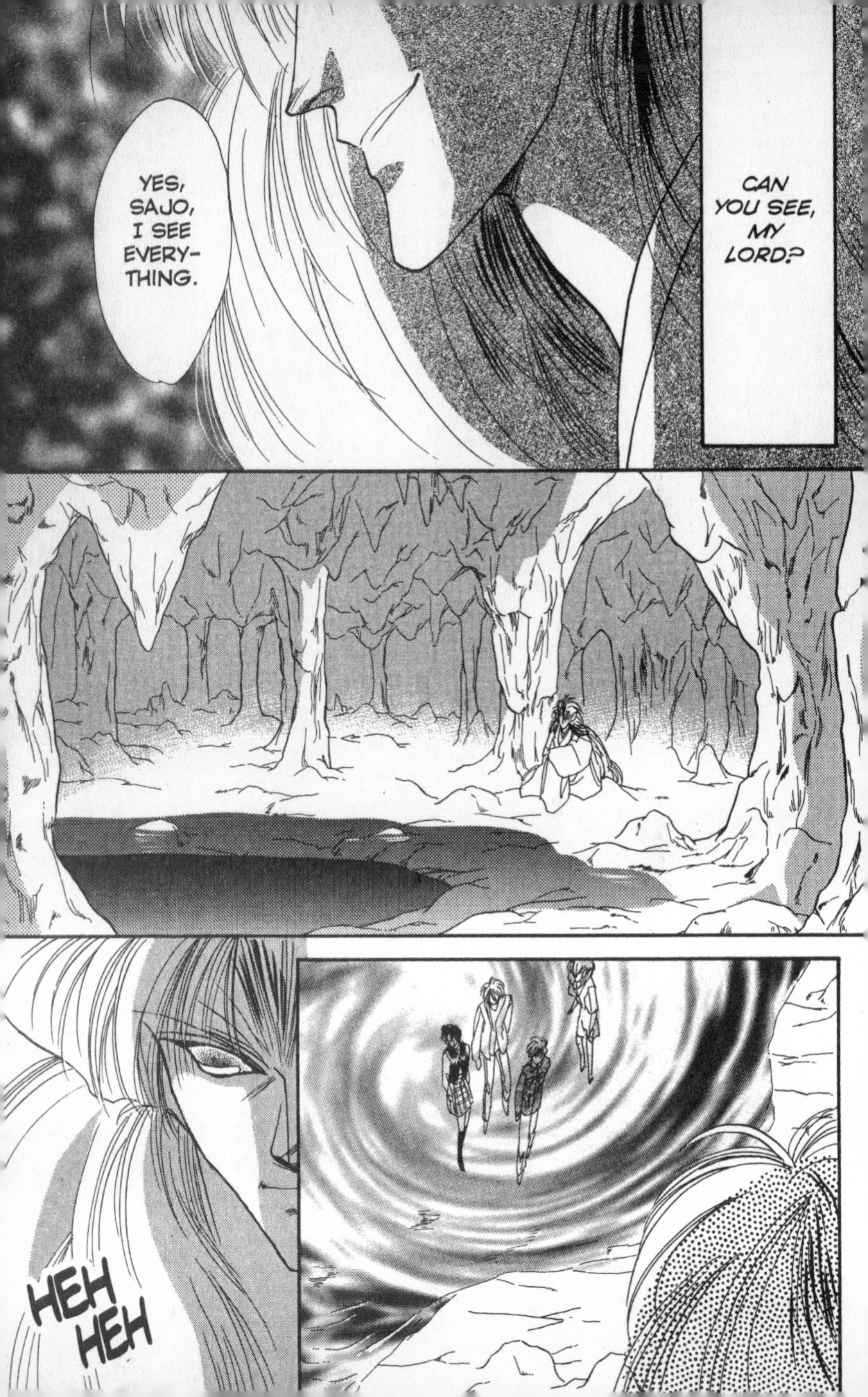
CAN YOU SEE, MY LORD?
YES, SAJO, I SEE EVERY-THING.
HEH HEH

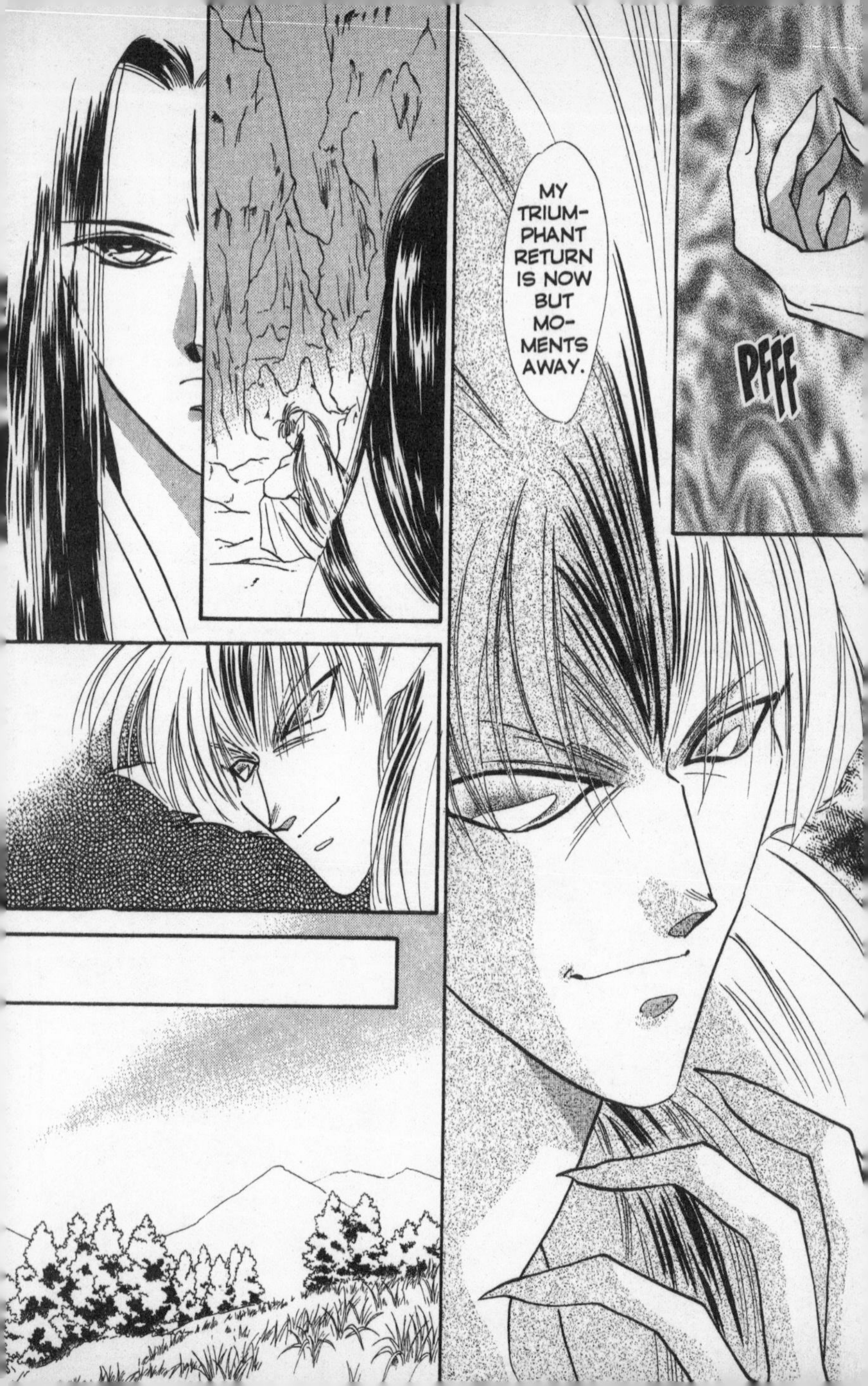
MY TRIUM-PHANT RETURN IS NOW BUT MO-MENTS AWAY.
PFFF

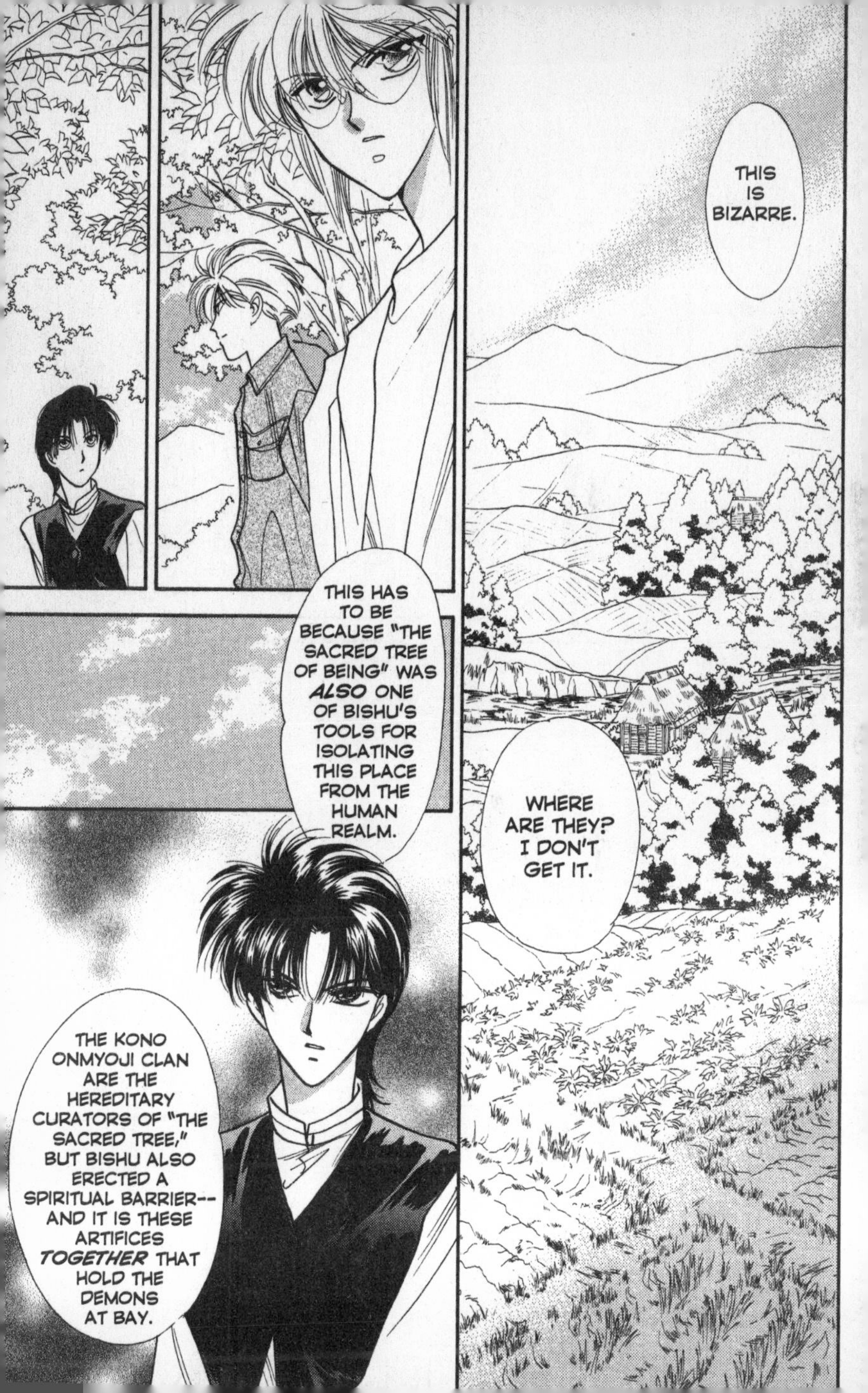
THIS IS BIZARRE.
WHERE ARE THEY? I DON'T GET IT.
THIS HAS TO BE BECAUSE "THE SACRED TREE OF BEING" WAS *ALSO* ONE OF BISHU'S TOOLS FOR ISOLATING THIS PLACE FROM THE HUMAN REALM.
THE KONO ONMYOJI CLAN ARE THE HEREDITARY CURATORS OF "THE SACRED TREE," BUT BISHU ALSO ERECTED A SPIRITUAL BARRIER-- AND IT IS THESE ARTIFICES *TOGETHER* THAT HOLD THE DEMONS AT BAY.

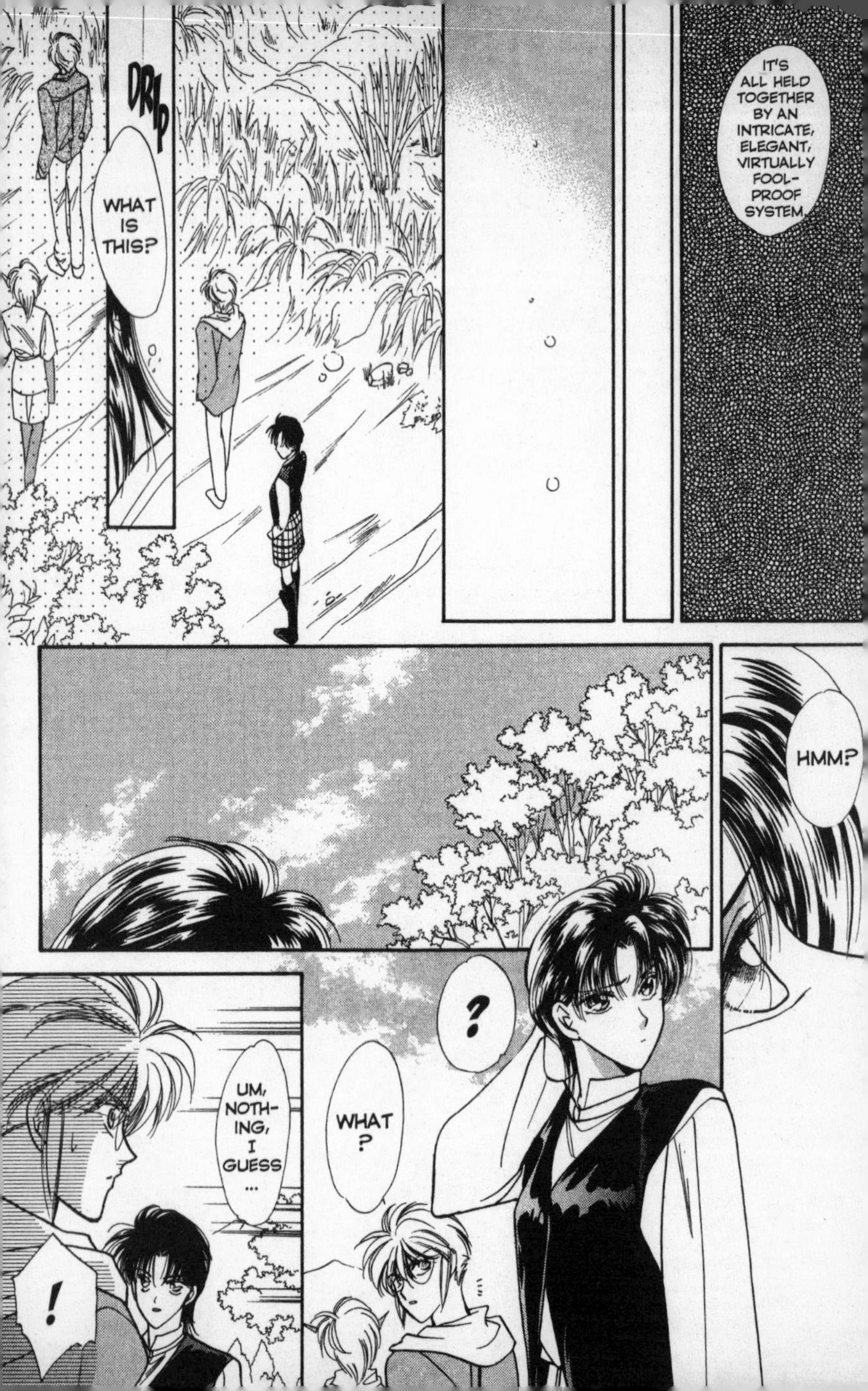
IT'S ALL HELD TOGETHER BY AN INTRICATE, ELEGANT, VIRTUALLY FOOL-PROOF SYSTEM.
DRIP
WHAT IS THIS?
HMM?
?
WHAT?
UM, NOTHING, I GUESS ...
!

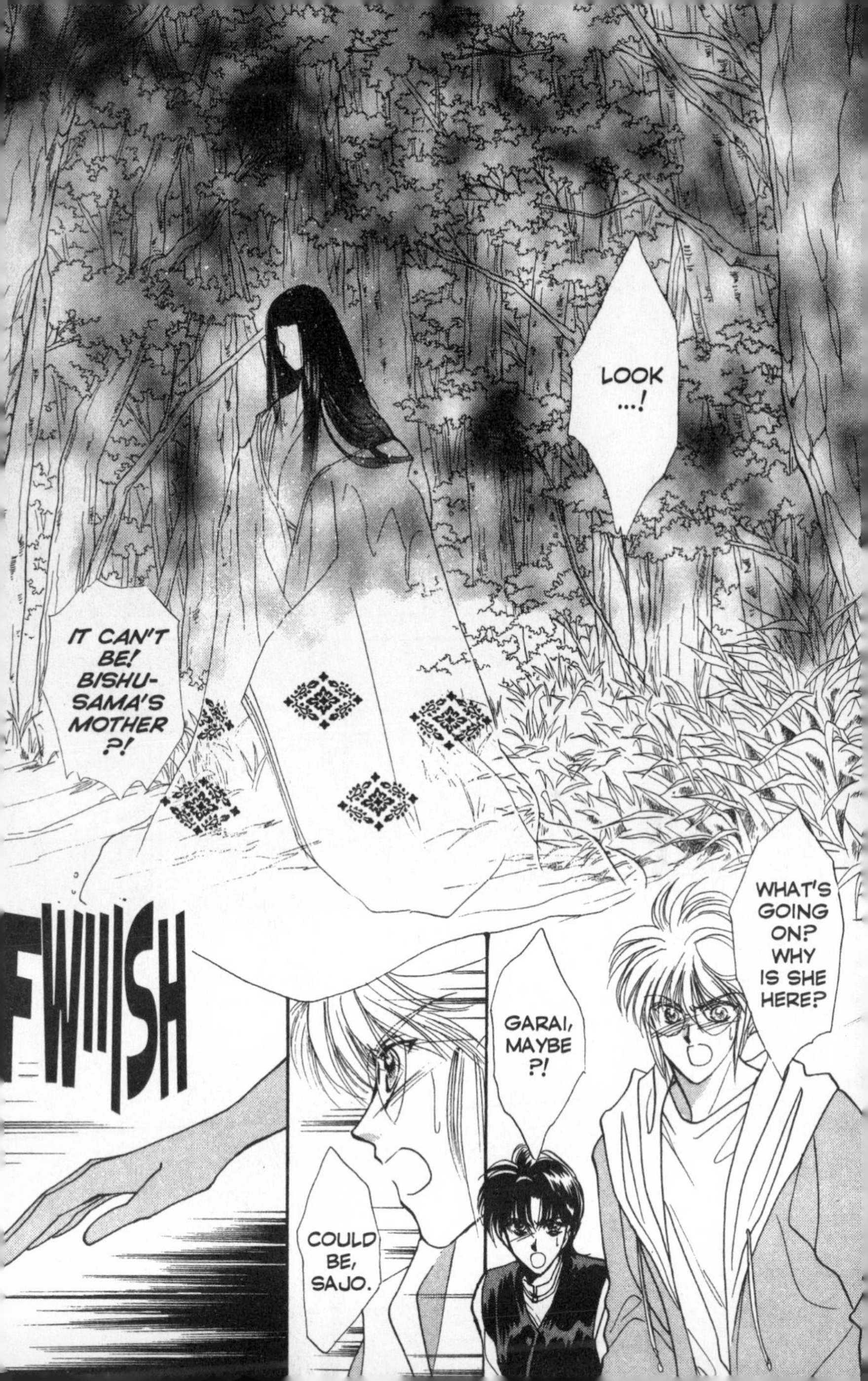
LOOK ...!
IT CAN'T BE! BISHU-SAMA'S MOTHER ?!
WHAT'S GOING ON? WHY IS SHE HERE?
GARAI, MAYBE ?!
COULD BE, SAJO.
FWIIISH

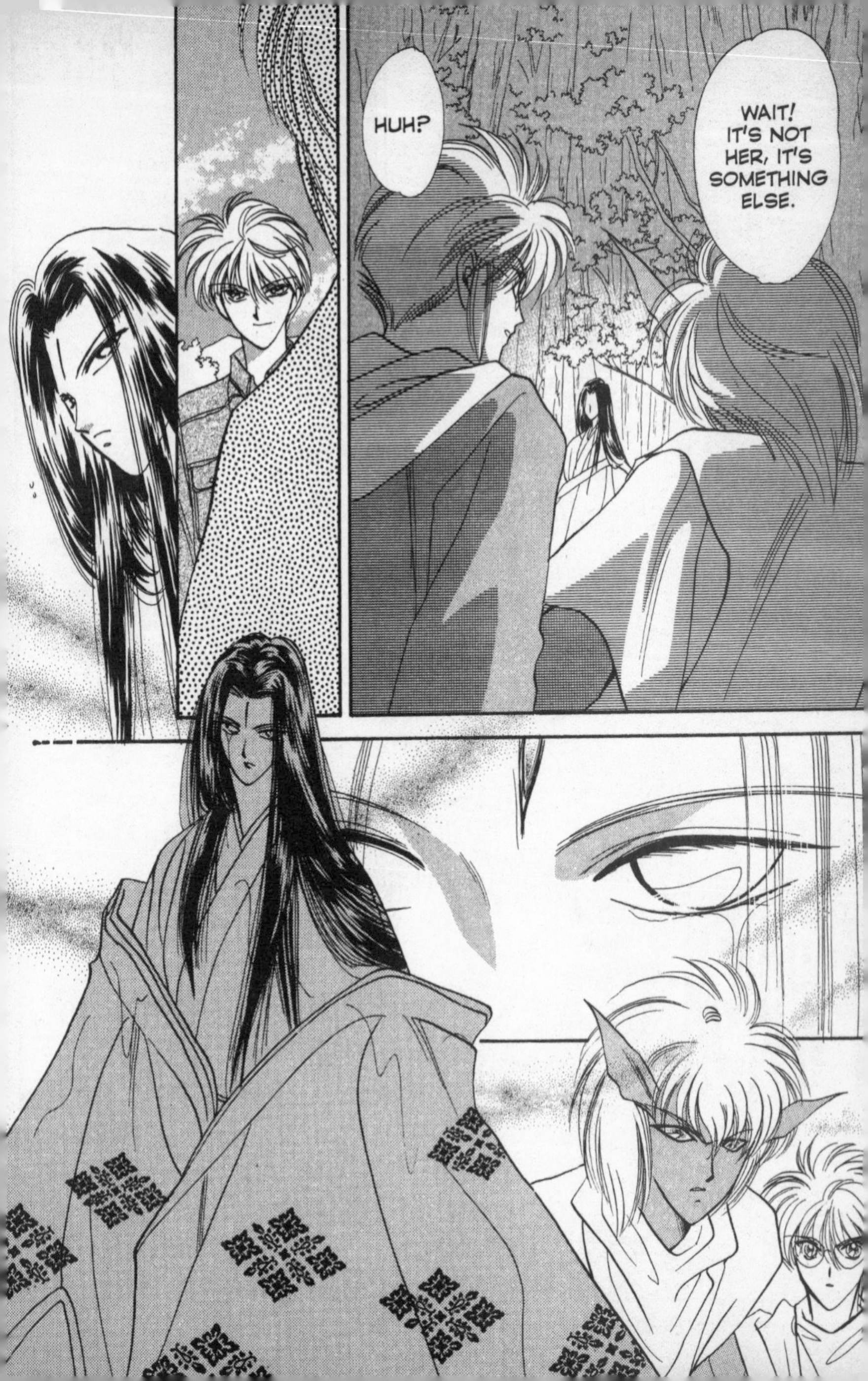
WAIT! IT'S NOT HER, IT'S SOMETHING ELSE.
HUH?

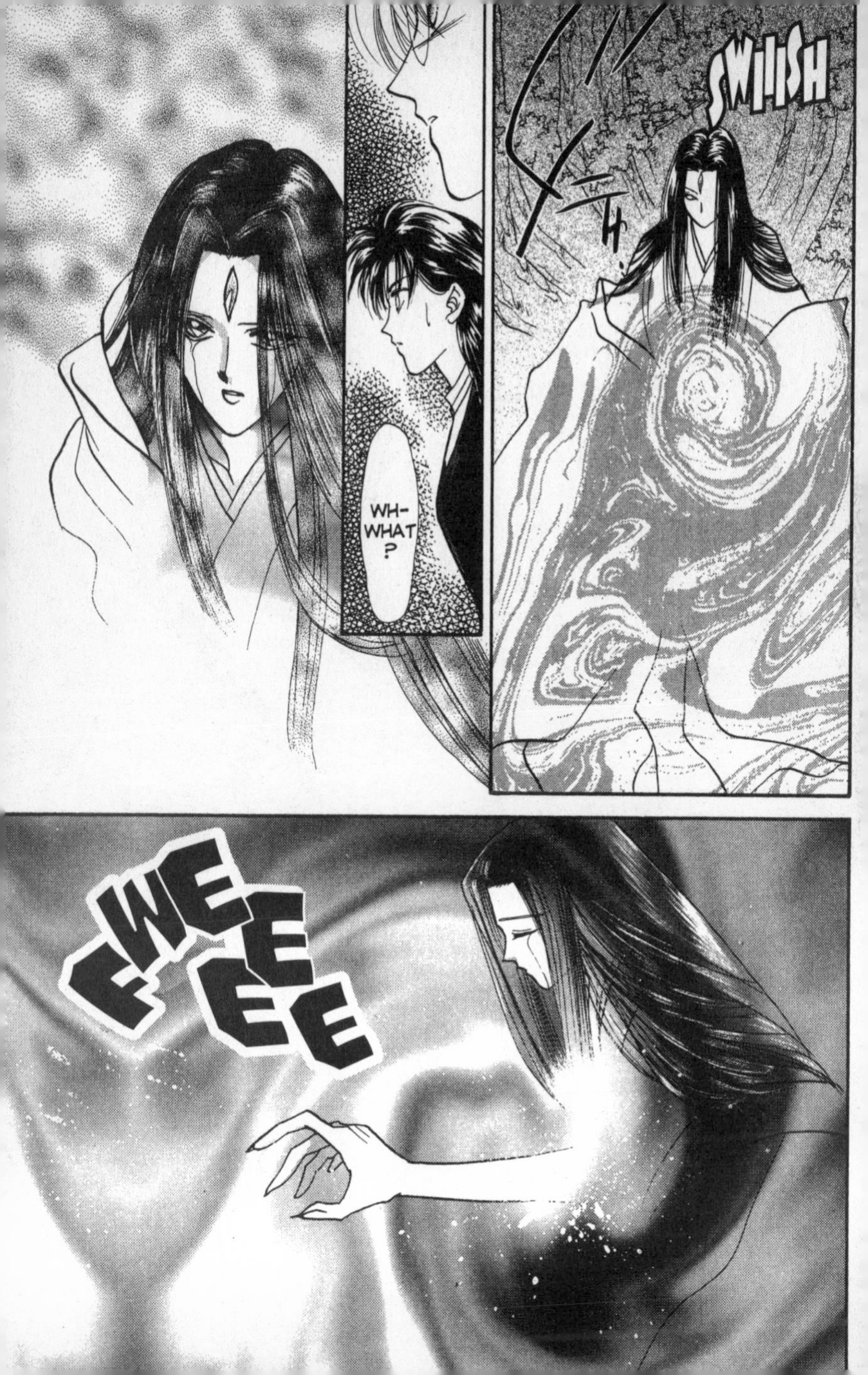
SWIISH
WH-WHAT?
FWEEEE

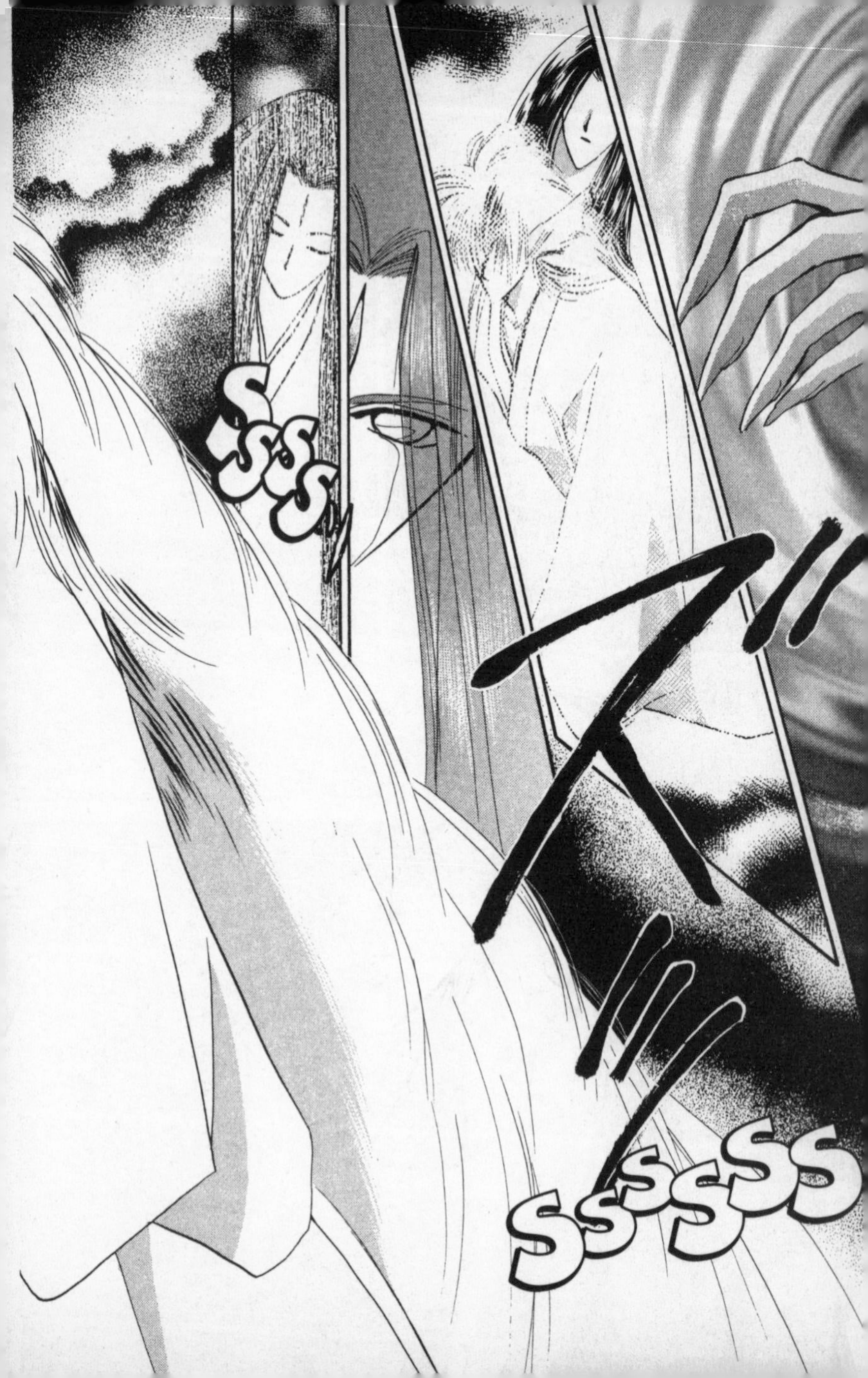
SSSS
SSSSSS

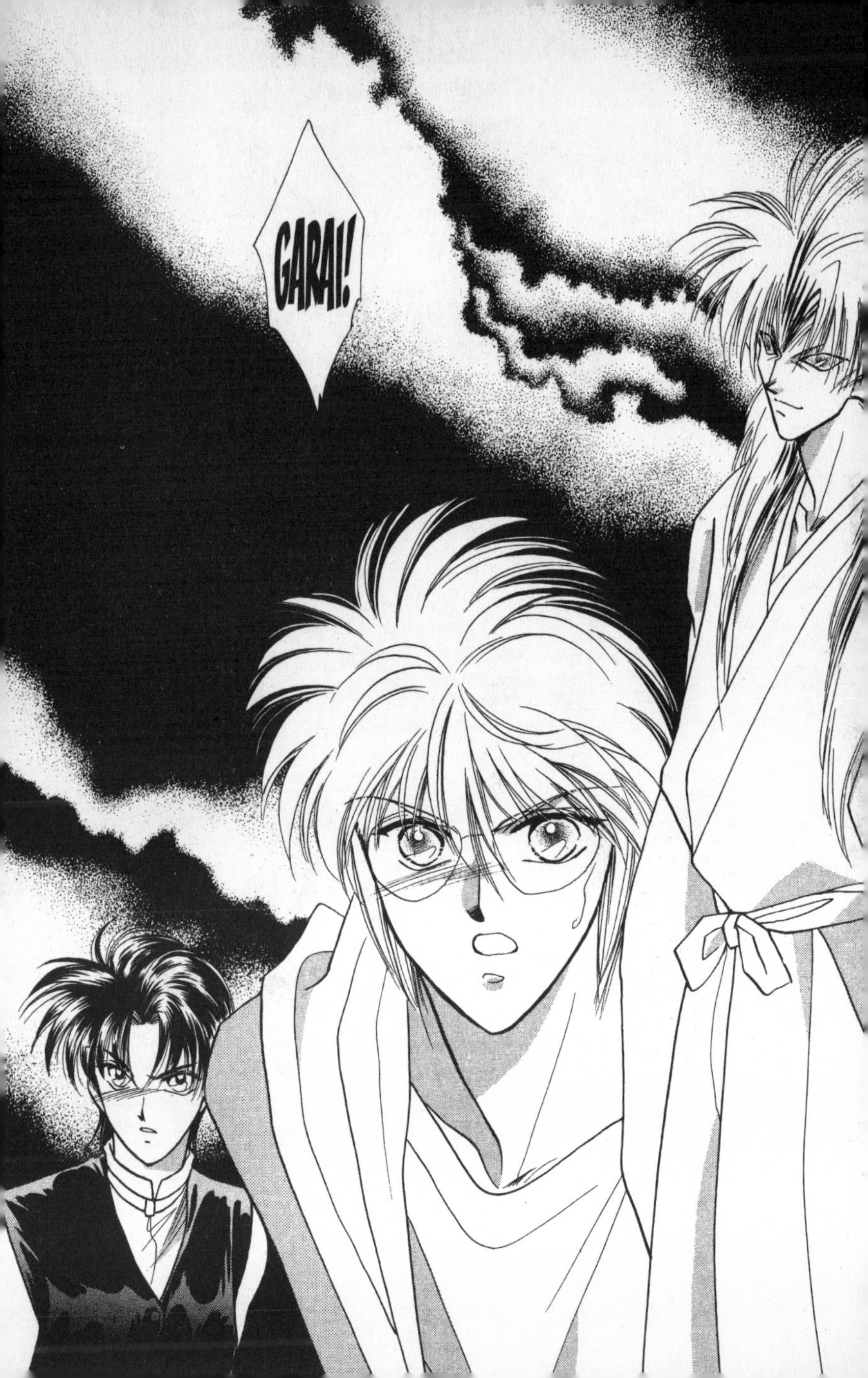
GARAI!

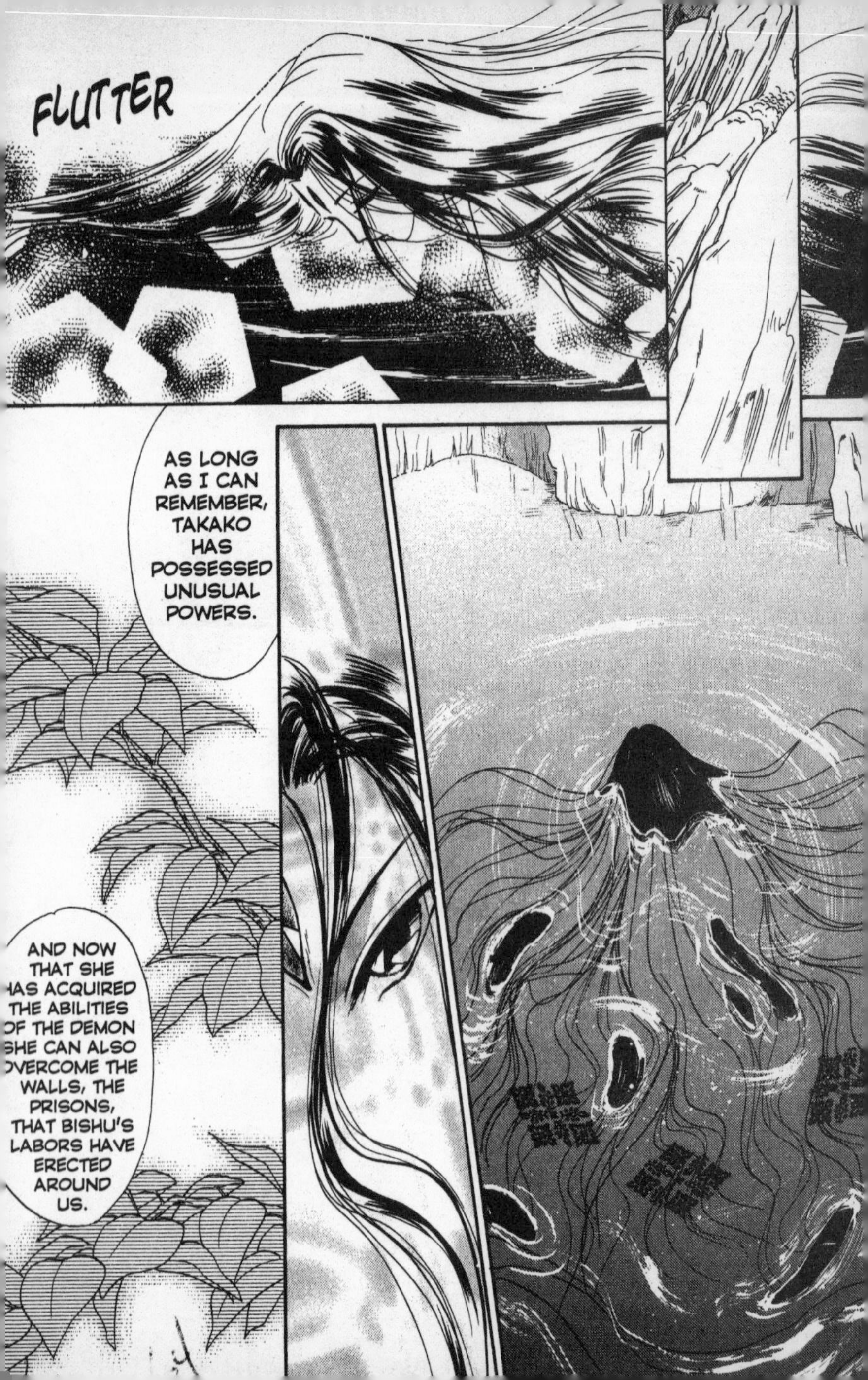
FLUTTER
AS LONG AS I CAN REMEMBER, TAKAKO HAS POSSESSED UNUSUAL POWERS.
AND NOW THAT SHE HAS ACQUIRED THE ABILITIES OF THE DEMON SHE CAN ALSO OVERCOME THE WALLS, THE PRISONS, THAT BISHU'S LABORS HAVE ERECTED AROUND US.

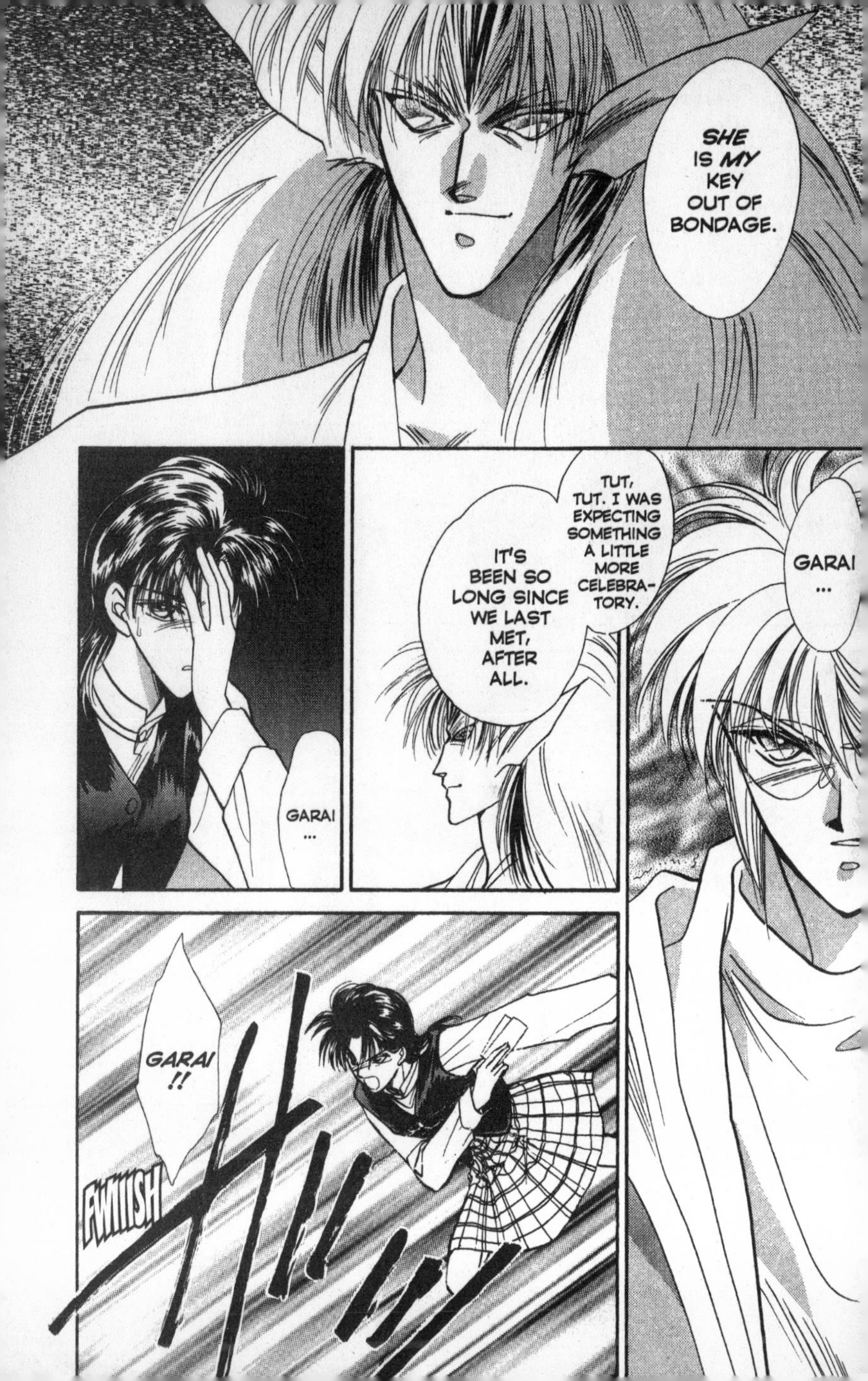
SHE IS MY KEY OUT OF BONDAGE.
GARAI ...
TUT, TUT. I WAS EXPECTING SOMETHING A LITTLE MORE CELEBRATORY.
IT'S BEEN SO LONG SINCE WE LAST MET, AFTER ALL.
GARAI ...
GARAI !!
FWIIISH

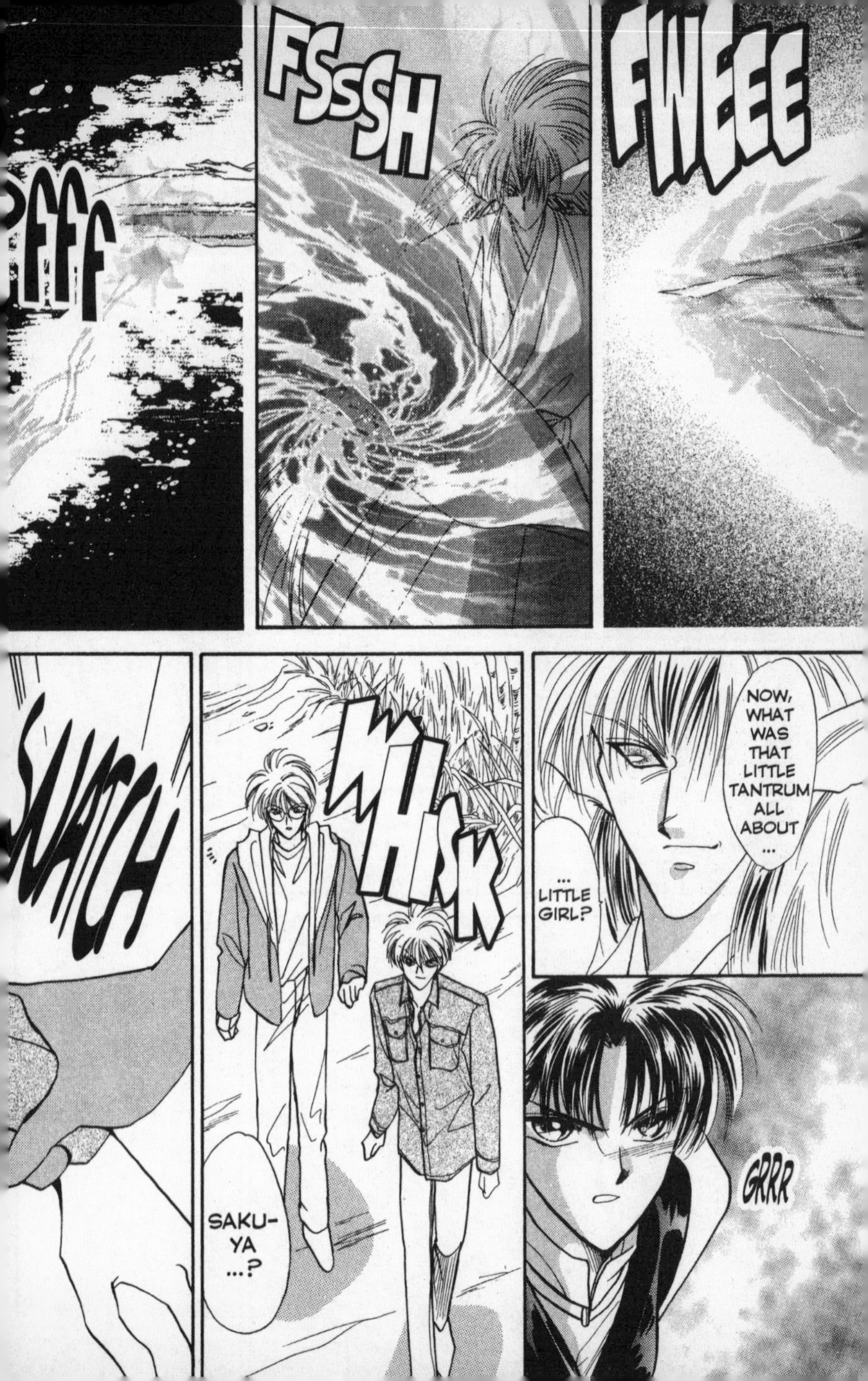
FWEEE
FSSSH
PFFF
NOW, WHAT WAS THAT LITTLE TANTRUM ALL ABOUT ...
... LITTLE GIRL?
GRRR
WHISK
SAKU-YA ...?
SNATCH

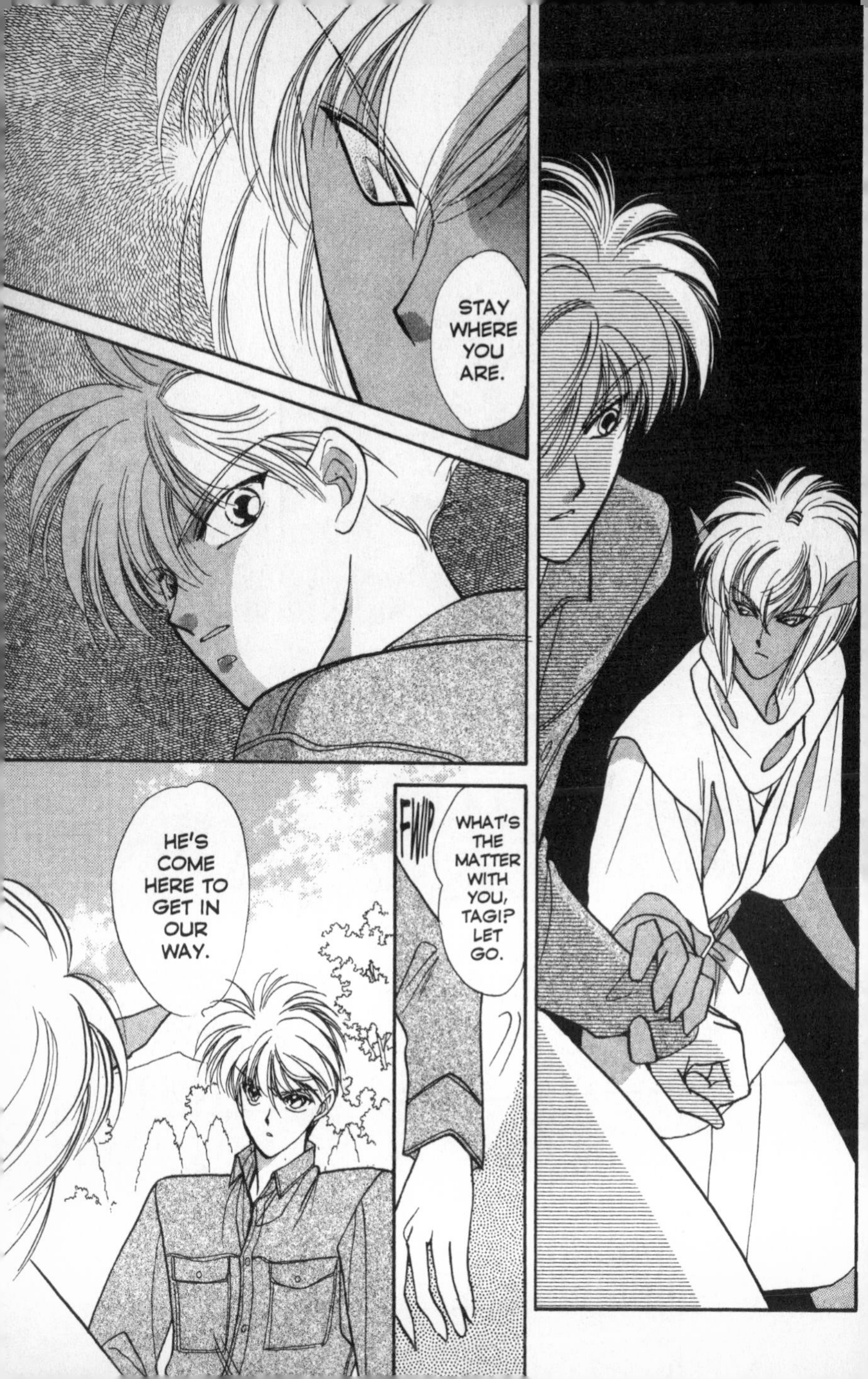
STAY WHERE YOU ARE.
FWIP
WHAT'S THE MATTER WITH YOU, TAGI? LET GO.
HE'S COME HERE TO GET IN OUR WAY.

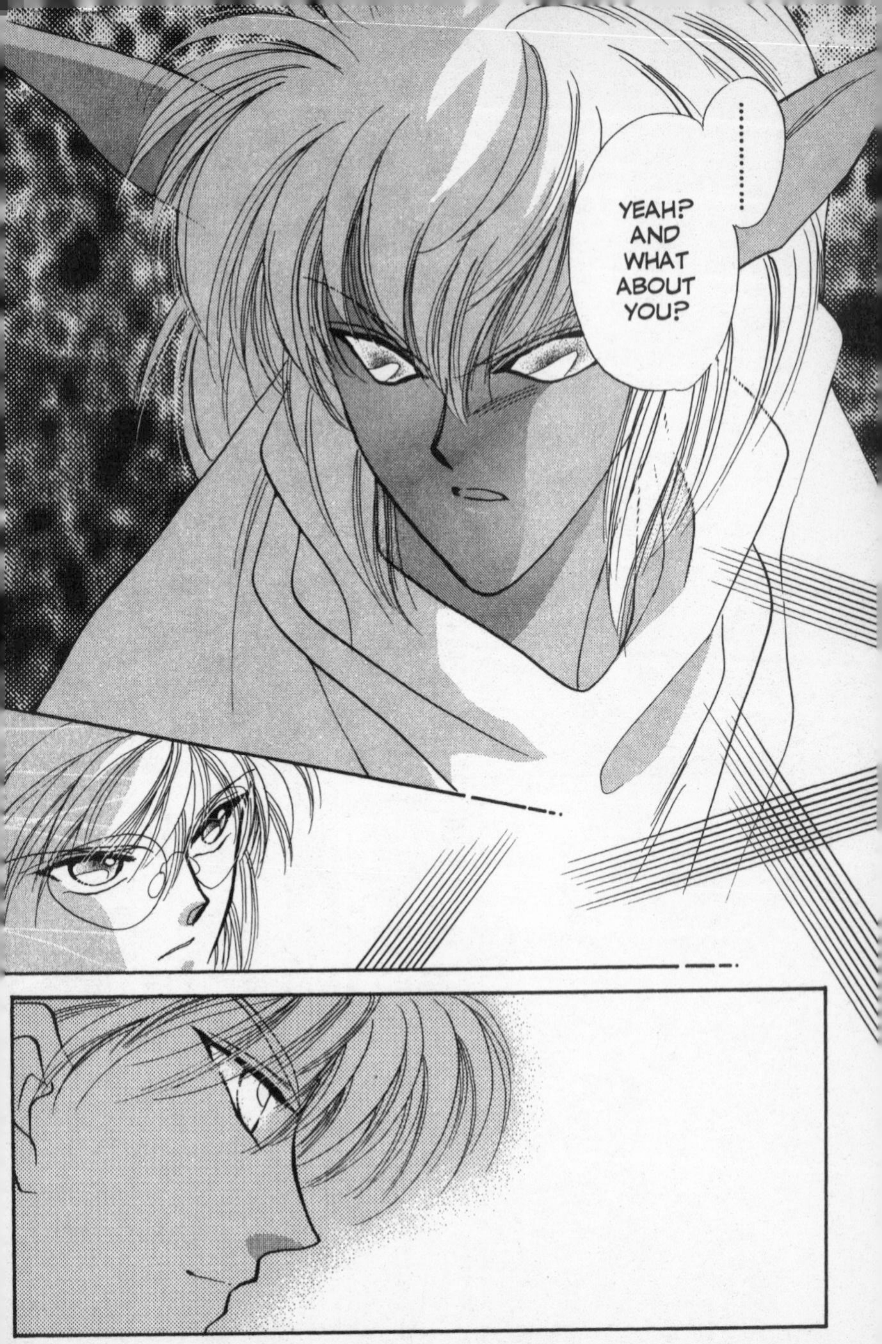
....
YEAH? AND WHAT ABOUT YOU?

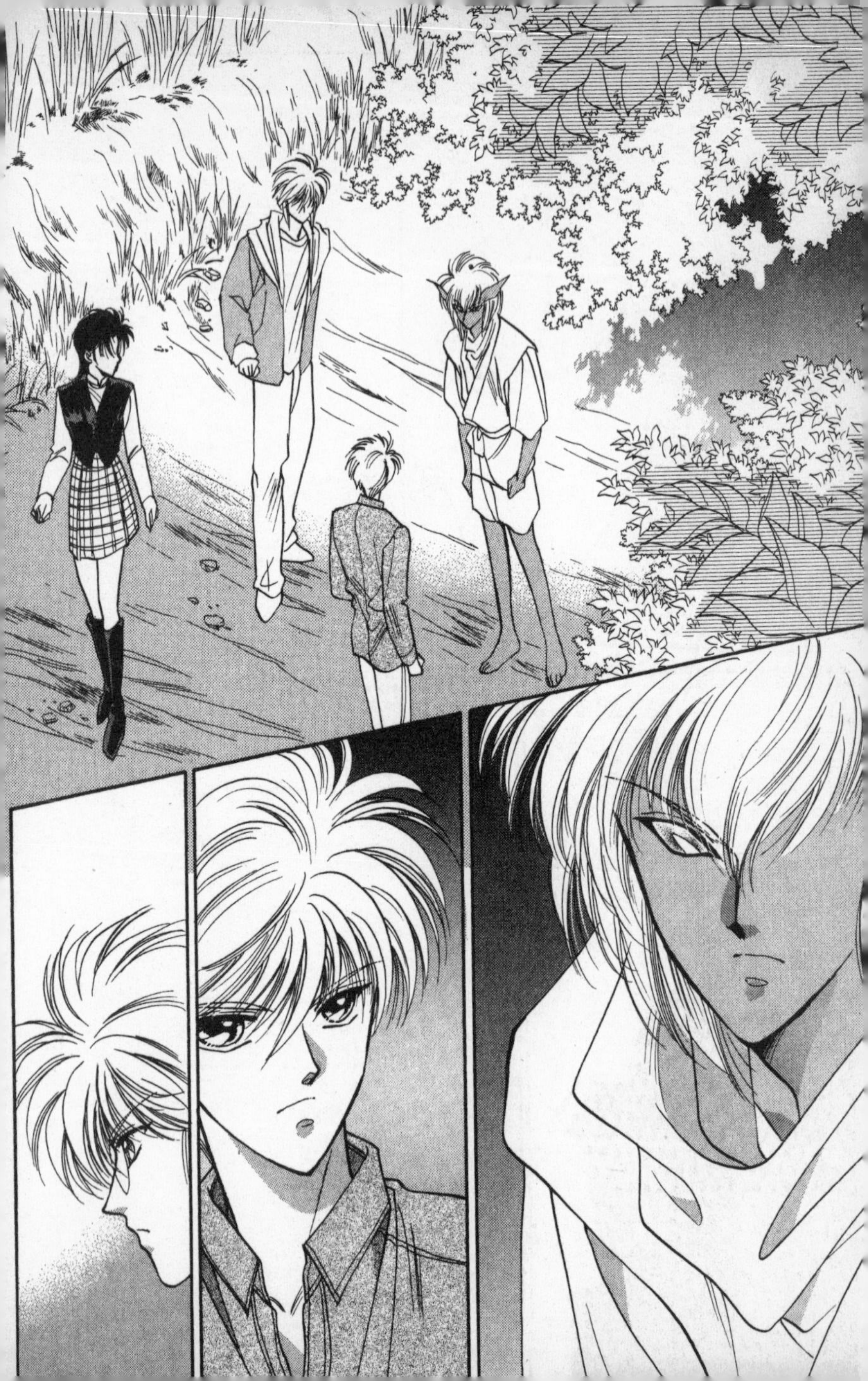

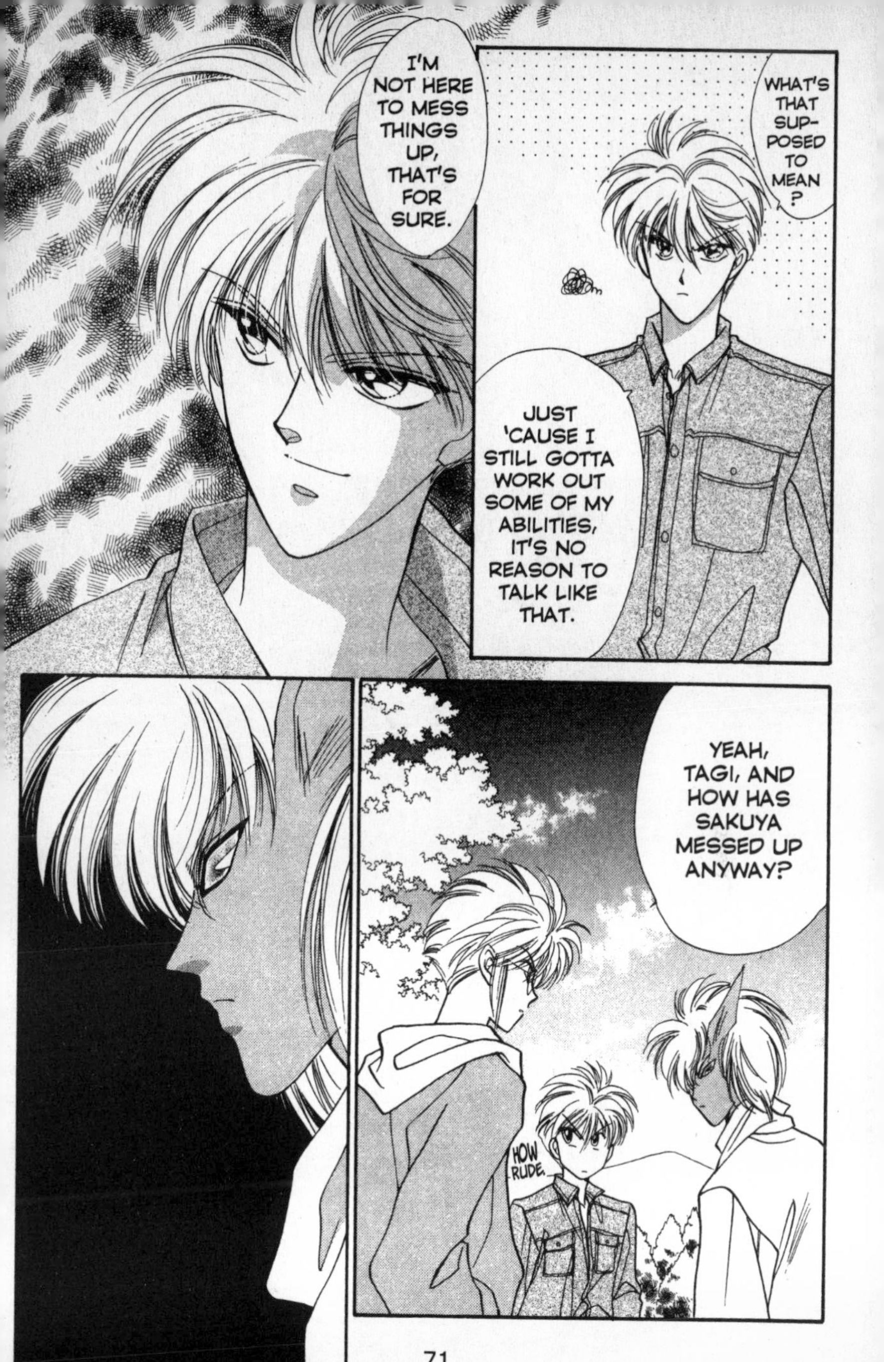
WHAT'S THAT SUP-POSED TO MEAN?
I'M NOT HERE TO MESS THINGS UP, THAT'S FOR SURE.
JUST 'CAUSE I STILL GOTTA WORK OUT SOME OF MY ABILITIES, IT'S NO REASON TO TALK LIKE THAT.
YEAH, TAGI, AND HOW HAS SAKUYA MESSED UP ANYWAY?
HOW RUDE.

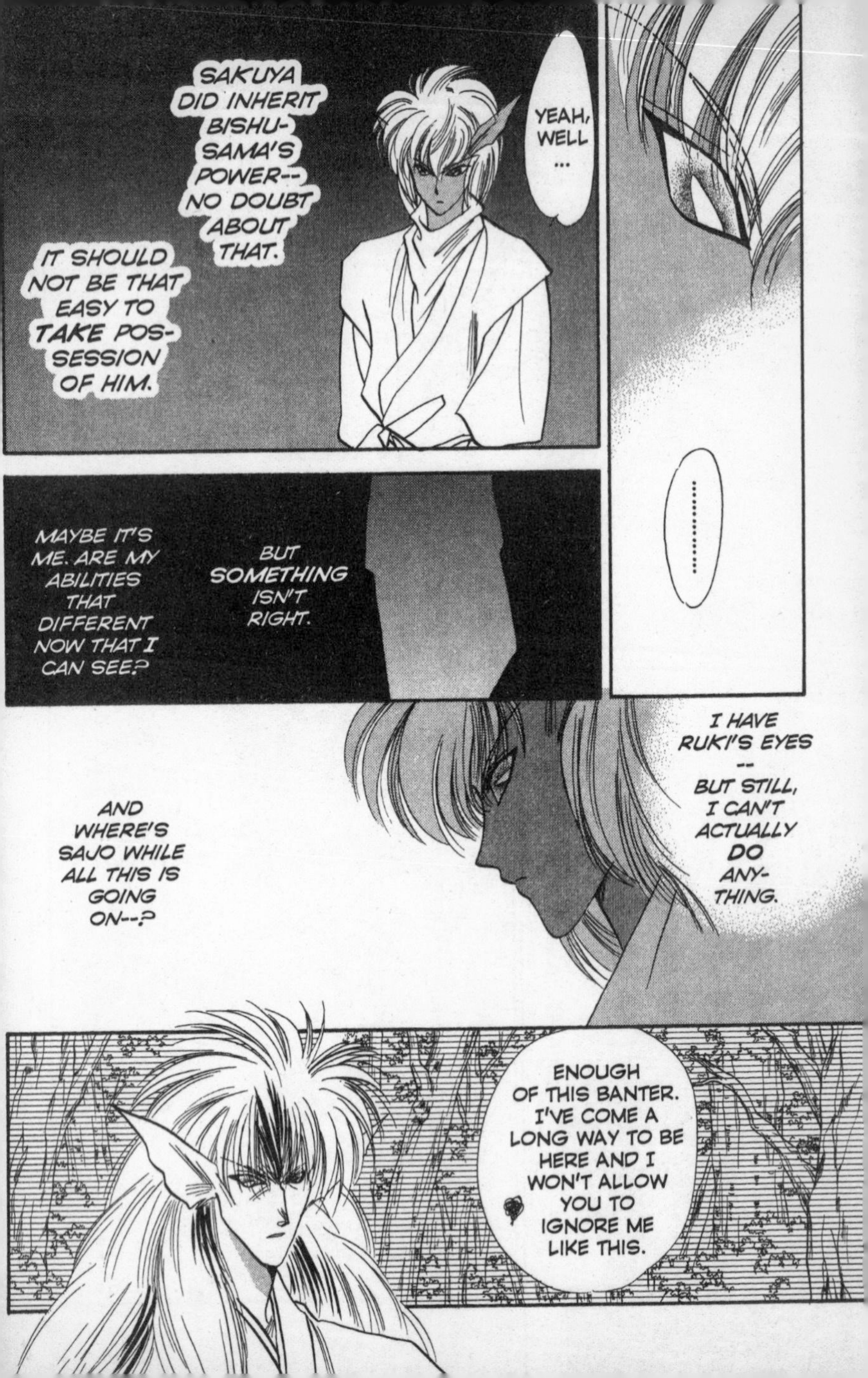
......
YEAH, WELL ...
SAKUYA DID INHERIT BISHU-SAMA'S POWER-- NO DOUBT ABOUT THAT.
IT SHOULD NOT BE THAT EASY TO TAKE POS-SESSION OF HIM.
BUT SOMETHING ISN'T RIGHT.
MAYBE IT'S ME. ARE MY ABILITIES THAT DIFFERENT NOW THAT I CAN SEE?
I HAVE RUKI'S EYES -- BUT STILL, I CAN'T ACTUALLY DO ANY-THING.
AND WHERE'S SAJO WHILE ALL THIS IS GOING ON--?
ENOUGH OF THIS BANTER. I'VE COME A LONG WAY TO BE HERE AND I WON'T ALLOW YOU TO IGNORE ME LIKE THIS.

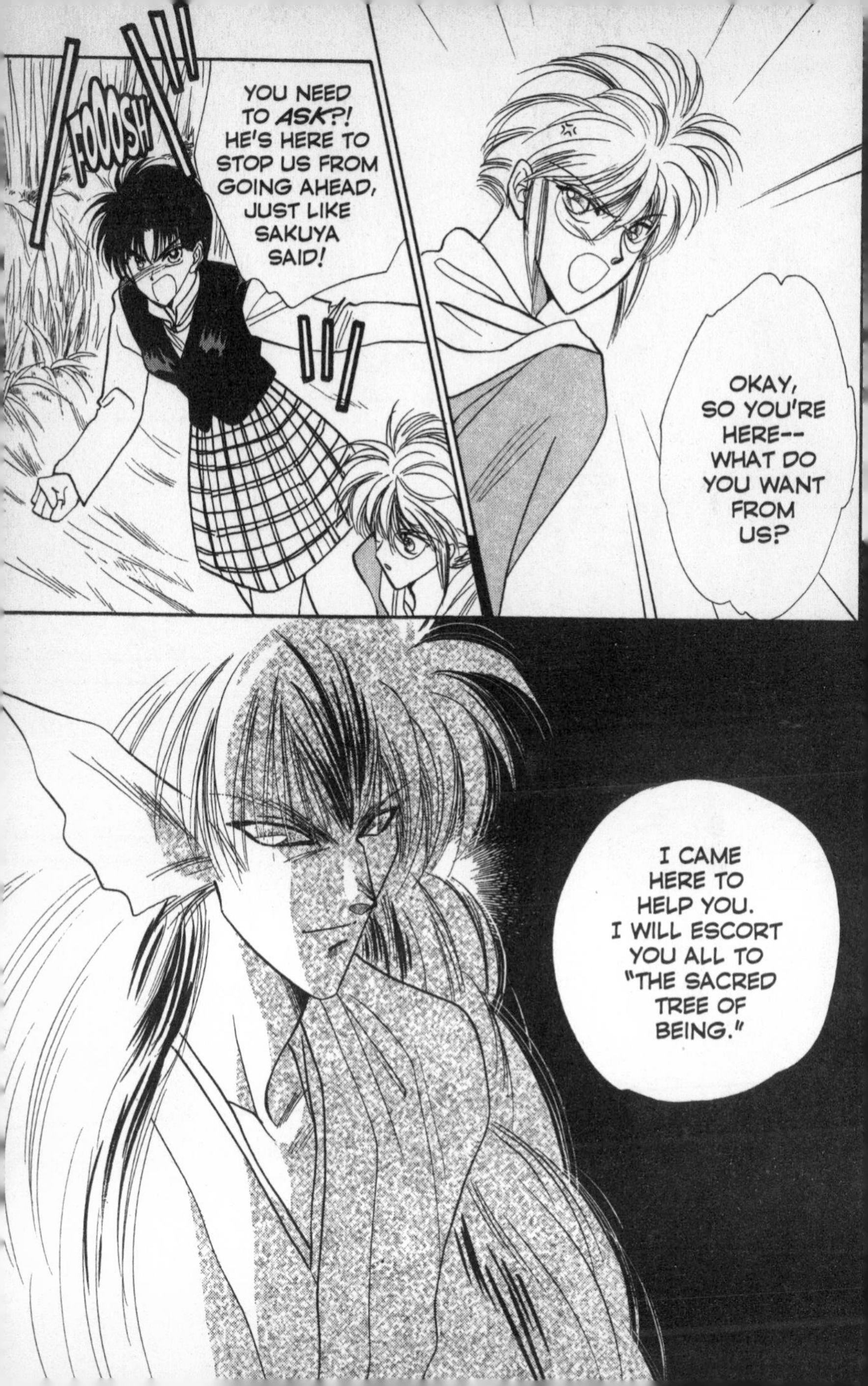
OKAY, SO YOU'RE HERE-- WHAT DO YOU WANT FROM US?
FOOOSH
YOU NEED TO ASK?! HE'S HERE TO STOP US FROM GOING AHEAD, JUST LIKE SAKUYA SAID!
I CAME HERE TO HELP YOU. I WILL ESCORT YOU ALL TO "THE SACRED TREE OF BEING."

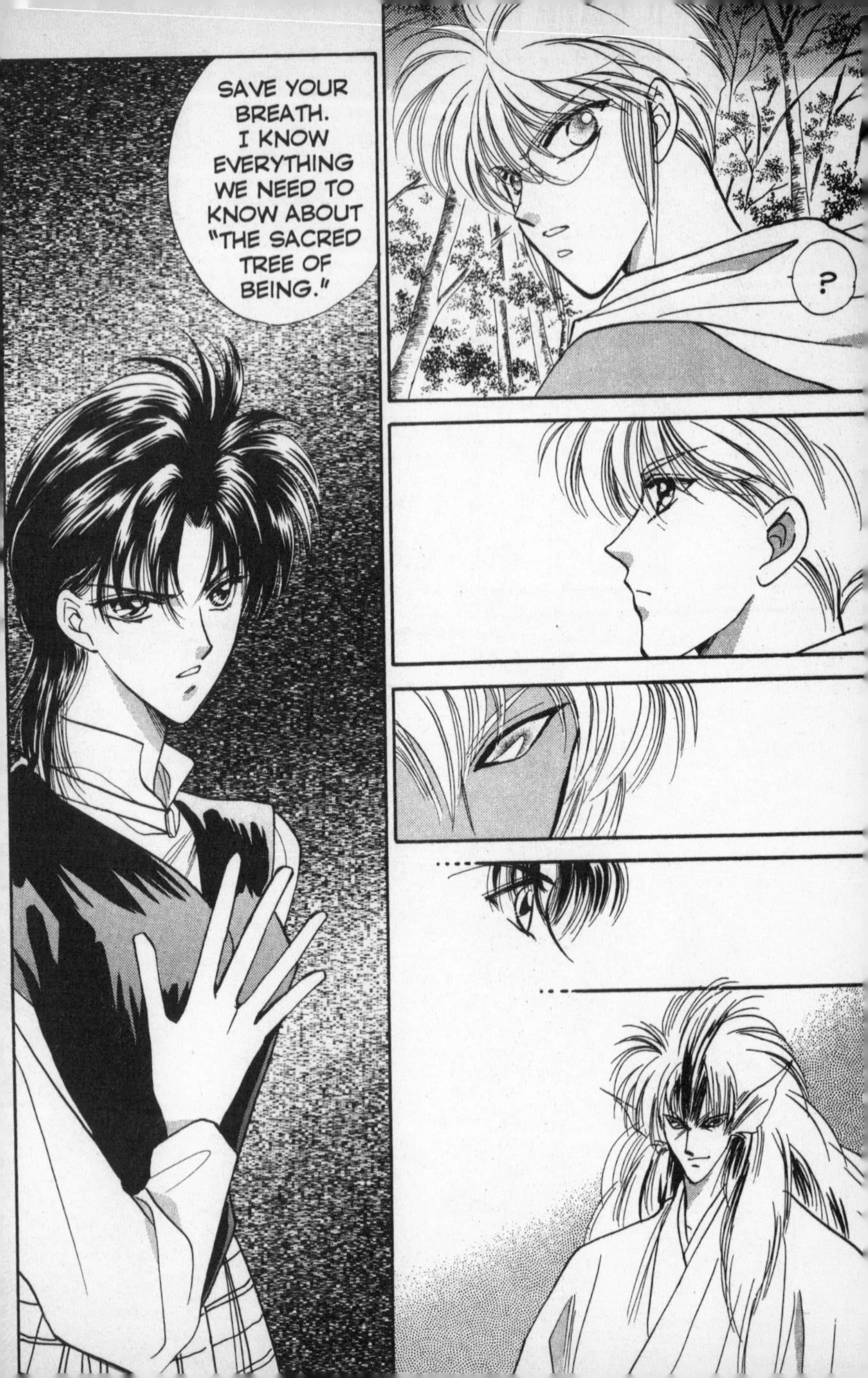
?
SAVE YOUR BREATH. I KNOW EVERYTHING WE NEED TO KNOW ABOUT "THE SACRED TREE OF BEING."

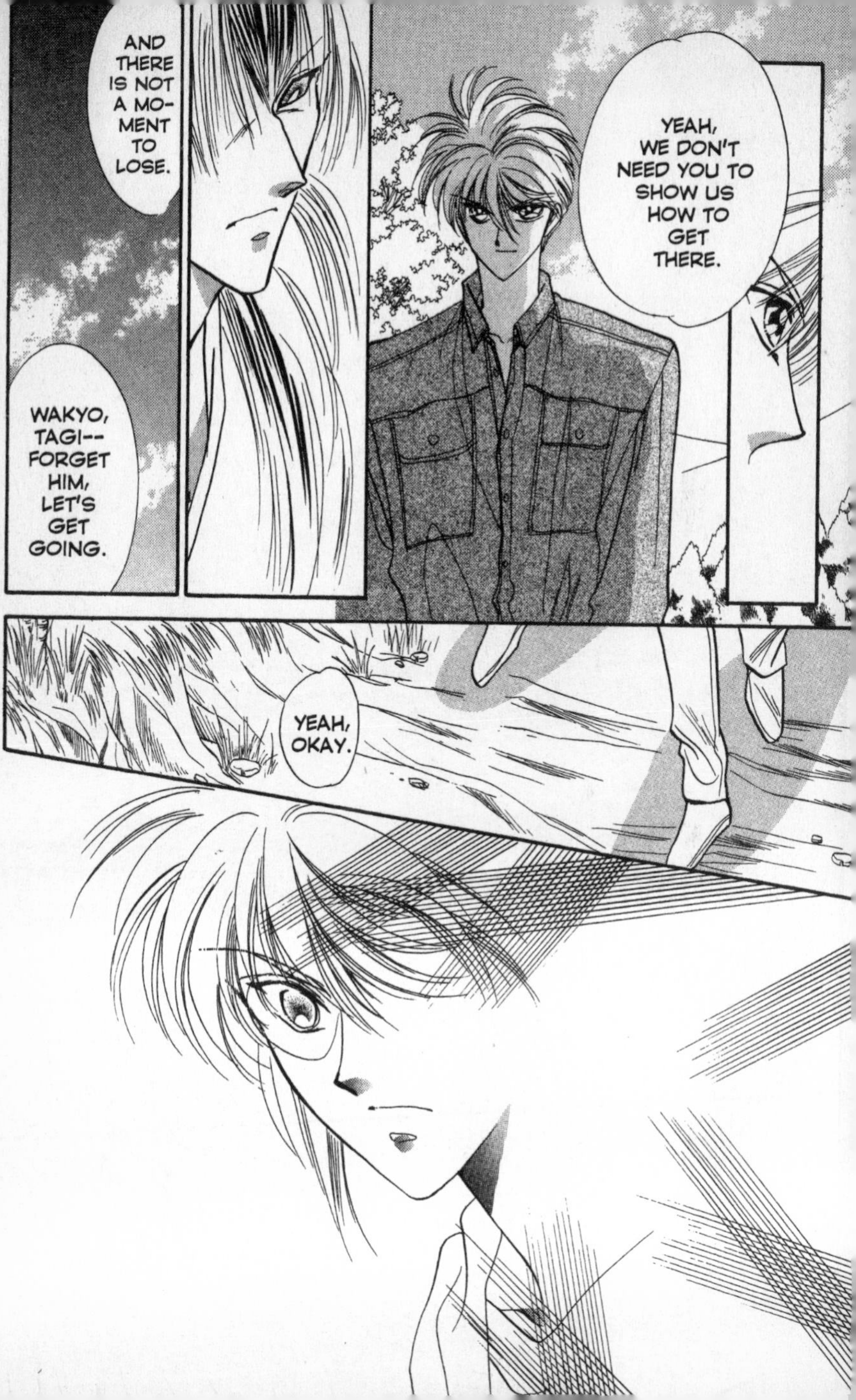
YEAH, WE DON'T NEED YOU TO SHOW US HOW TO GET THERE.
AND THERE IS NOT A MO-MENT TO LOSE.
WAKYO, TAGI-- FORGET HIM, LET'S GET GOING.
YEAH, OKAY.

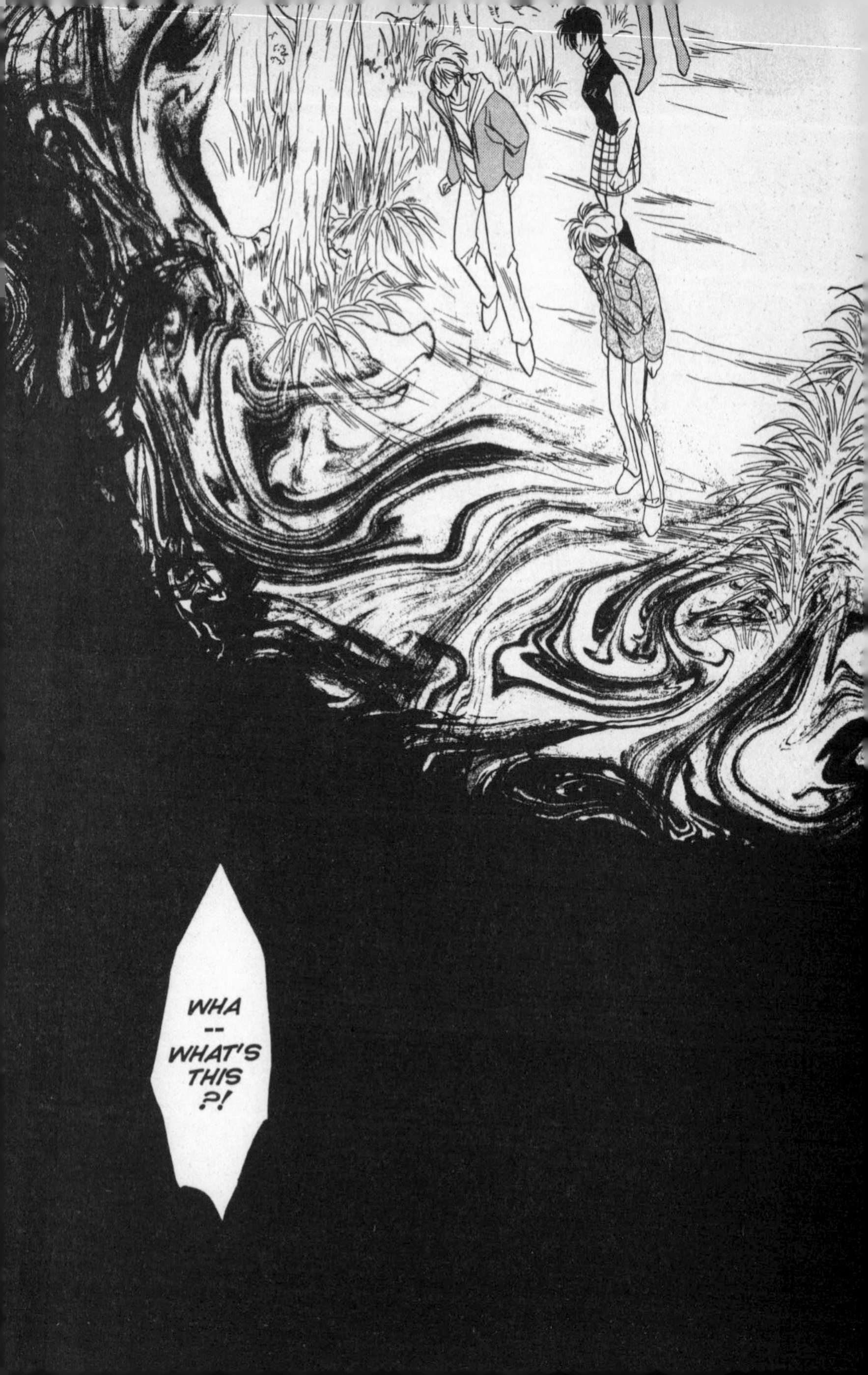
WHA -- WHAT'S THIS ?!

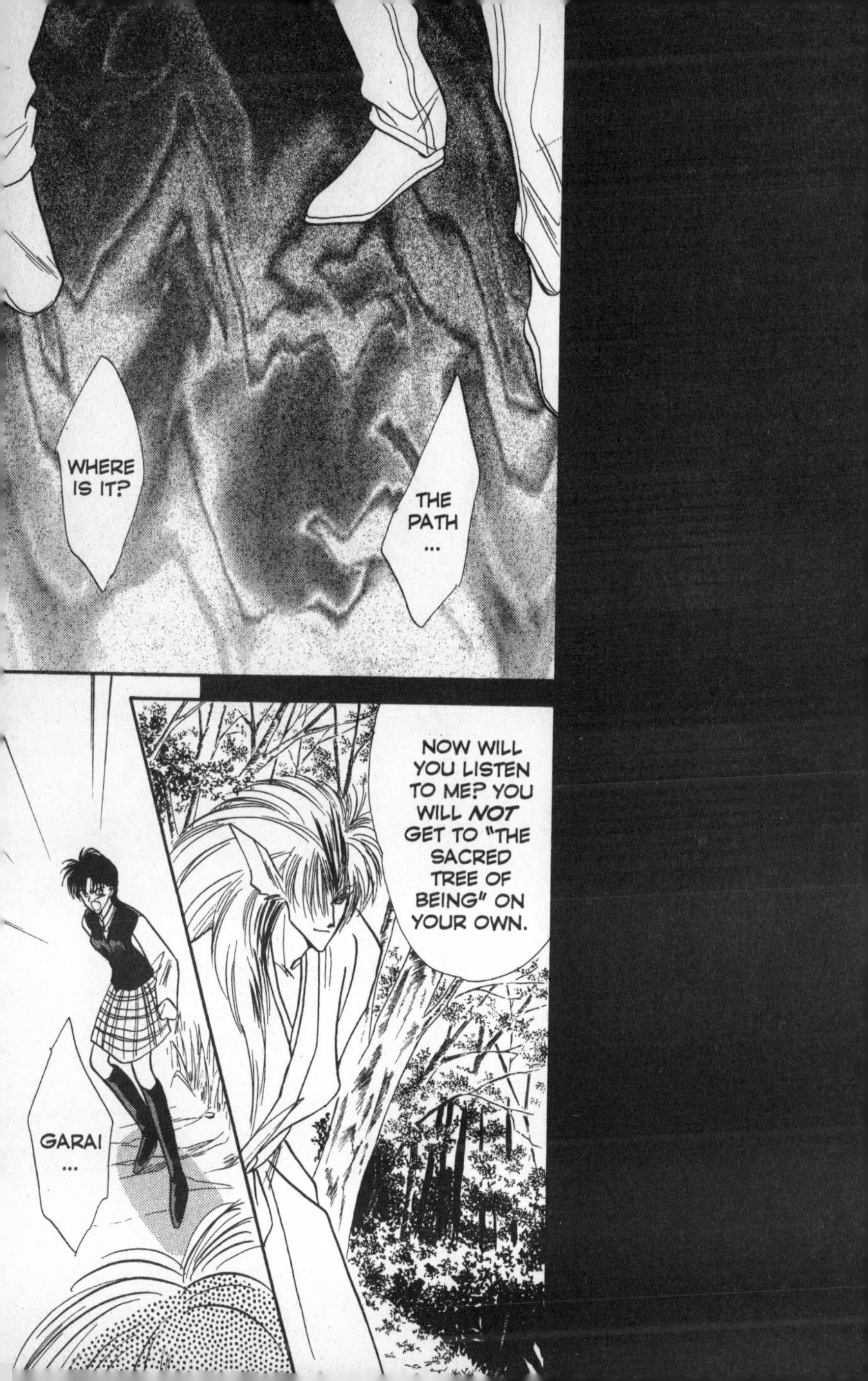
THE PATH ...
WHERE IS IT?
NOW WILL YOU LISTEN TO ME? YOU WILL *NOT* GET TO "THE SACRED TREE OF BEING" ON YOUR OWN.
GARAI ...

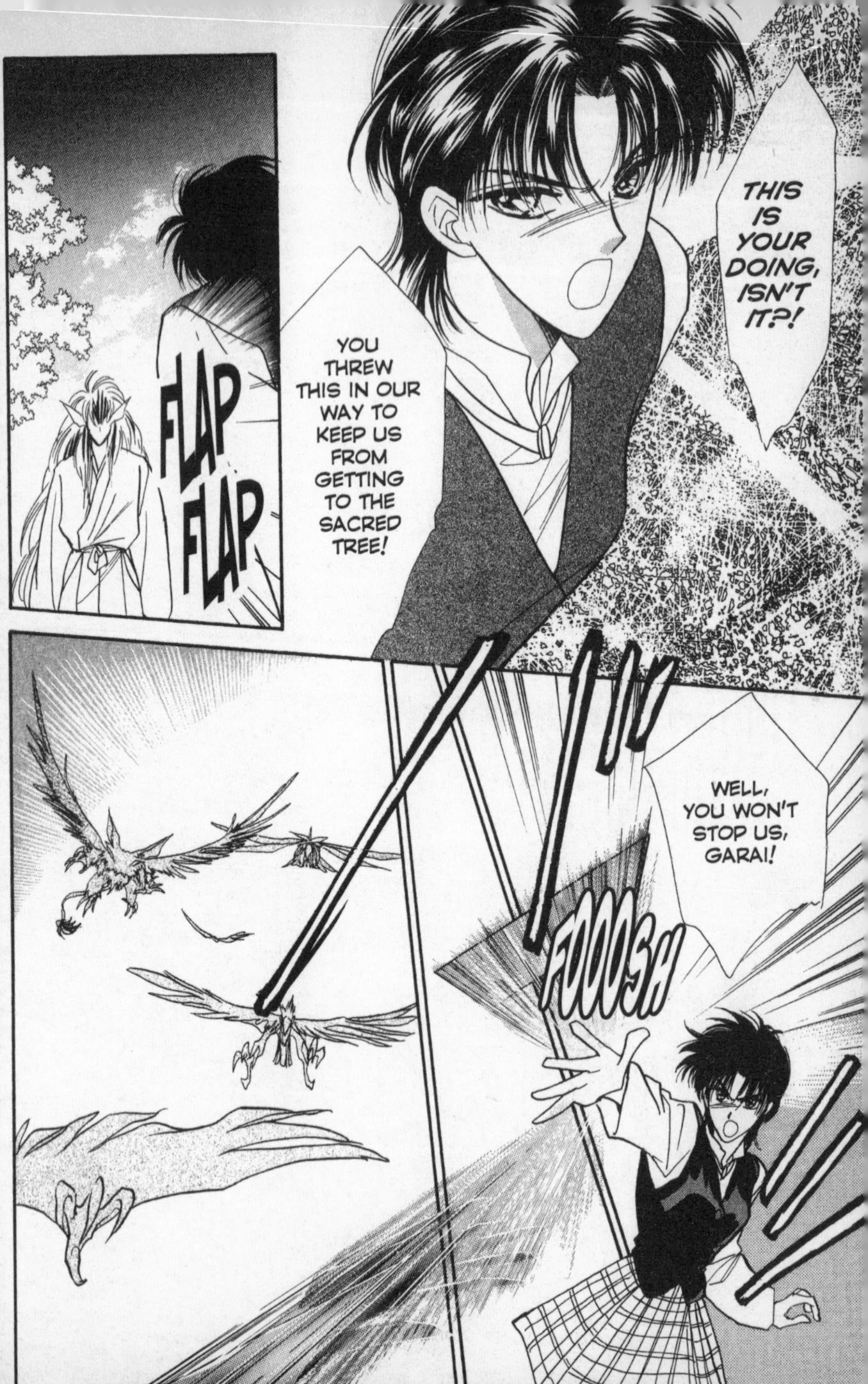
THIS IS YOUR DOING, ISN'T IT?!
YOU THREW THIS IN OUR WAY TO KEEP US FROM GETTING TO THE SACRED TREE!
FLAP FLAP
WELL, YOU WON'T STOP US, GARAI!
FOOOSH

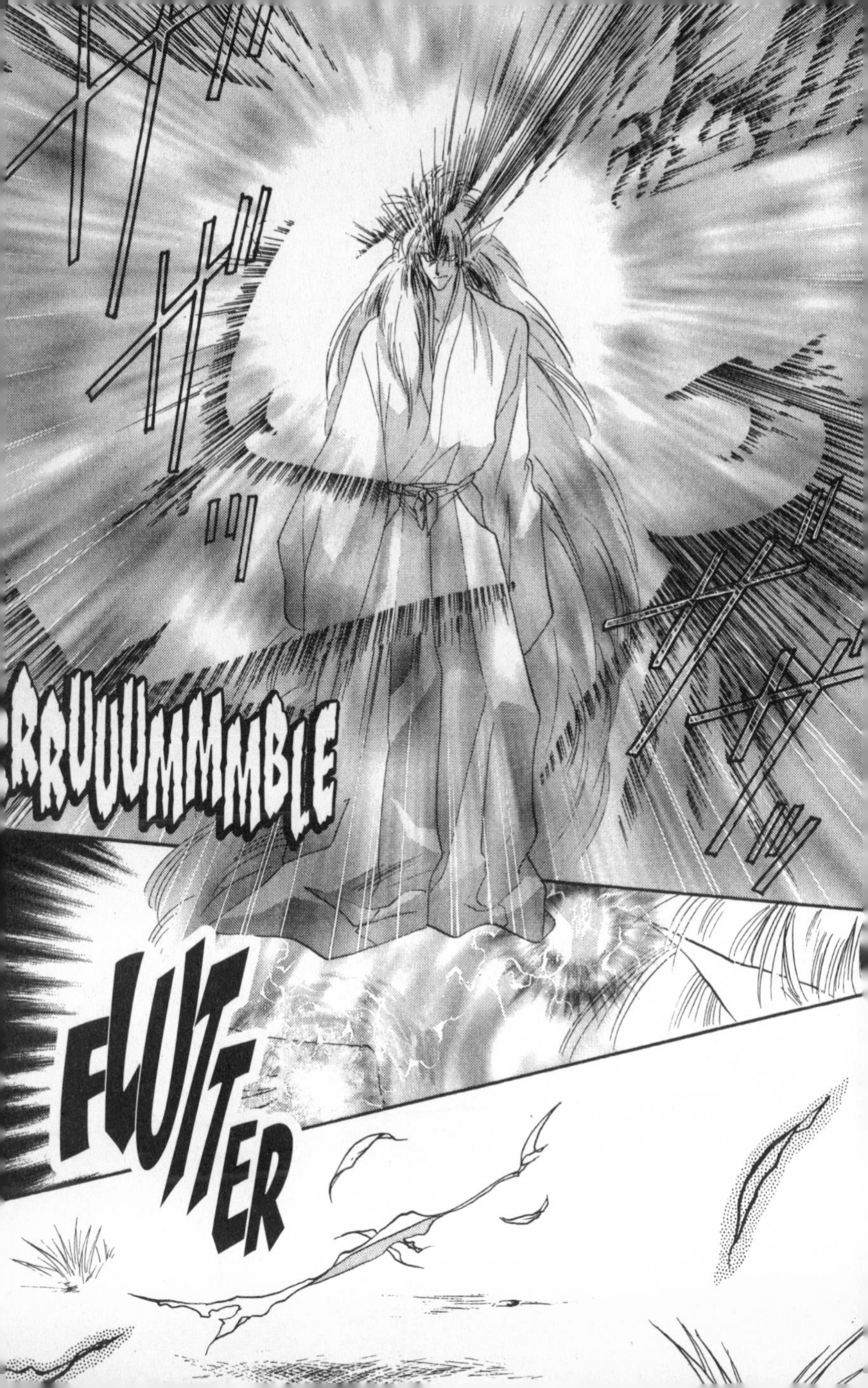
RRUUUMMMBLE
FLUTTER

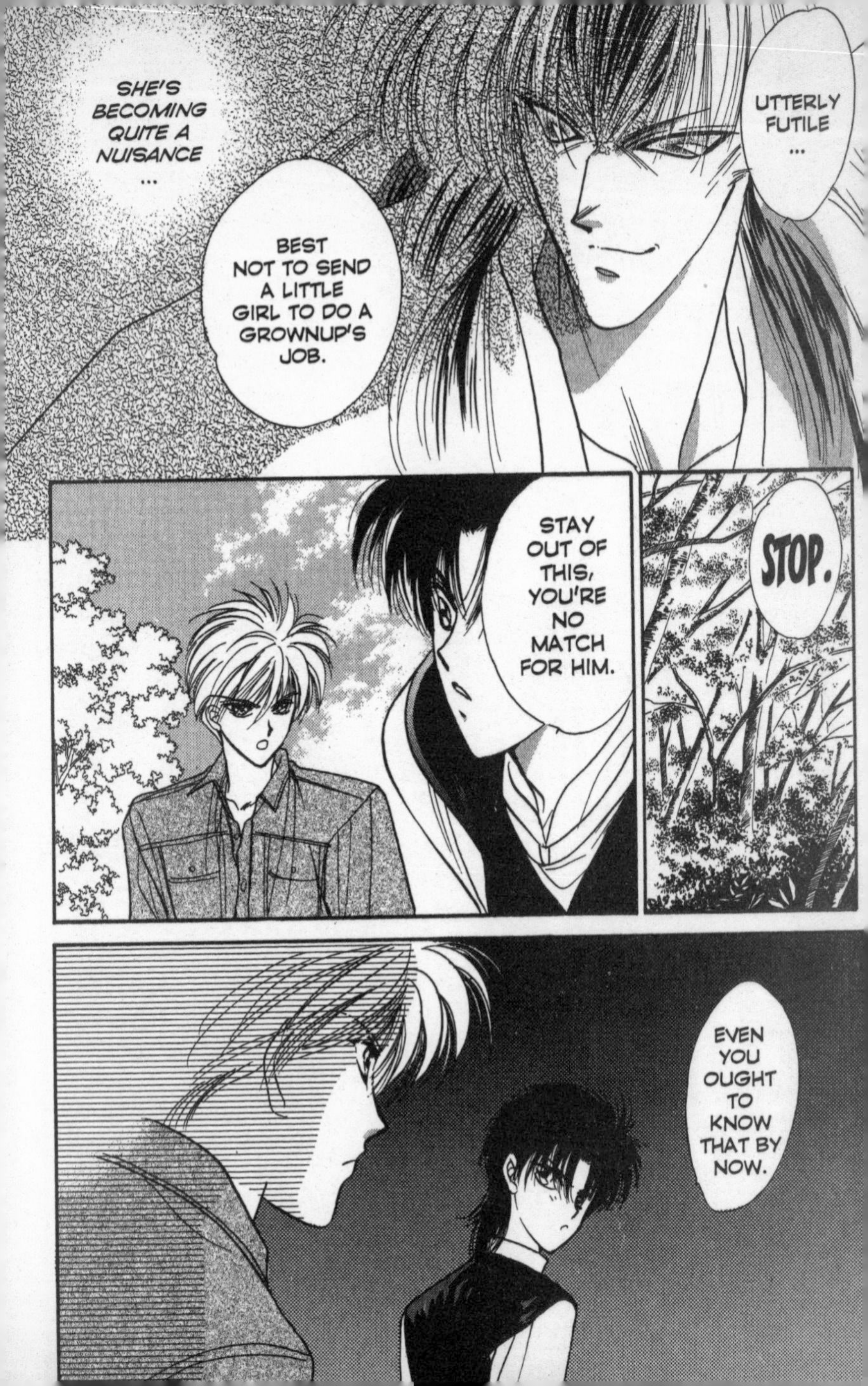
UTTERLY FUTILE ...
SHE'S BECOMING QUITE A NUISANCE ...
BEST NOT TO SEND A LITTLE GIRL TO DO A GROWNUP'S JOB.
STOP.
STAY OUT OF THIS, YOU'RE NO MATCH FOR HIM.
EVEN YOU OUGHT TO KNOW THAT BY NOW.

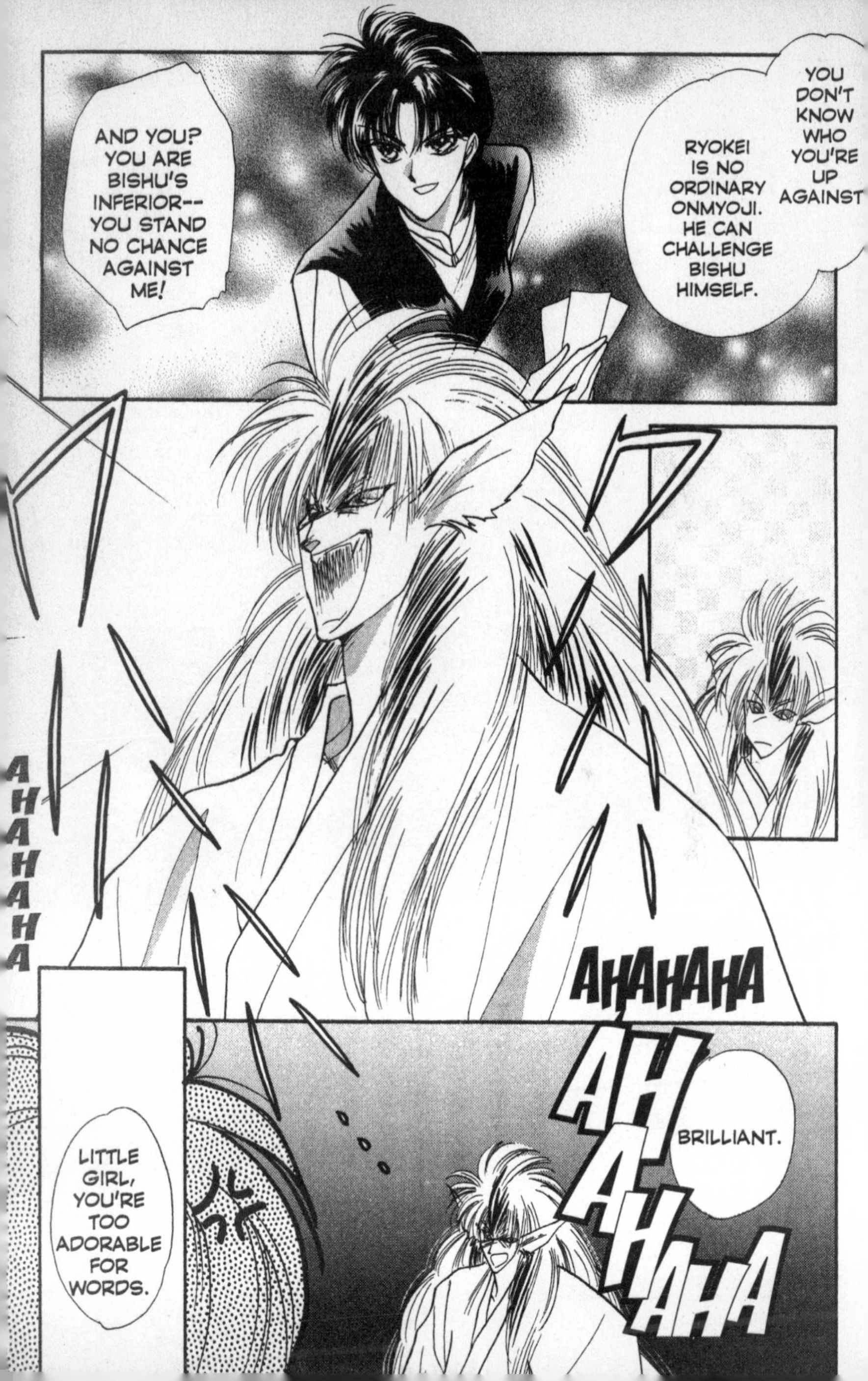

YOU DON'T KNOW WHO YOU'RE UP AGAINST
RYOKEI IS NO ORDINARY ONMYOJI. HE CAN CHALLENGE BISHU HIMSELF.
AND YOU? YOU ARE BISHU'S INFERIOR-- YOU STAND NO CHANCE AGAINST ME!
AHAHAHA
AHAHAHA
AHAHAHA
BRILLIANT.
LITTLE GIRL, YOU'RE TOO ADORABLE FOR WORDS.

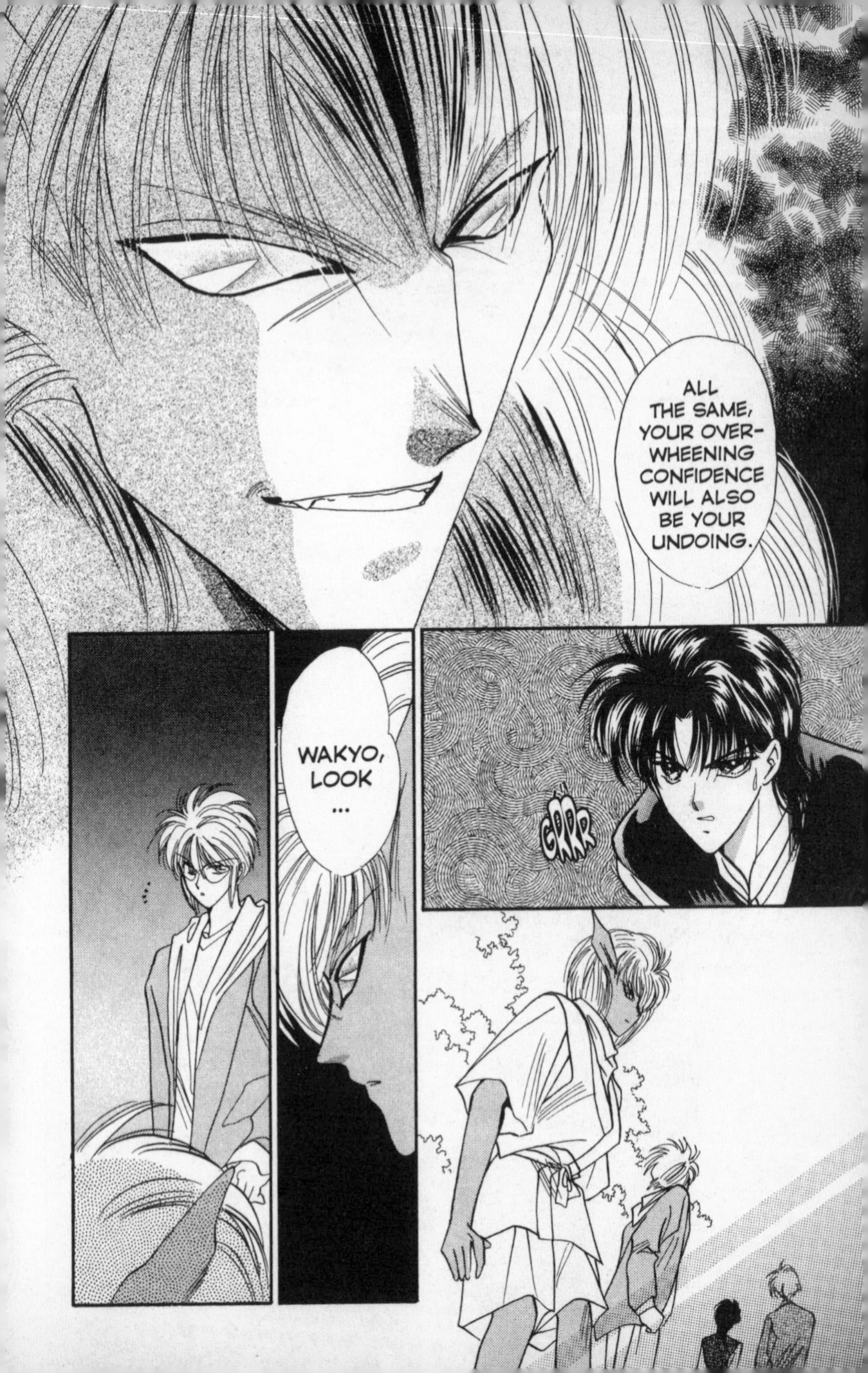
ALL THE SAME, YOUR OVER-WHEENING CONFIDENCE WILL ALSO BE YOUR UNDOING.
GRRR
WAKYO, LOOK ...

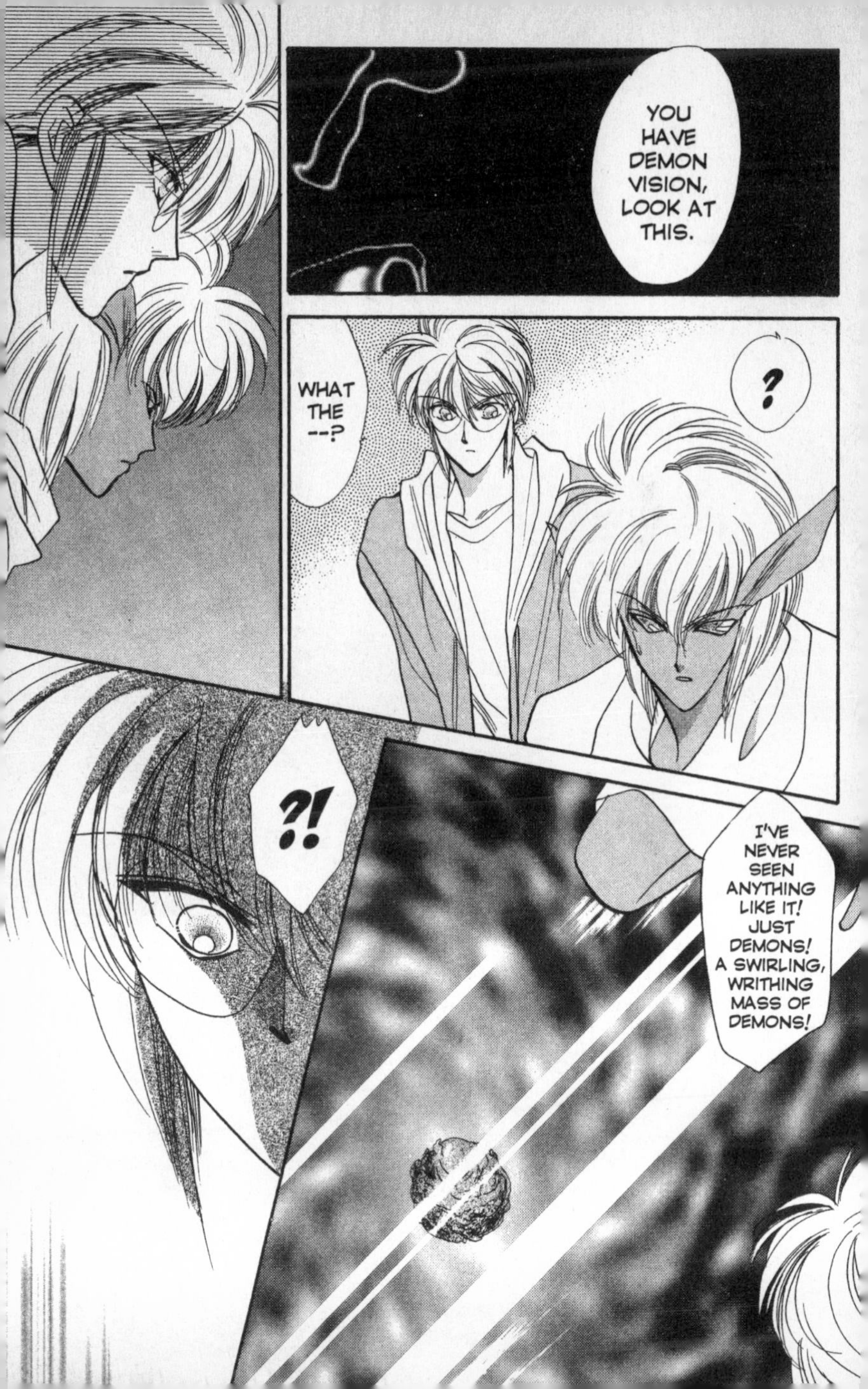
YOU HAVE DEMON VISION, LOOK AT THIS.
?
WHAT THE --?
I'VE NEVER SEEN ANYTHING LIKE IT! JUST DEMONS! A SWIRLING, WRITHING MASS OF DEMONS!
?!

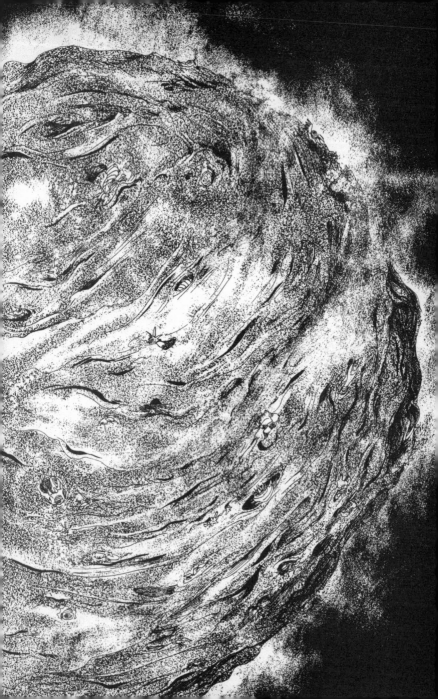

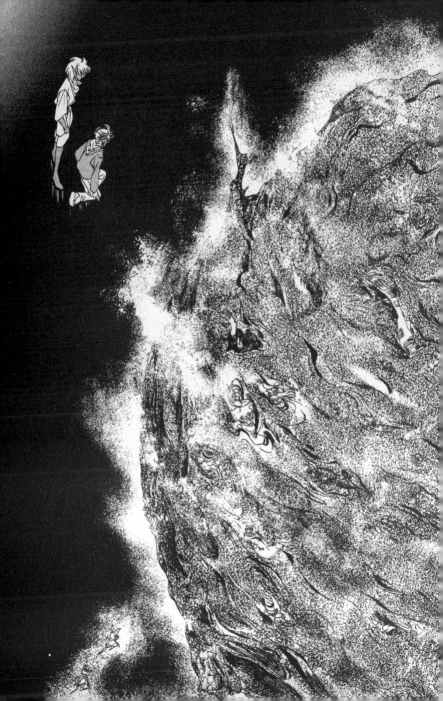

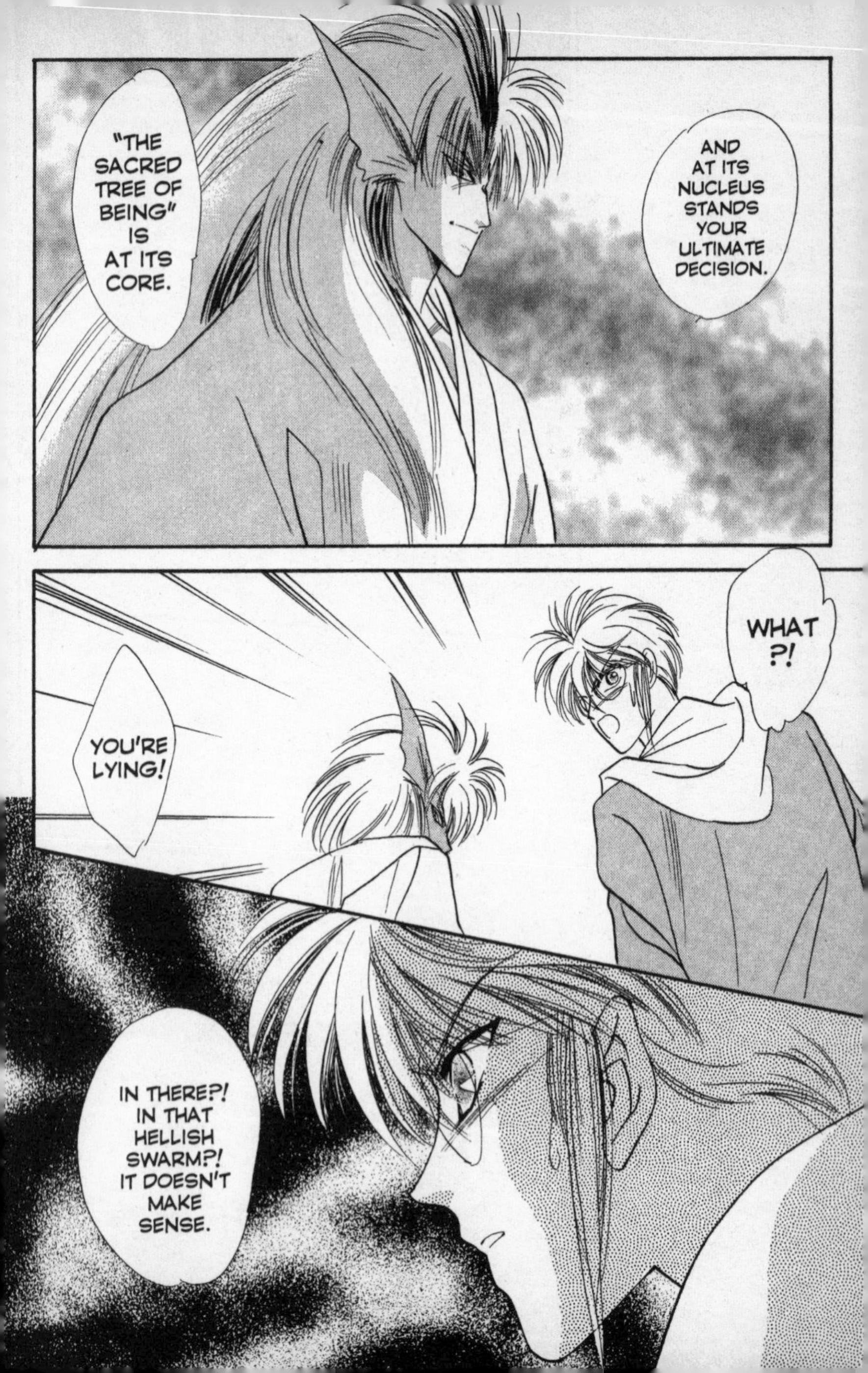
AND AT ITS NUCLEUS STANDS YOUR ULTIMATE DECISION.
"THE SACRED TREE OF BEING" IS AT ITS CORE.
WHAT ?!
YOU'RE LYING!
IN THERE?! IN THAT HELLISH SWARM?! IT DOESN'T MAKE SENSE.

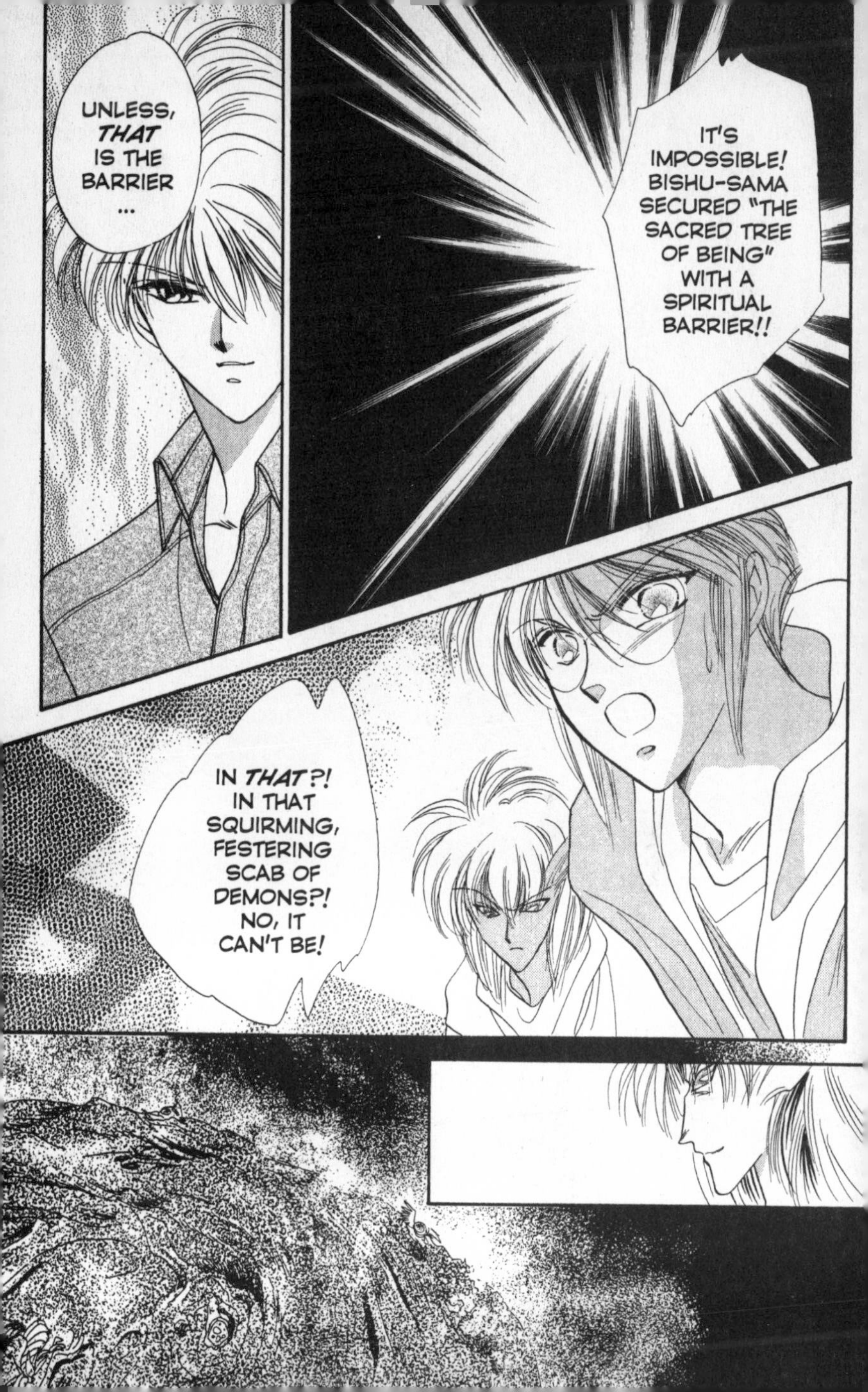
IT'S IMPOSSIBLE! BISHU-SAMA SECURED "THE SACRED TREE OF BEING" WITH A SPIRITUAL BARRIER!!
UNLESS, *THAT* IS THE BARRIER ...
IN *THAT*?! IN THAT SQUIRMING, FESTERING SCAB OF DEMONS?! NO, IT CAN'T BE!

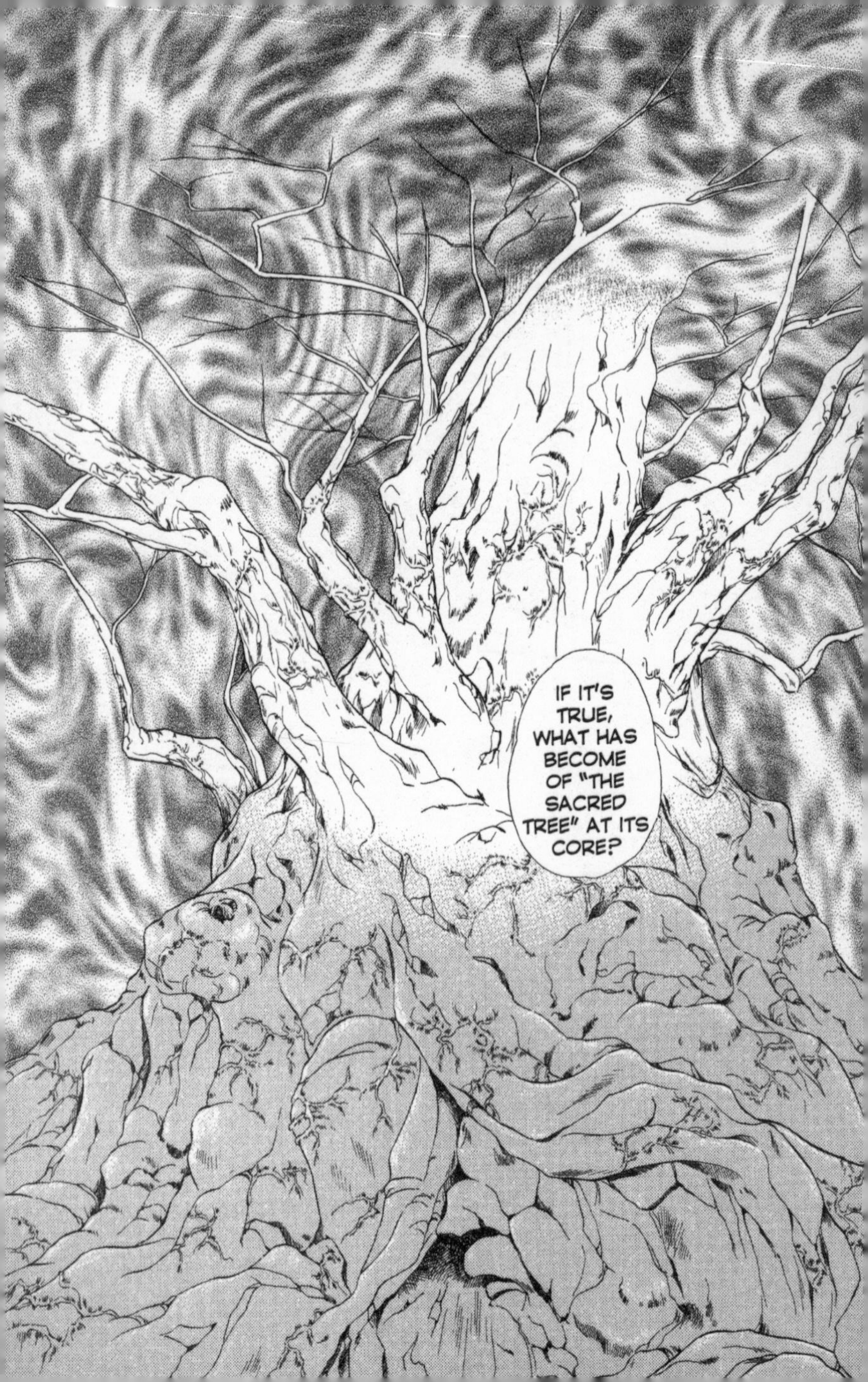
IF IT'S TRUE, WHAT HAS BECOME OF "THE SACRED TREE" AT ITS CORE?

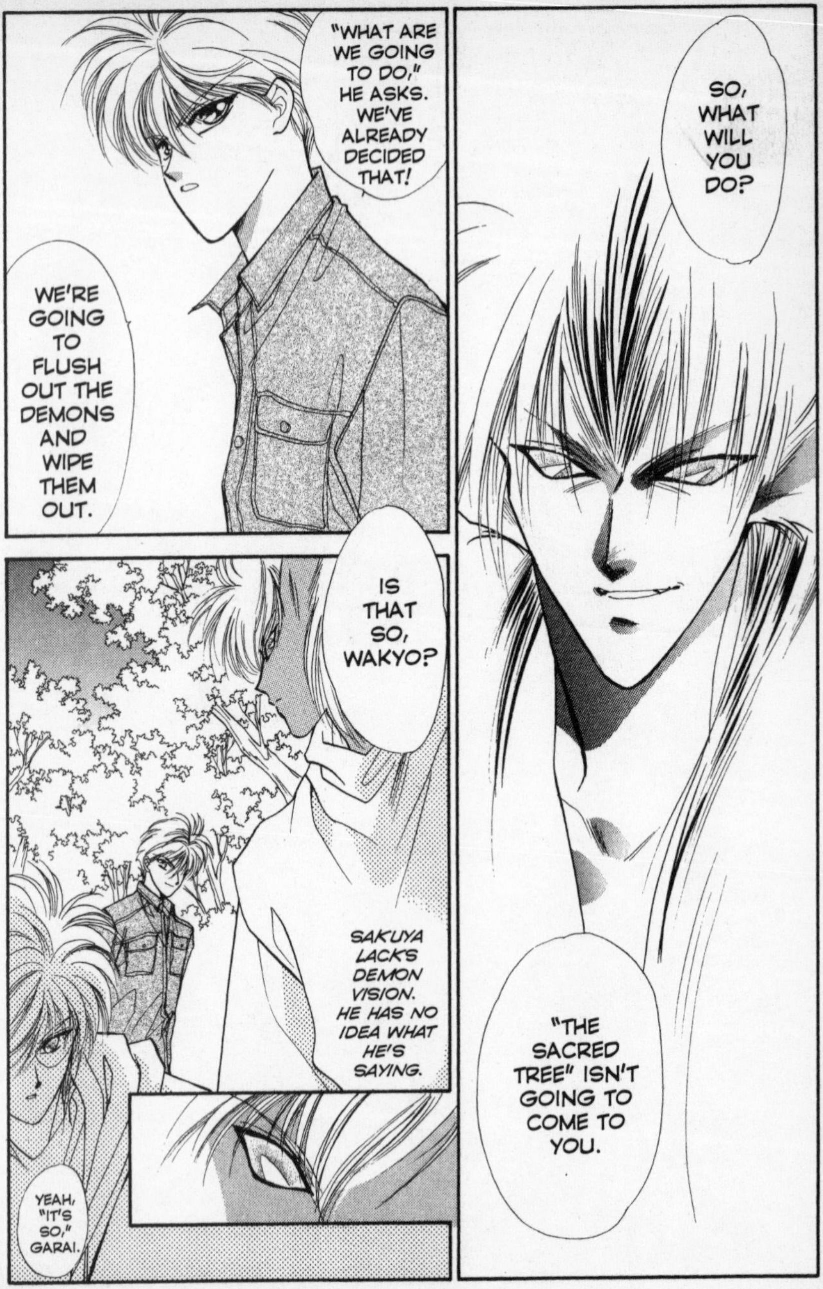
SO, WHAT WILL YOU DO?
"THE SACRED TREE" ISN'T GOING TO COME TO YOU.
"WHAT ARE WE GOING TO DO," HE ASKS. WE'VE ALREADY DECIDED THAT!
WE'RE GOING TO FLUSH OUT THE DEMONS AND WIPE THEM OUT.
IS THAT SO, WAKYO?
SAKUYA LACKS DEMON VISION. HE HAS NO IDEA WHAT HE'S SAYING.
YEAH, "IT'S SO," GARAI.

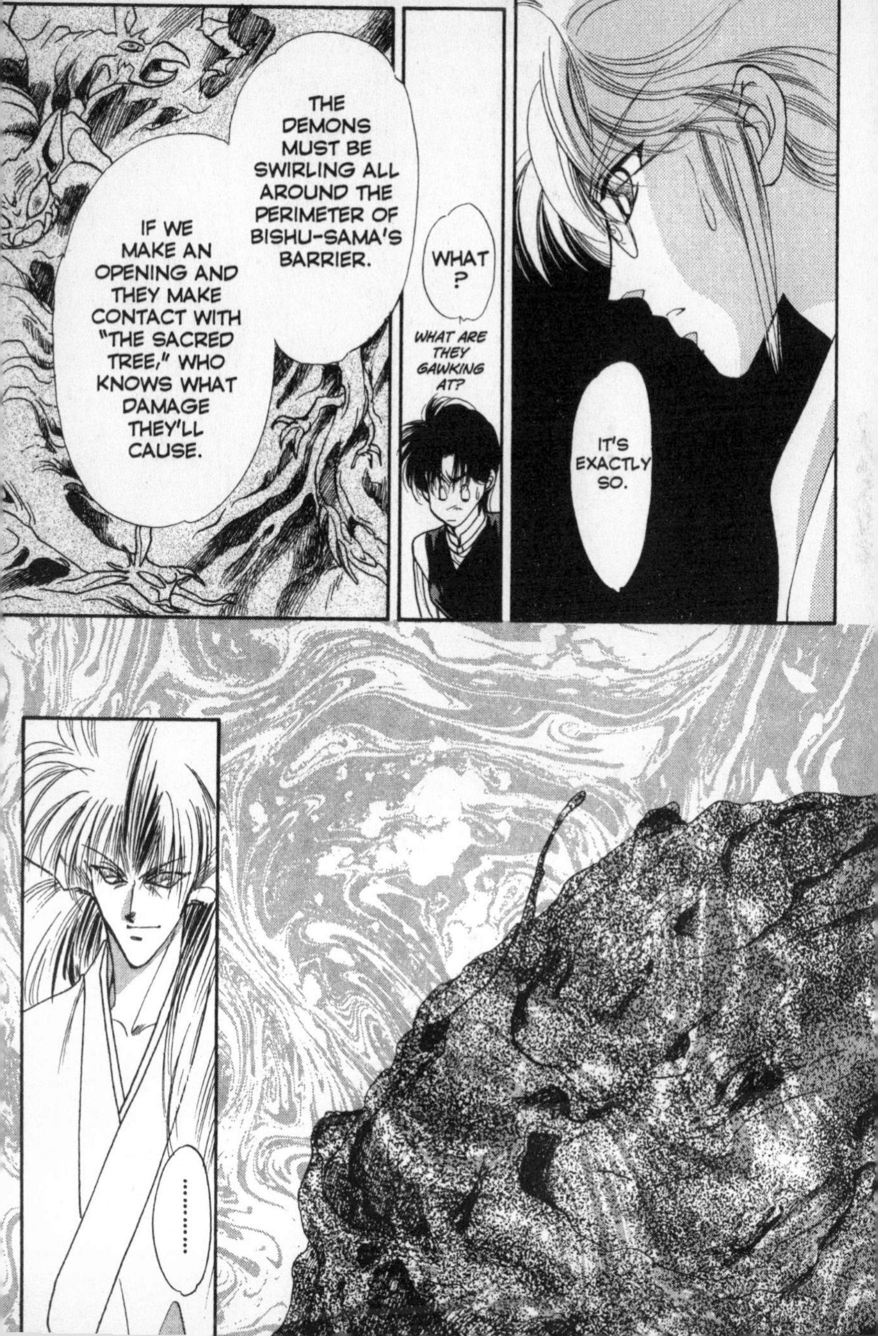
IT'S EXACTLY SO.
WHAT ?
WHAT ARE THEY GAWKING AT?
THE DEMONS MUST BE SWIRLING ALL AROUND THE PERIMETER OF BISHU-SAMA'S BARRIER.
IF WE MAKE AN OPENING AND THEY MAKE CONTACT WITH "THE SACRED TREE," WHO KNOWS WHAT DAMAGE THEY'LL CAUSE.
....

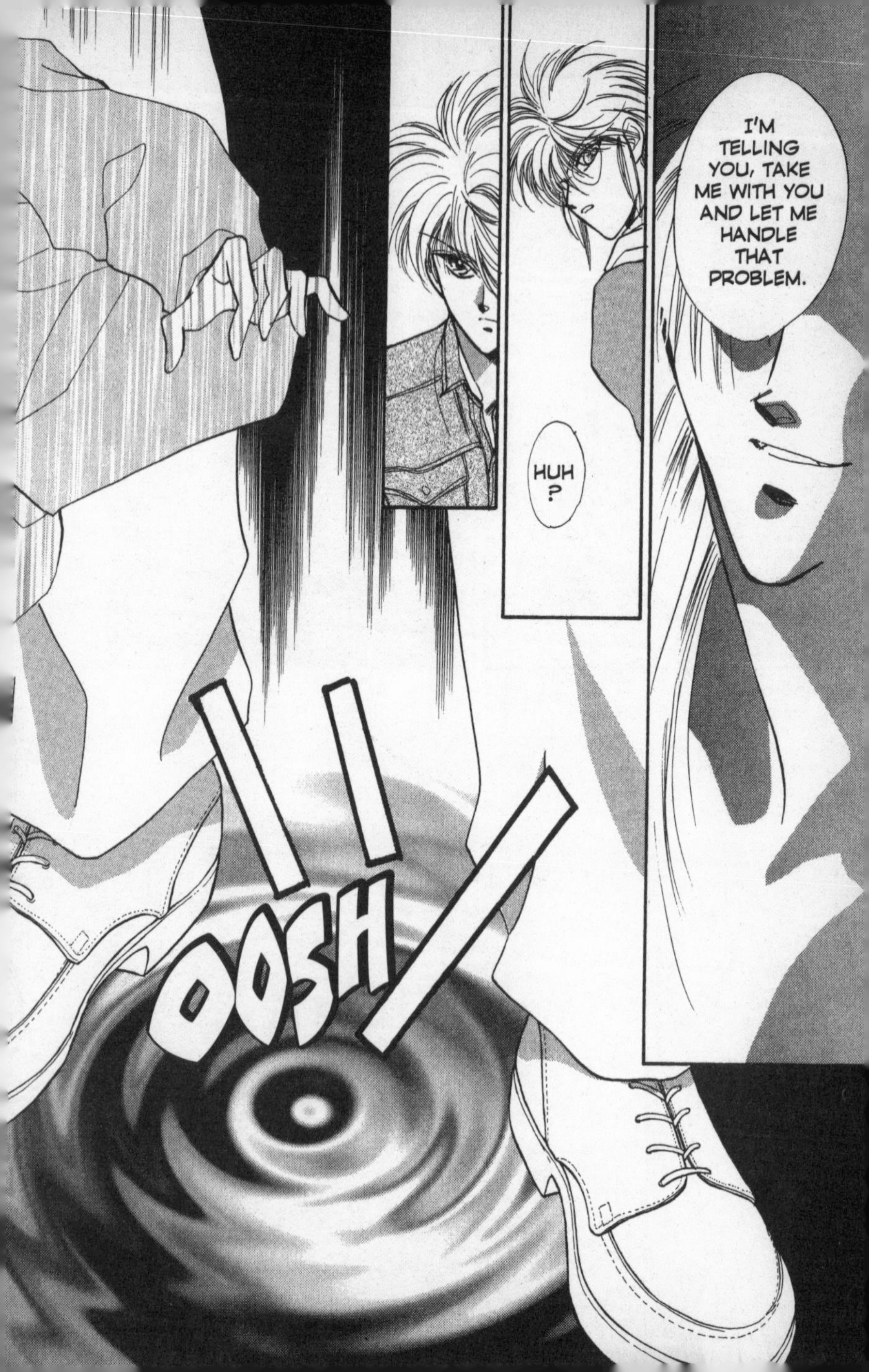
I'M TELLING YOU, TAKE ME WITH YOU AND LET ME HANDLE THAT PROBLEM.
HUH?
OOSH

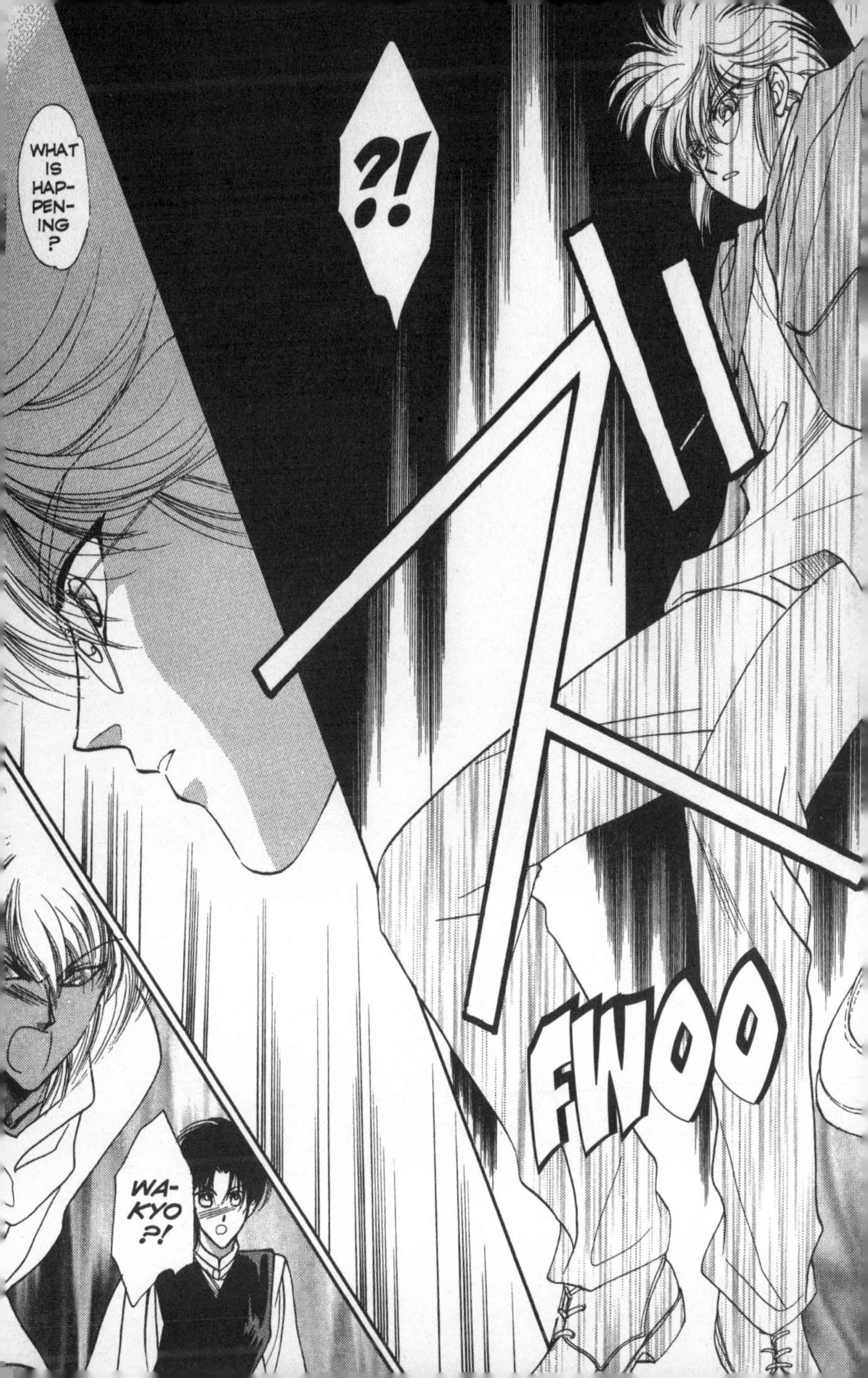
?!
WHAT IS HAP-PEN-ING?
FWOO
WA-KYO?!

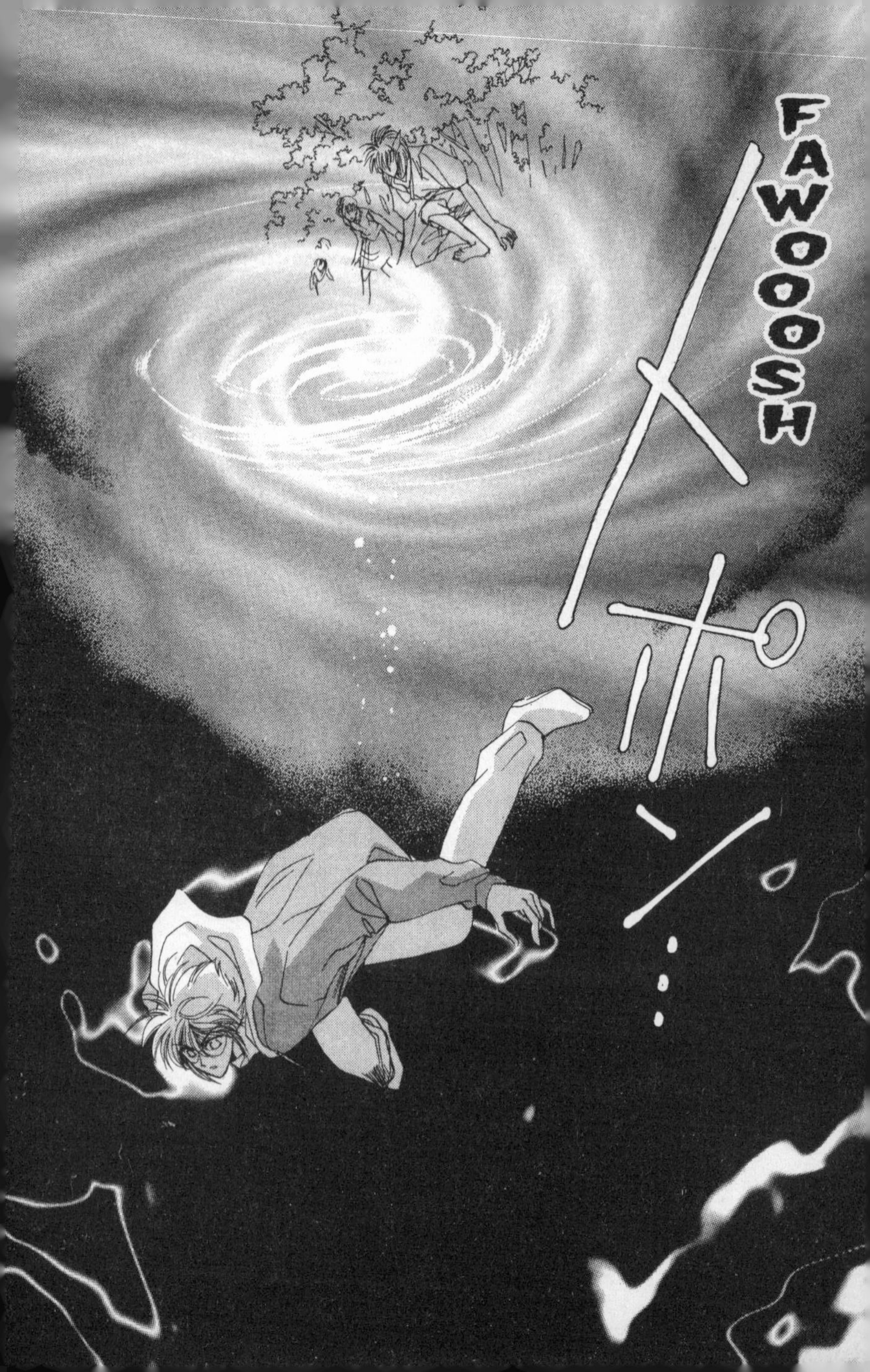
FAWOOOSH
ドボン…

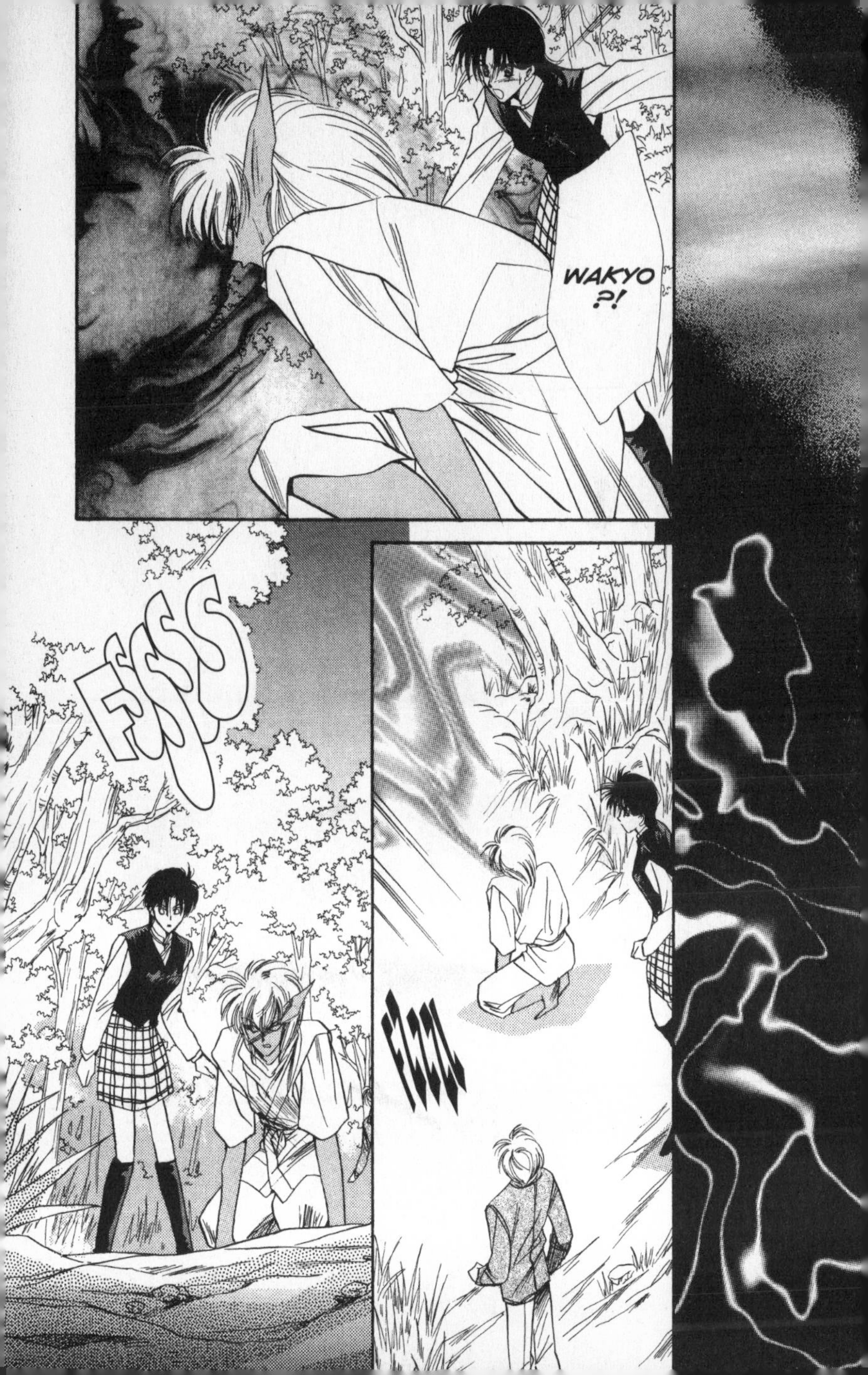
WAKYO
?!
FZZZ
FSSS

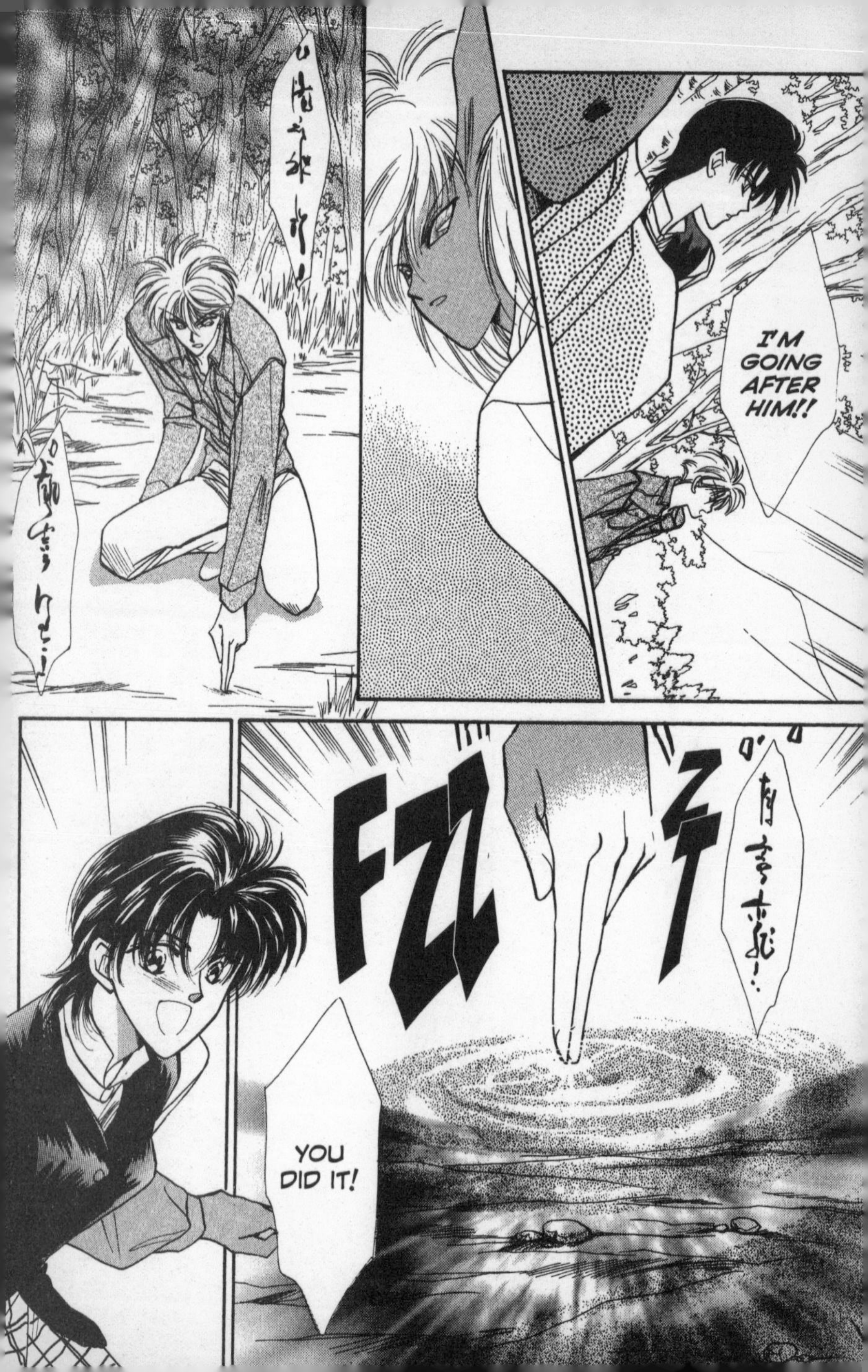
I'M GOING AFTER HIM!!
FZZZT
YOU DID IT!

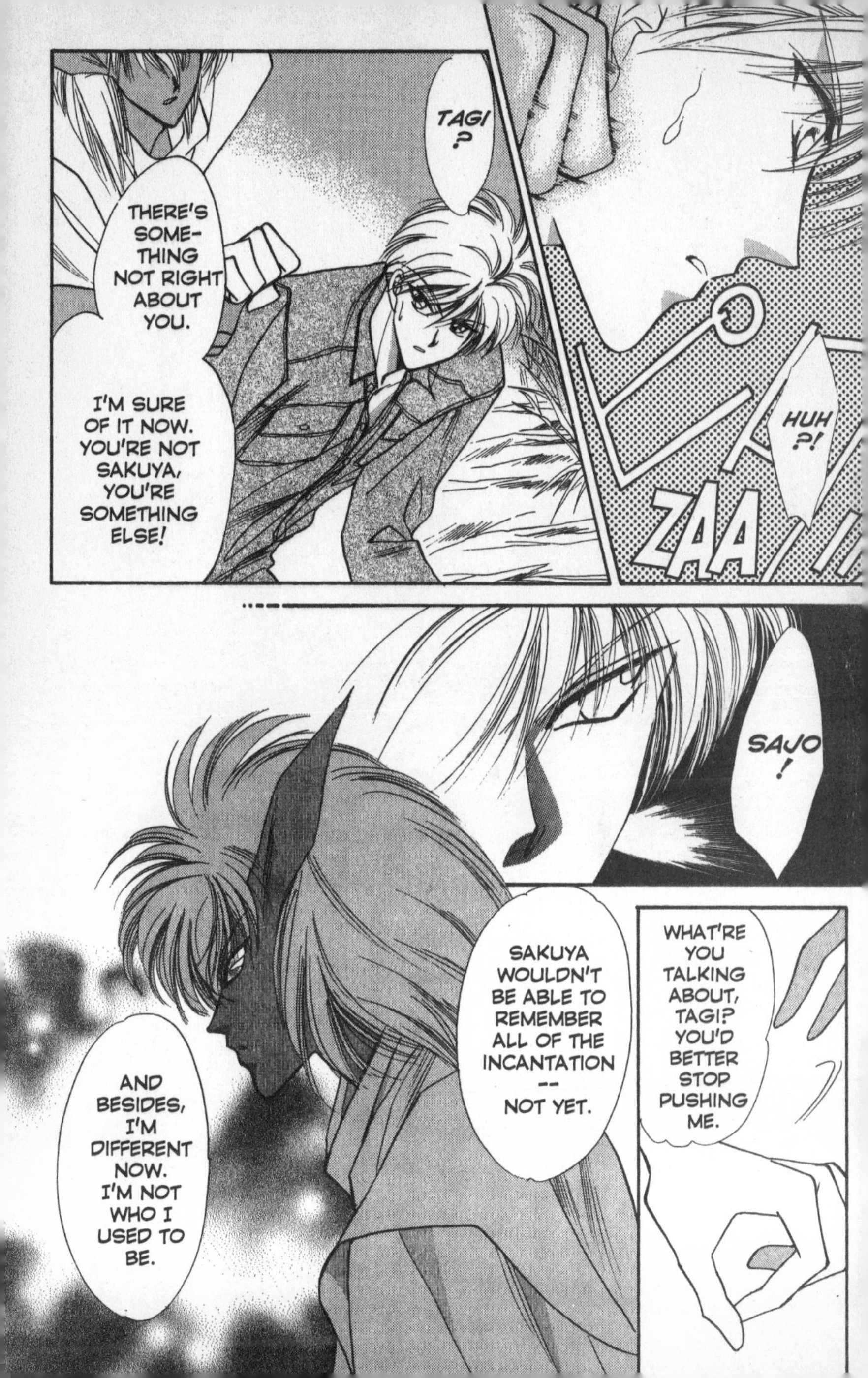
HUH ?!
ZAA
TAGI ?
THERE'S SOME-THING NOT RIGHT ABOUT YOU.
I'M SURE OF IT NOW. YOU'RE NOT SAKUYA, YOU'RE SOMETHING ELSE!
SAJO !
WHAT'RE YOU TALKING ABOUT, TAGI? YOU'D BETTER STOP PUSHING ME.
SAKUYA WOULDN'T BE ABLE TO REMEMBER ALL OF THE INCANTATION -- NOT YET.
AND BESIDES, I'M DIFFERENT NOW. I'M NOT WHO I USED TO BE.

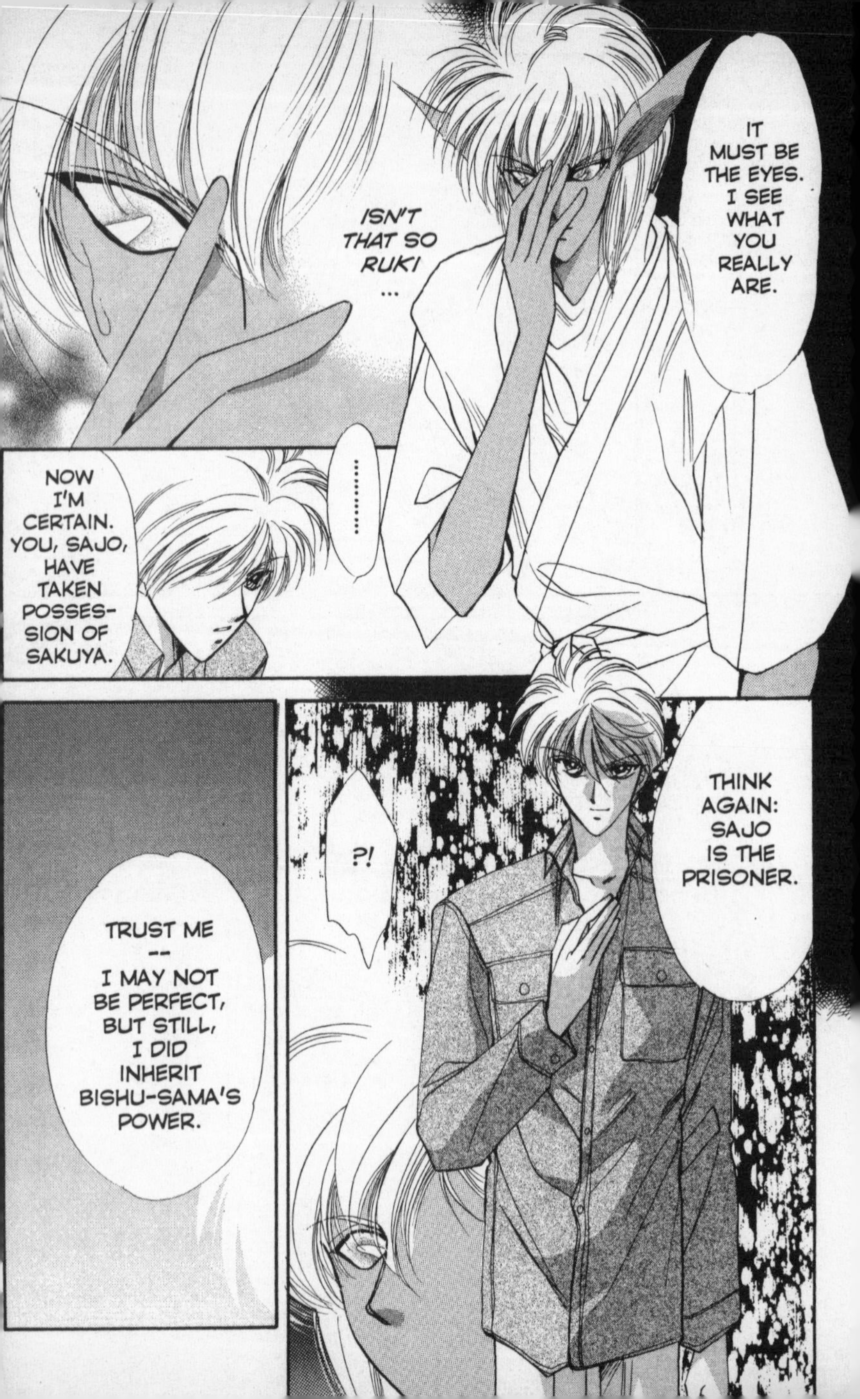
IT MUST BE THE EYES. I SEE WHAT YOU REALLY ARE.
ISN'T THAT SO RUKI ...
......
NOW I'M CERTAIN. YOU, SAJO, HAVE TAKEN POSSES-SION OF SAKUYA.
THINK AGAIN: SAJO IS THE PRISONER.
?!
TRUST ME -- I MAY NOT BE PERFECT, BUT STILL, I DID INHERIT BISHU-SAMA'S POWER.

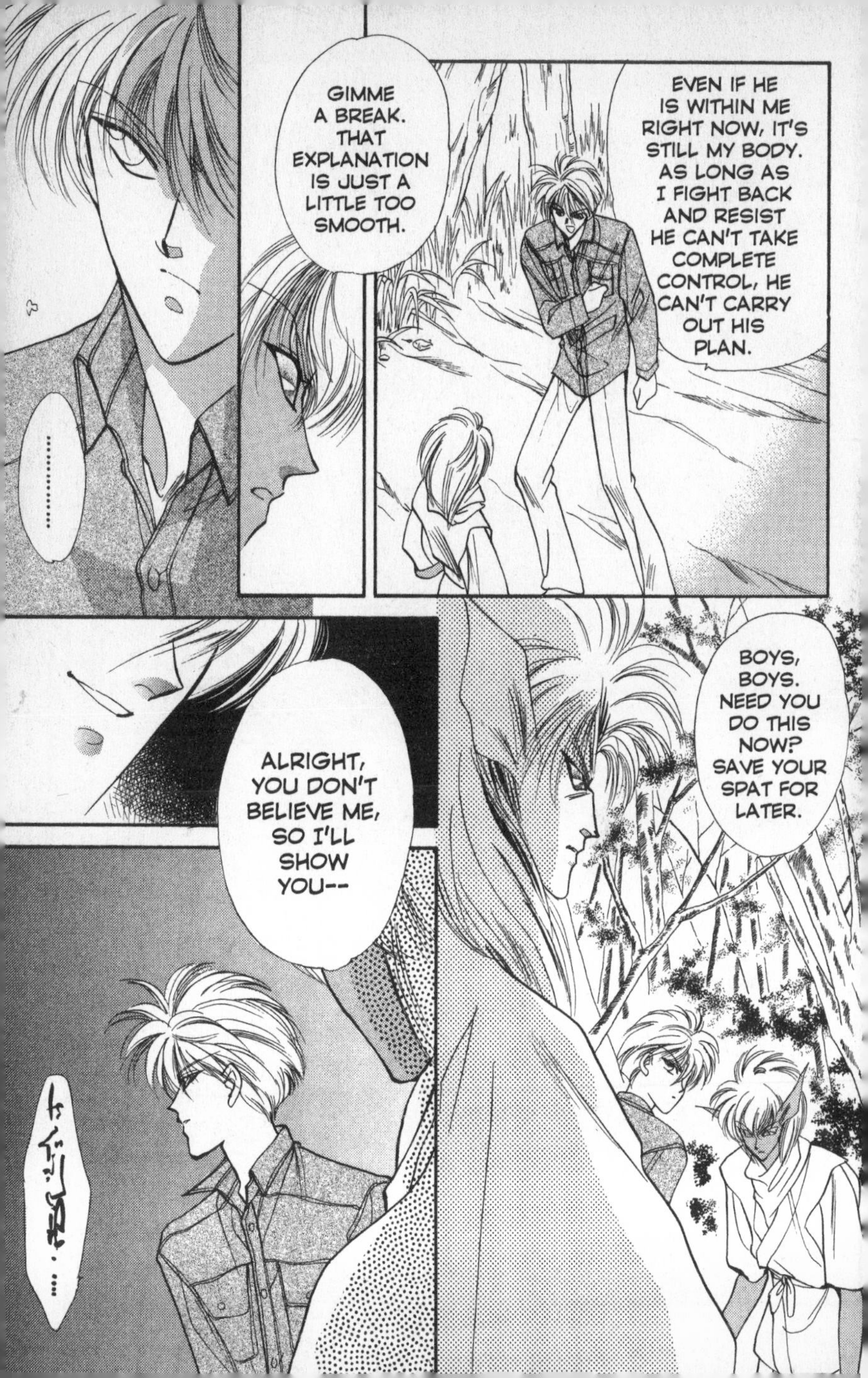
EVEN IF HE IS WITHIN ME RIGHT NOW, IT'S STILL MY BODY. AS LONG AS I FIGHT BACK AND RESIST HE CAN'T TAKE COMPLETE CONTROL, HE CAN'T CARRY OUT HIS PLAN.
GIMME A BREAK. THAT EXPLANATION IS JUST A LITTLE TOO SMOOTH.
....
BOYS, BOYS. NEED YOU DO THIS NOW? SAVE YOUR SPAT FOR LATER.
ALRIGHT, YOU DON'T BELIEVE ME, SO I'LL SHOW YOU--

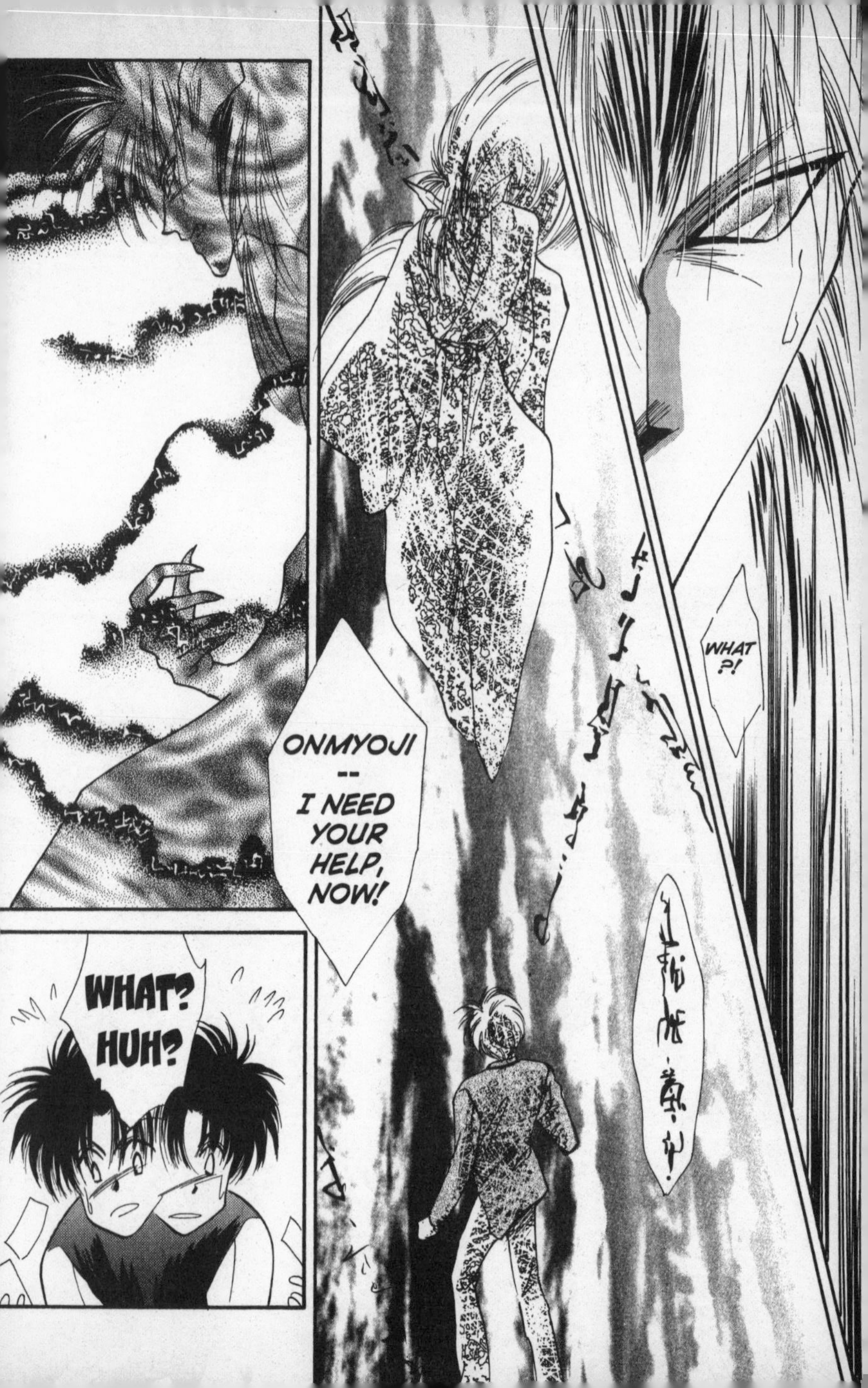
WHAT?!
ONMYOJI -- I NEED YOUR HELP, NOW!
WHAT? HUH?

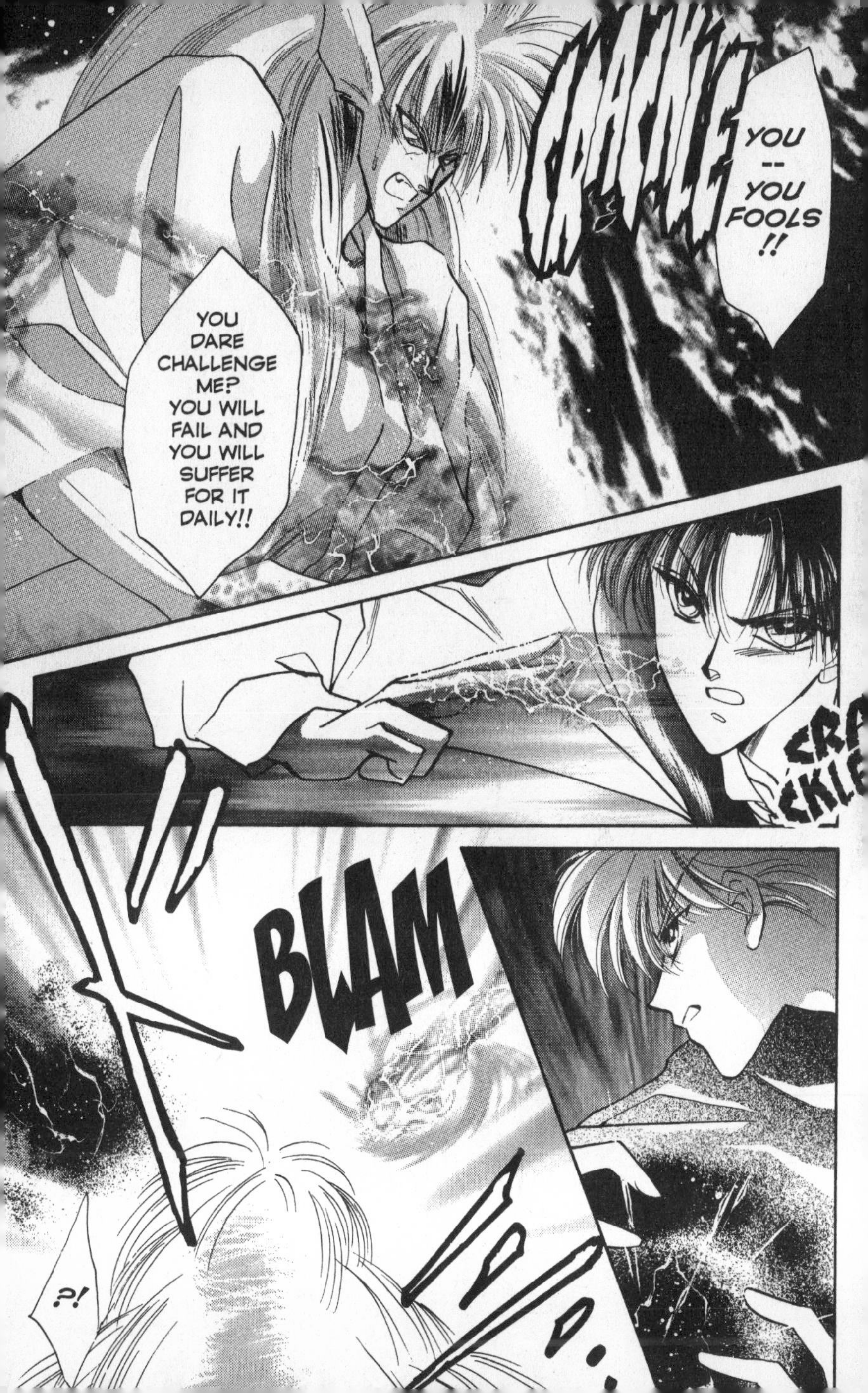
YOU -- YOU FOOLS!!
YOU DARE CHALLENGE ME? YOU WILL FAIL AND YOU WILL SUFFER FOR IT DAILY!!
CRA
CKLE
BLAM
?!

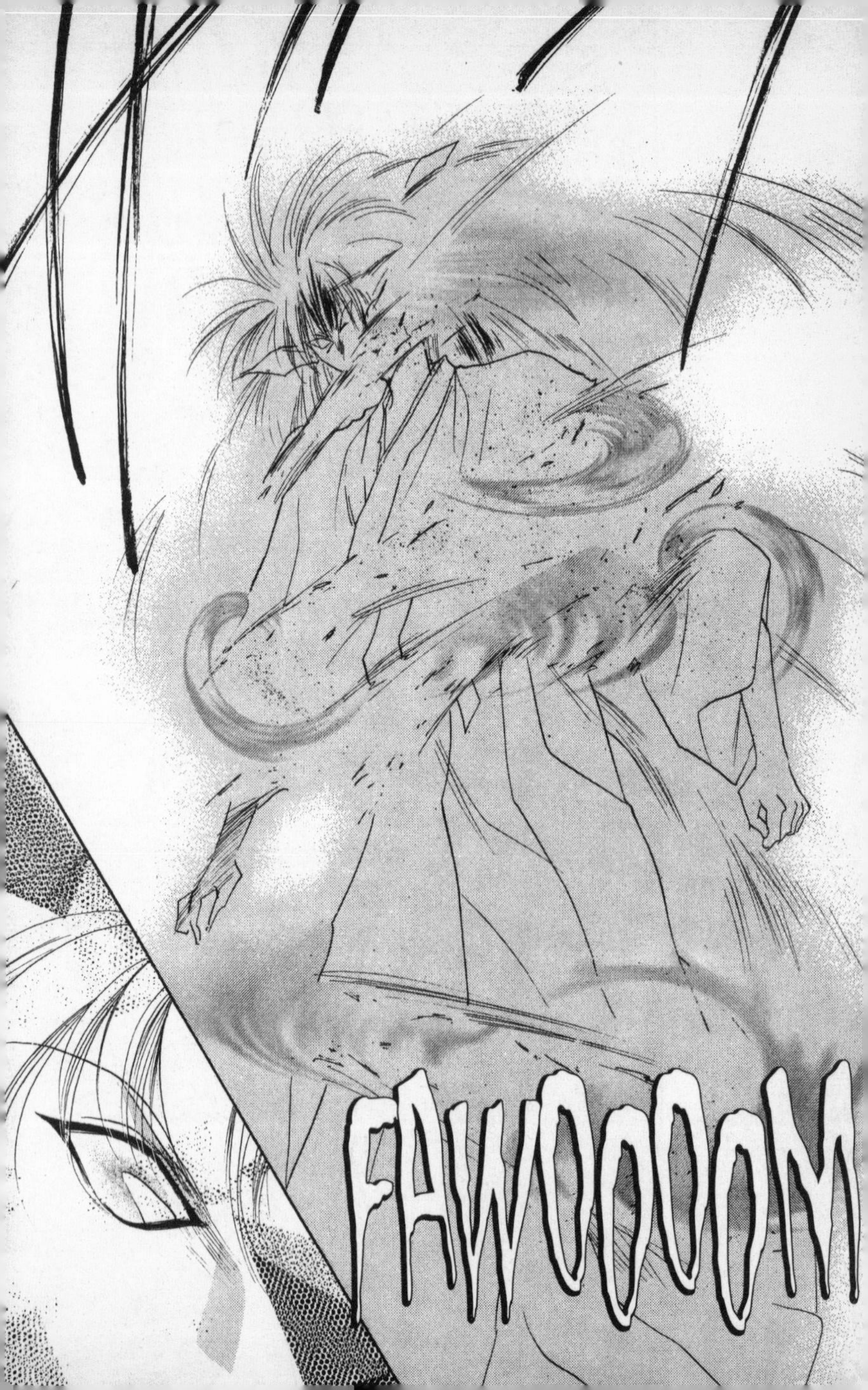
FAWOOOOM

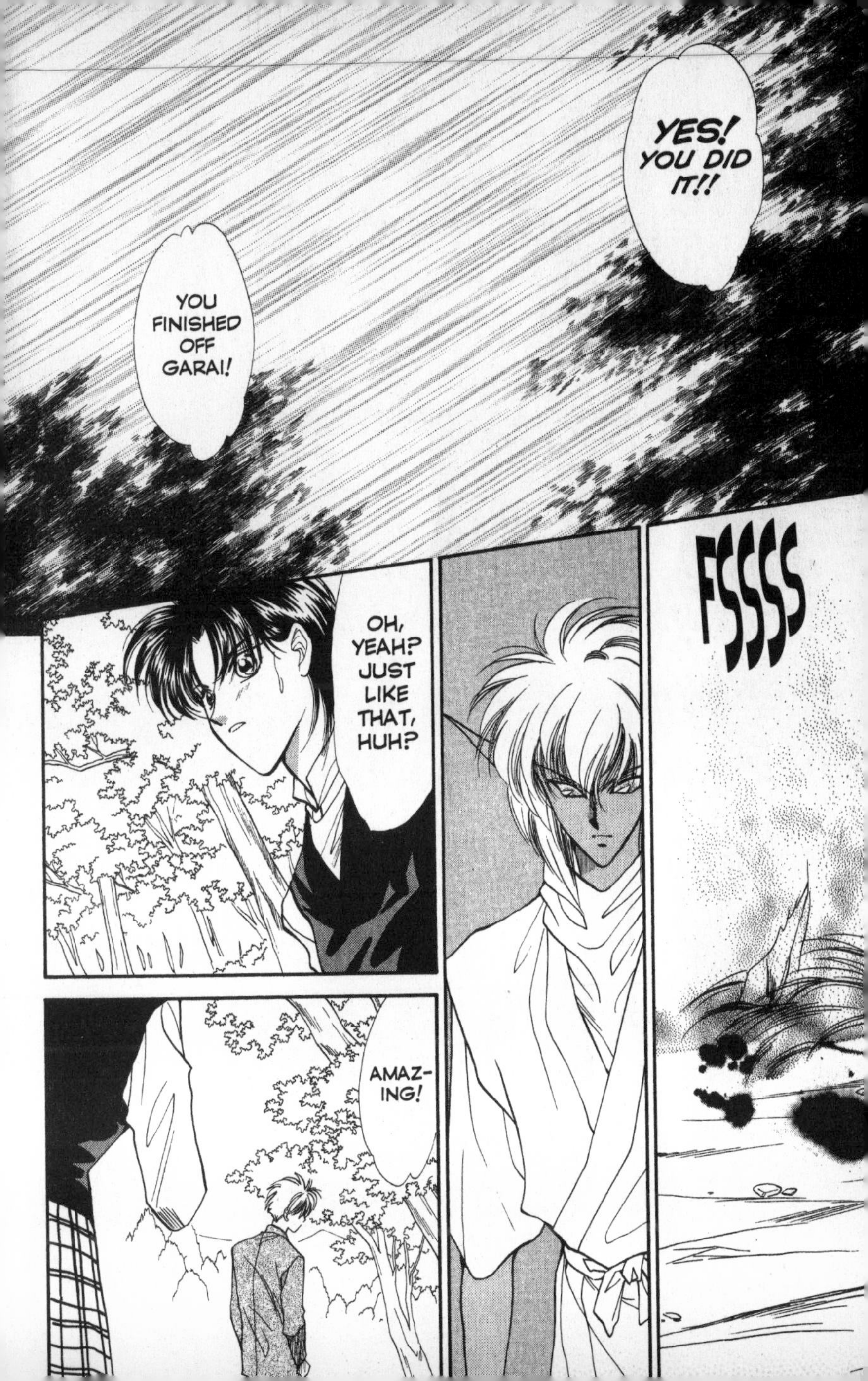
YES! YOU DID IT!!
YOU FINISHED OFF GARAI!
FSSSS
OH, YEAH? JUST LIKE THAT, HUH?
AMAZ-ING!

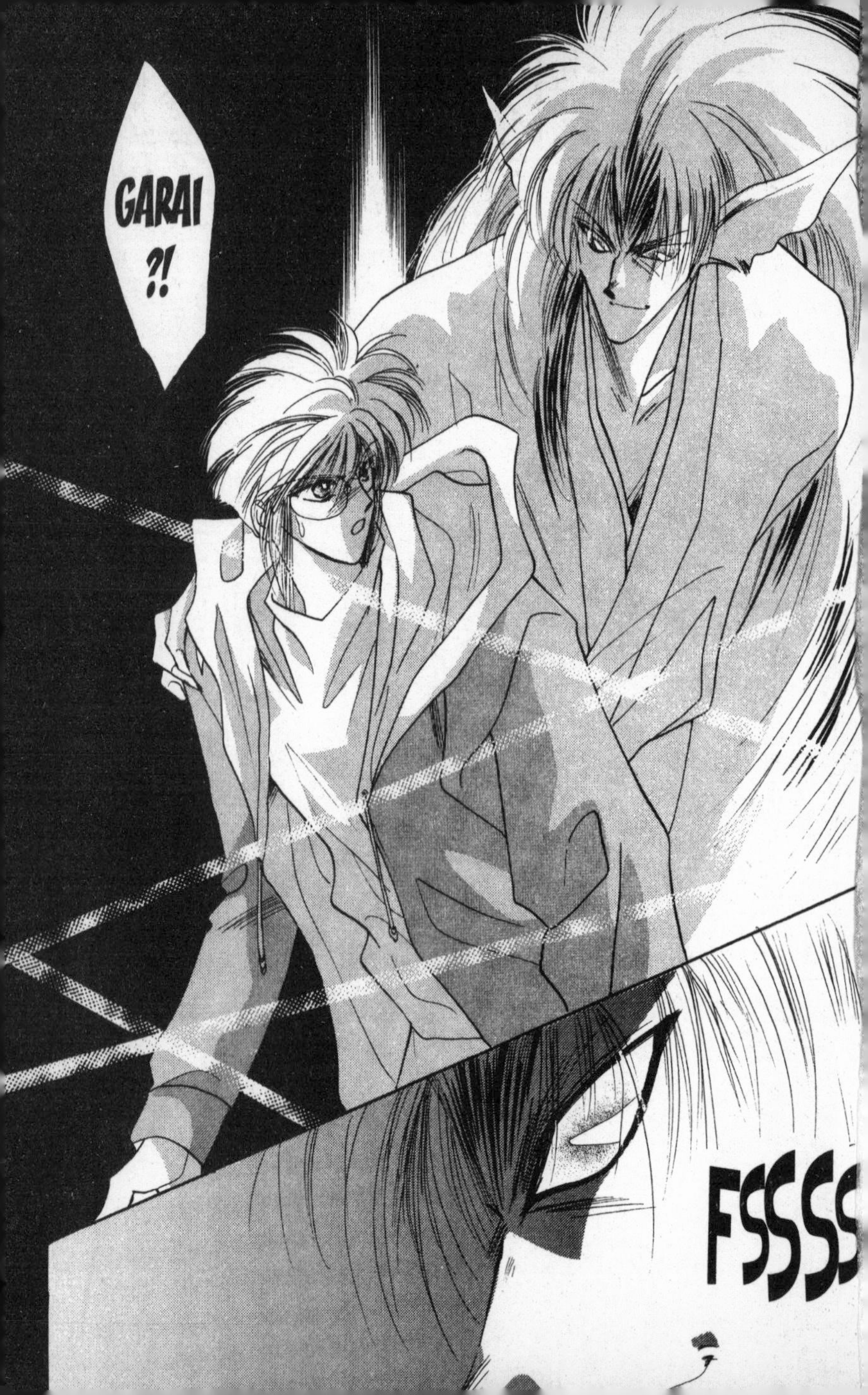
GARAI ?!
FSSSS

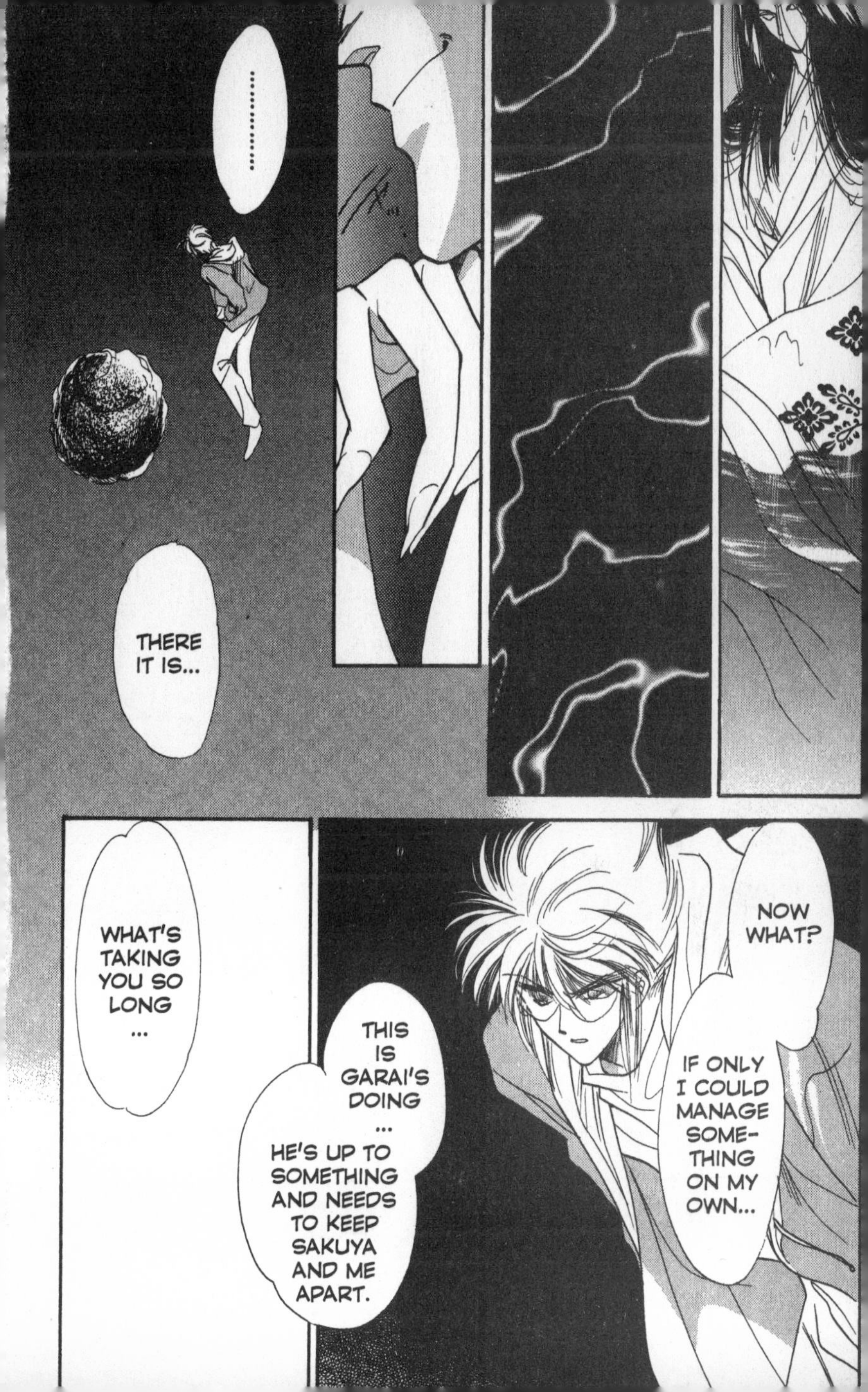
……
THERE IT IS...
NOW WHAT?
IF ONLY I COULD MANAGE SOMETHING ON MY OWN...
THIS IS GARAI'S DOING...
HE'S UP TO SOMETHING AND NEEDS TO KEEP SAKUYA AND ME APART.
WHAT'S TAKING YOU SO LONG...

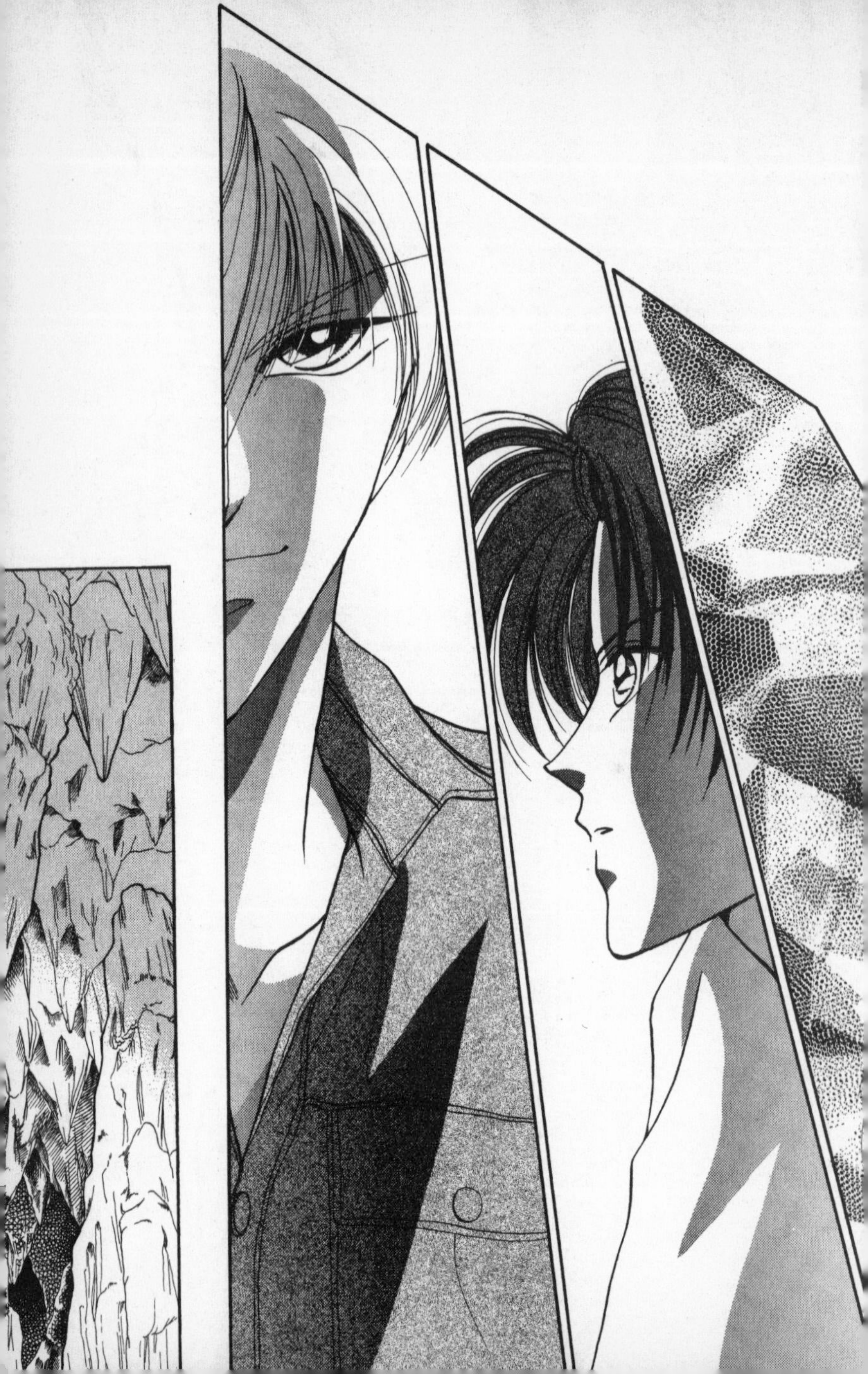

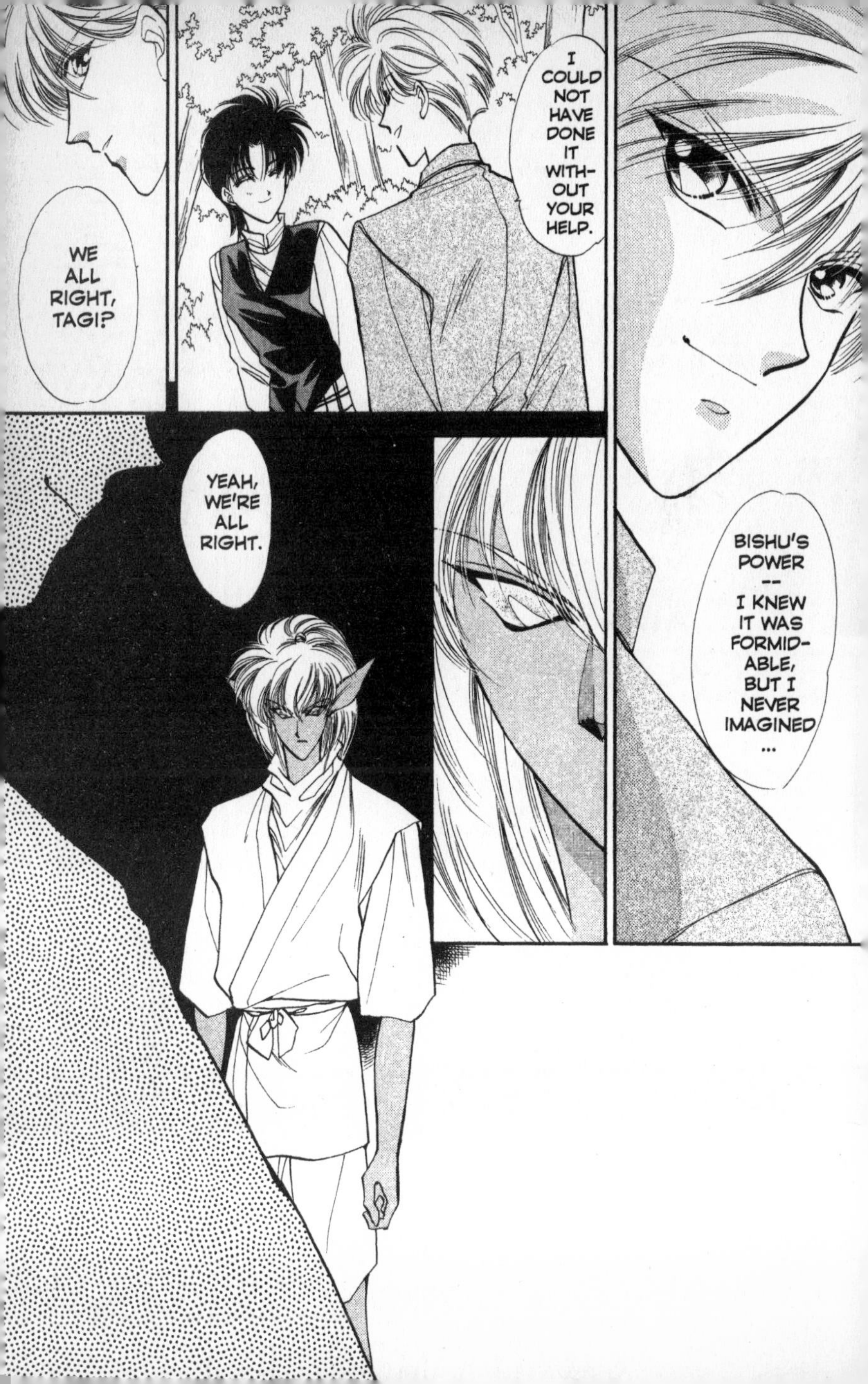
BISHU'S POWER -- I KNEW IT WAS FORMID-ABLE, BUT I NEVER IMAGINED ...
I COULD NOT HAVE DONE IT WITH-OUT YOUR HELP.
WE ALL RIGHT, TAGI?
YEAH, WE'RE ALL RIGHT.

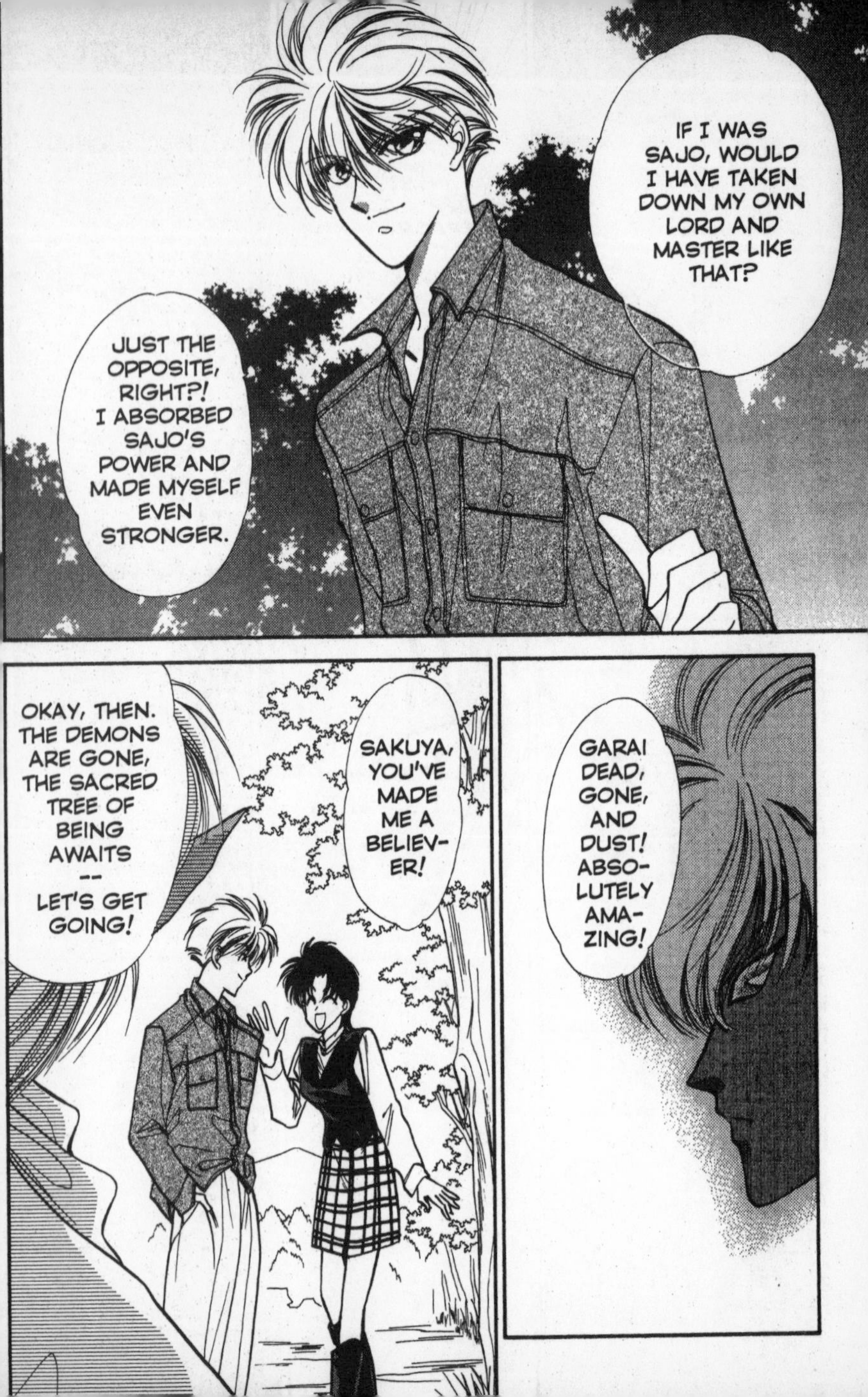
IF I WAS SAJO, WOULD I HAVE TAKEN DOWN MY OWN LORD AND MASTER LIKE THAT?
JUST THE OPPOSITE, RIGHT?! I ABSORBED SAJO'S POWER AND MADE MYSELF EVEN STRONGER.
GARAI DEAD, GONE, AND DUST! ABSO-LUTELY AMA-ZING!
SAKUYA, YOU'VE MADE ME A BELIEV-ER!
OKAY, THEN. THE DEMONS ARE GONE, THE SACRED TREE OF BEING AWAITS -- LET'S GET GOING!

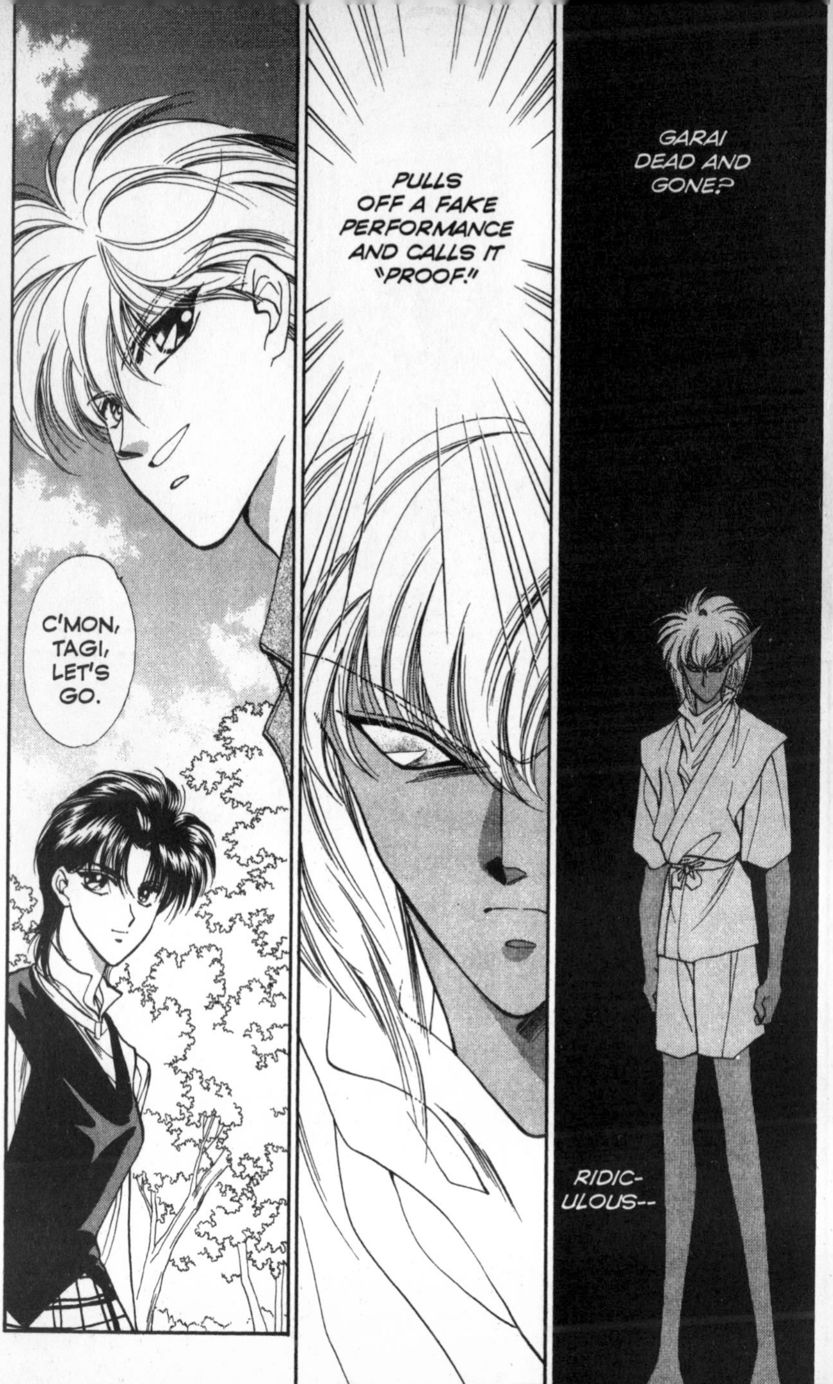
GARAI DEAD AND GONE?
RIDIC-ULOUS--
PULLS OFF A FAKE PERFORMANCE AND CALLS IT "PROOF."
C'MON, TAGI, LET'S GO.

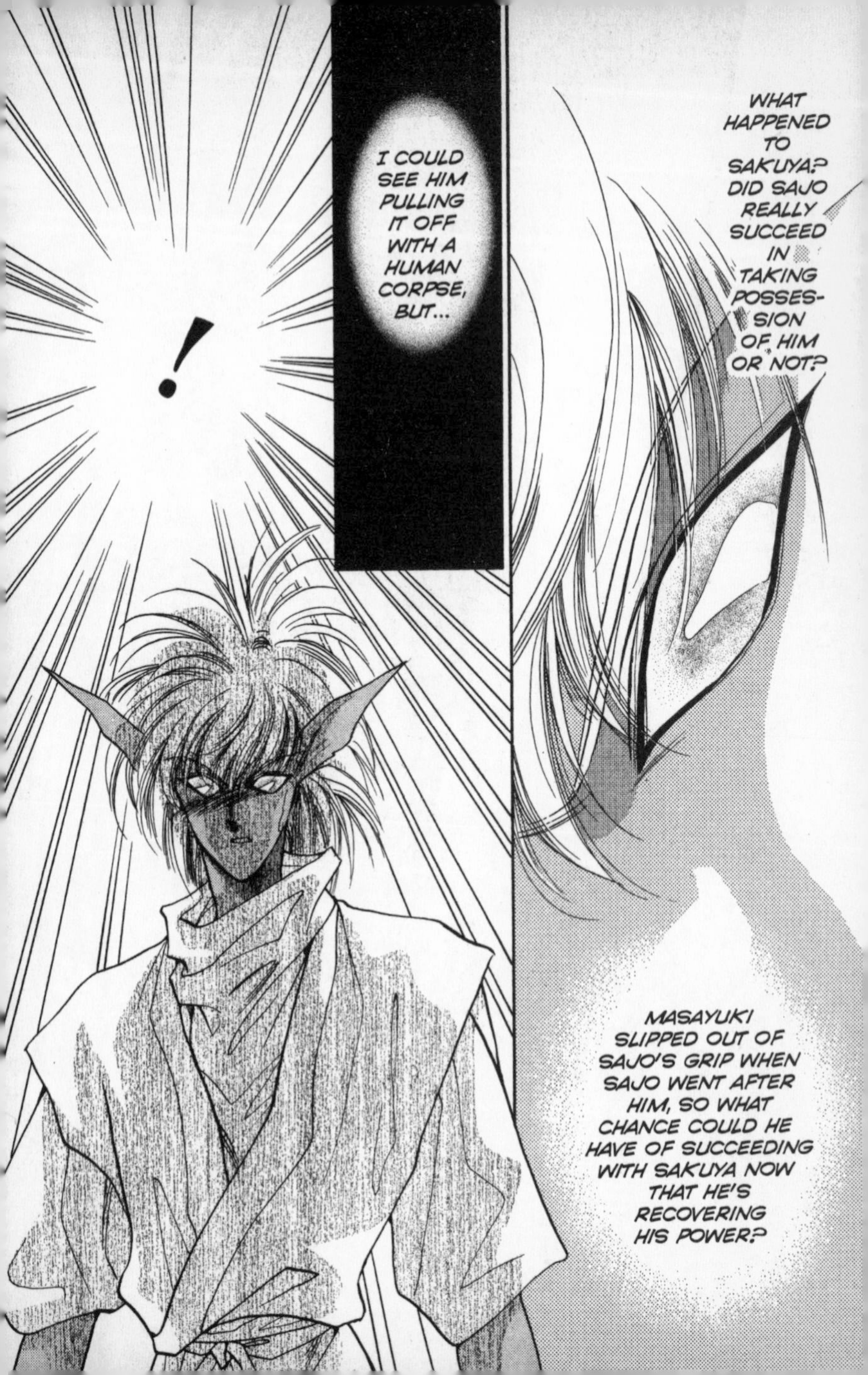
WHAT HAPPENED TO SAKUYA? DID SAJO REALLY SUCCEED IN TAKING POSSES-SION OF HIM OR NOT?
MASAYUKI SLIPPED OUT OF SAJO'S GRIP WHEN SAJO WENT AFTER HIM, SO WHAT CHANCE COULD HE HAVE OF SUCCEEDING WITH SAKUYA NOW THAT HE'S RECOVERING HIS POWER?
I COULD SEE HIM PULLING IT OFF WITH A HUMAN CORPSE, BUT...
!

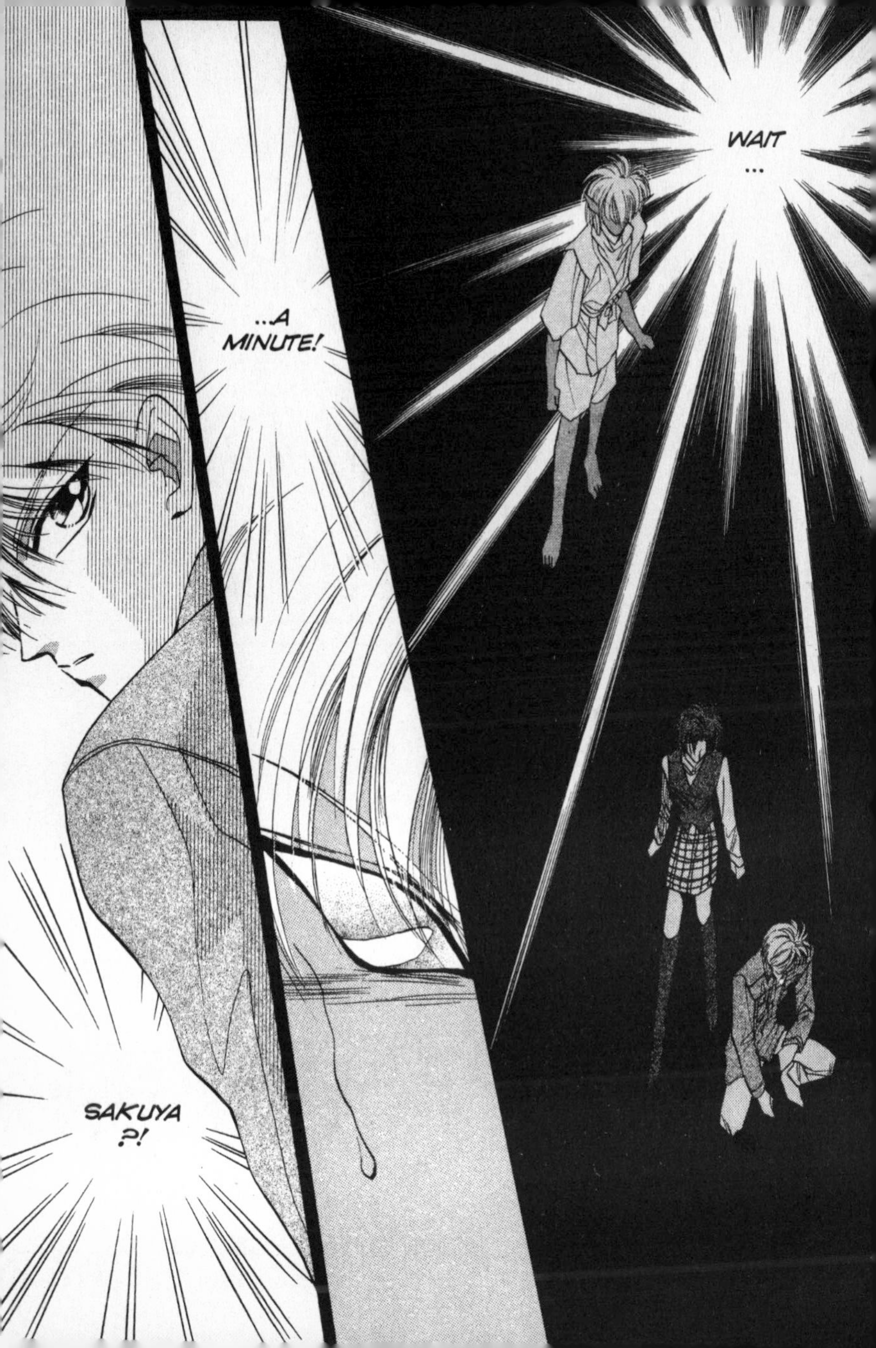
WAIT ...
...A MINUTE!
SAKUYA ?!

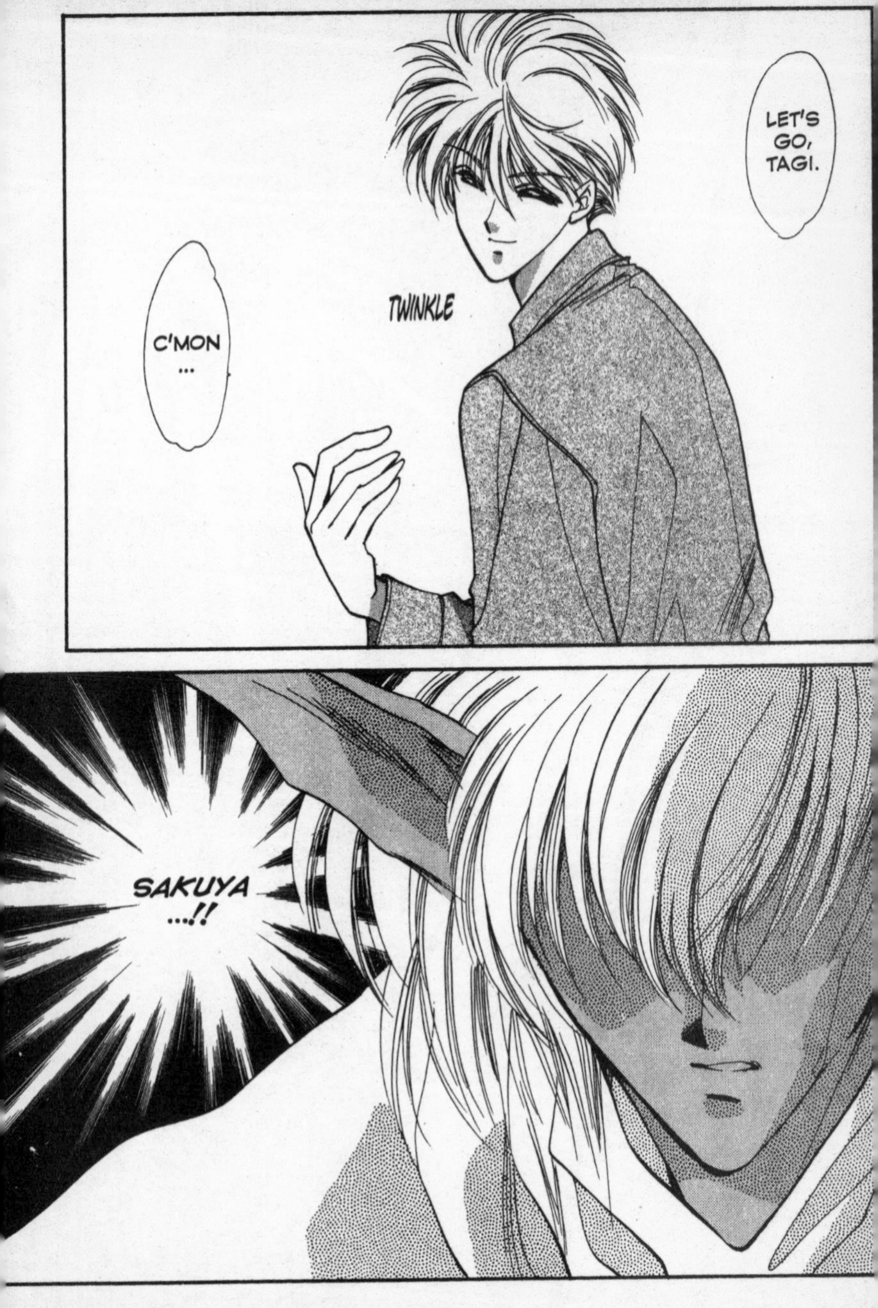
LET'S GO, TAGI.
TWINKLE
C'MON ...
SAKUYA ...!!

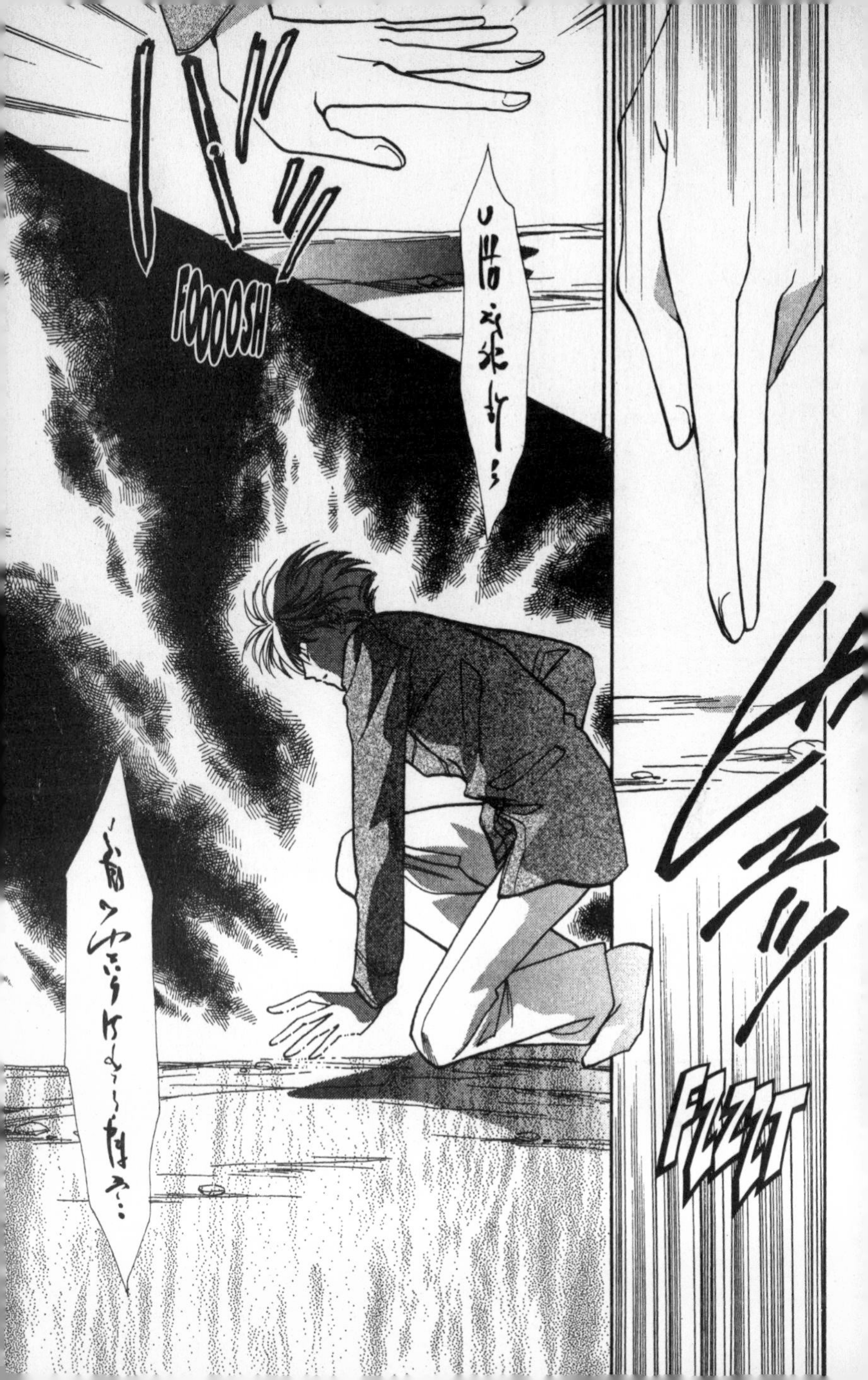
FZZZT
FOOOOSH

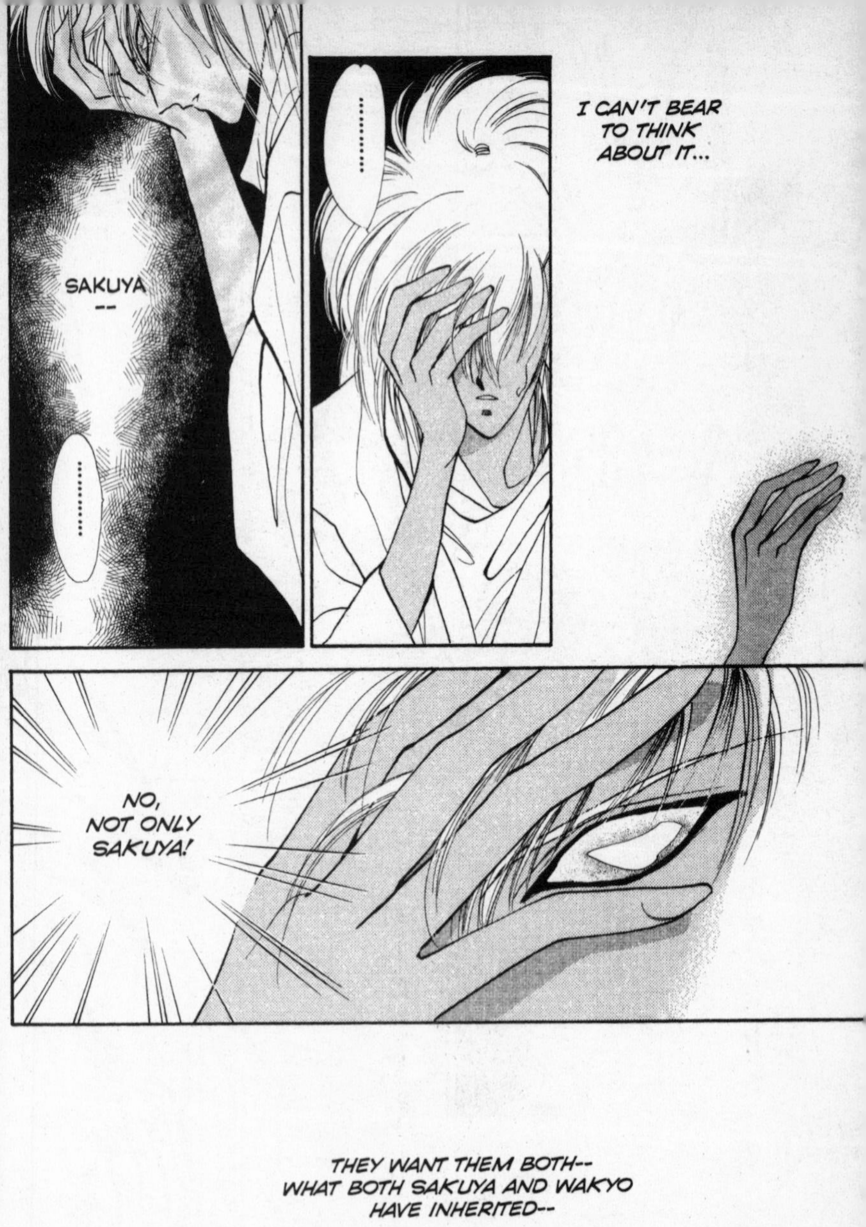
I CAN'T BEAR TO THINK ABOUT IT...
....
SAKUYA --
....
NO, NOT ONLY SAKUYA!
THEY WANT THEM BOTH-- WHAT BOTH SAKUYA AND WAKYO HAVE INHERITED--

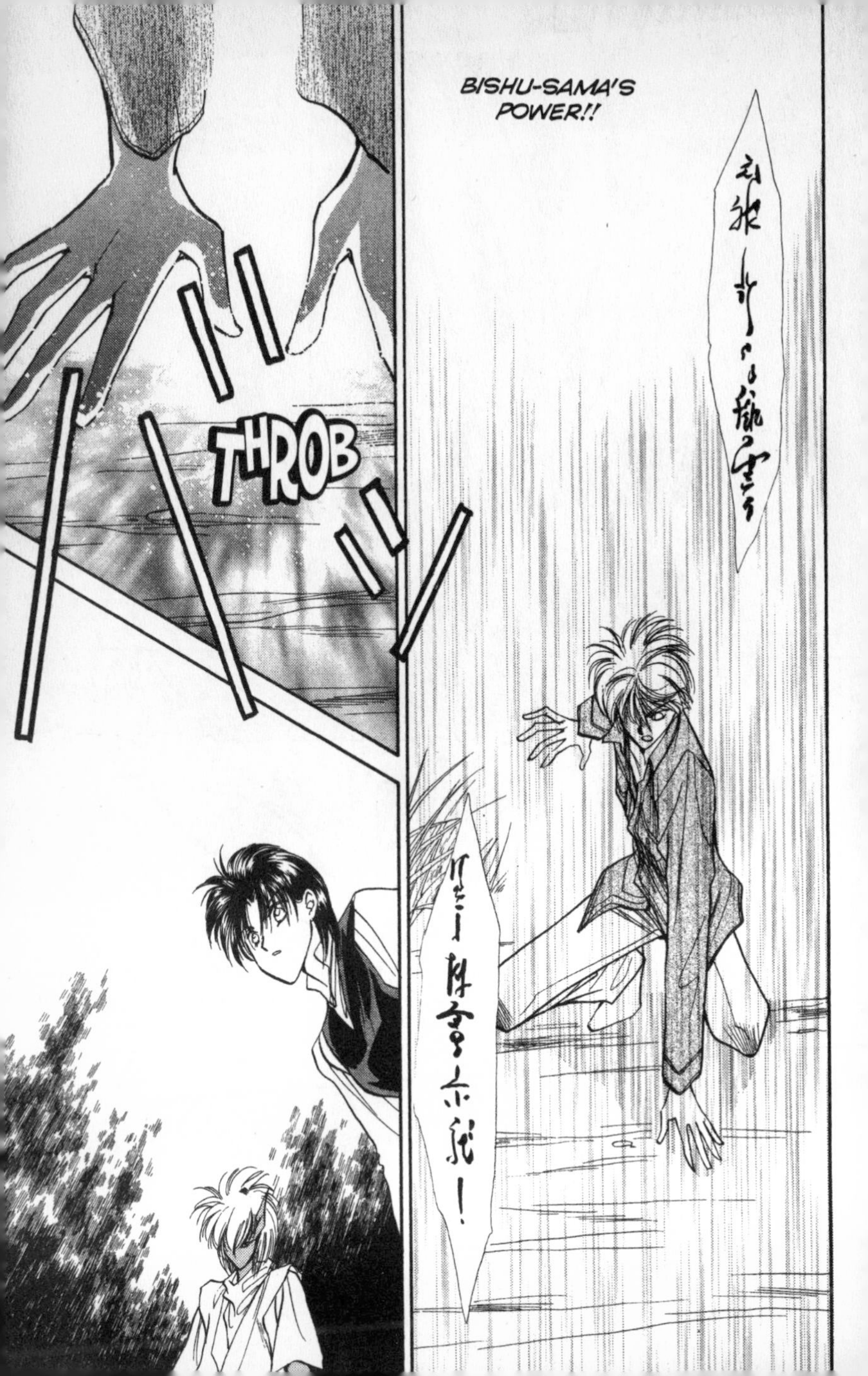
BISHU-SAMA'S POWER!!
THROB

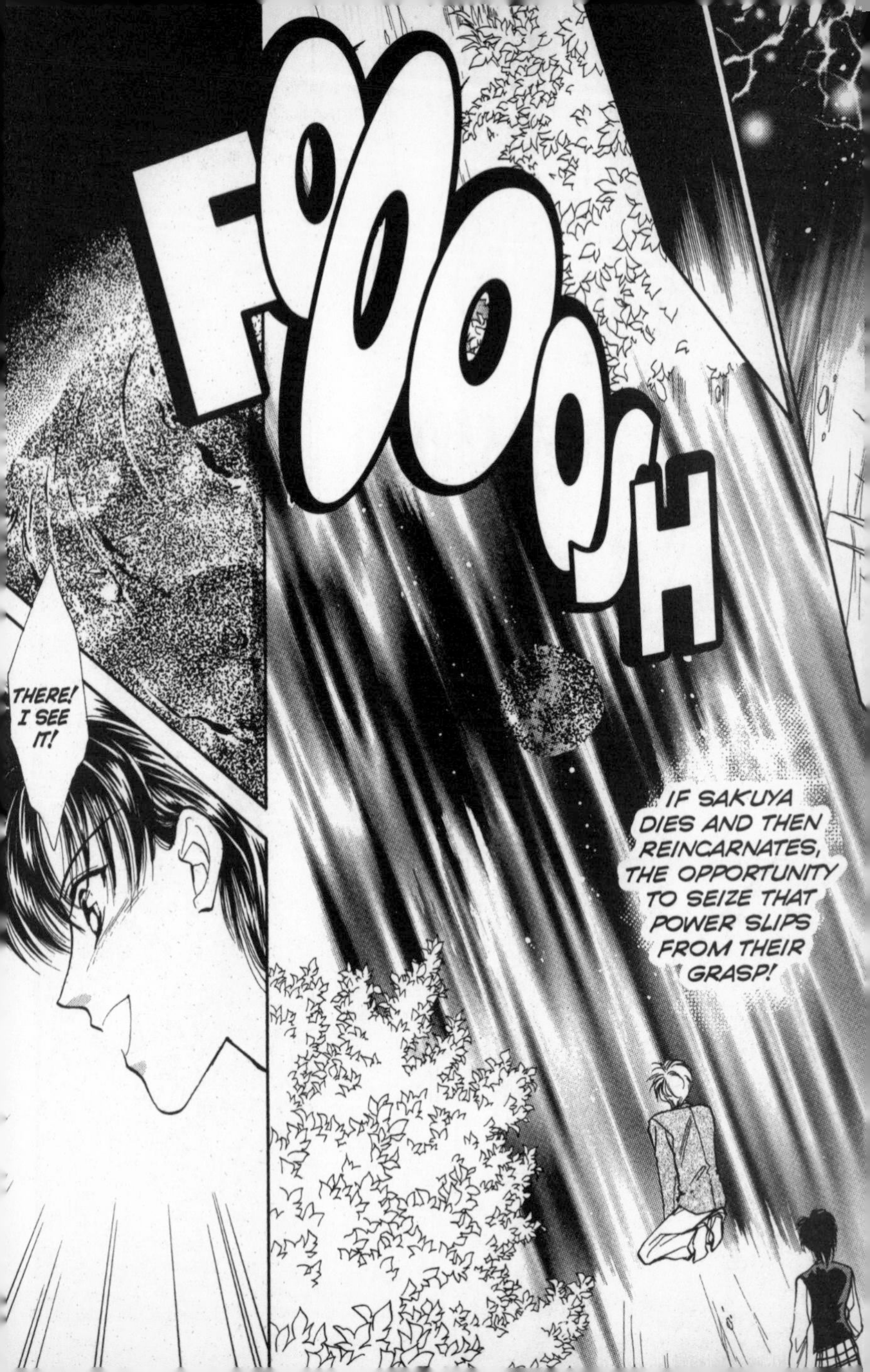
FOOOOSH
IF SAKUYA DIES AND THEN REINCARNATES, THE OPPORTUNITY TO SEIZE THAT POWER SLIPS FROM THEIR GRASP!
THERE! I SEE IT!

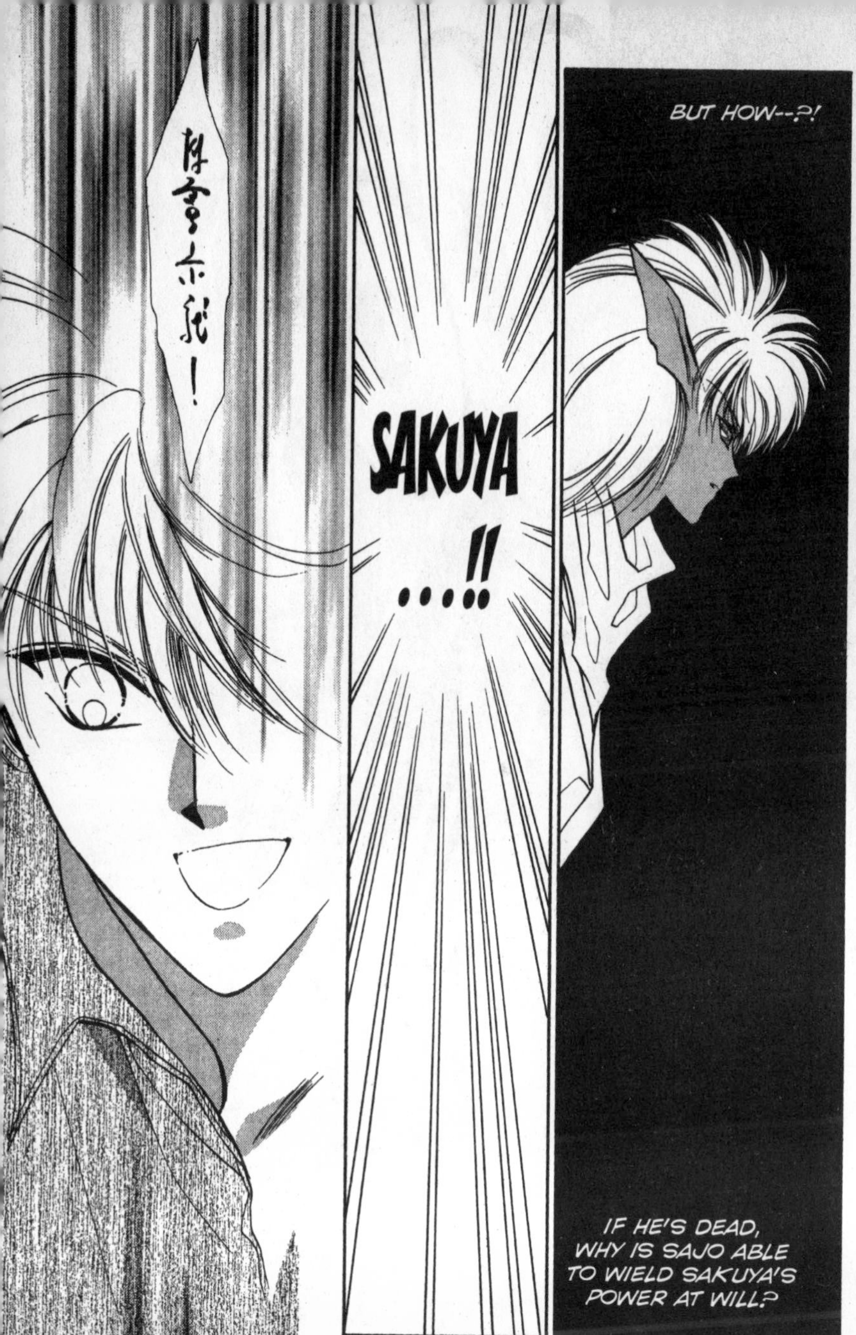
BUT HOW--?!
IF HE'S DEAD, WHY IS SAJO ABLE TO WIELD SAKUYA'S POWER AT WILL?
SAKUYA ...!!

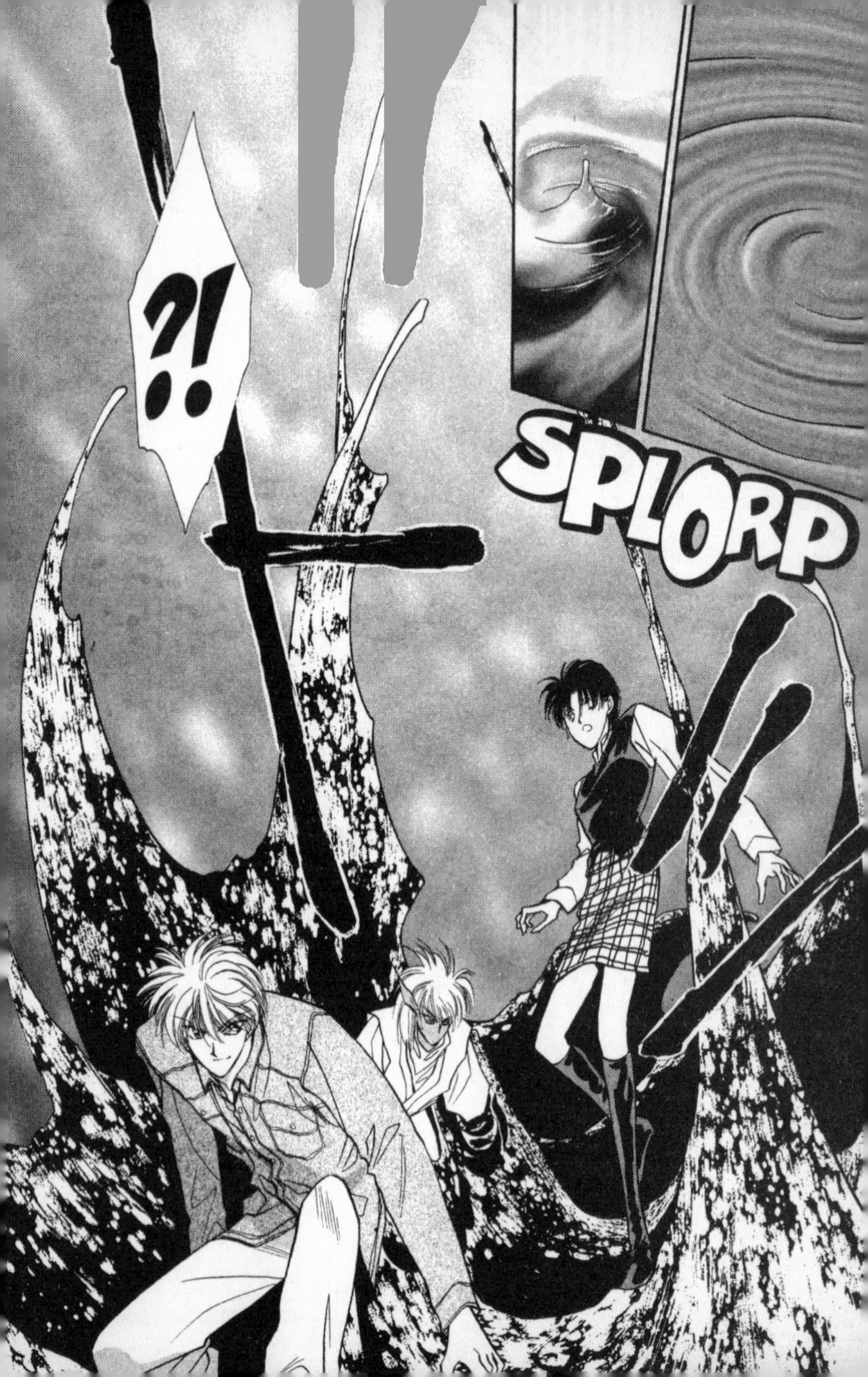
SPLORP
?!

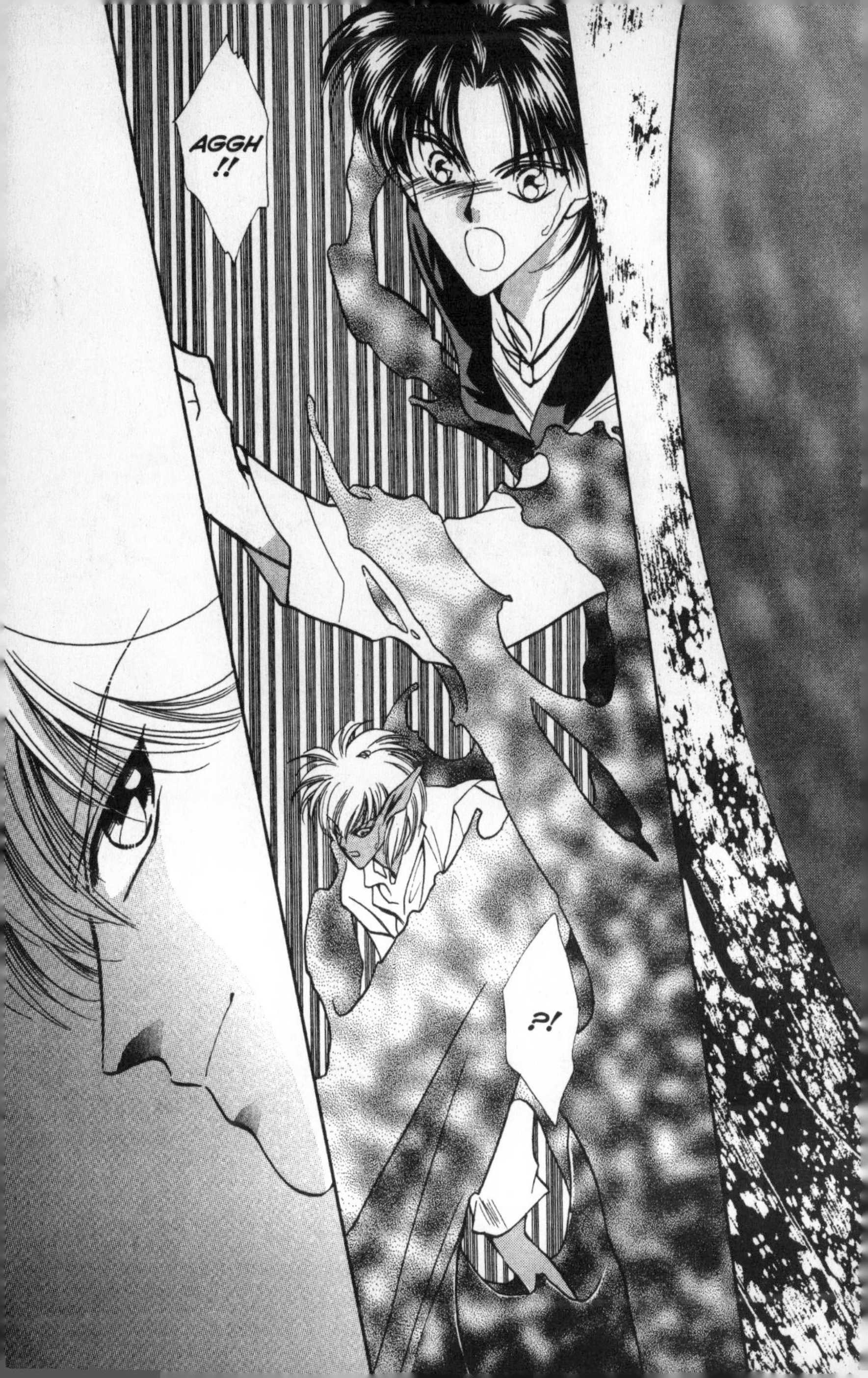
AGGH !!
?!

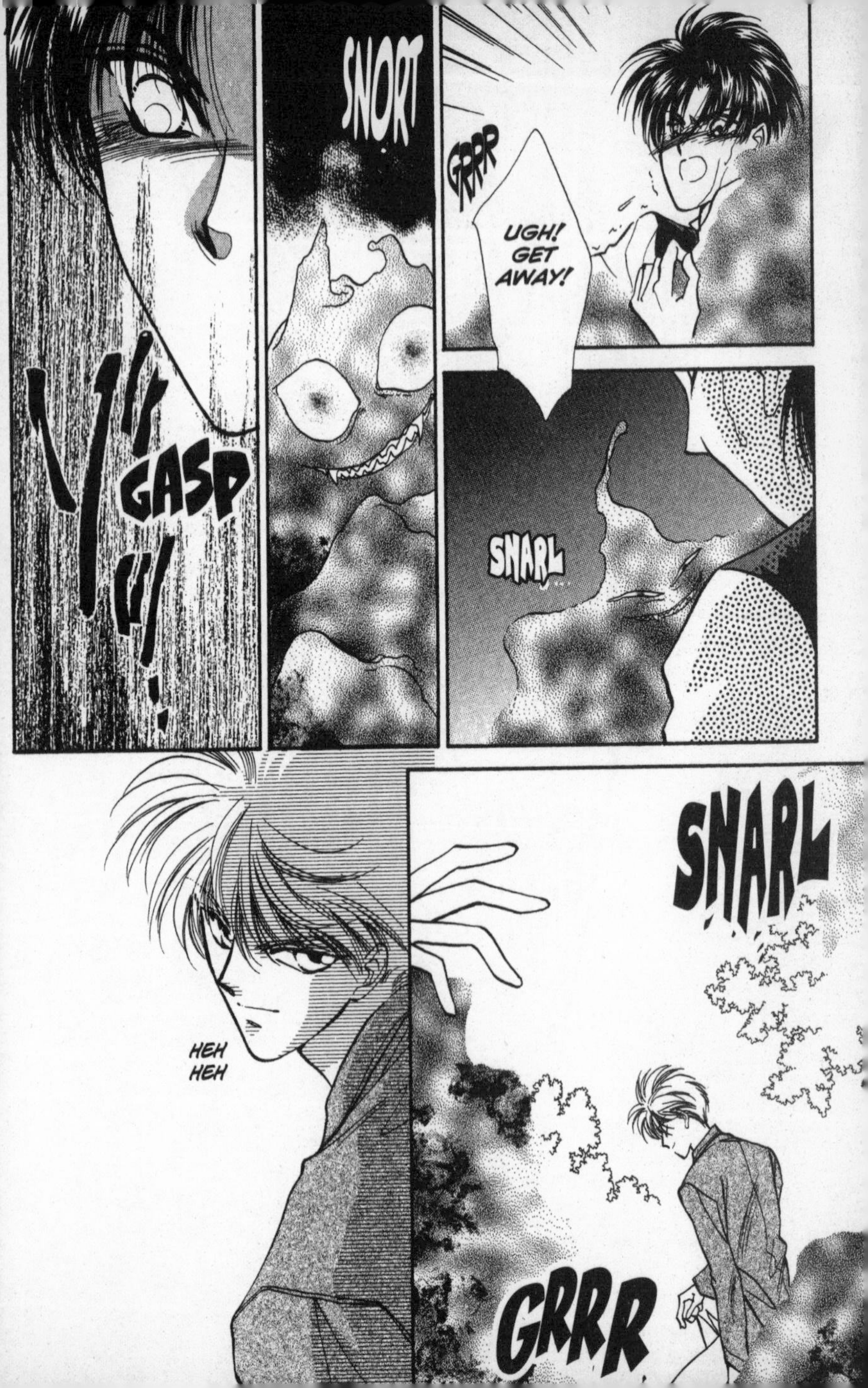
GRRR
UGH! GET AWAY!
SNARL
SNORT
GASP
SNARL
GRRR
HEH HEH

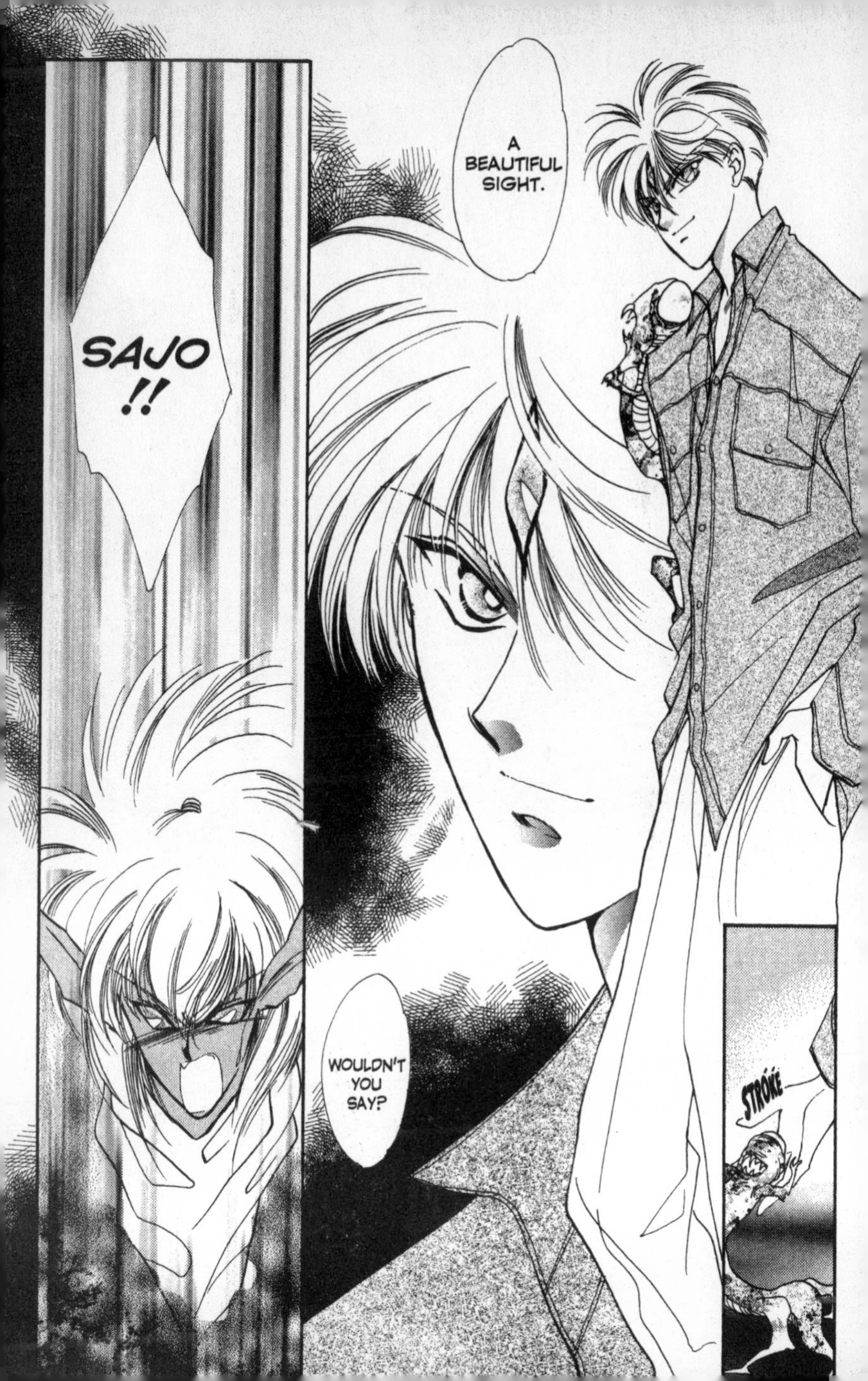
A BEAUTIFUL SIGHT.
WOULDN'T YOU SAY?
STROKE
SAJO!!

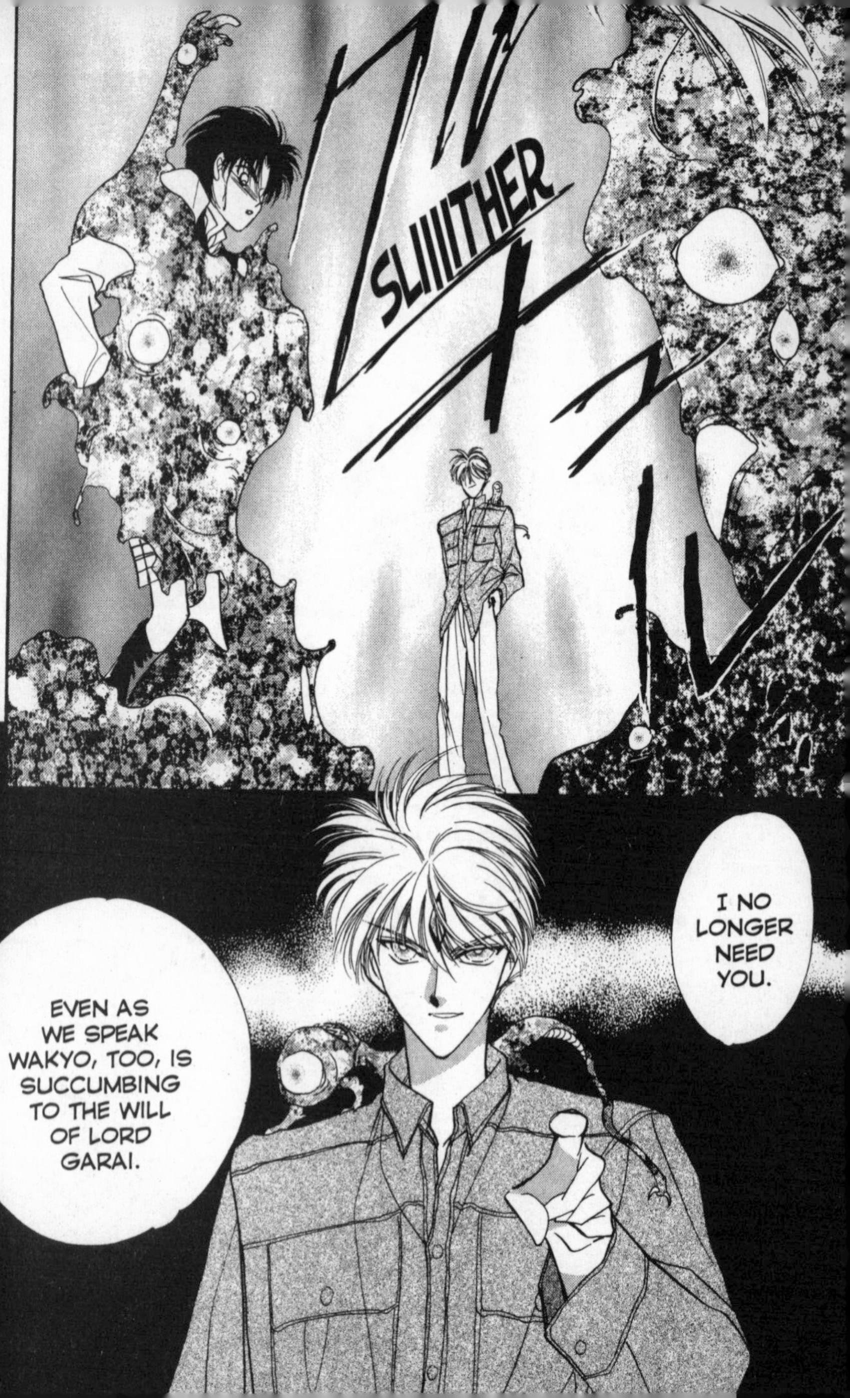
SLIIIITHER
I NO LONGER NEED YOU.
EVEN AS WE SPEAK WAKYO, TOO, IS SUCCUMBING TO THE WILL OF LORD GARAI.

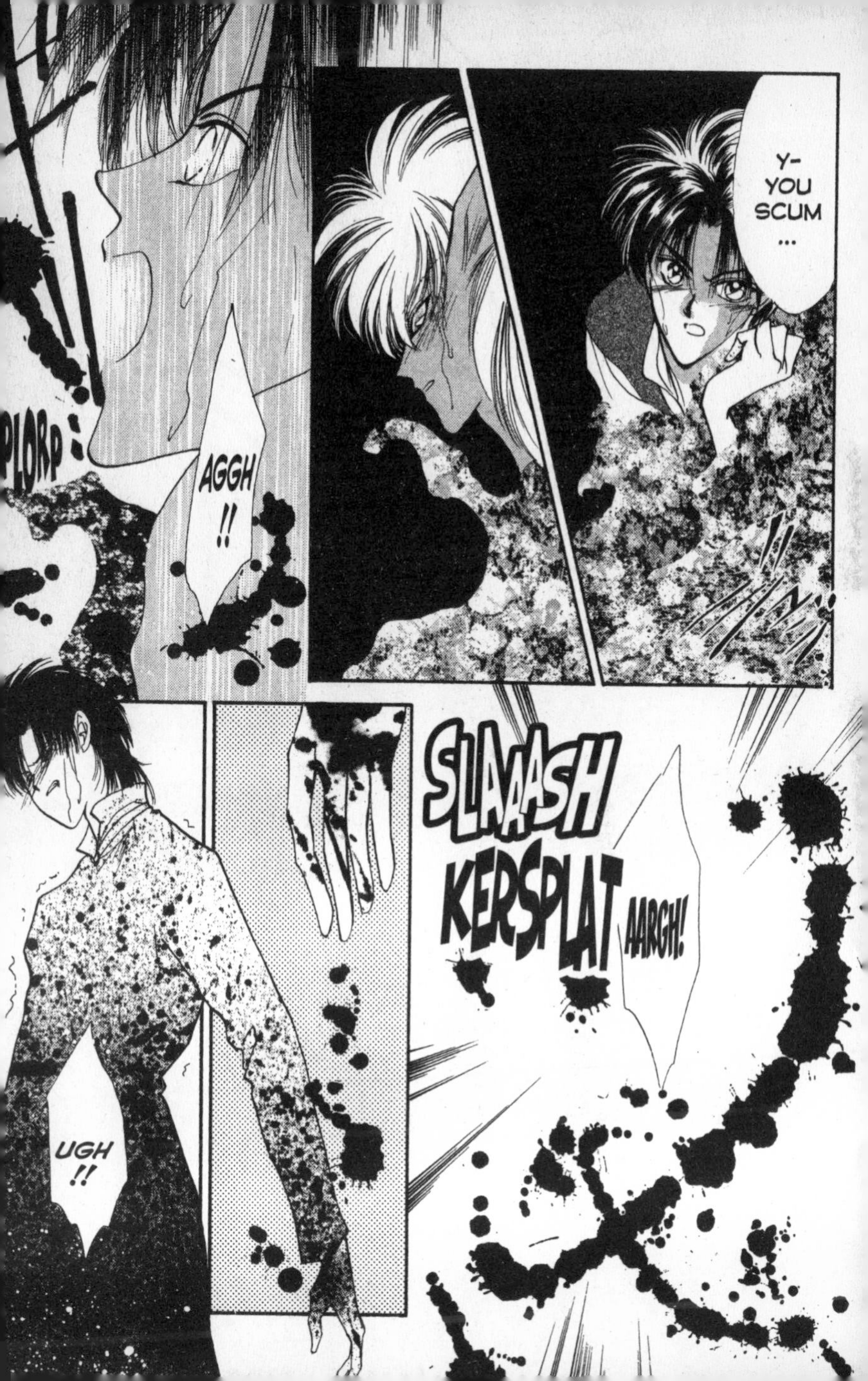
Y-
YOU SCUM
...
PLORP
AGGH !!
SLAAASH
KERSPLAT
AARGH!
UGH !!

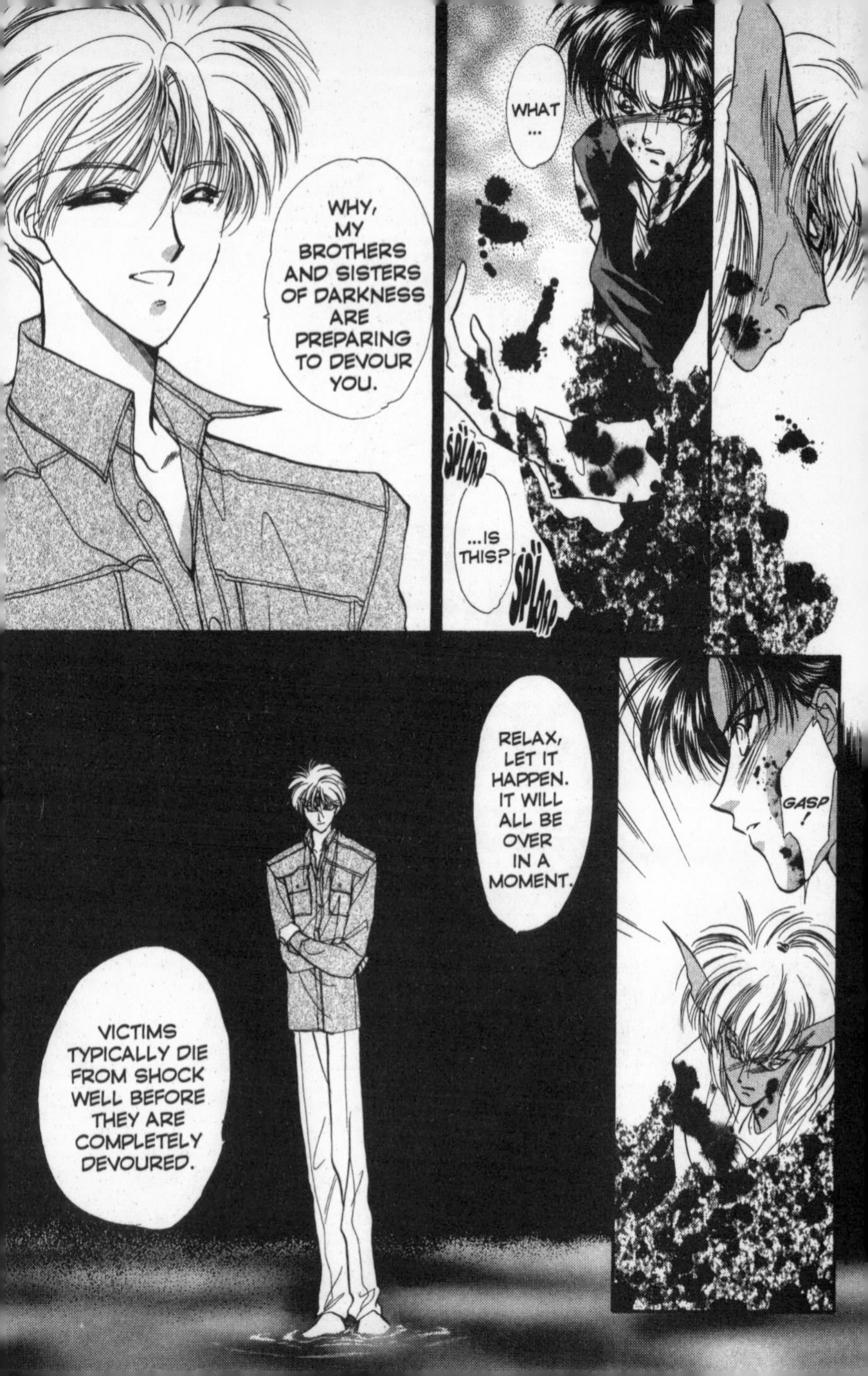
WHAT ...
SPLORP
...IS THIS?
SPLORP
WHY, MY BROTHERS AND SISTERS OF DARKNESS ARE PREPARING TO DEVOUR YOU.
GASP!
RELAX, LET IT HAPPEN. IT WILL ALL BE OVER IN A MOMENT.
VICTIMS TYPICALLY DIE FROM SHOCK WELL BEFORE THEY ARE COMPLETELY DEVOURED.

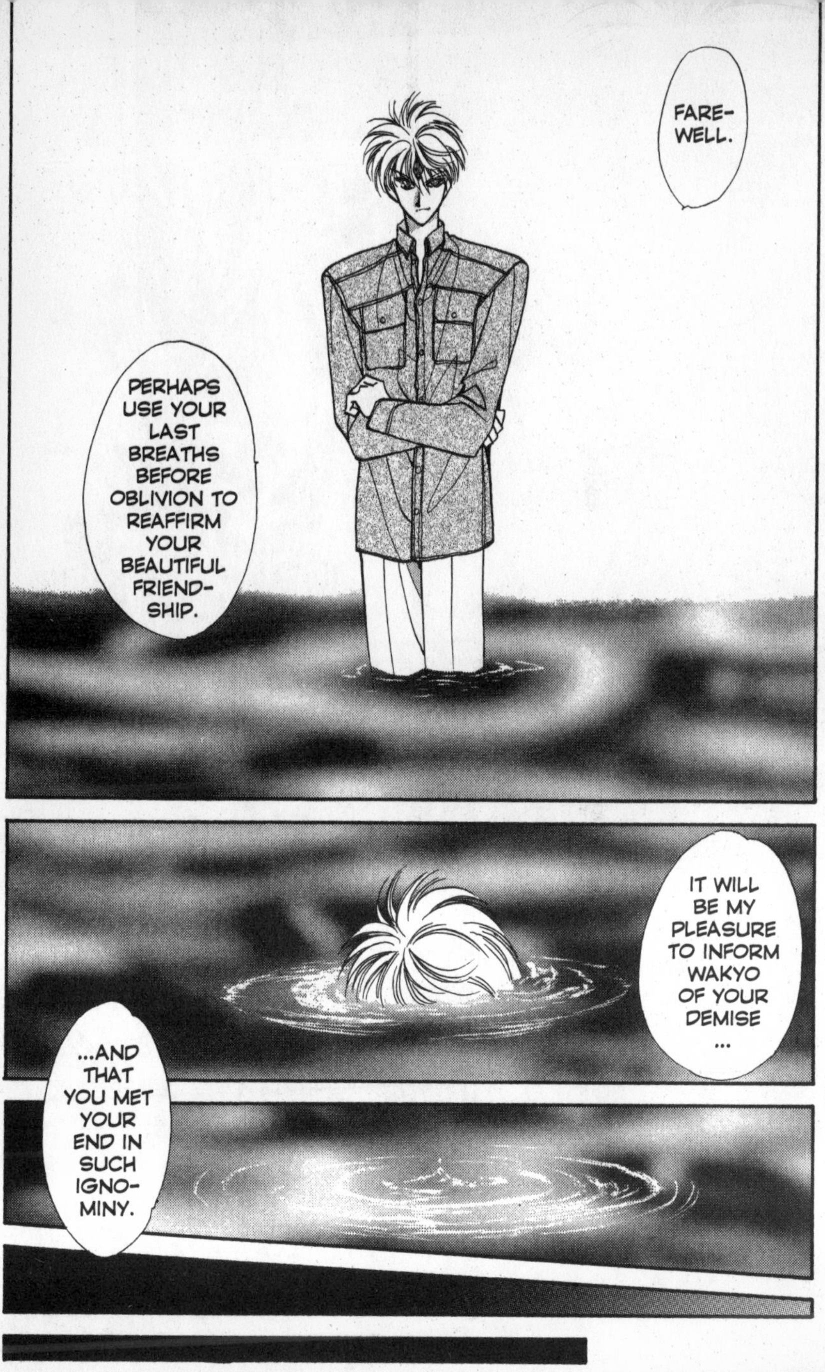
FARE-WELL.
PERHAPS USE YOUR LAST BREATHS BEFORE OBLIVION TO REAFFIRM YOUR BEAUTIFUL FRIEND-SHIP.
IT WILL BE MY PLEASURE TO INFORM WAKYO OF YOUR DEMISE ...
...AND THAT YOU MET YOUR END IN SUCH IGNO-MINY.

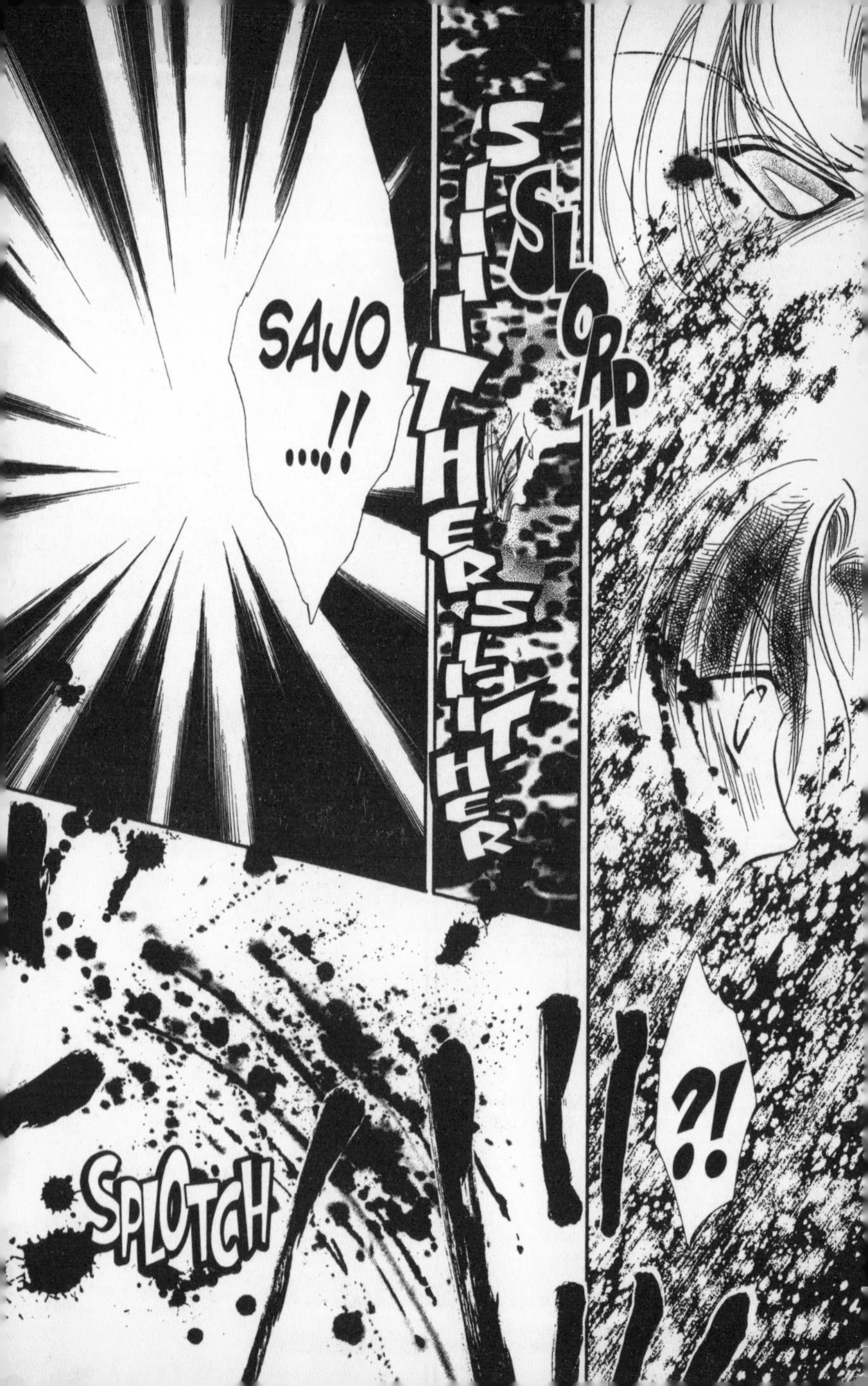
?!
SLORP
SLIIITHER SLITHER
SAJO ...!!
SPLOTCH

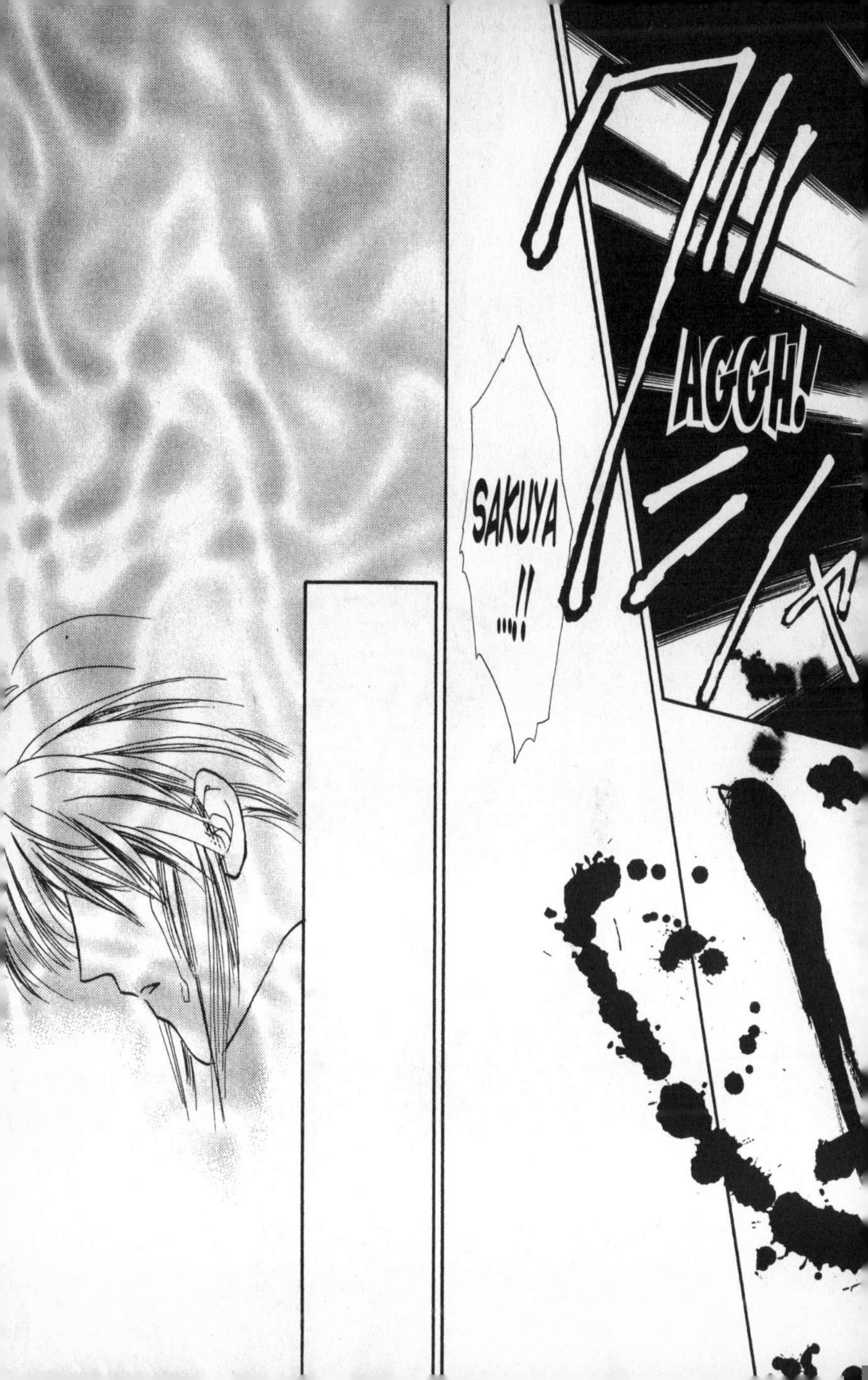
AGGH!
SAKUYA ...!!

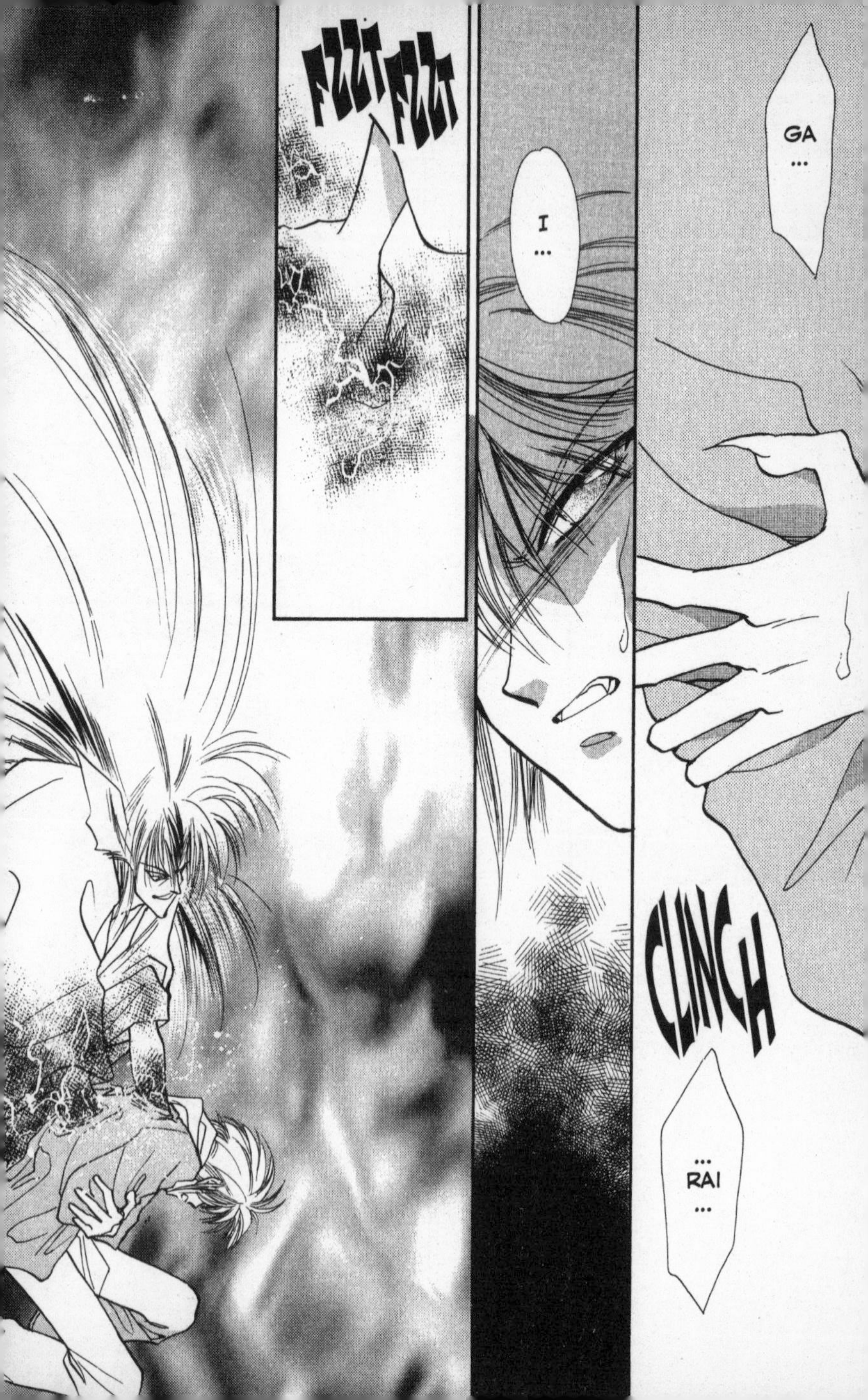
GA ...
CLINCH
... RAI ...
I ...
FZZT FZZT

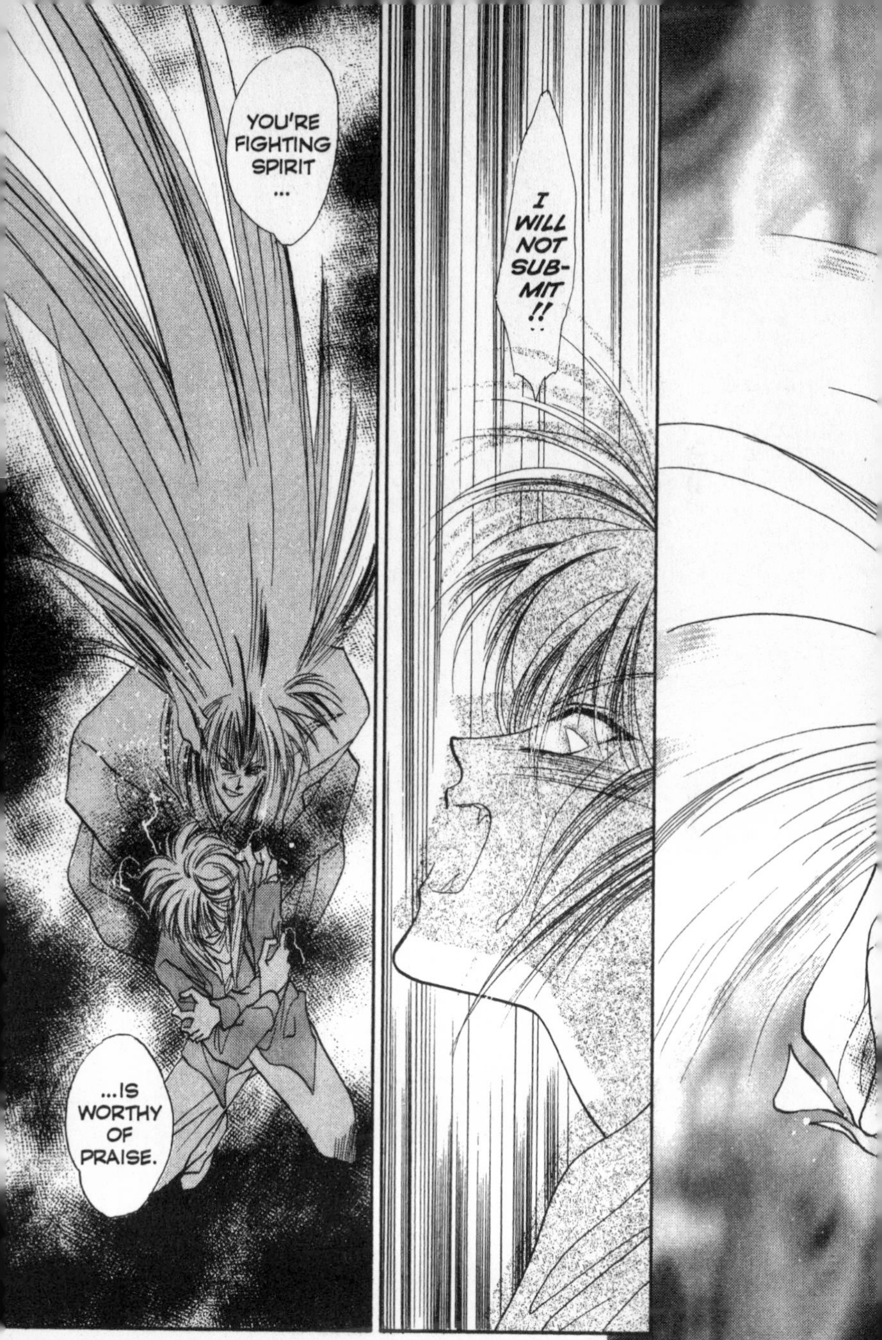
YOU'RE FIGHTING SPIRIT ...
I WILL NOT SUB-MIT!!
...IS WORTHY OF PRAISE.

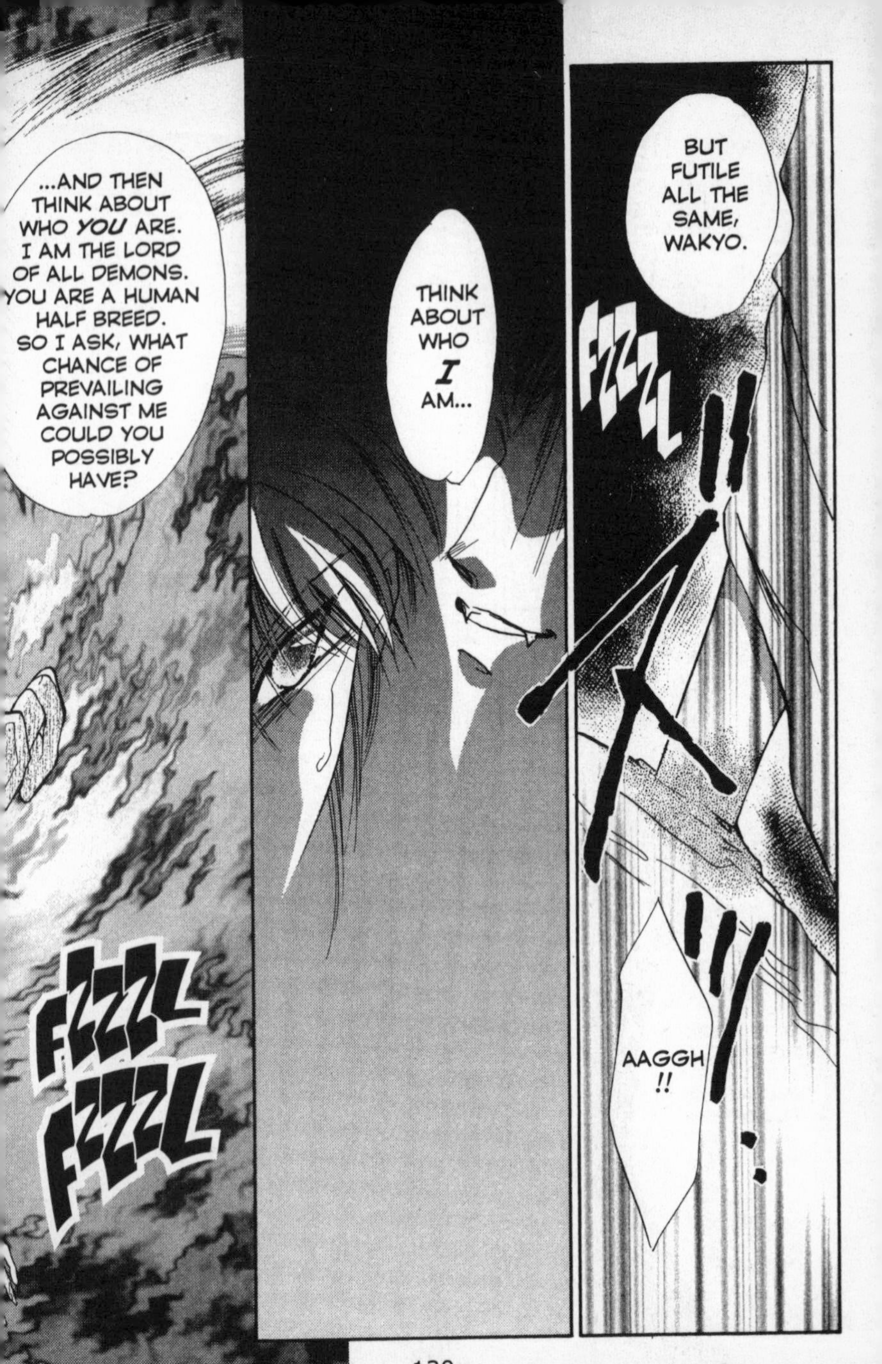
BUT FUTILE ALL THE SAME, WAKYO.
FZZZL!!
AAGGH!!
THINK ABOUT WHO I AM...
...AND THEN THINK ABOUT WHO YOU ARE. I AM THE LORD OF ALL DEMONS. YOU ARE A HUMAN HALF BREED. SO I ASK, WHAT CHANCE OF PREVAILING AGAINST ME COULD YOU POSSIBLY HAVE?
FZZZL FZZZL

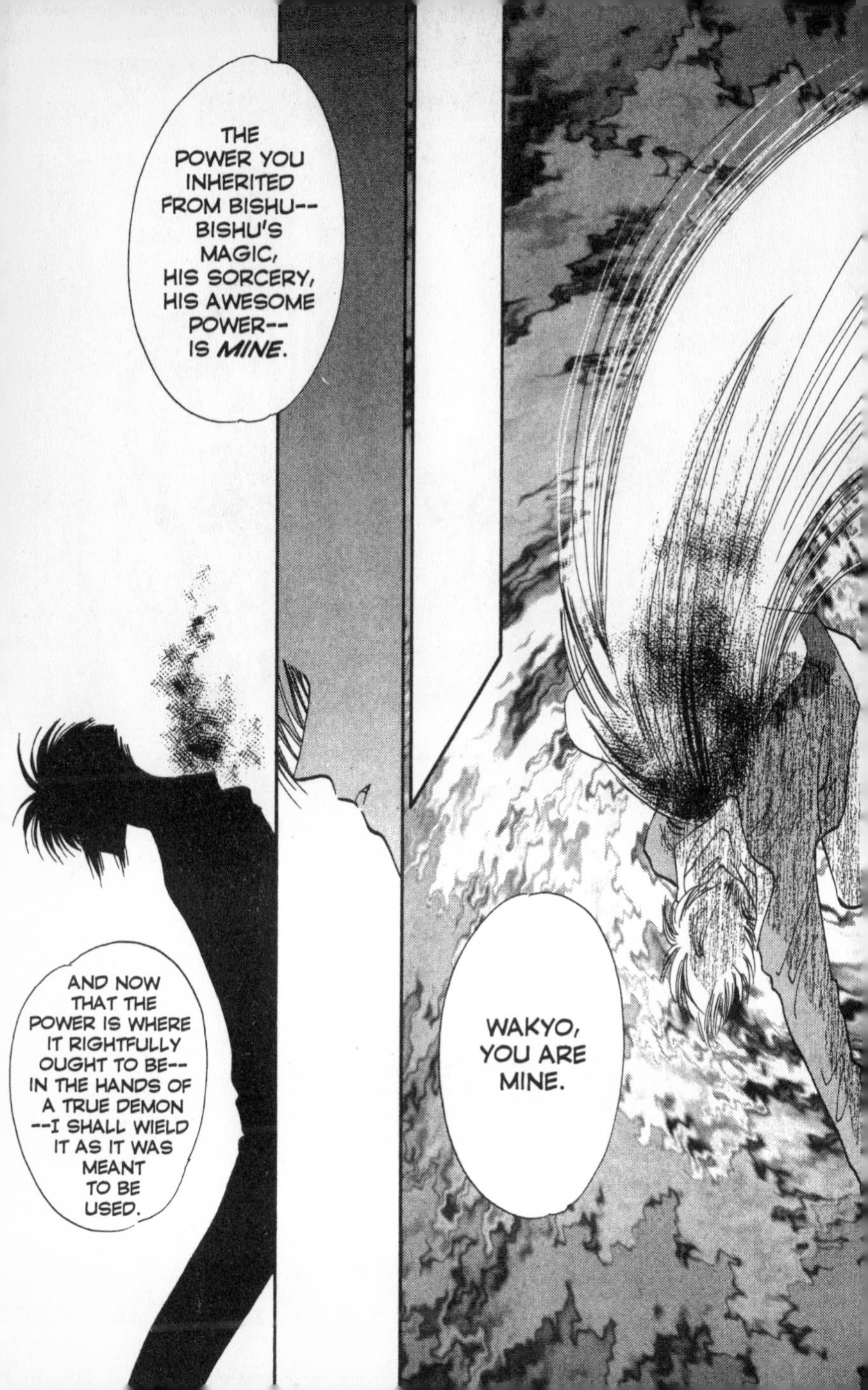
WAKYO, YOU ARE MINE.
THE POWER YOU INHERITED FROM BISHU-- BISHU'S MAGIC, HIS SORCERY, HIS AWESOME POWER-- IS *MINE*.
AND NOW THAT THE POWER IS WHERE IT RIGHTFULLY OUGHT TO BE-- IN THE HANDS OF A TRUE DEMON --I SHALL WIELD IT AS IT WAS MEANT TO BE USED.

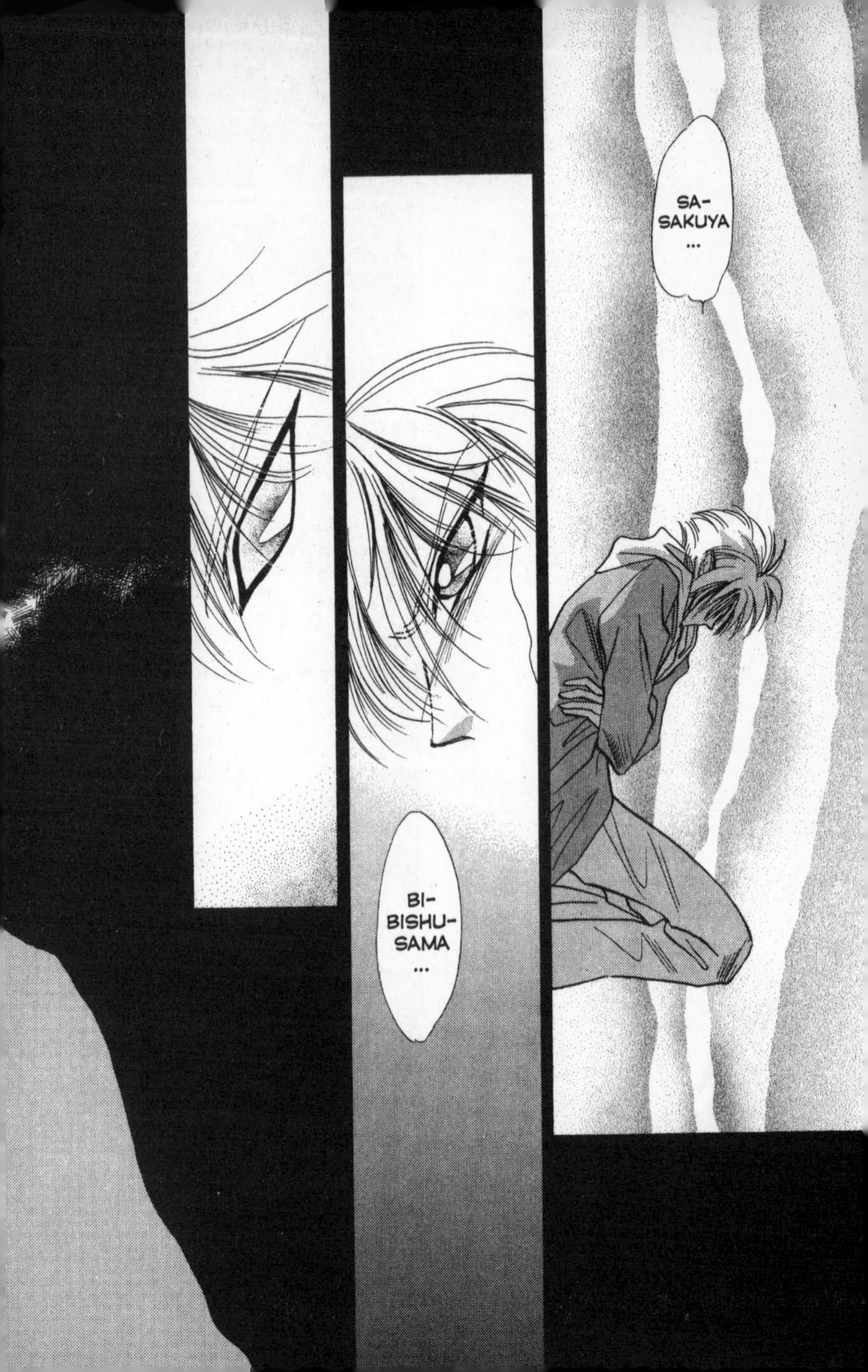
SA-SAKUYA ...
BI-BISHU-SAMA ...

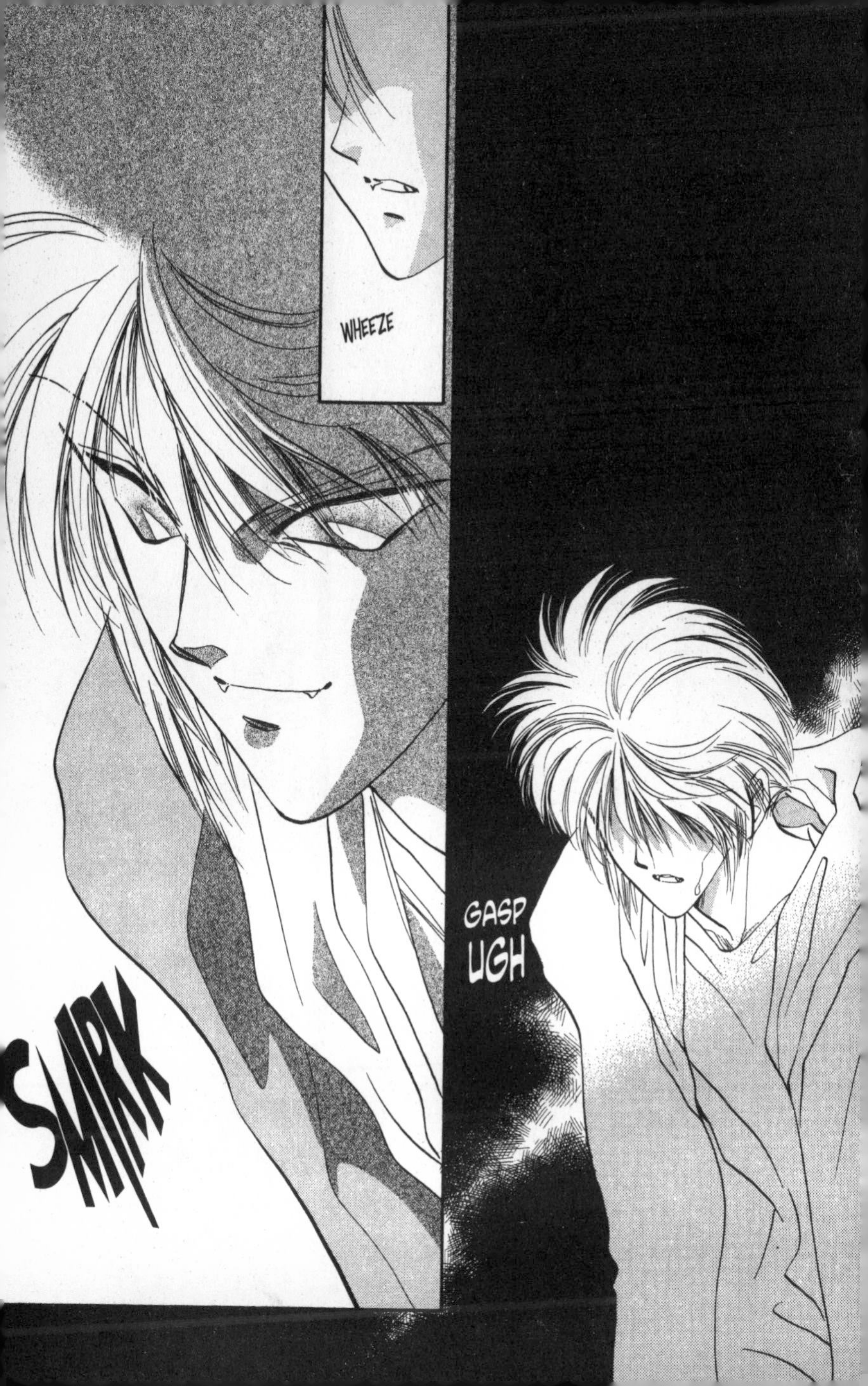
GASP
UGH
WHEEZE
SMIRK

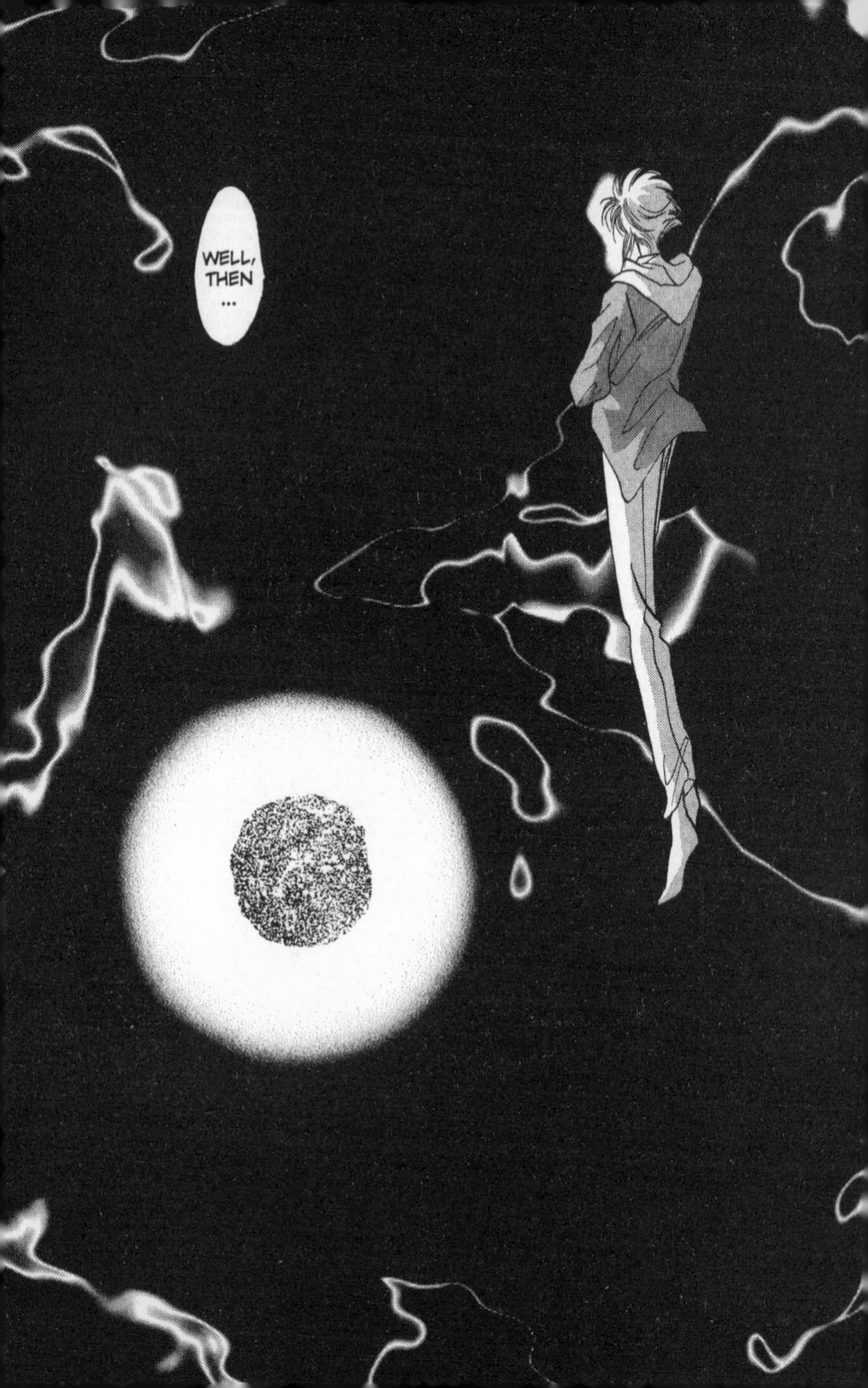
WELL, THEN ...

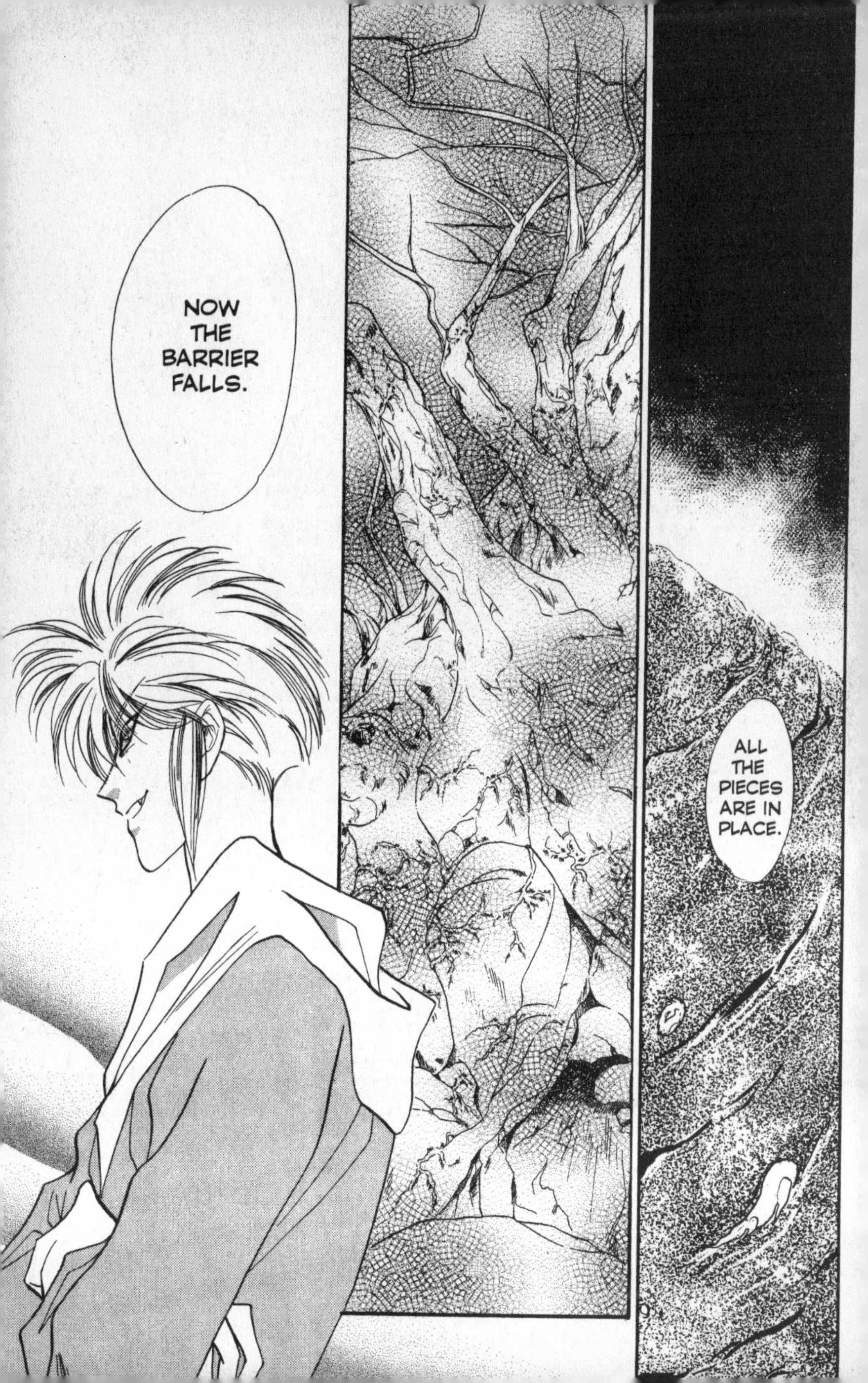
ALL THE PIECES ARE IN PLACE.
NOW THE BARRIER FALLS.

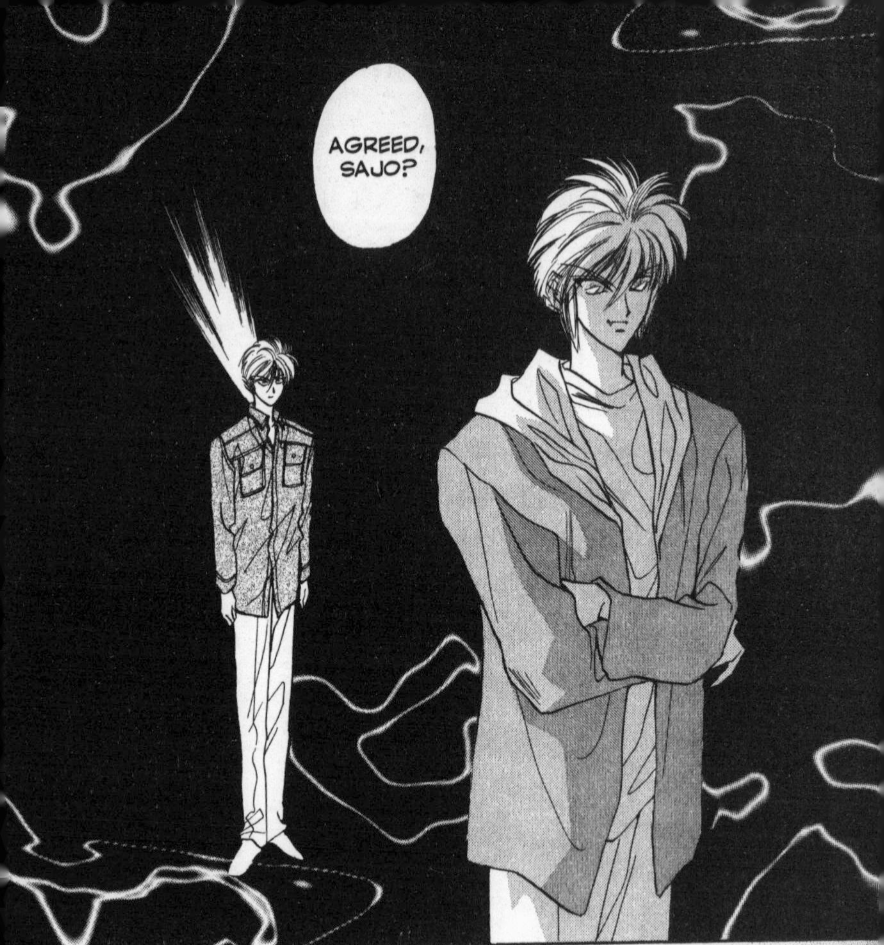
AGREED, SAJO?

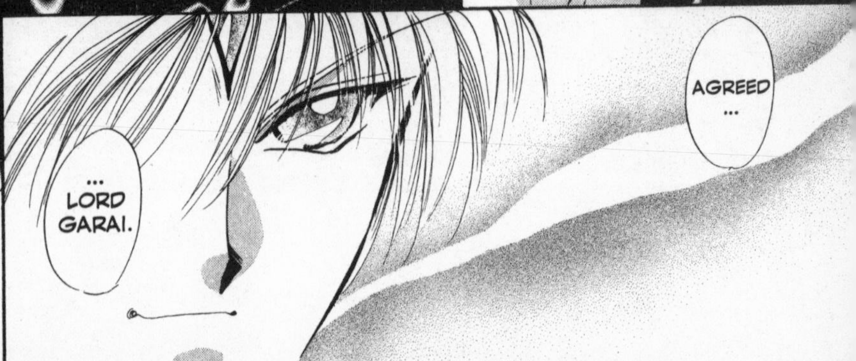
AGREED ...
... LORD GARAI.

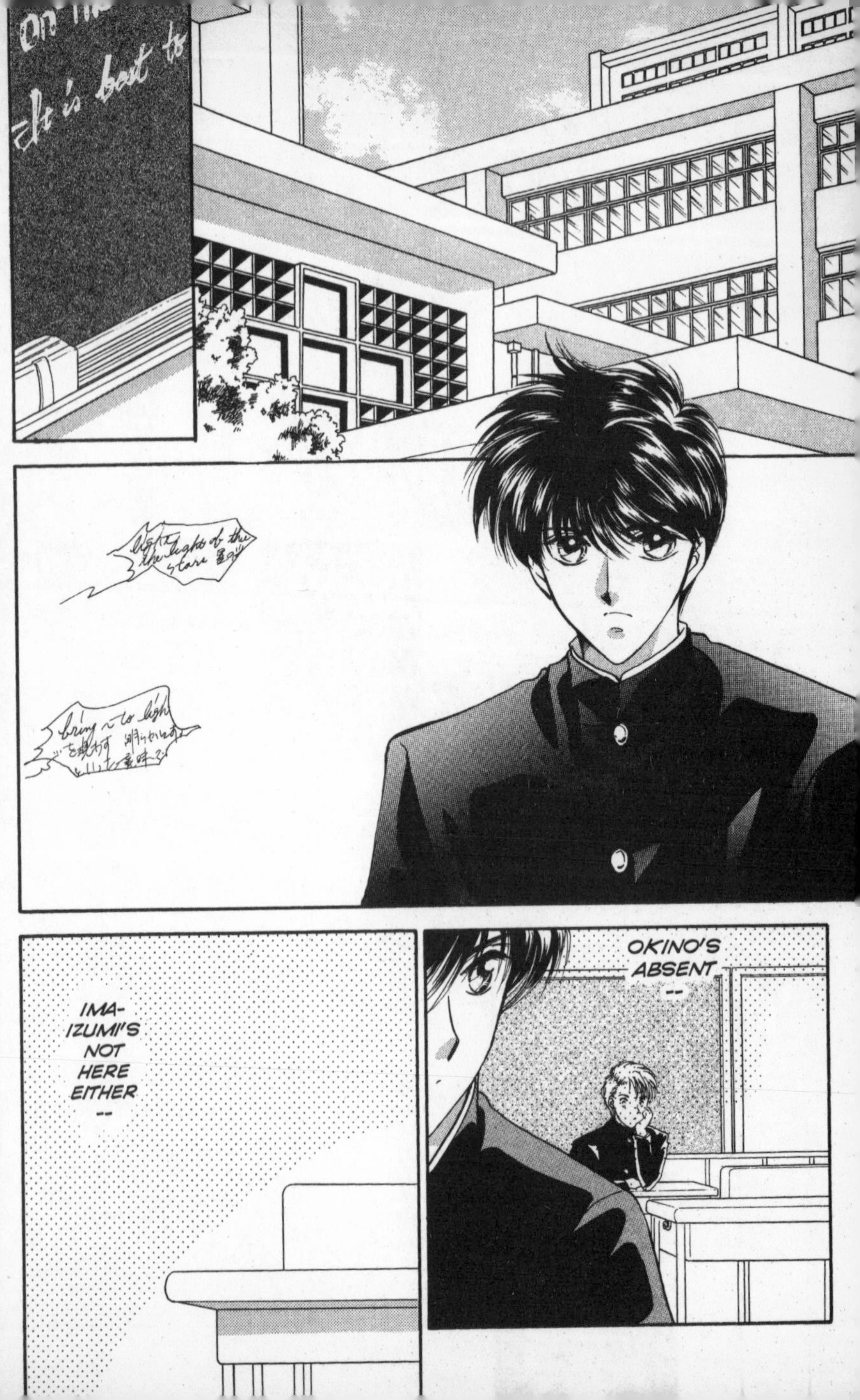
It is best to
OKINO'S ABSENT --
IMA-IZUMI'S NOT HERE EITHER --

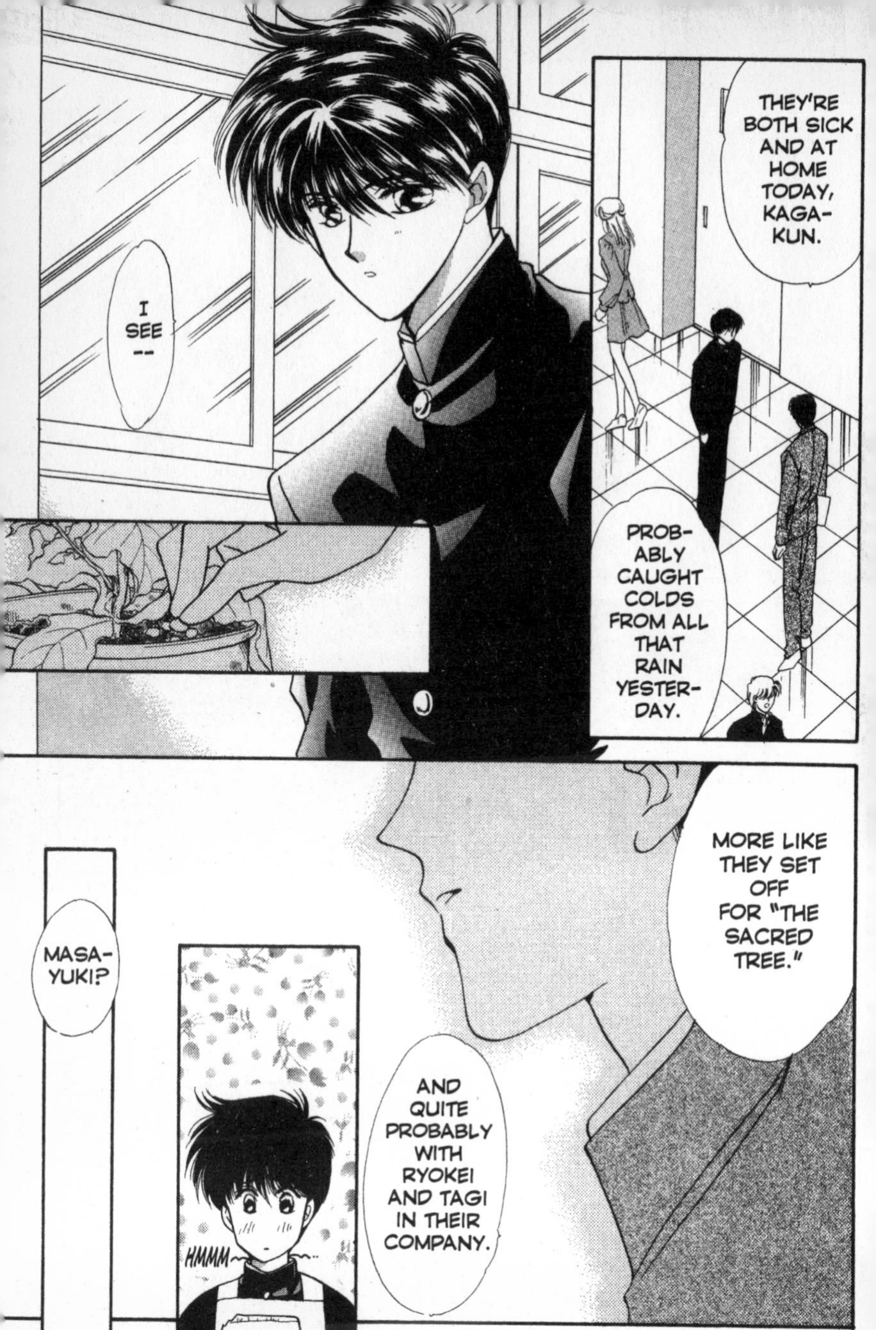
THEY'RE BOTH SICK AND AT HOME TODAY, KAGA-KUN.
PROB-ABLY CAUGHT COLDS FROM ALL THAT RAIN YESTER-DAY.
I SEE --
MORE LIKE THEY SET OFF FOR "THE SACRED TREE."
AND QUITE PROBABLY WITH RYOKEI AND TAGI IN THEIR COMPANY.
MASA-YUKI?
HMMM~
TAKING OVER

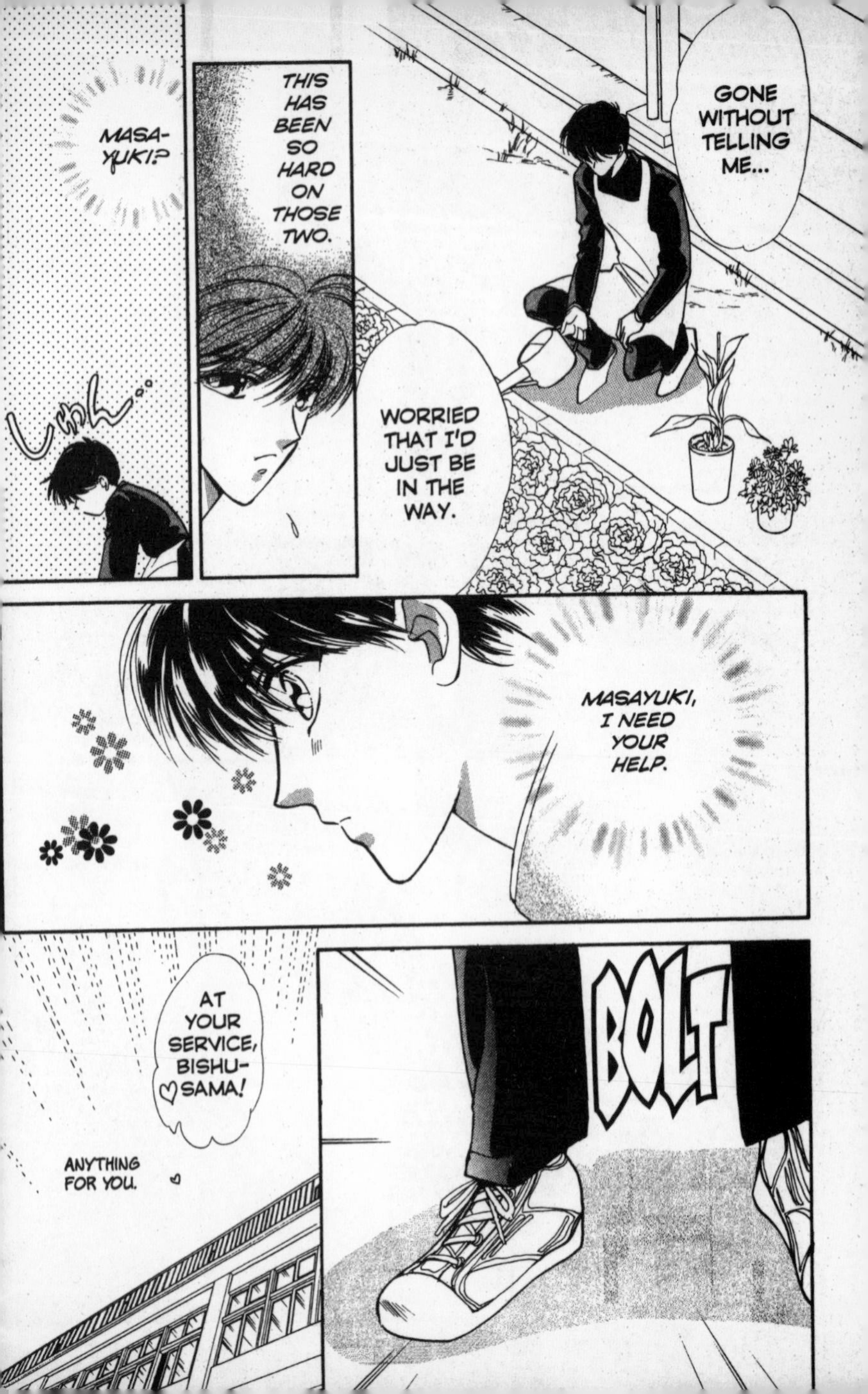
GONE WITHOUT TELLING ME...
WORRIED THAT I'D JUST BE IN THE WAY.
THIS HAS BEEN SO HARD ON THOSE TWO.
MASA-YUKI?
しゅん...
MASAYUKI, I NEED YOUR HELP.
BOLT
AT YOUR SERVICE, BISHU-SAMA! ♡
ANYTHING FOR YOU. ♡

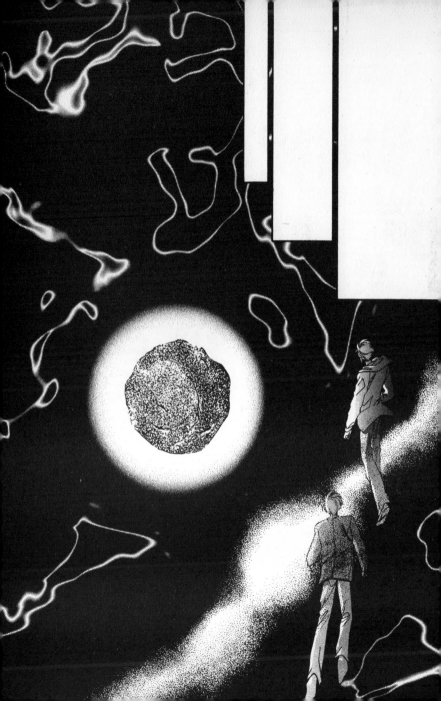

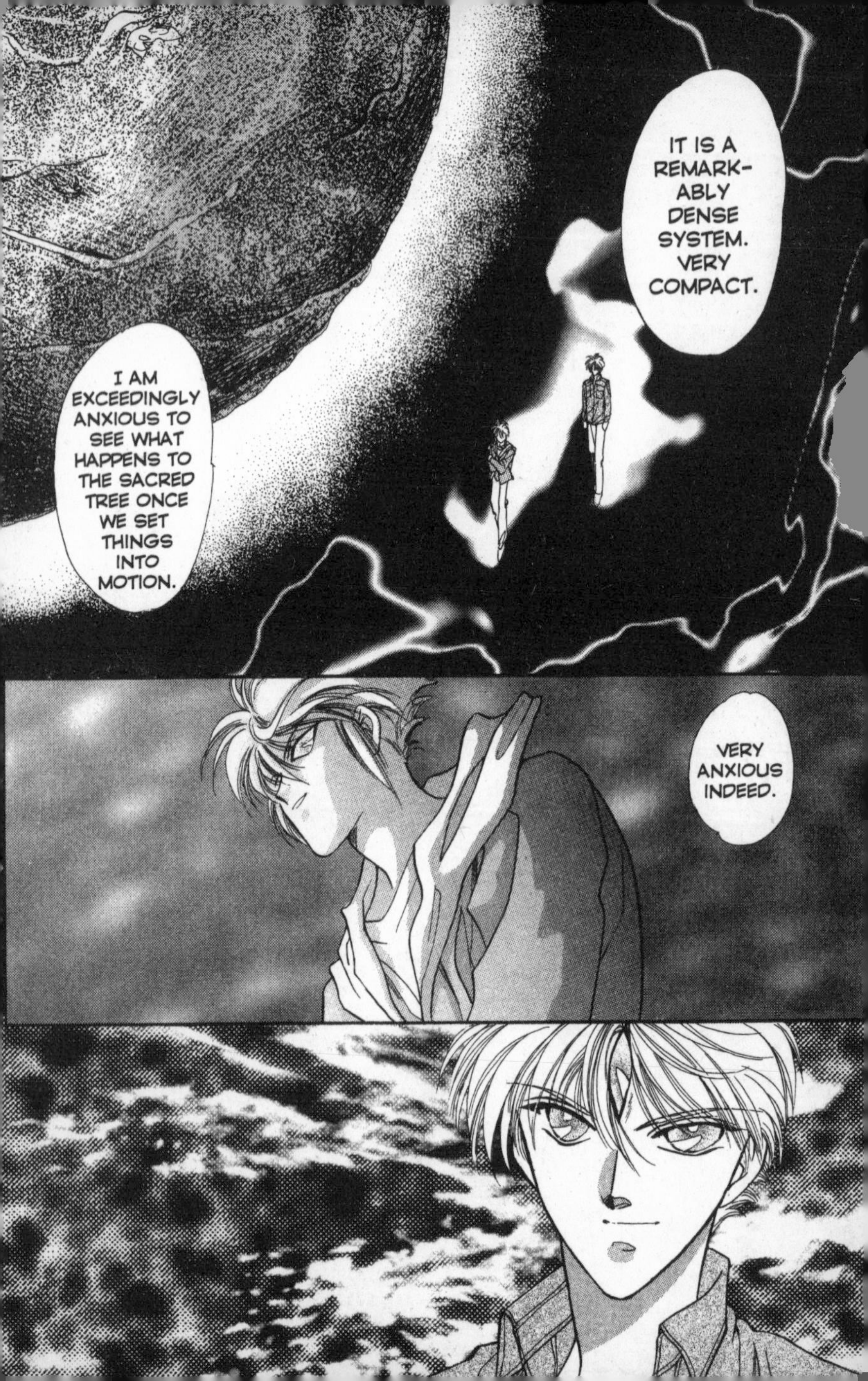
IT IS A REMARKABLY DENSE SYSTEM. VERY COMPACT.
I AM EXCEEDINGLY ANXIOUS TO SEE WHAT HAPPENS TO THE SACRED TREE ONCE WE SET THINGS INTO MOTION.
VERY ANXIOUS INDEED.

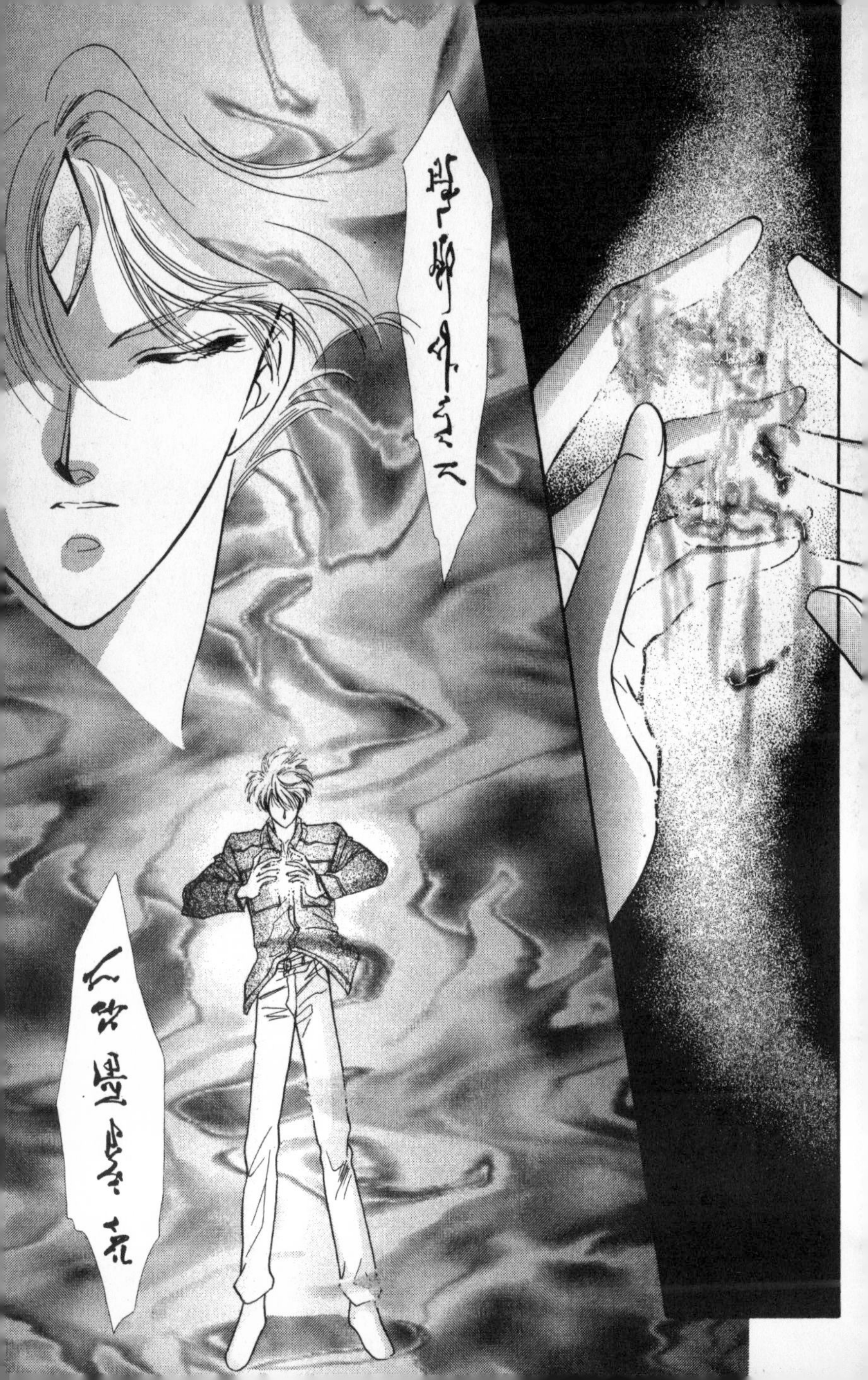

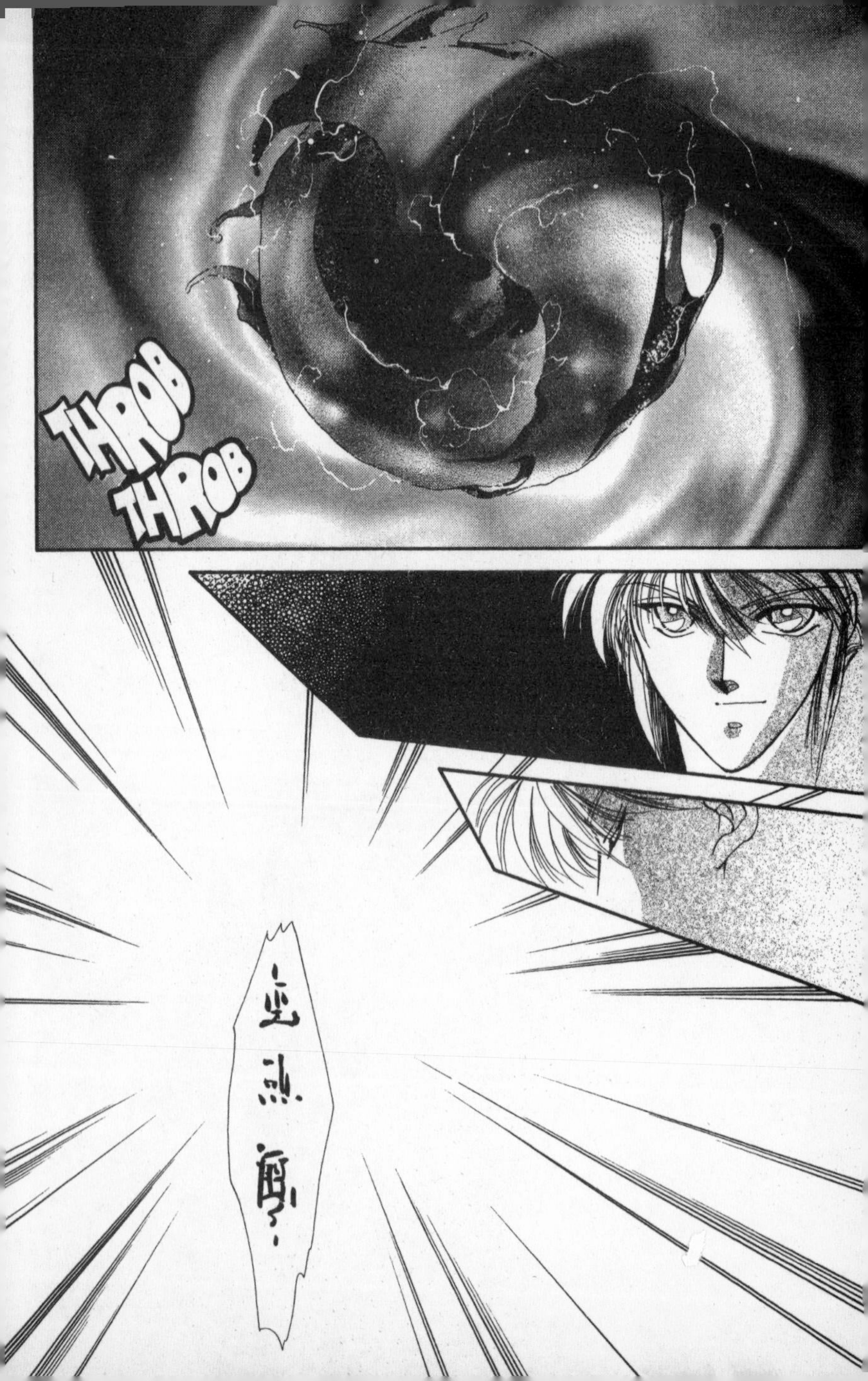
THROB THROB

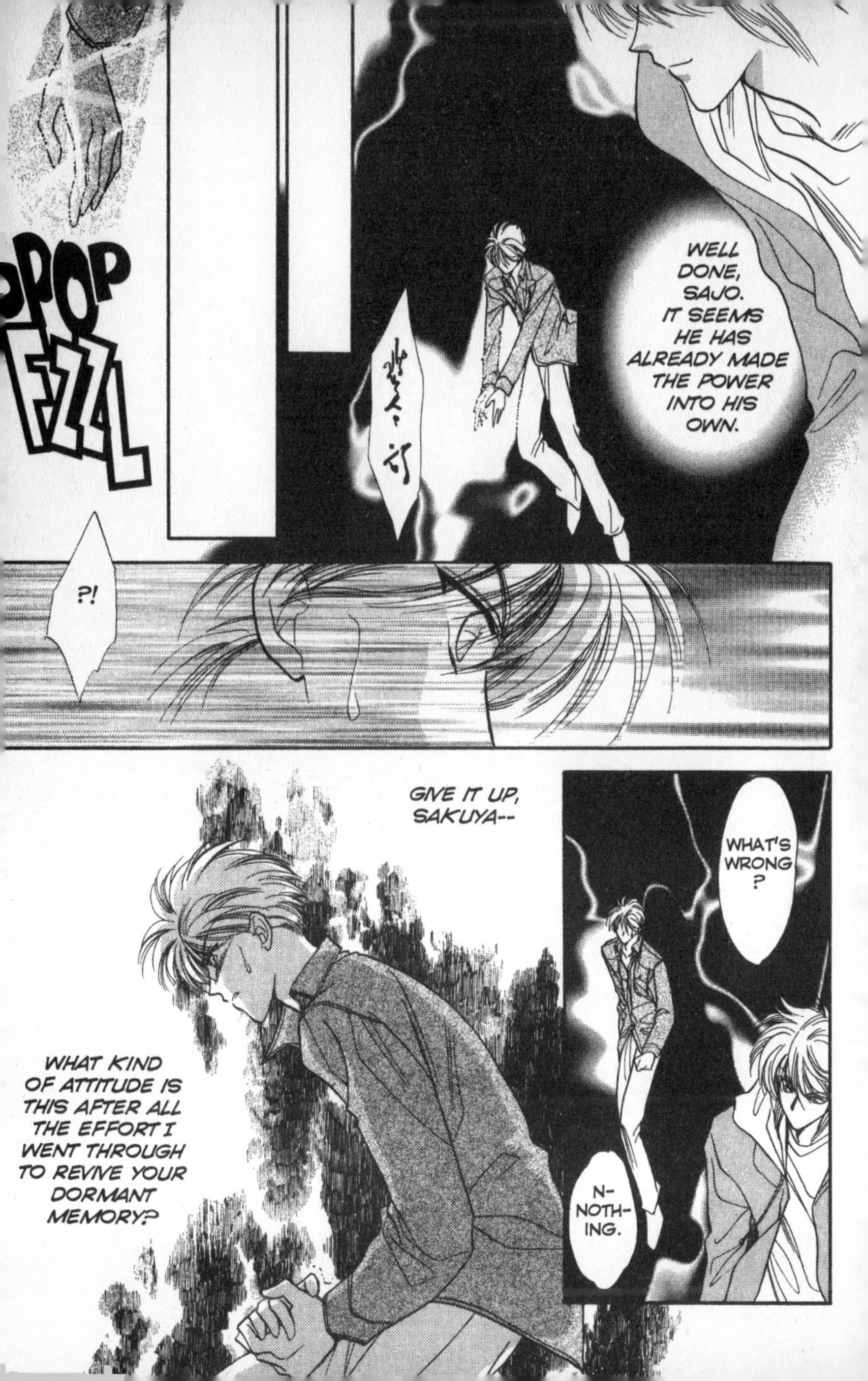
WELL DONE, SAJO. IT SEEMS HE HAS ALREADY MADE THE POWER INTO HIS OWN.
POP FIZZL
?!
WHAT'S WRONG?
N-NOTHING.
GIVE IT UP, SAKUYA--
WHAT KIND OF ATTITUDE IS THIS AFTER ALL THE EFFORT I WENT THROUGH TO REVIVE YOUR DORMANT MEMORY?

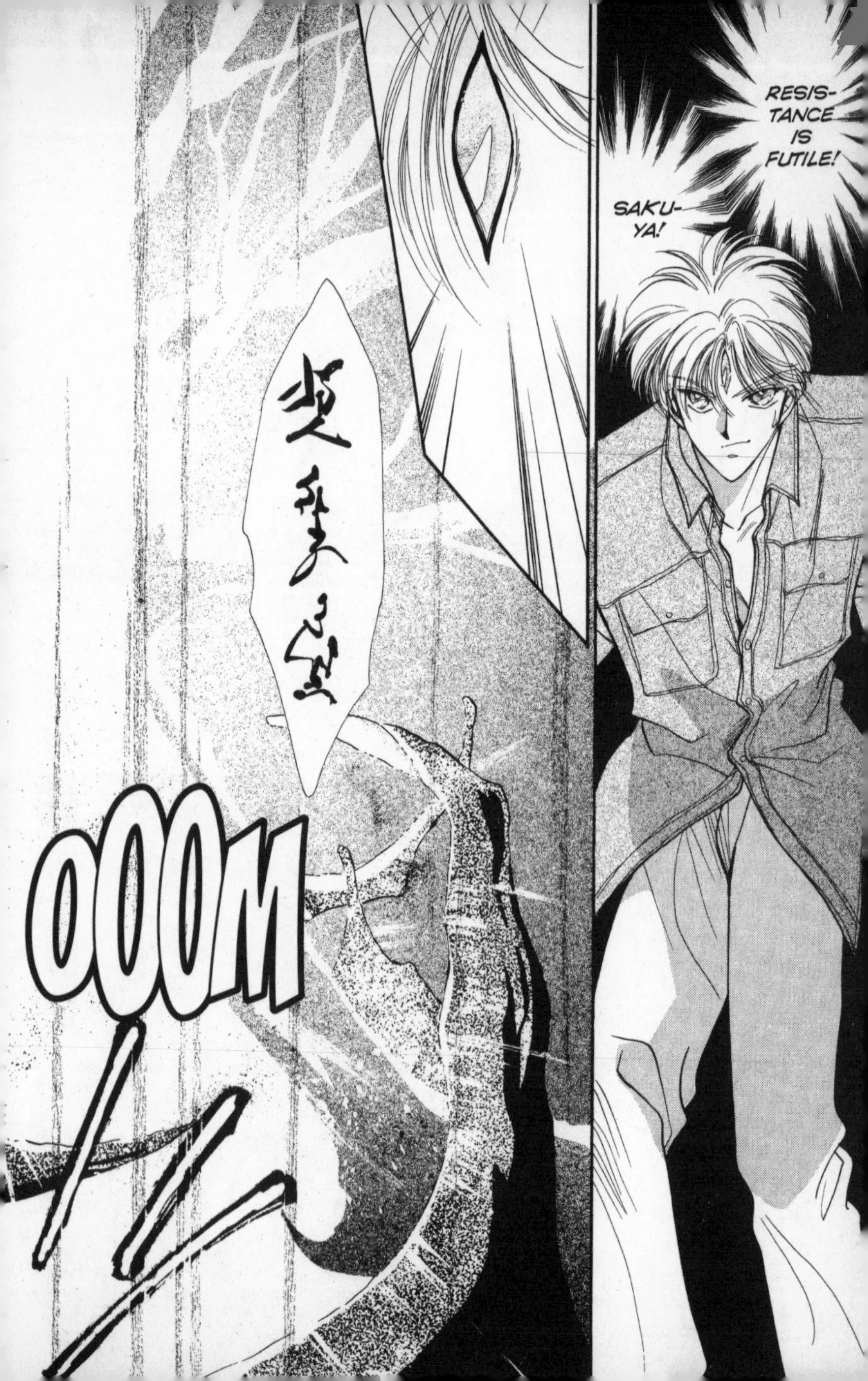
RESIS-TANCE IS FUTILE!
SAKU-YA!
OOOM

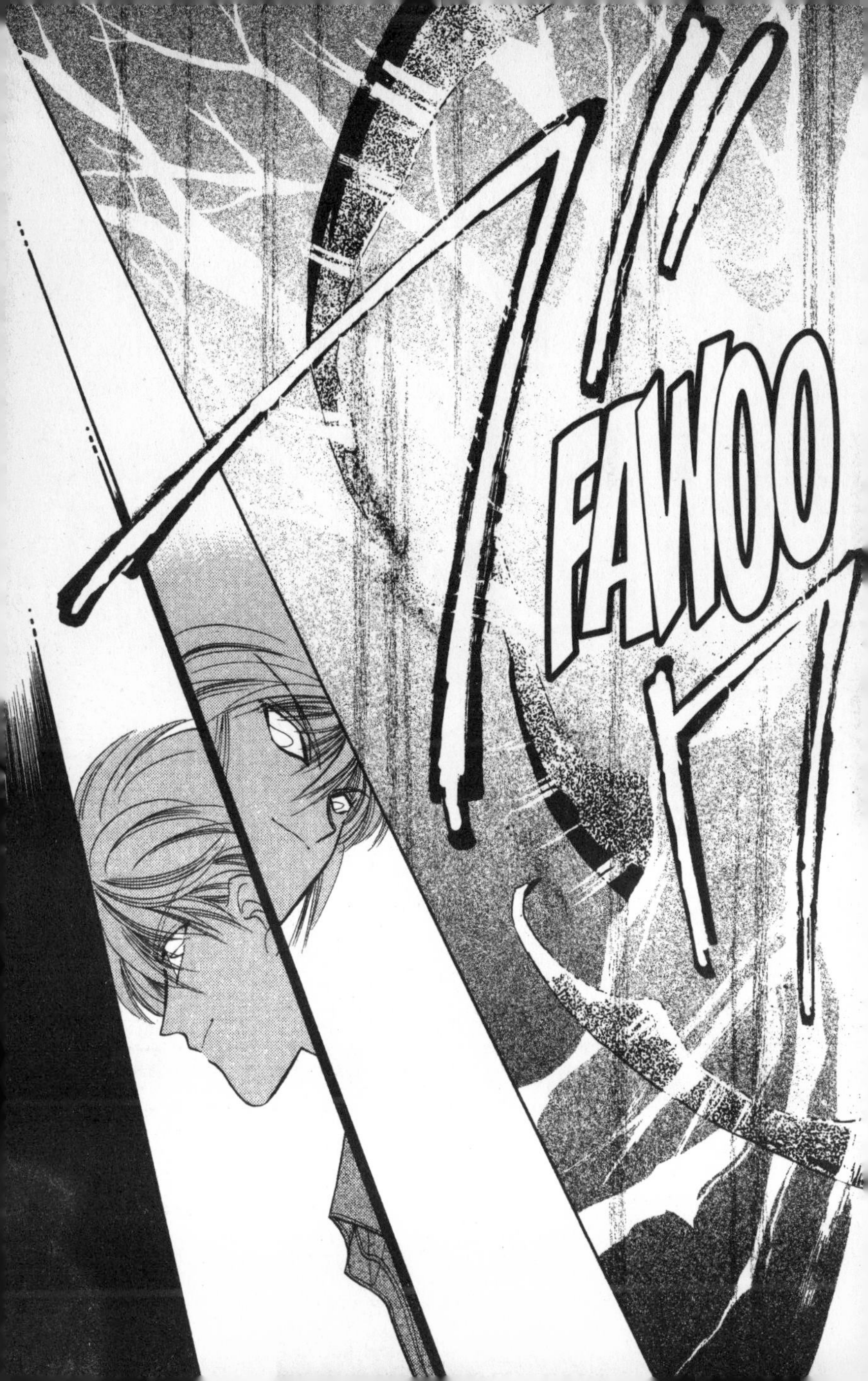
FAWOO

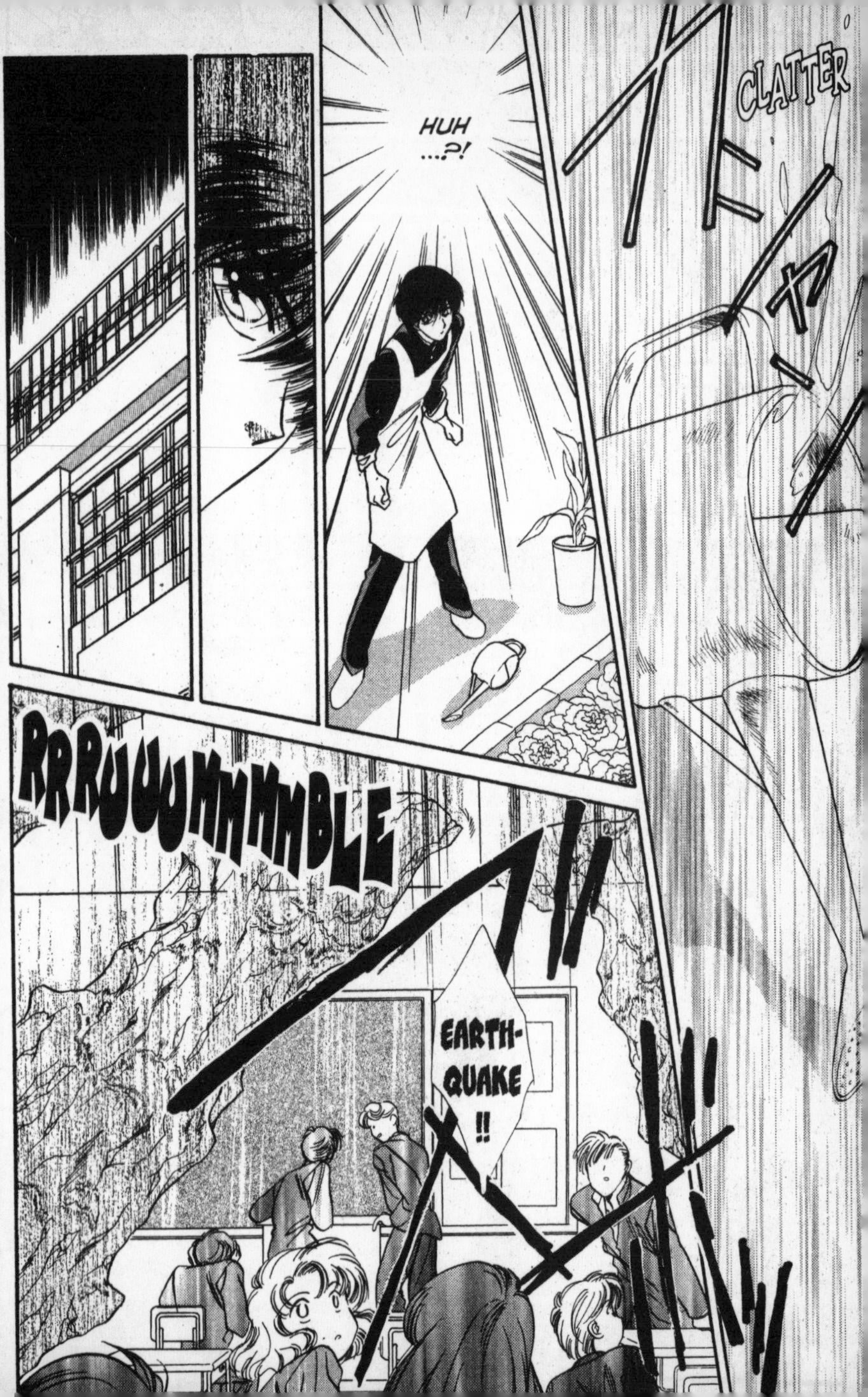
CLATTER
HUH ...?!
RRRUUUMMMMBLE
EARTH-QUAKE !!

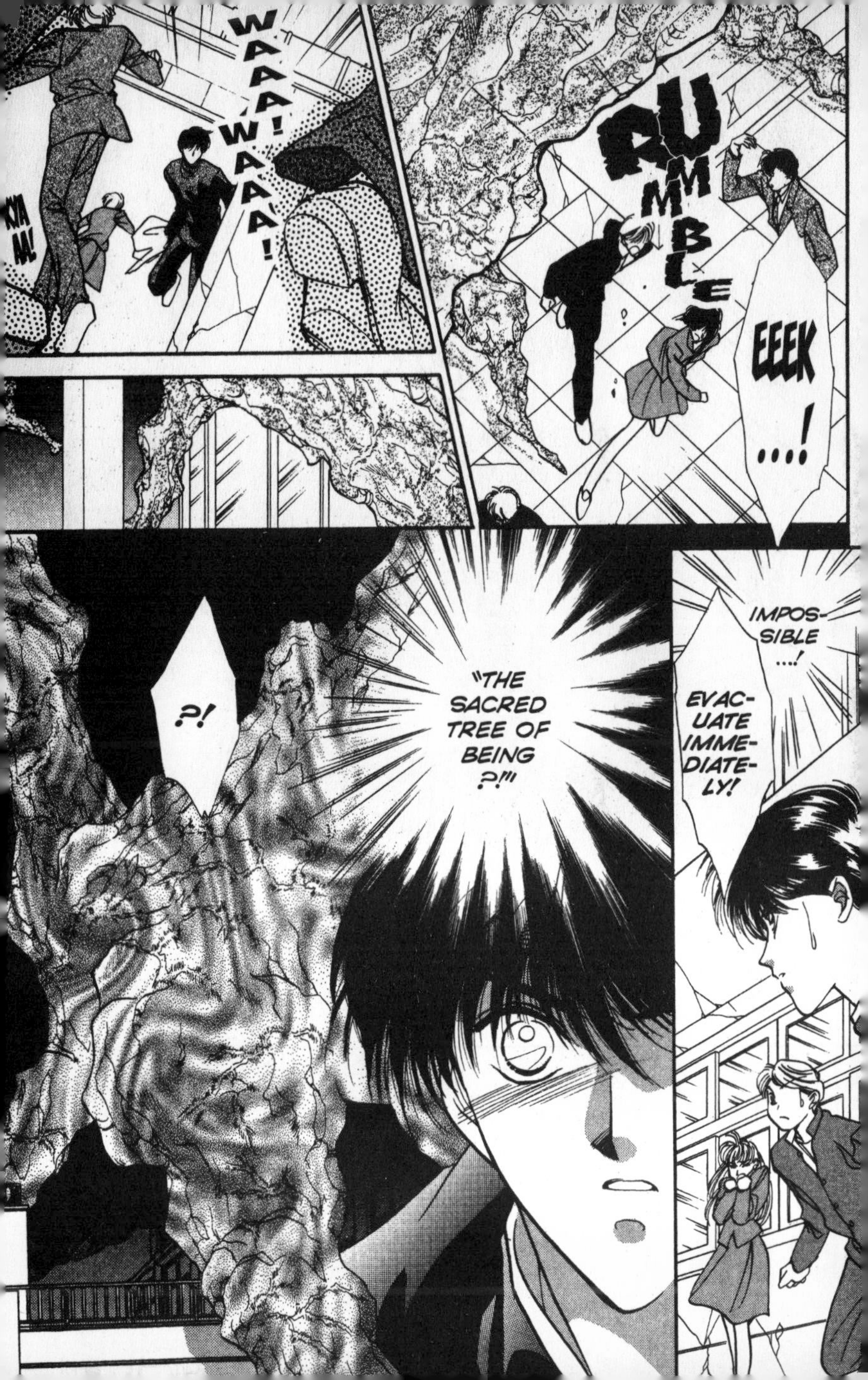
RUMMMBLE
EEEK ...!
WAAAA! WAAAA!
KYAAA!
IMPOSSIBLE ...!
EVACUATE IMMEDIATELY!
"THE SACRED TREE OF BEING ?!"
?!

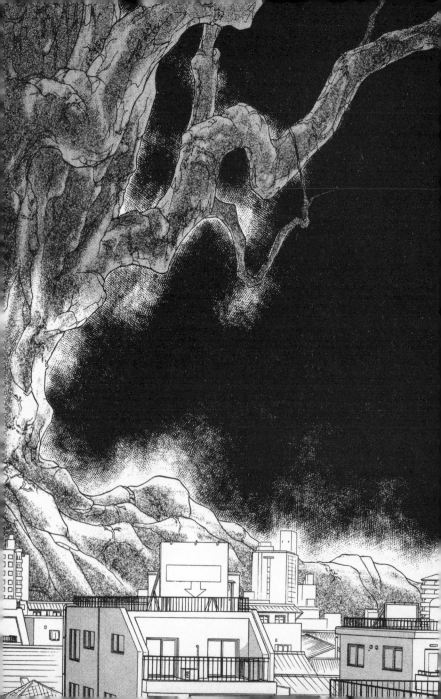

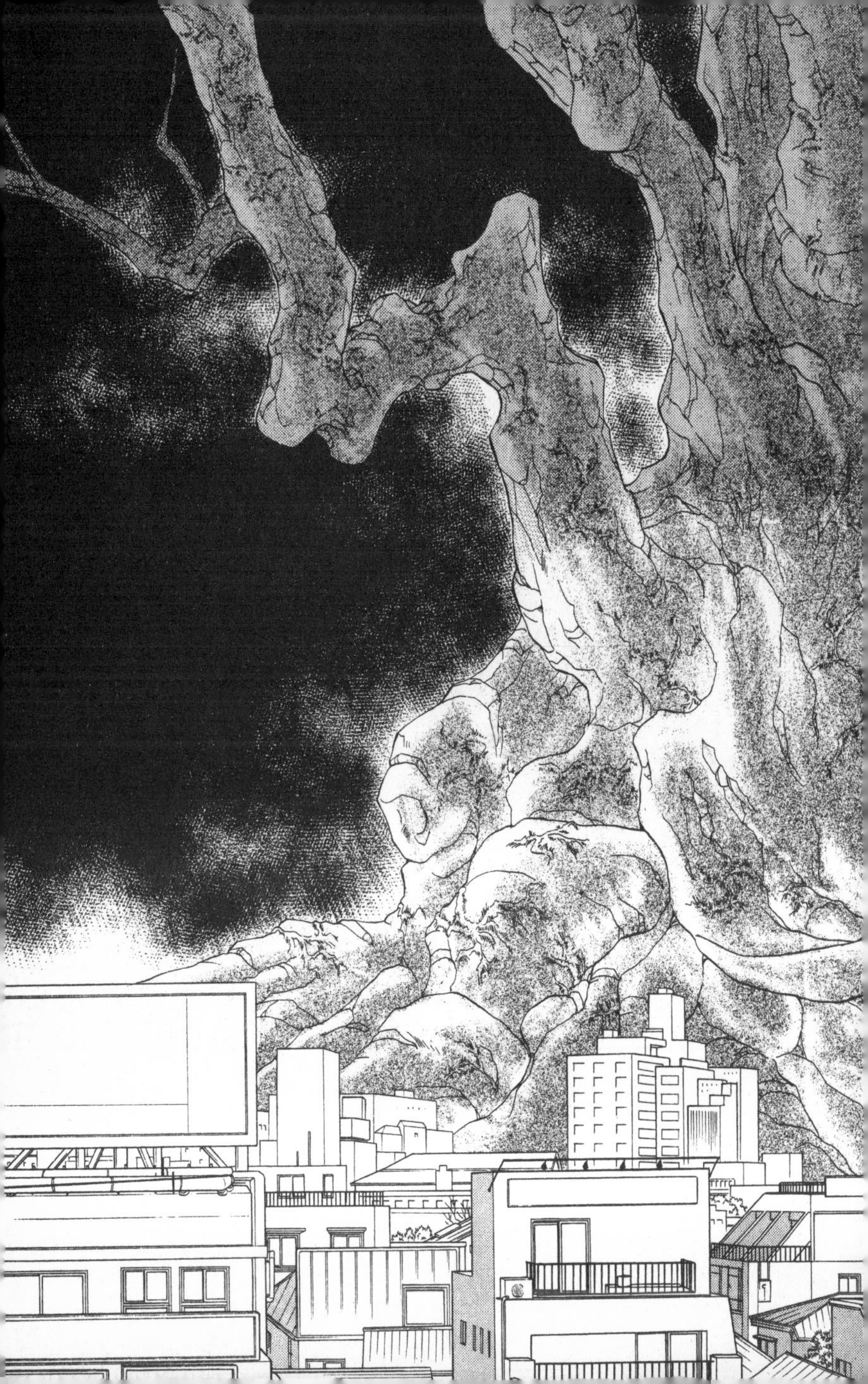

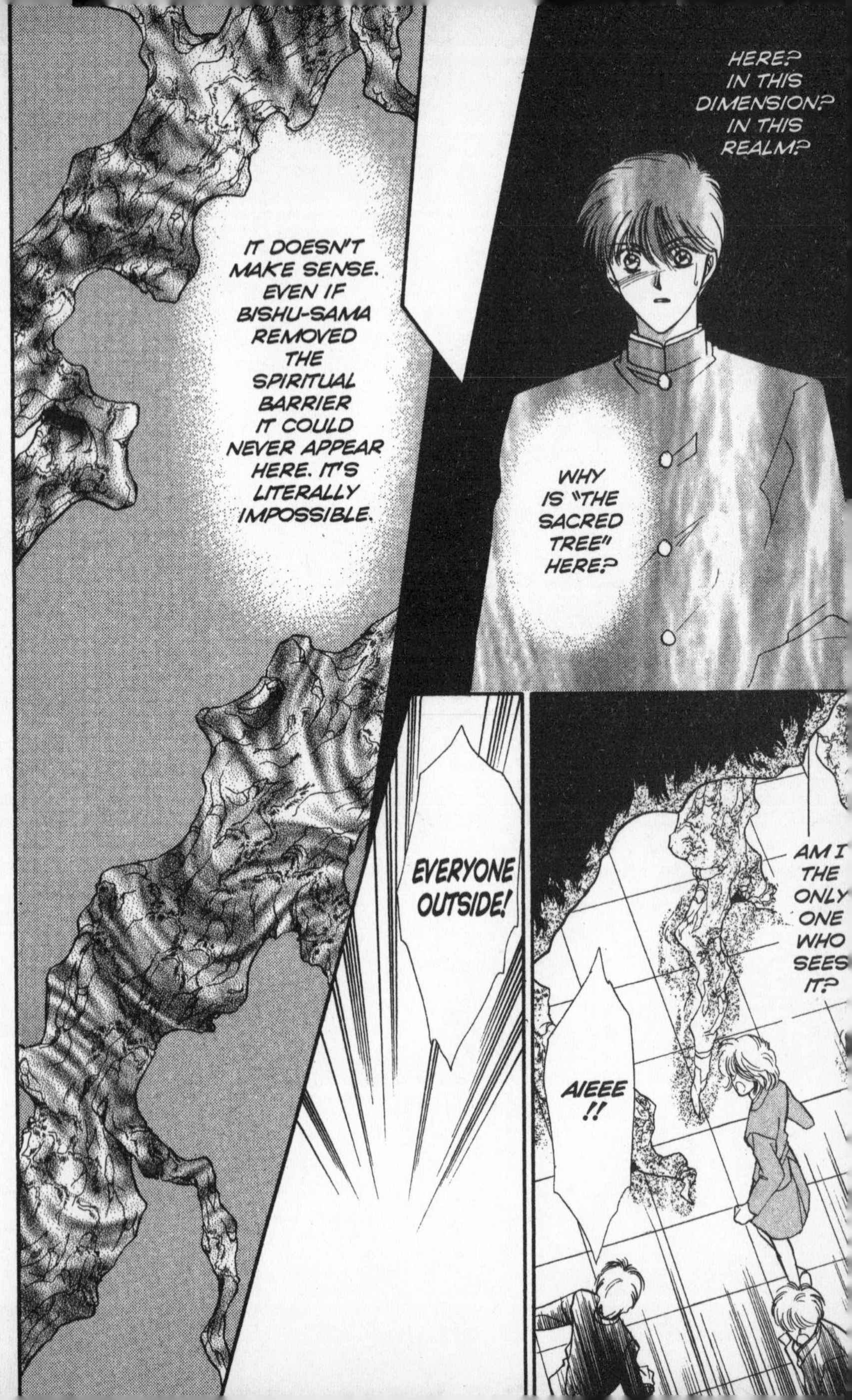
HERE? IN THIS DIMENSION? IN THIS REALM?
WHY IS "THE SACRED TREE" HERE?
AM I THE ONLY ONE WHO SEES IT?
AIEEE !!
EVERYONE OUTSIDE!
IT DOESN'T MAKE SENSE. EVEN IF BISHU-SAMA REMOVED THE SPIRITUAL BARRIER IT COULD NEVER APPEAR HERE. IT'S LITERALLY IMPOSSIBLE.

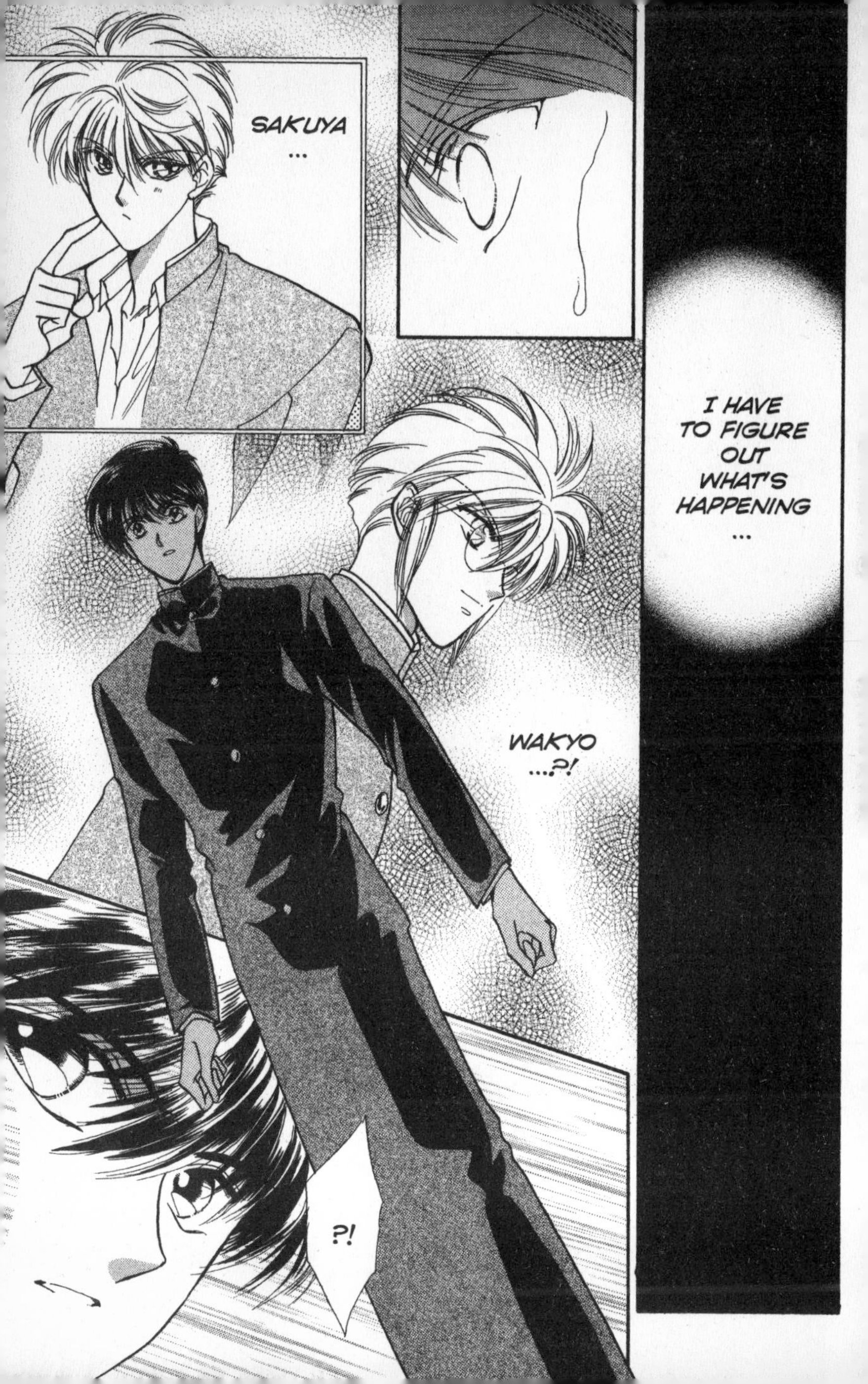
I HAVE TO FIGURE OUT WHAT'S HAPPENING ...
SAKUYA ...
WAKYO ...?!
?!

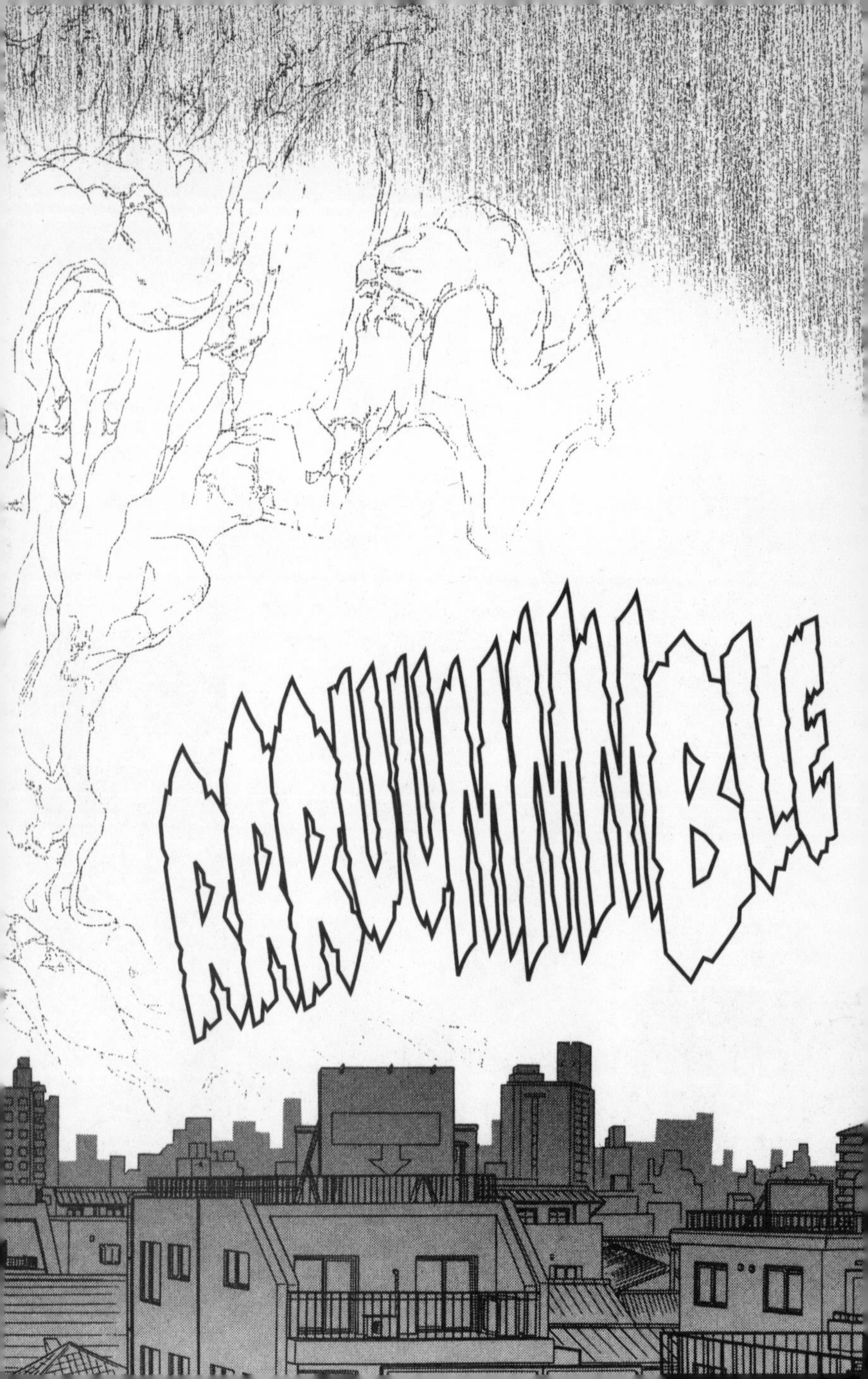
RRRUUMMMBLE

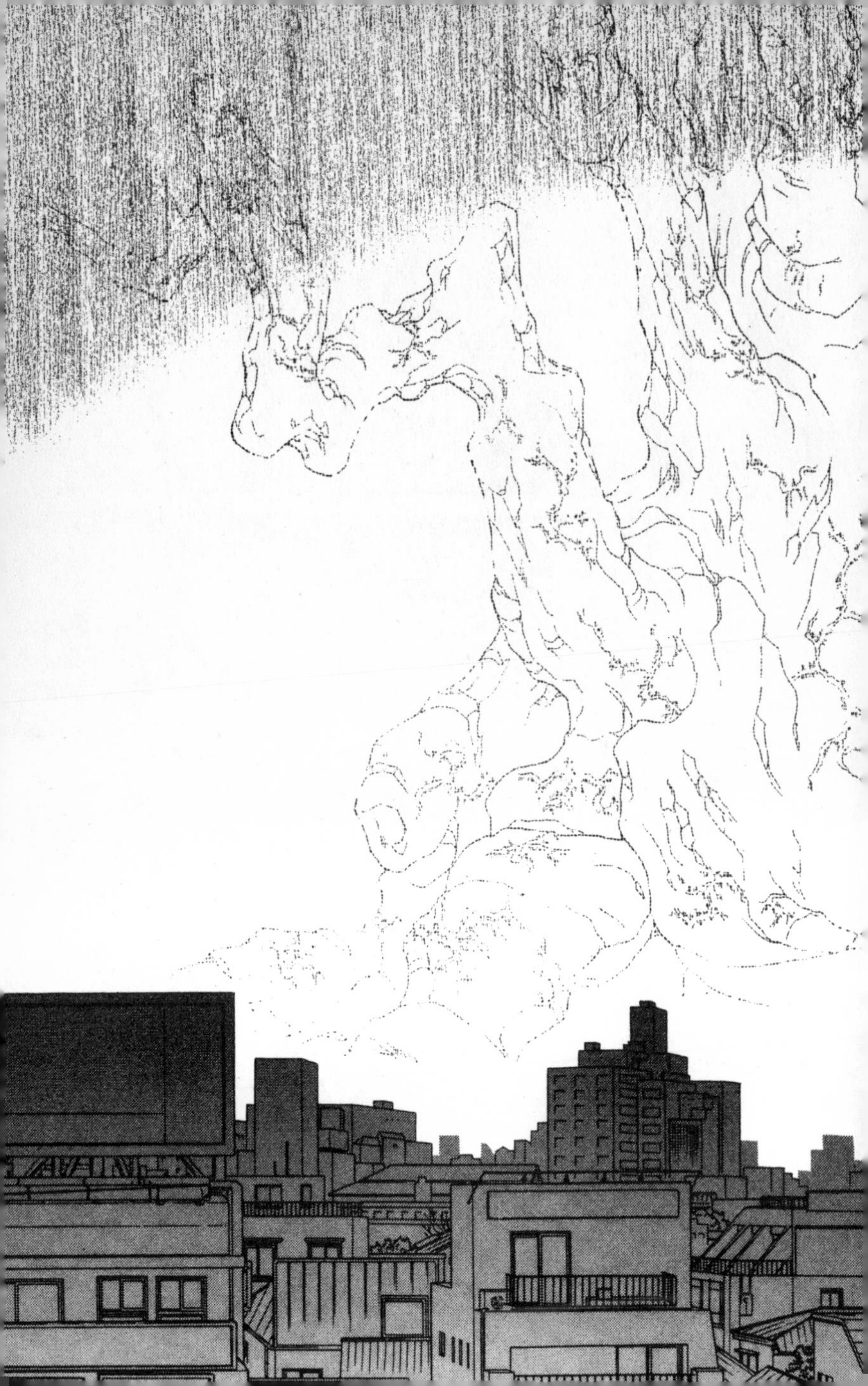

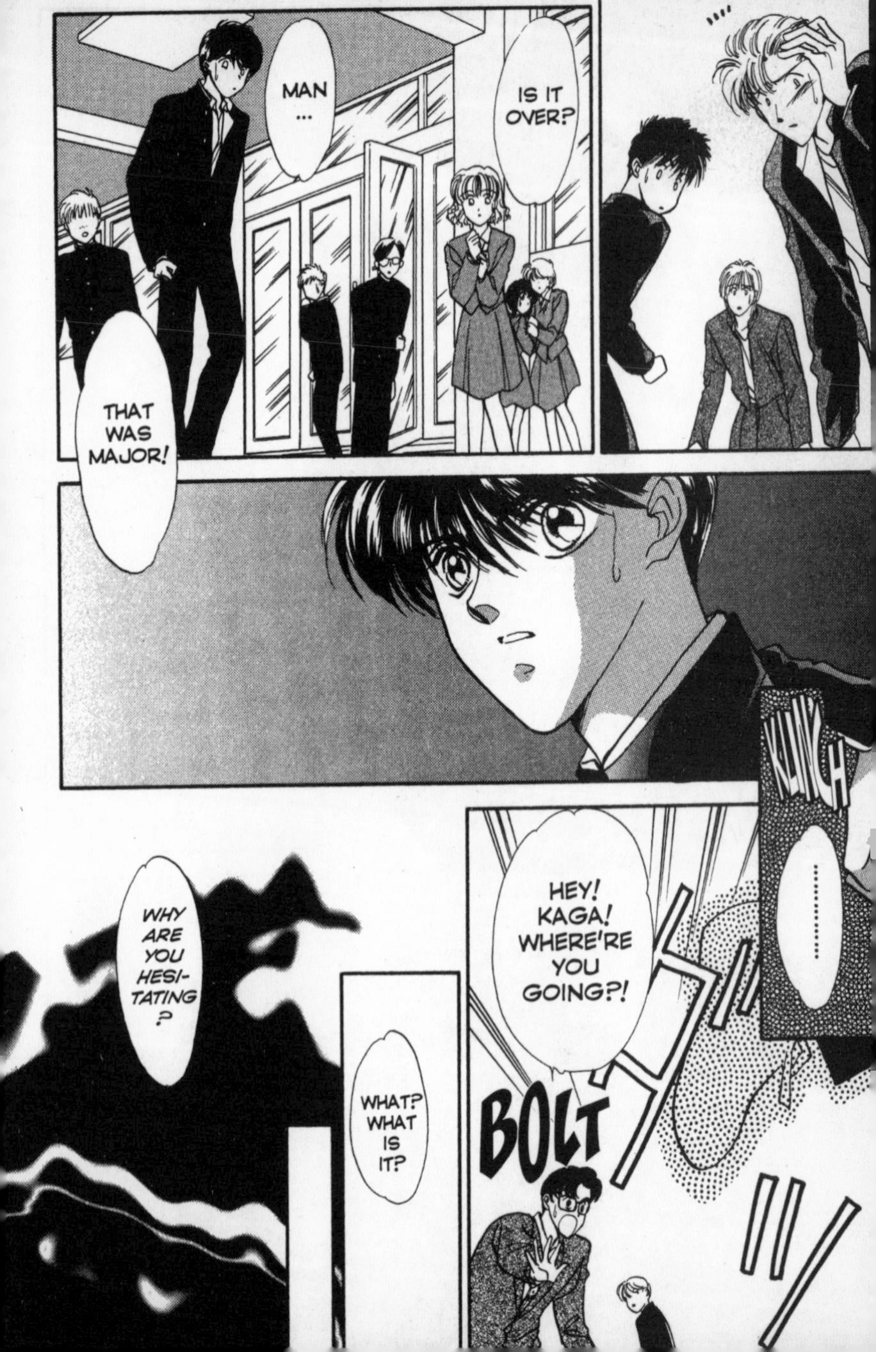
IS IT OVER?
MAN ...
THAT WAS MAJOR!
....
HEY! KAGA! WHERE'RE YOU GOING?!
BOLT
WHAT? WHAT IS IT?
WHY ARE YOU HESI-TATING?

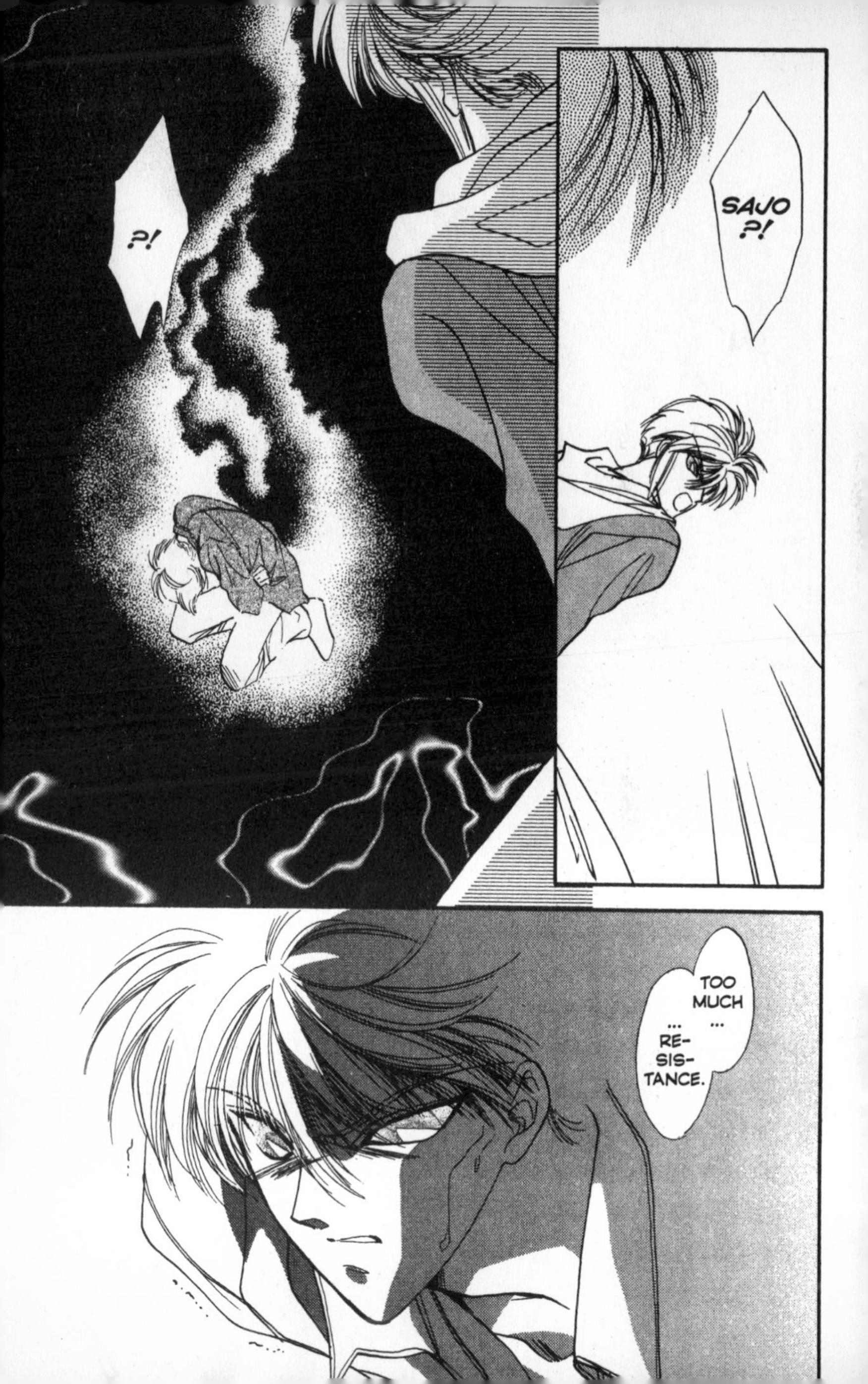
SAJO ?!
?!
TOO MUCH ... ... RE-SIS-TANCE.

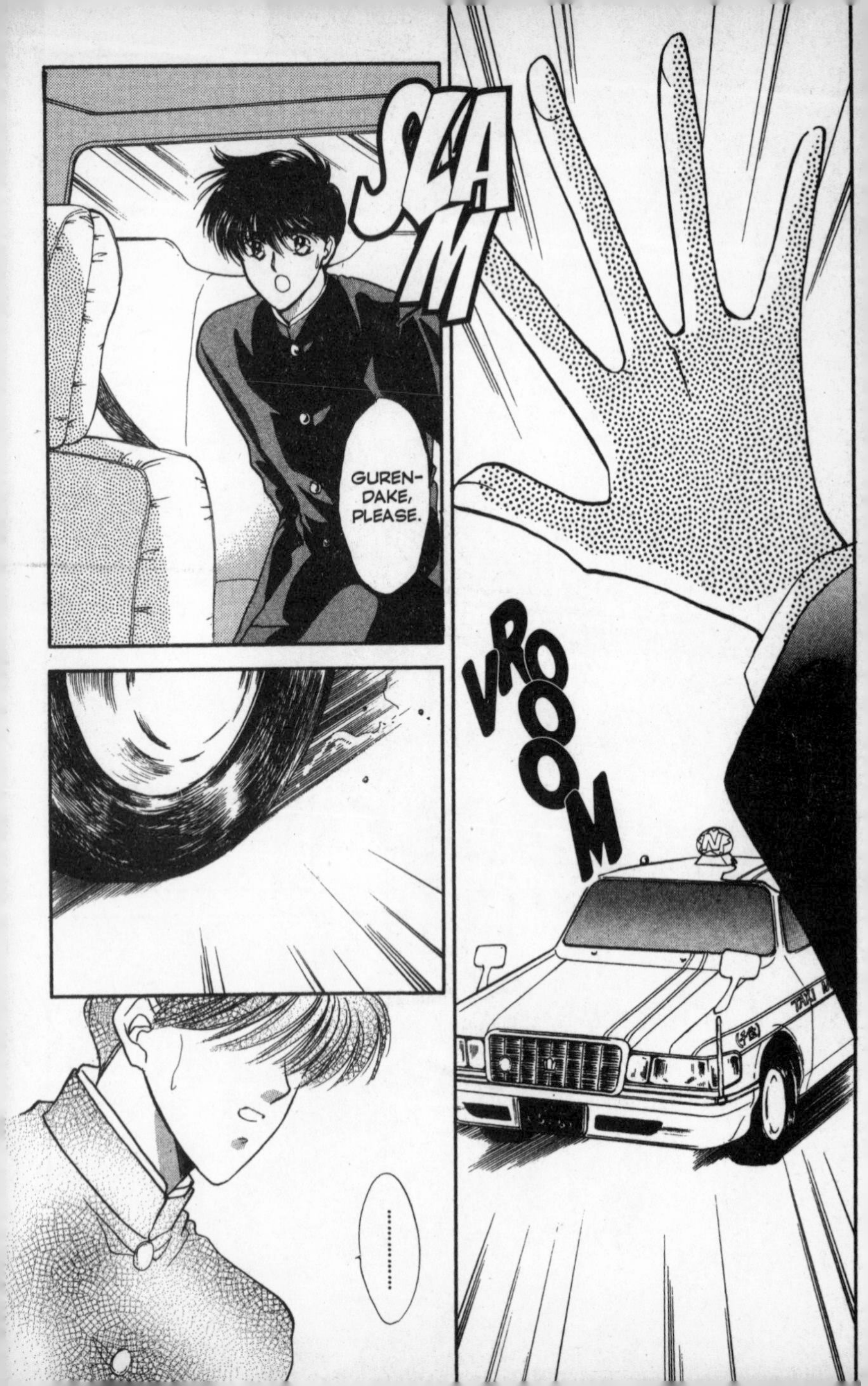
SLAM
VROOOM
GUREN-DAKE, PLEASE.
....

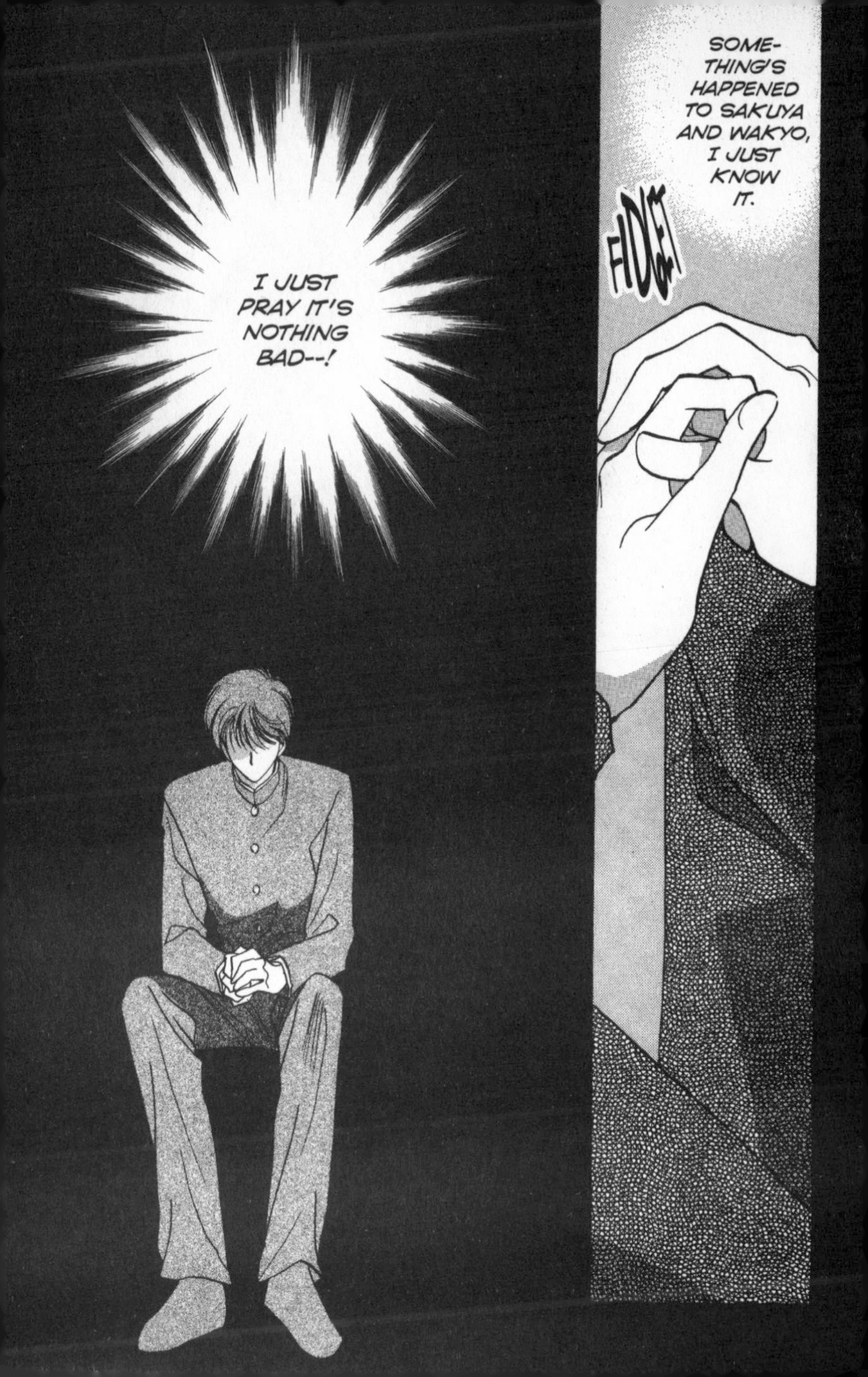
SOME-THING'S HAPPENED TO SAKUYA AND WAKYO, I JUST KNOW IT.
FIDGET
I JUST PRAY IT'S NOTHING BAD--!

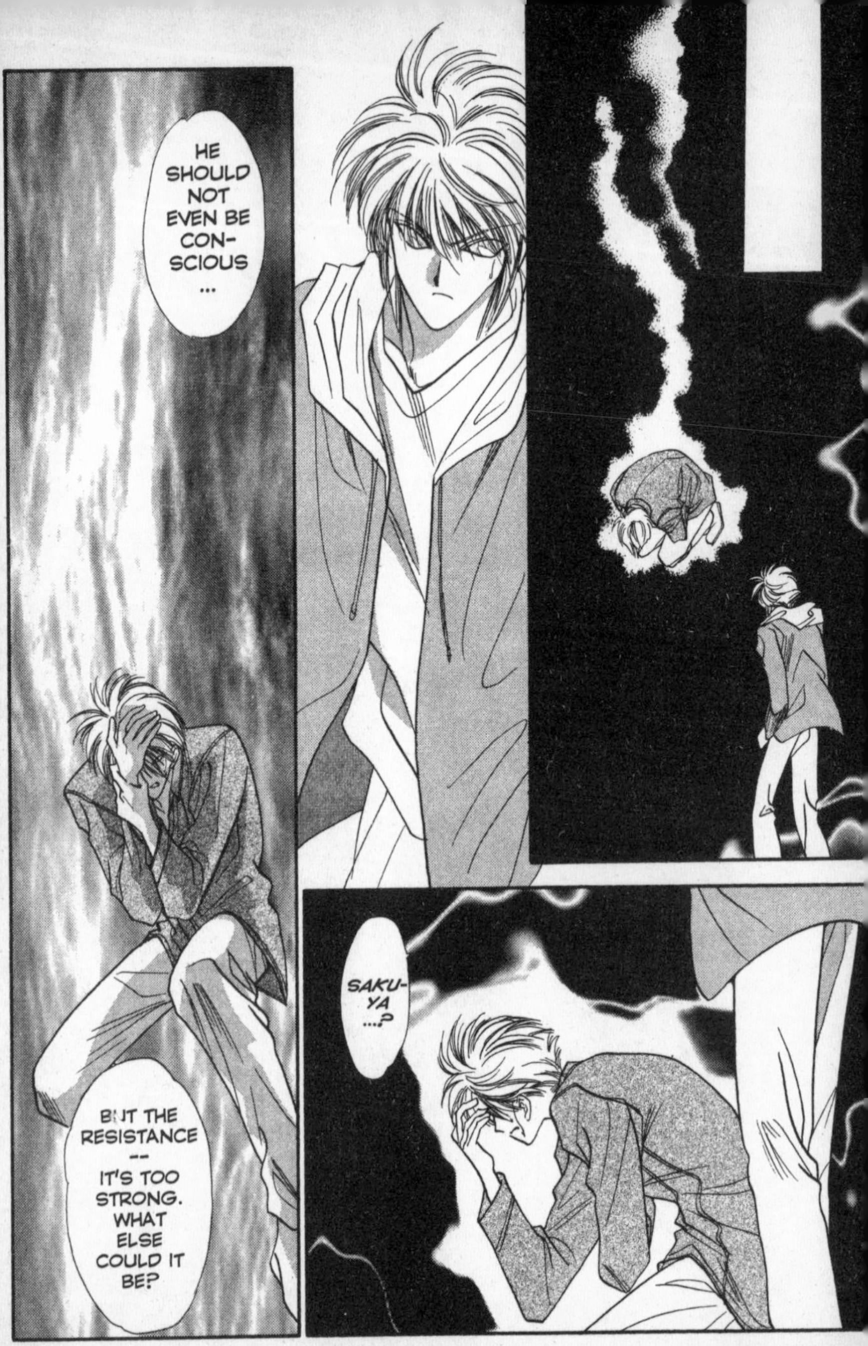
SAKU-YA ...?
HE SHOULD NOT EVEN BE CON-SCIOUS ...
BUT THE RESISTANCE -- IT'S TOO STRONG. WHAT ELSE COULD IT BE?

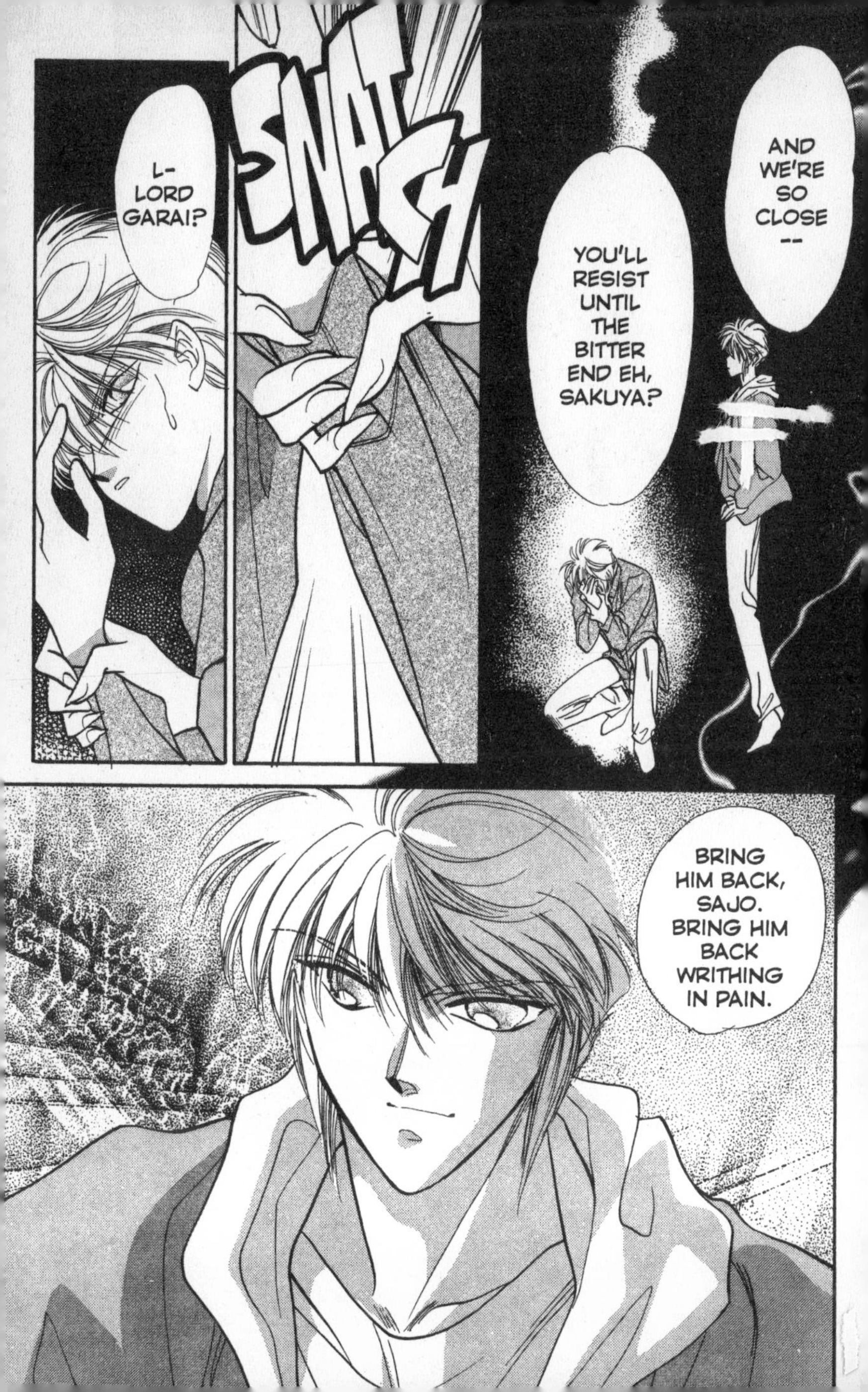
AND WE'RE SO CLOSE --
YOU'LL RESIST UNTIL THE BITTER END EH, SAKUYA?
SNATCH
L-LORD GARAI?
BRING HIM BACK, SAJO. BRING HIM BACK WRITHING IN PAIN.

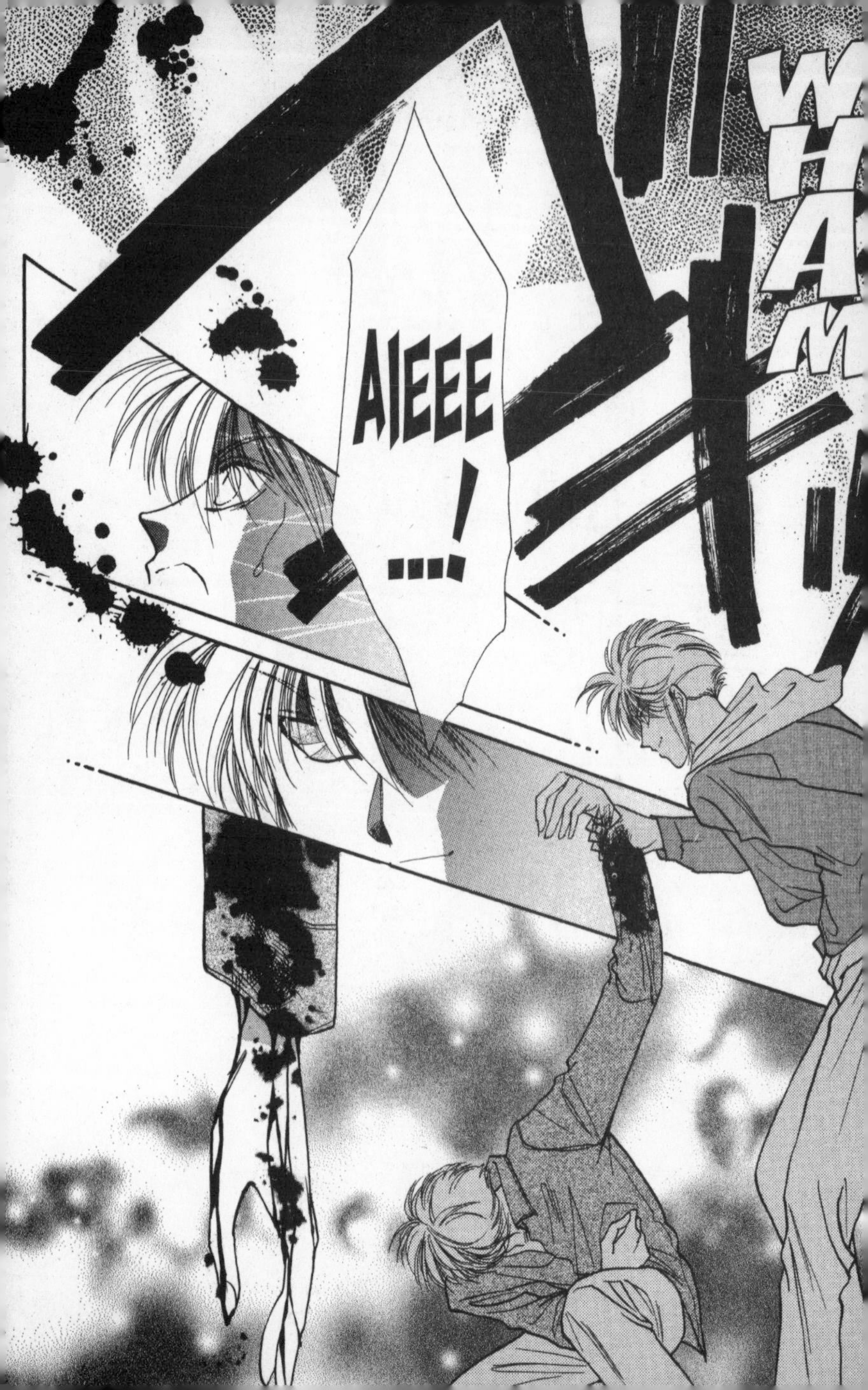
WHAM
AIEEE ...!

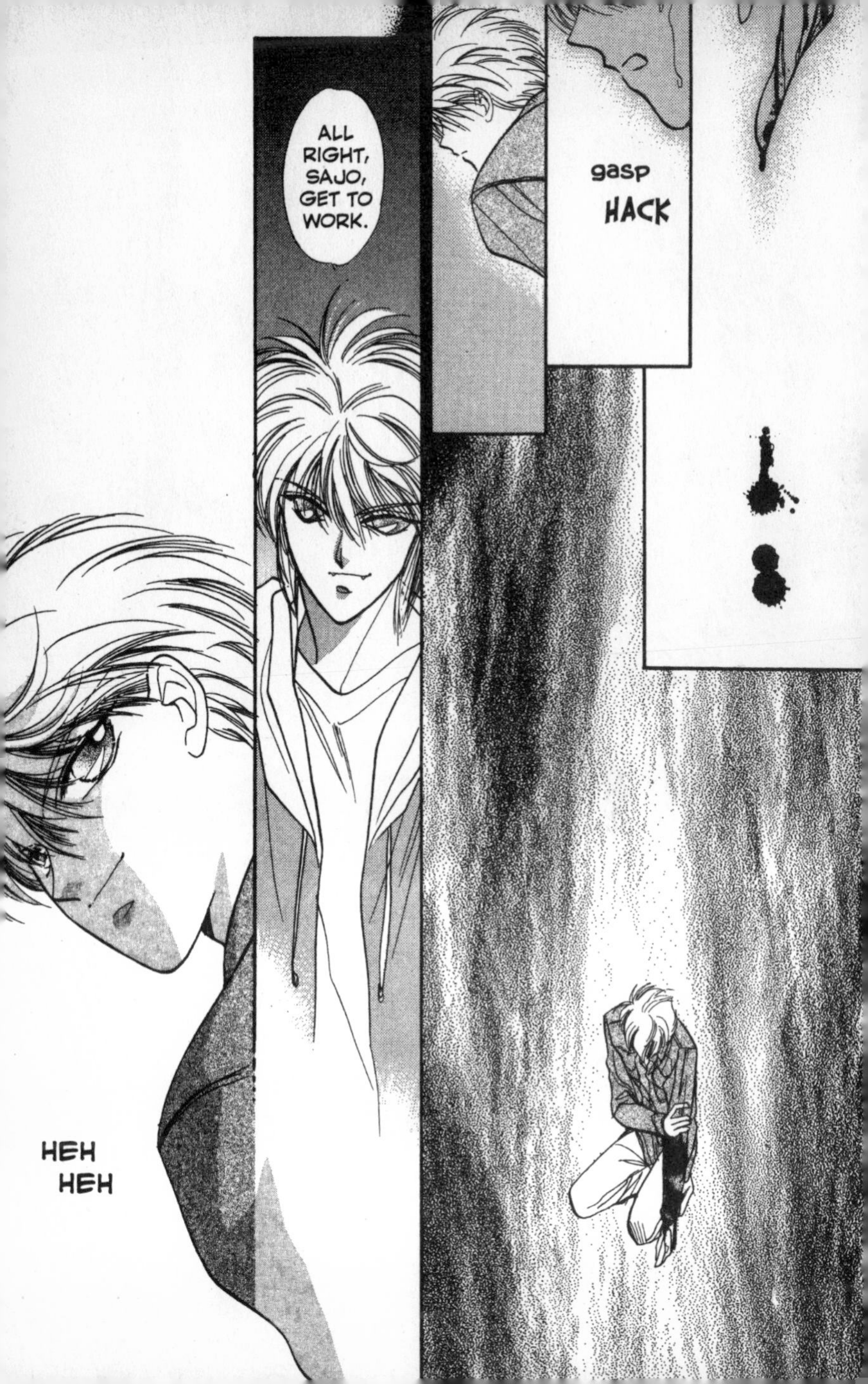
gasp
HACK
ALL RIGHT, SAJO, GET TO WORK.
HEH HEH

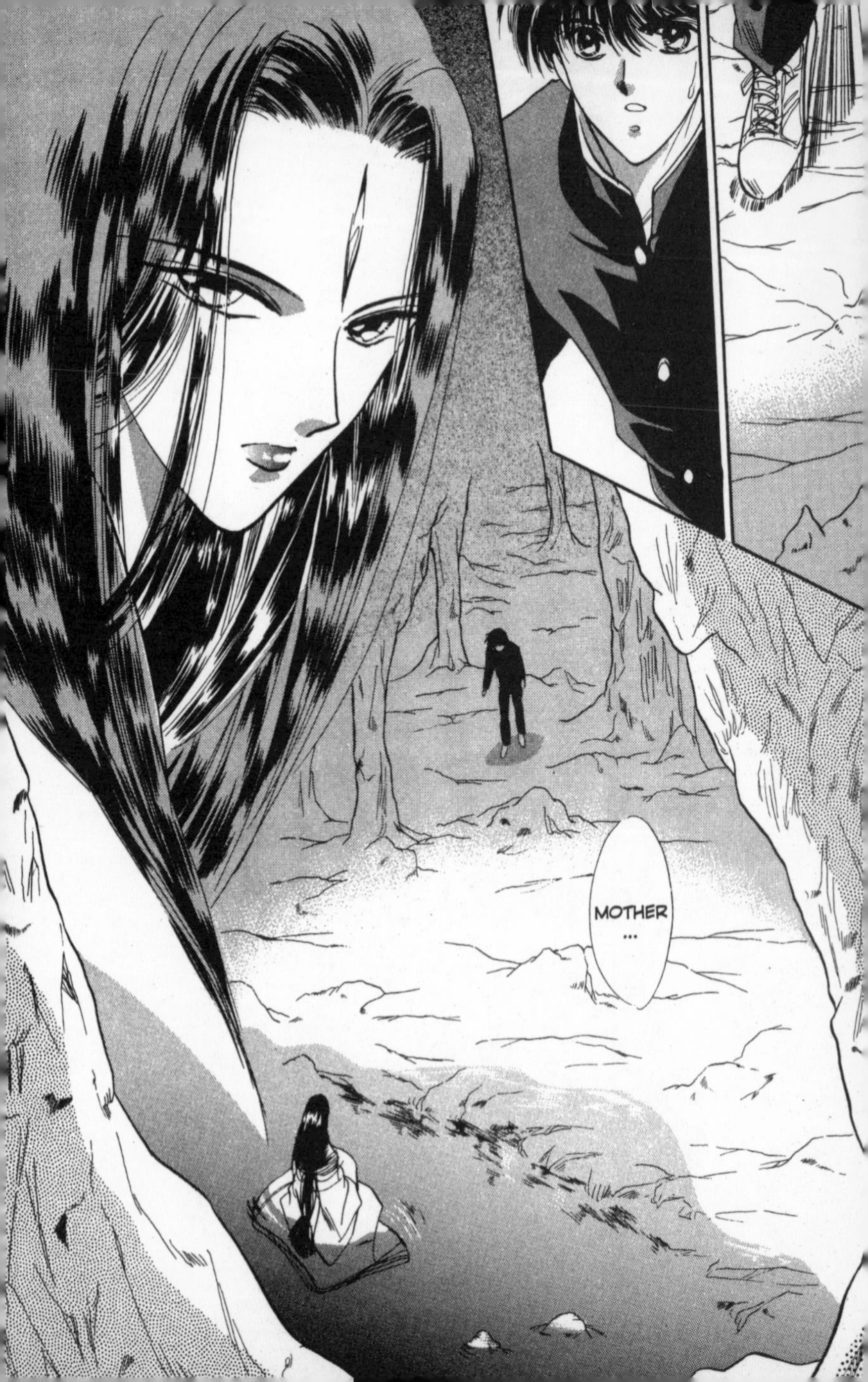
MOTHER
...

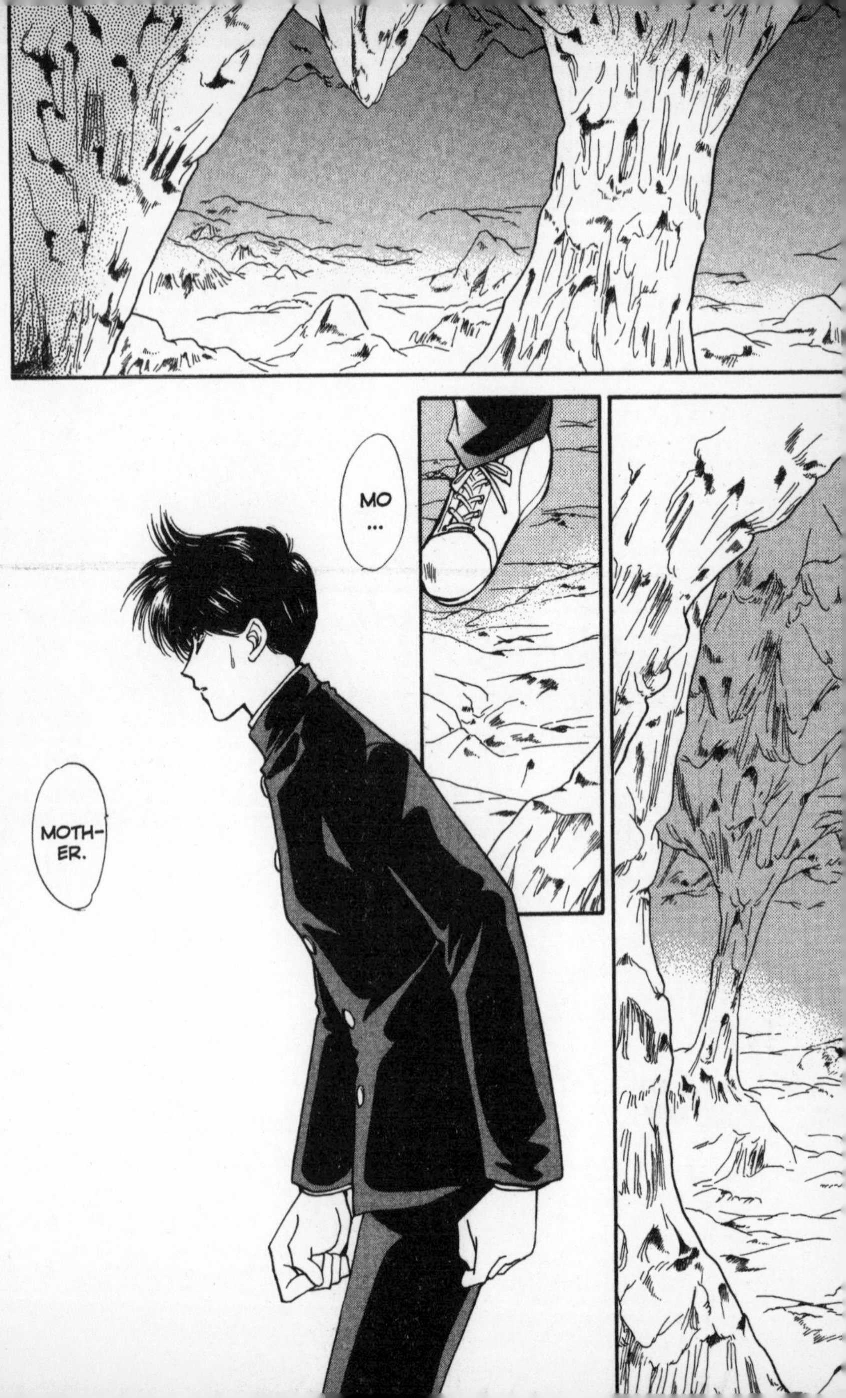
MO ...
MOTH-ER.

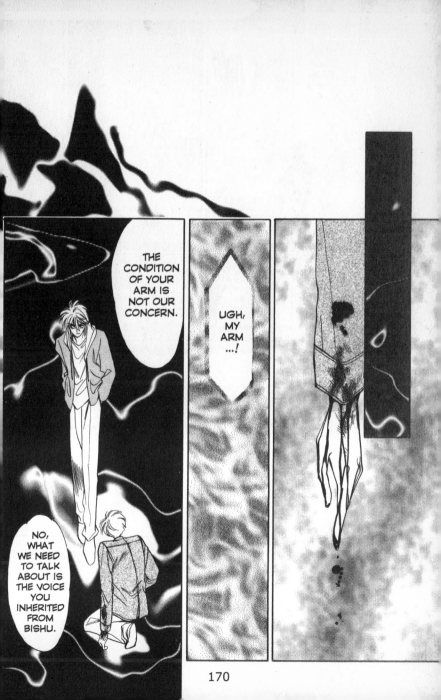

THE CONDITION OF YOUR ARM IS NOT OUR CONCERN.

NO, WHAT WE NEED TO TALK ABOUT IS THE VOICE YOU INHERITED FROM BISHU.

UGH, MY ARM ...!

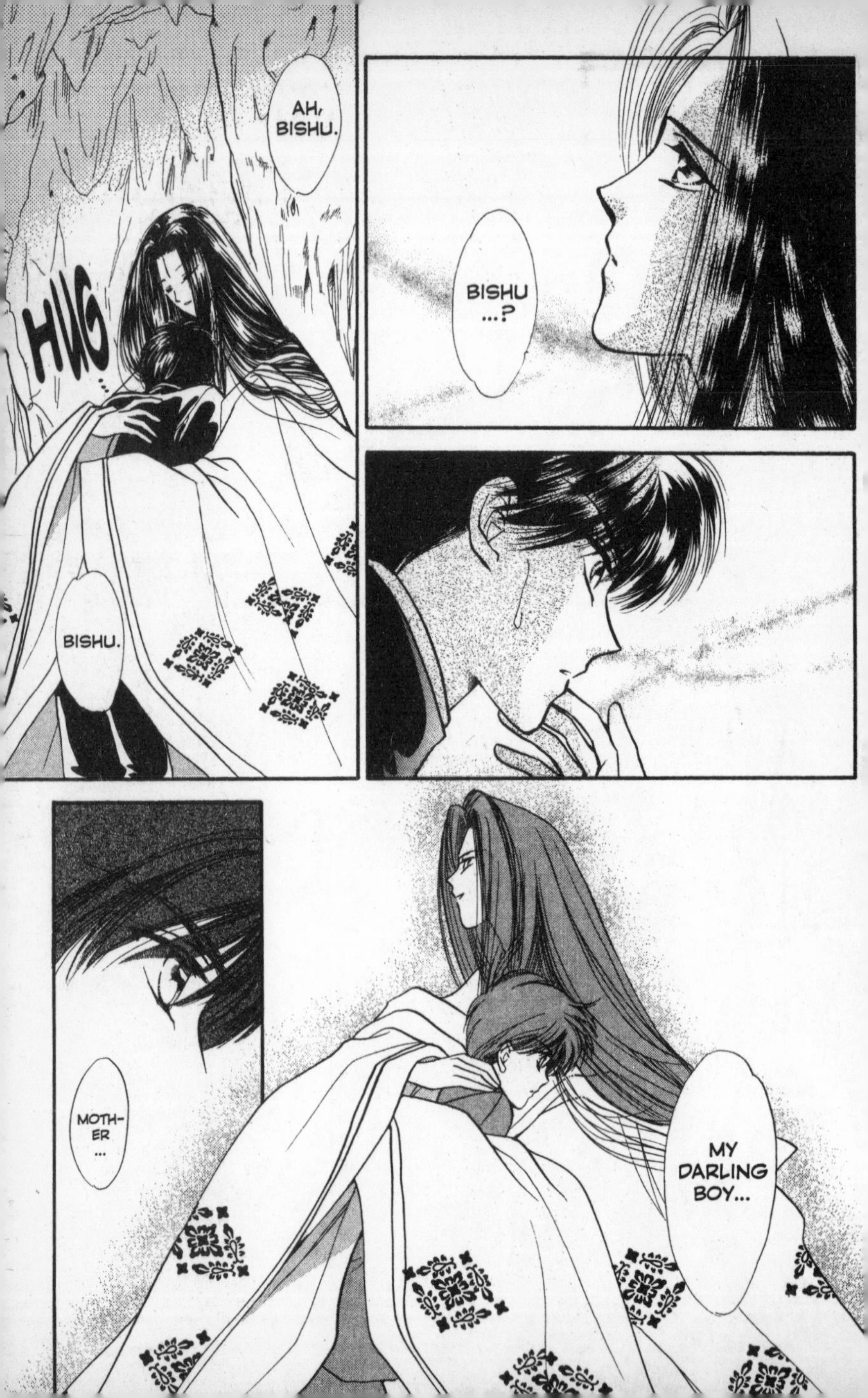
BISHU ...?
AH, BISHU.
HUG...
BISHU.
MY DARLING BOY...
MOTHER-ER ...

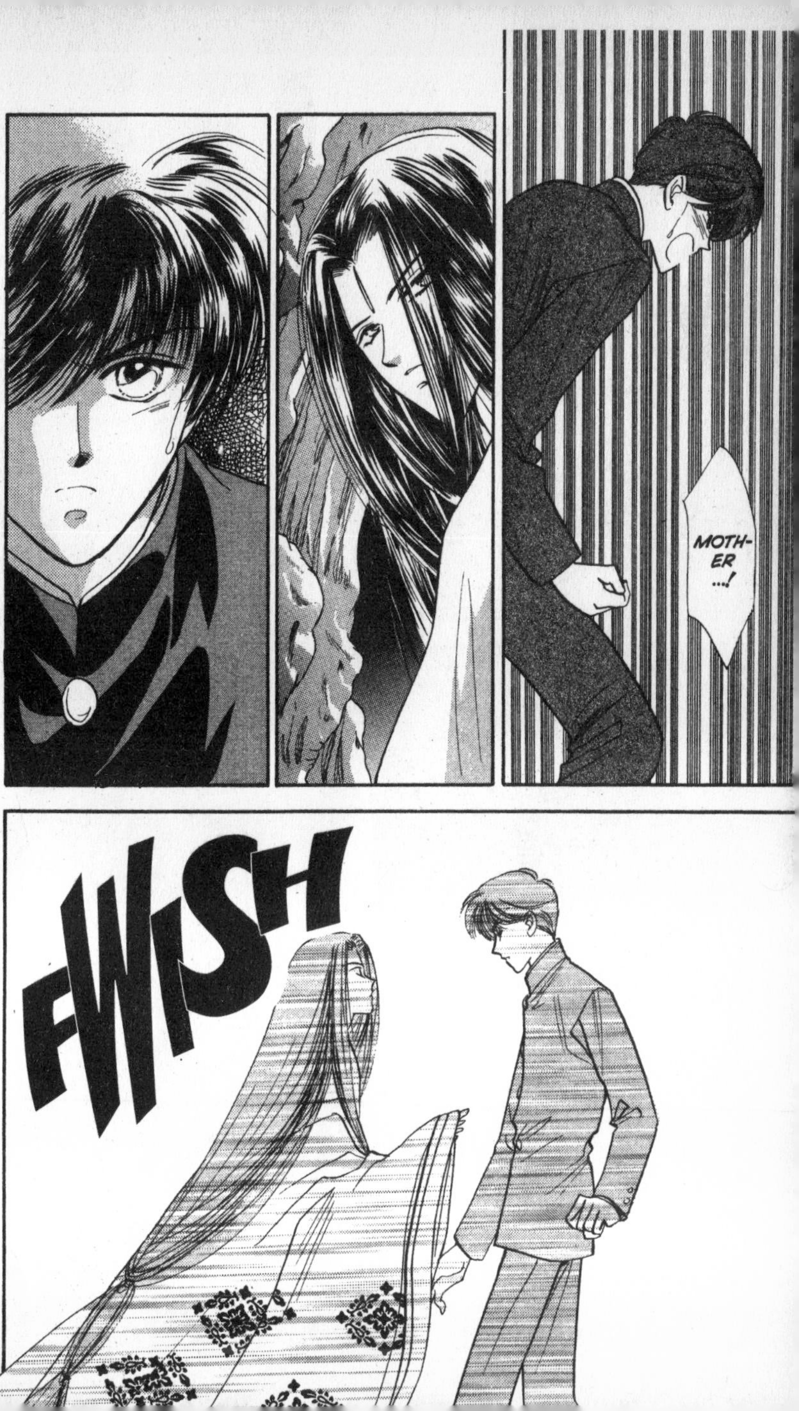
MOTH-
ER
...!
FWISH

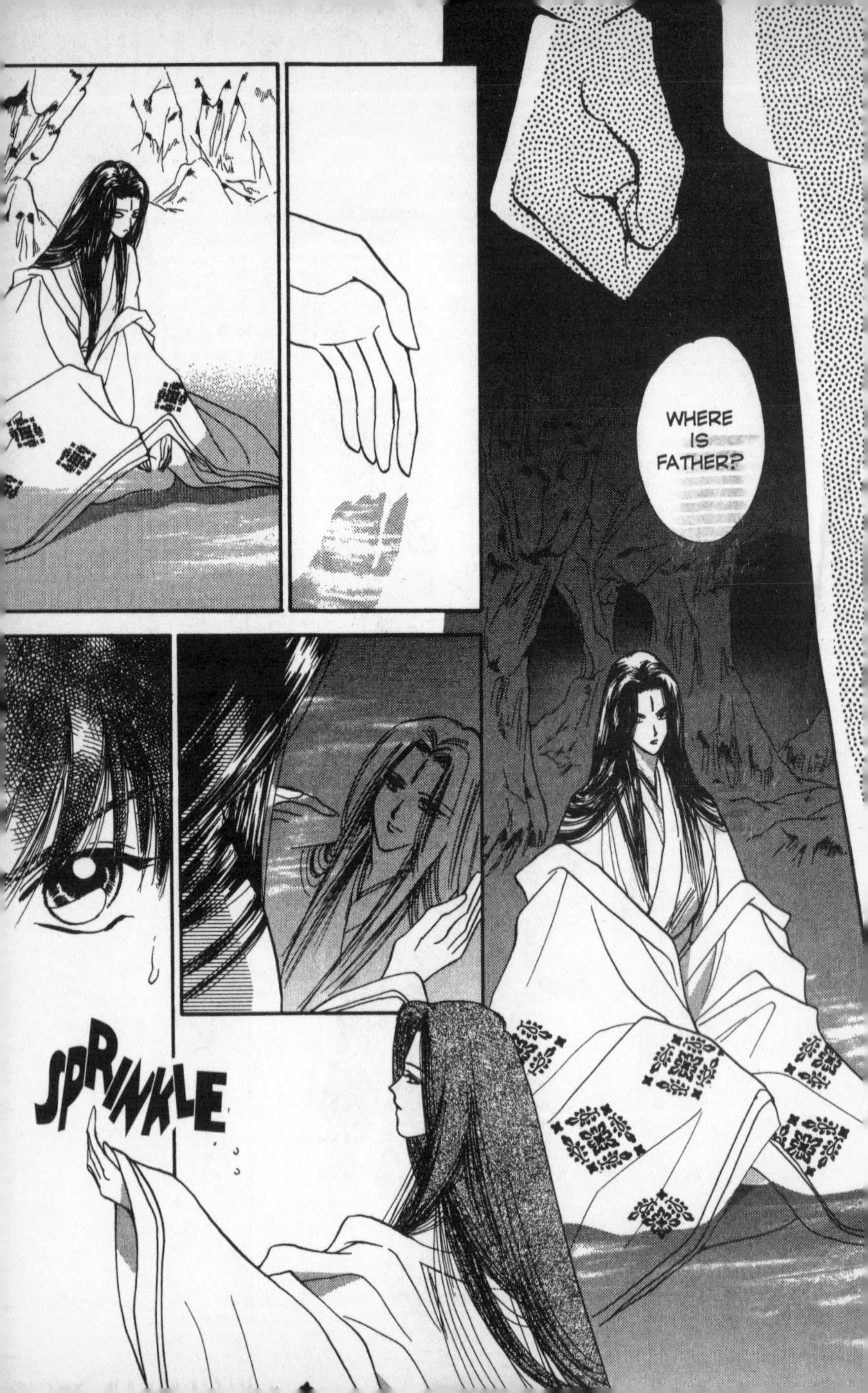
WHERE IS FATHER?
SPRINKLE

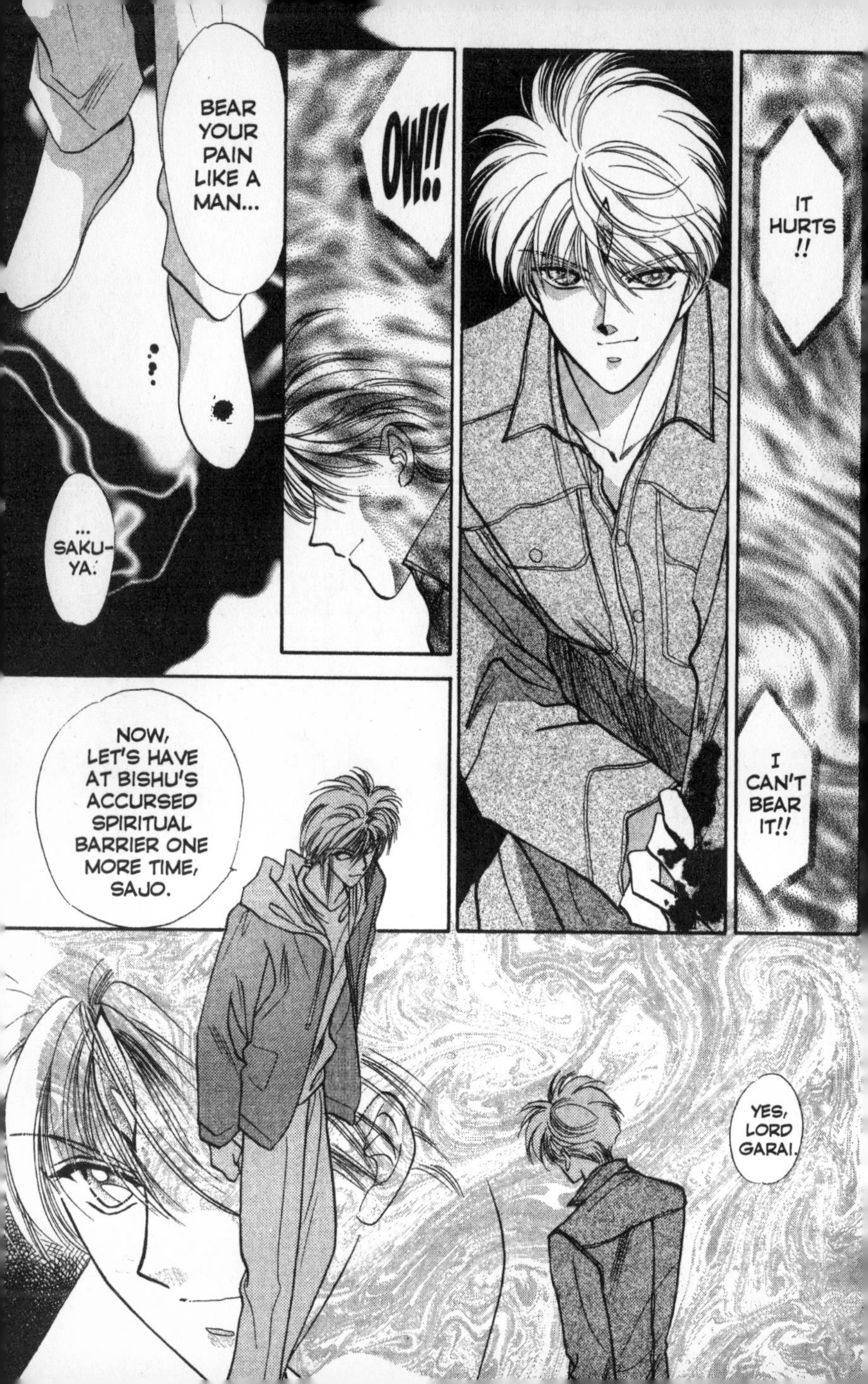
IT HURTS!!
I CAN'T BEAR IT!!
OW!!
BEAR YOUR PAIN LIKE A MAN...
... SAKU-YA.
NOW, LET'S HAVE AT BISHU'S ACCURSED SPIRITUAL BARRIER ONE MORE TIME, SAJO.
YES, LORD GARAI.

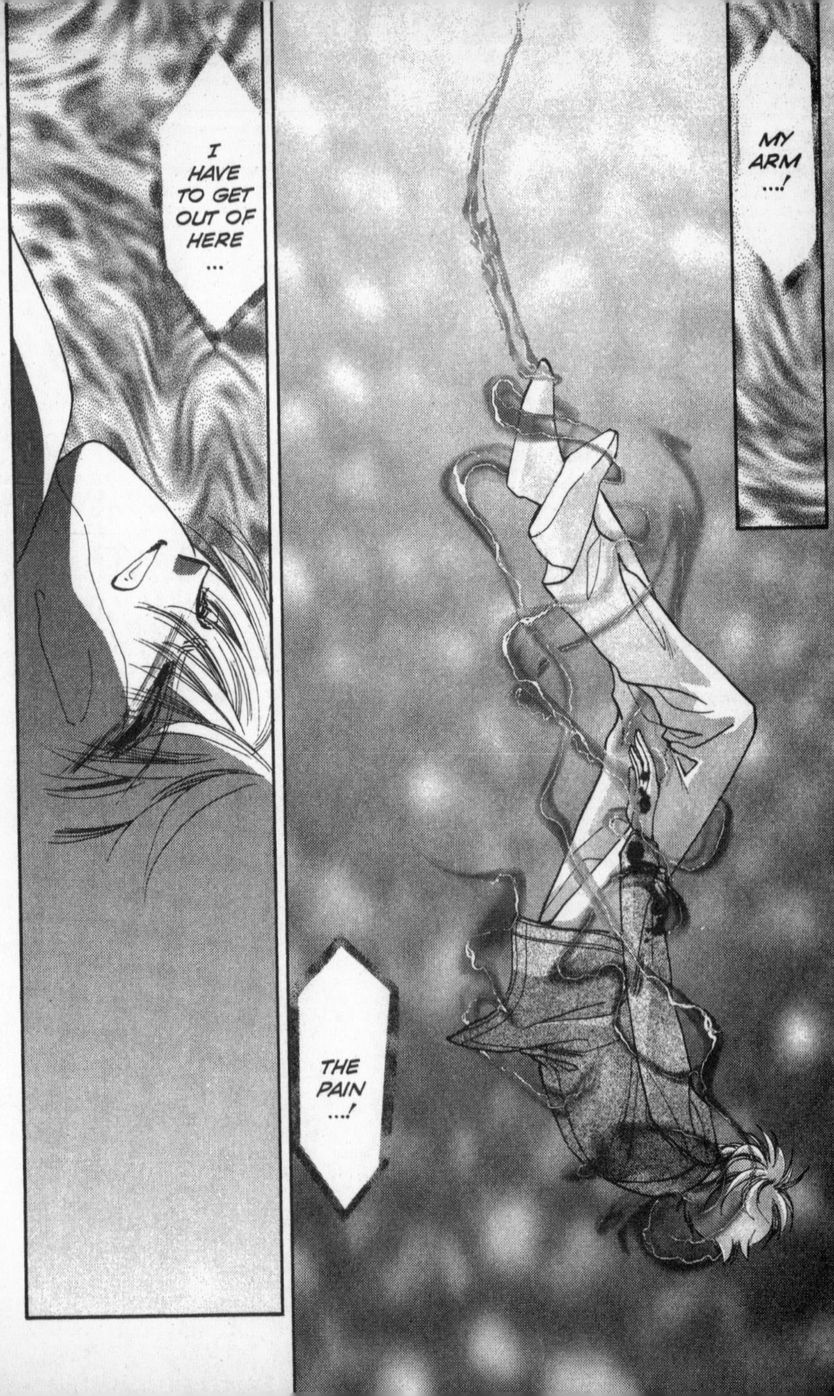
MY ARM ...!
THE PAIN ...!
I HAVE TO GET OUT OF HERE ...

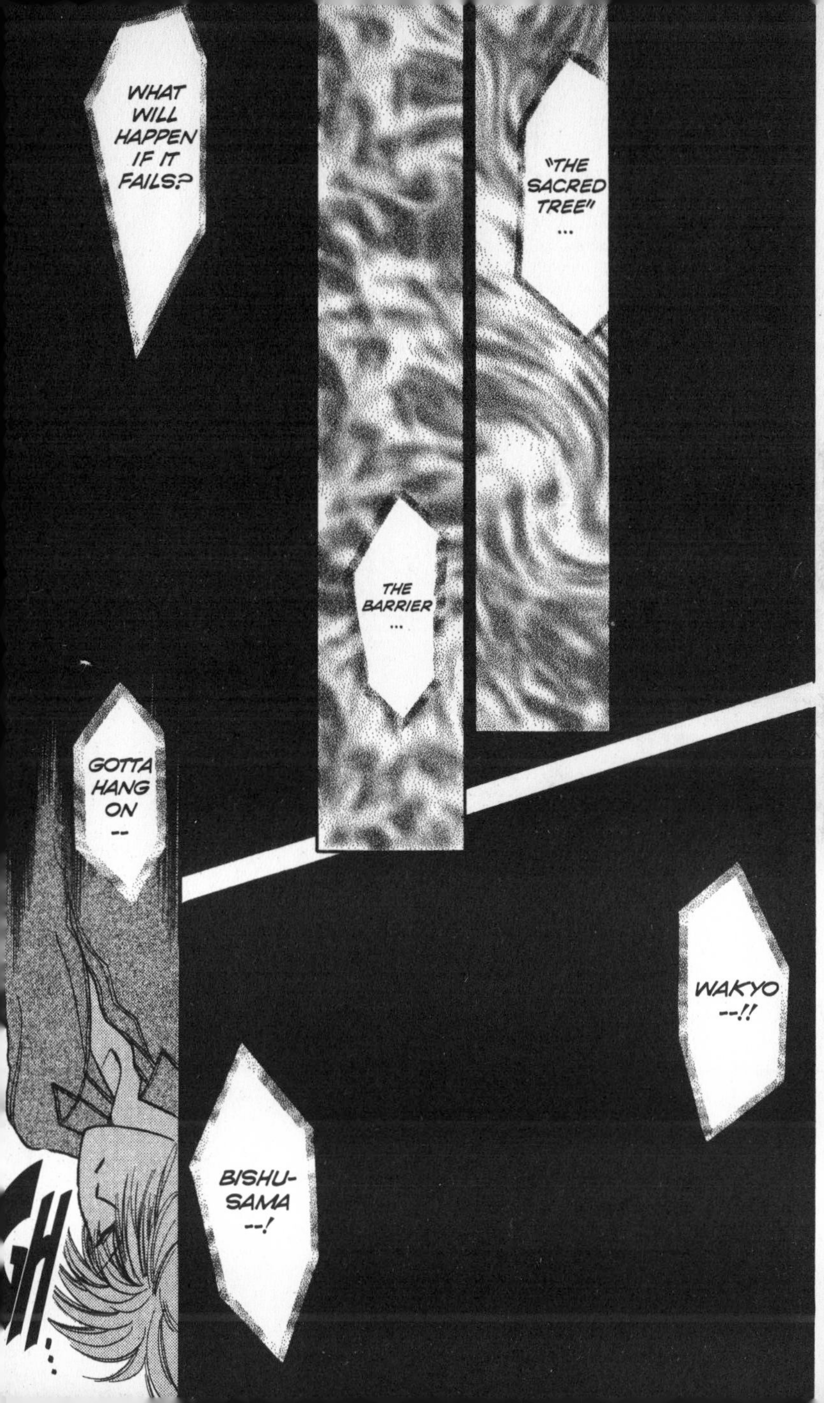
"THE SACRED TREE" ...
THE BARRIER ...
WHAT WILL HAPPEN IF IT FAILS?
WAKYO --!!
GOTTA HANG ON --
BISHU-SAMA --!

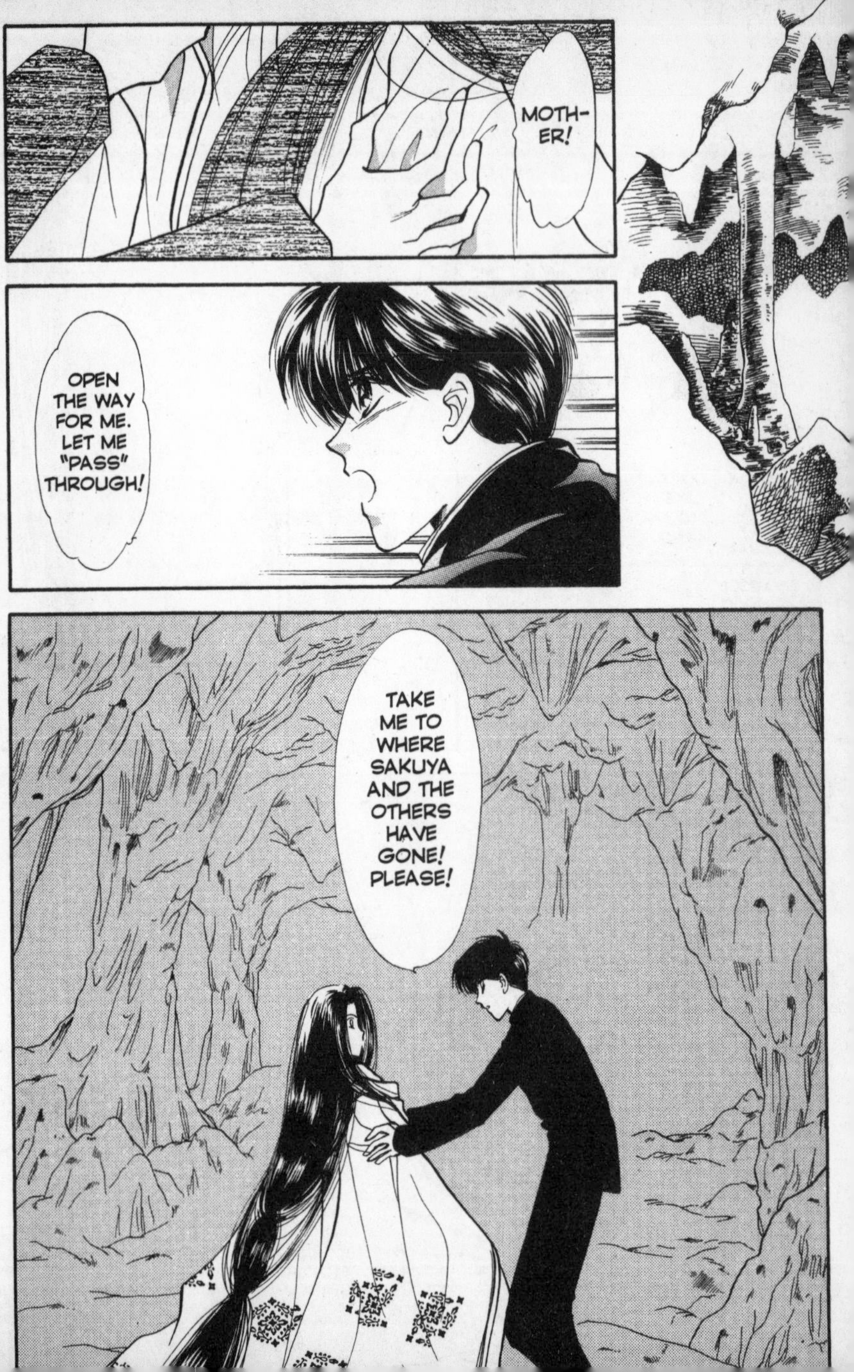
MOTH-
ER!
OPEN THE WAY FOR ME. LET ME "PASS" THROUGH!
TAKE ME TO WHERE SAKUYA AND THE OTHERS HAVE GONE! PLEASE!

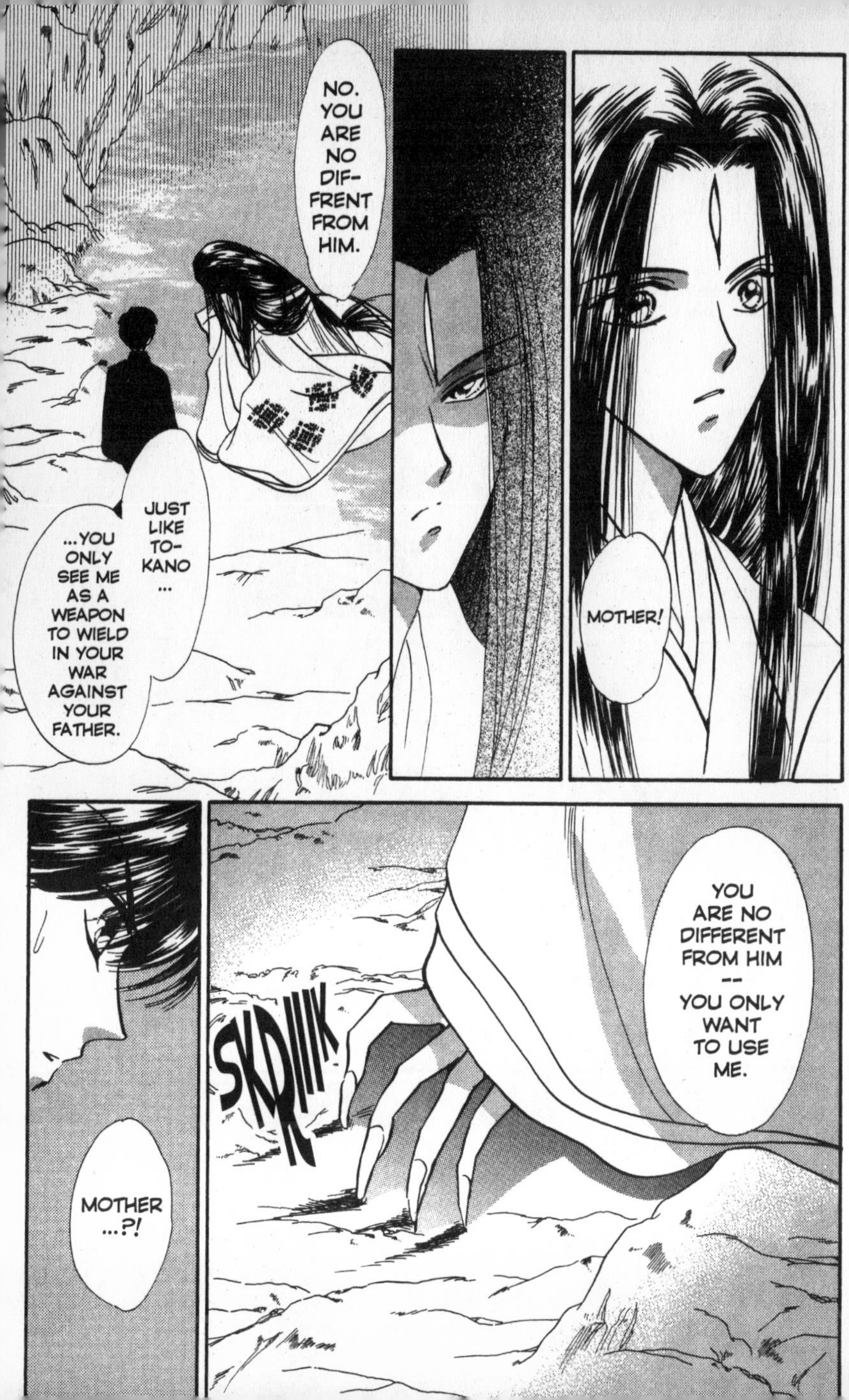
MOTHER!
NO. YOU ARE NO DIF-FRENT FROM HIM.
JUST LIKE TO-KANO ...
...YOU ONLY SEE ME AS A WEAPON TO WIELD IN YOUR WAR AGAINST YOUR FATHER.
YOU ARE NO DIFFERENT FROM HIM -- YOU ONLY WANT TO USE ME.
SKRIIIIK
MOTHER ...?!

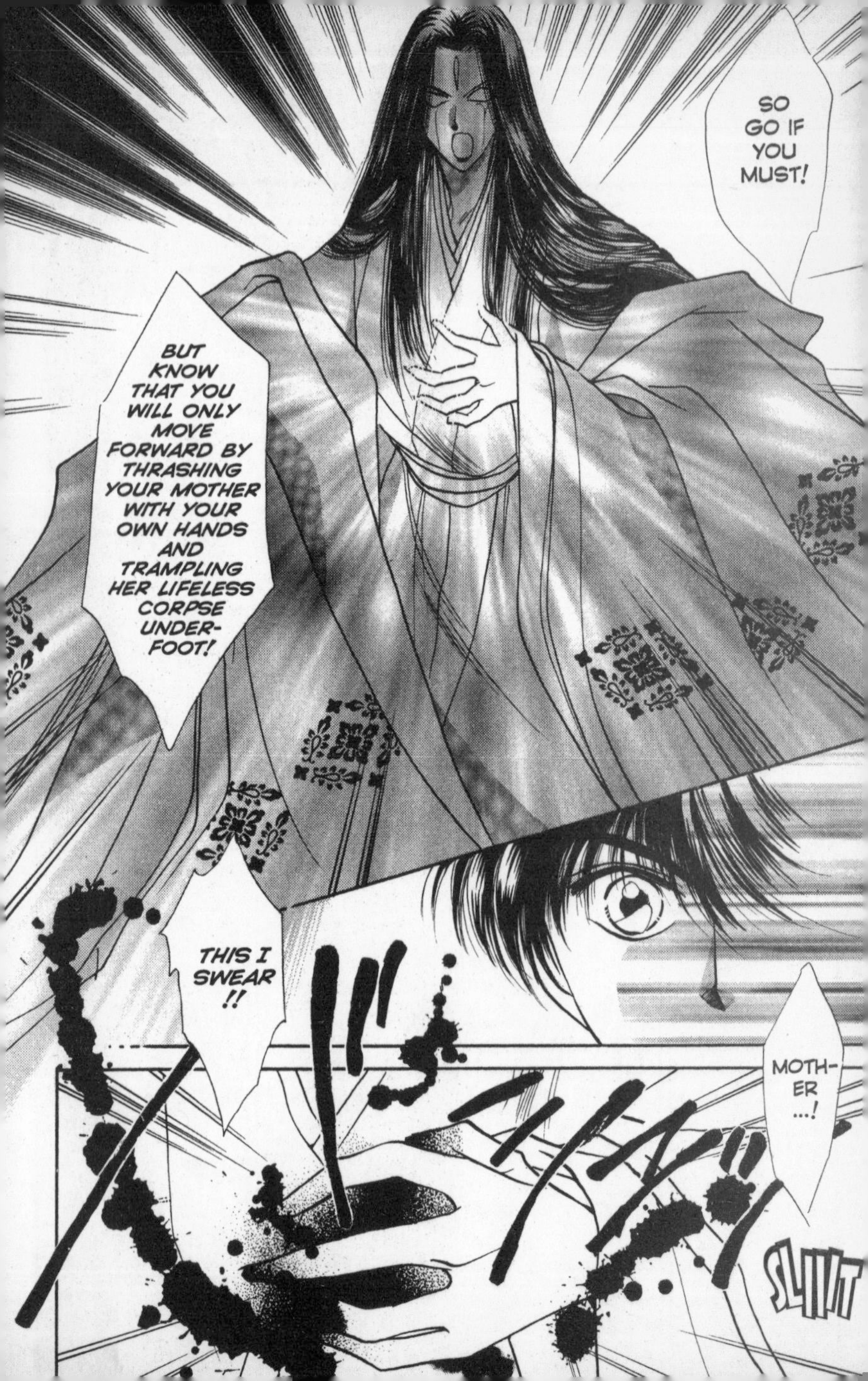
SO GO IF YOU MUST!
BUT KNOW THAT YOU WILL ONLY MOVE FORWARD BY THRASHING YOUR MOTHER WITH YOUR OWN HANDS AND TRAMPLING HER LIFELESS CORPSE UNDER-FOOT!
THIS I SWEAR !!
MOTH-ER ...!
SLIIIT

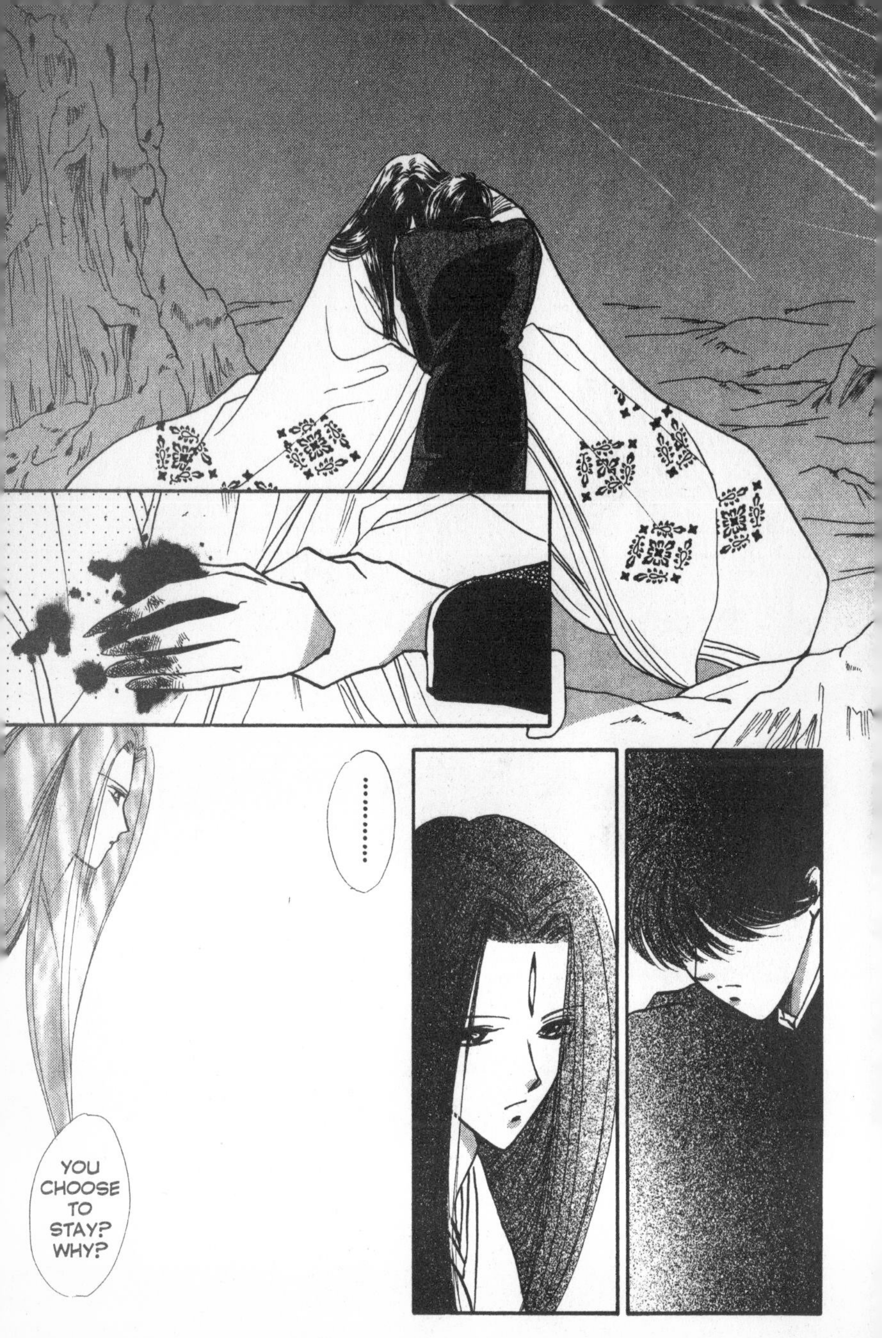
....
YOU CHOOSE TO STAY? WHY?

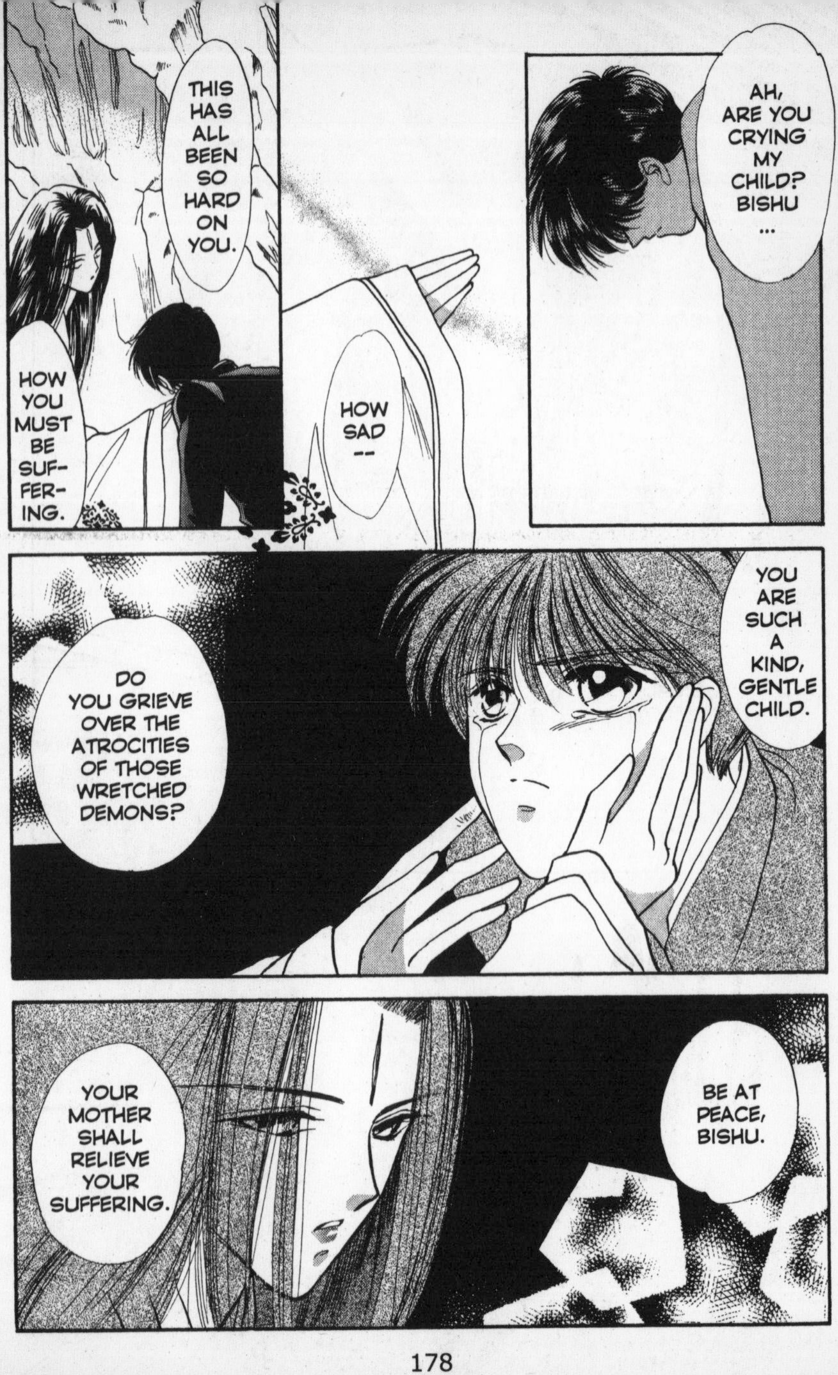
AH, ARE YOU CRYING MY CHILD? BISHU ...
HOW SAD --
THIS HAS ALL BEEN SO HARD ON YOU.
HOW YOU MUST BE SUF-FER-ING.
YOU ARE SUCH A KIND, GENTLE CHILD.
DO YOU GRIEVE OVER THE ATROCITIES OF THOSE WRETCHED DEMONS?
BE AT PEACE, BISHU.
YOUR MOTHER SHALL RELIEVE YOUR SUFFERING.

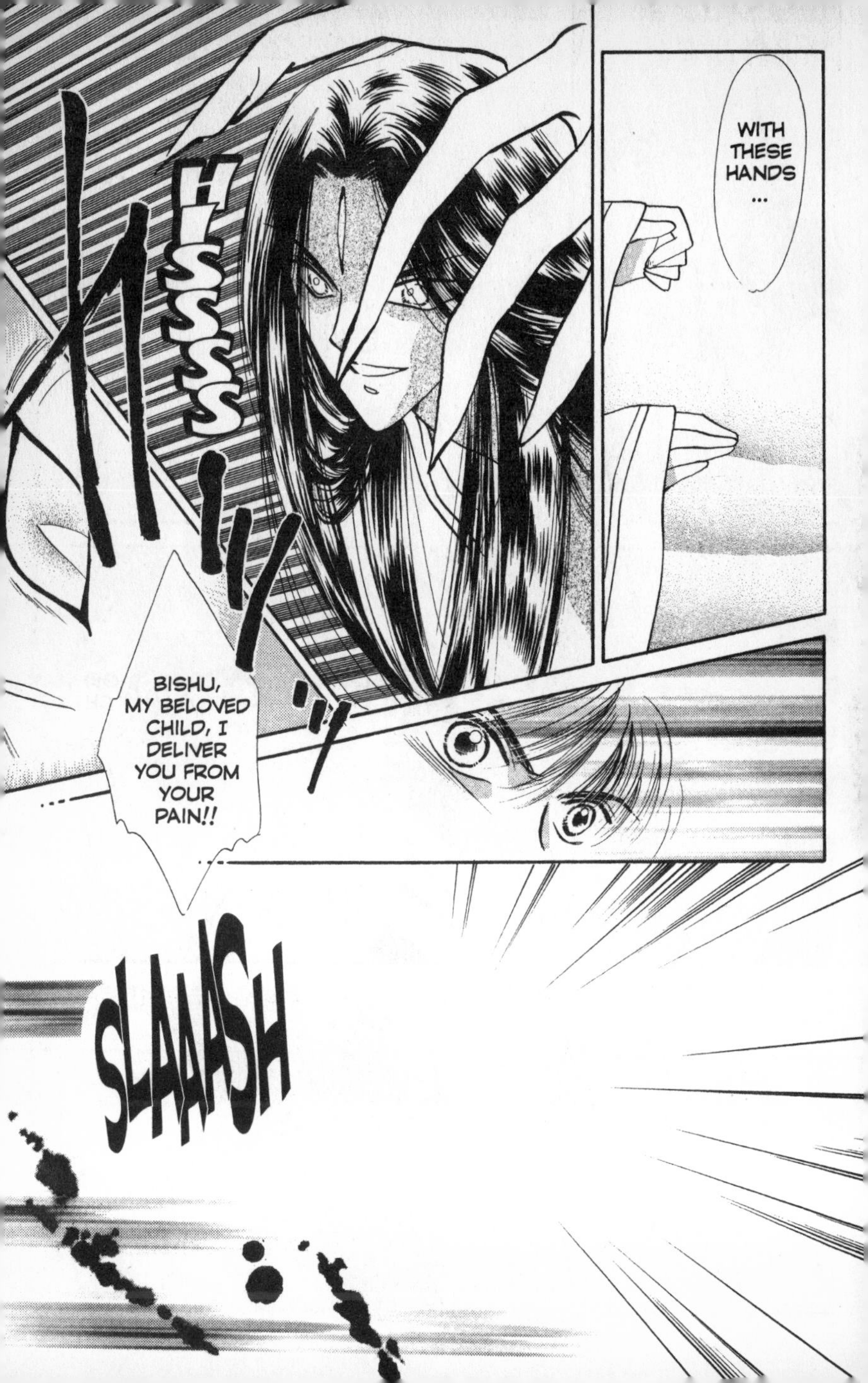
WITH THESE HANDS ...
HISSSS
BISHU, MY BELOVED CHILD, I DELIVER YOU FROM YOUR PAIN!!
SLAAASH

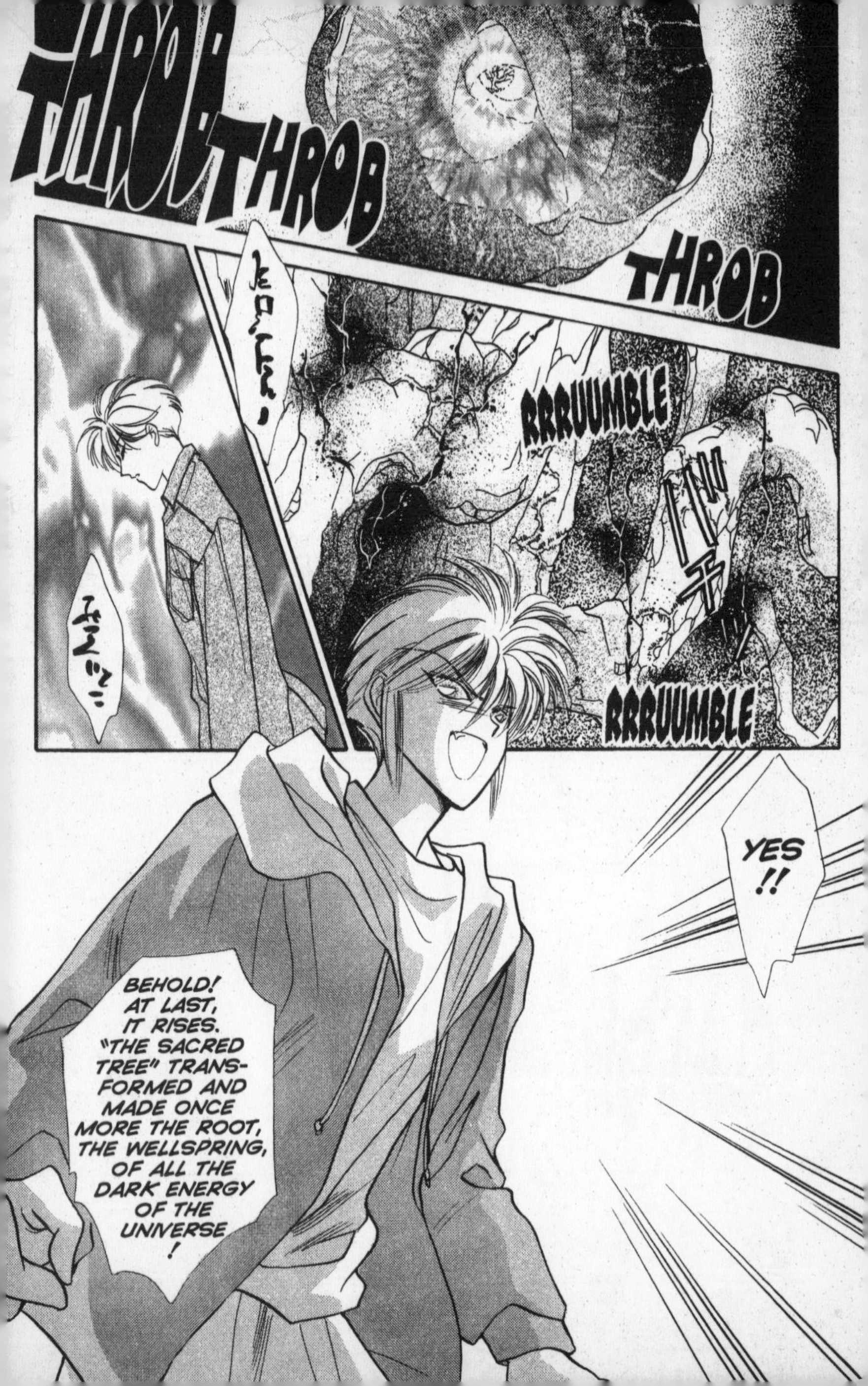
THROB
THROB
THROB
RRRUUMBLE
RRRUUMBLE
YES!!
BEHOLD! AT LAST, IT RISES. "THE SACRED TREE" TRANS-FORMED AND MADE ONCE MORE THE ROOT, THE WELLSPRING, OF ALL THE DARK ENERGY OF THE UNIVERSE!

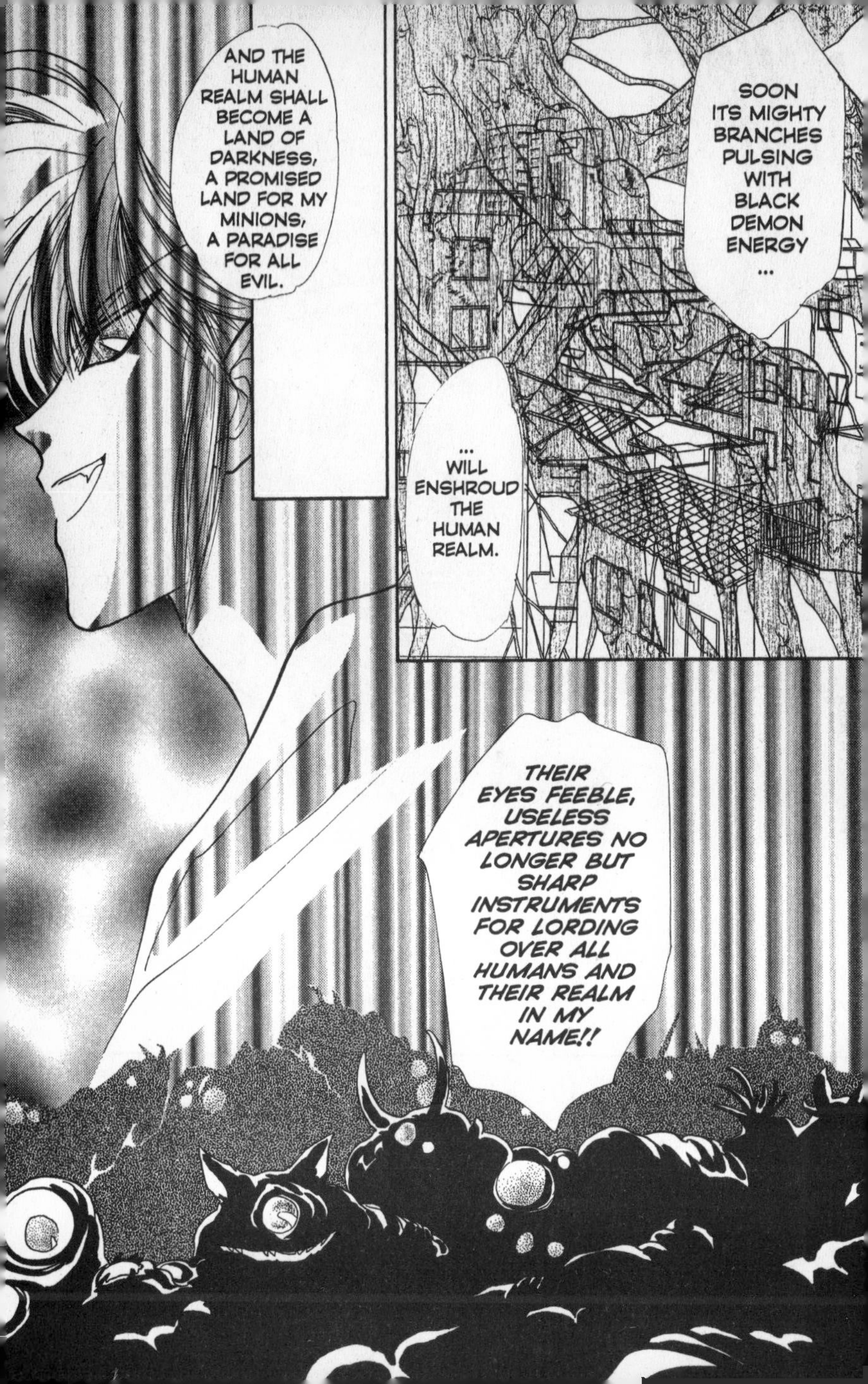
SOON ITS MIGHTY BRANCHES PULSING WITH BLACK DEMON ENERGY ...
... WILL ENSHROUD THE HUMAN REALM.
AND THE HUMAN REALM SHALL BECOME A LAND OF DARKNESS, A PROMISED LAND FOR MY MINIONS, A PARADISE FOR ALL EVIL.
THEIR EYES FEEBLE, USELESS APERTURES NO LONGER BUT SHARP INSTRUMENTS FOR LORDING OVER ALL HUMANS AND THEIR REALM IN MY NAME!!

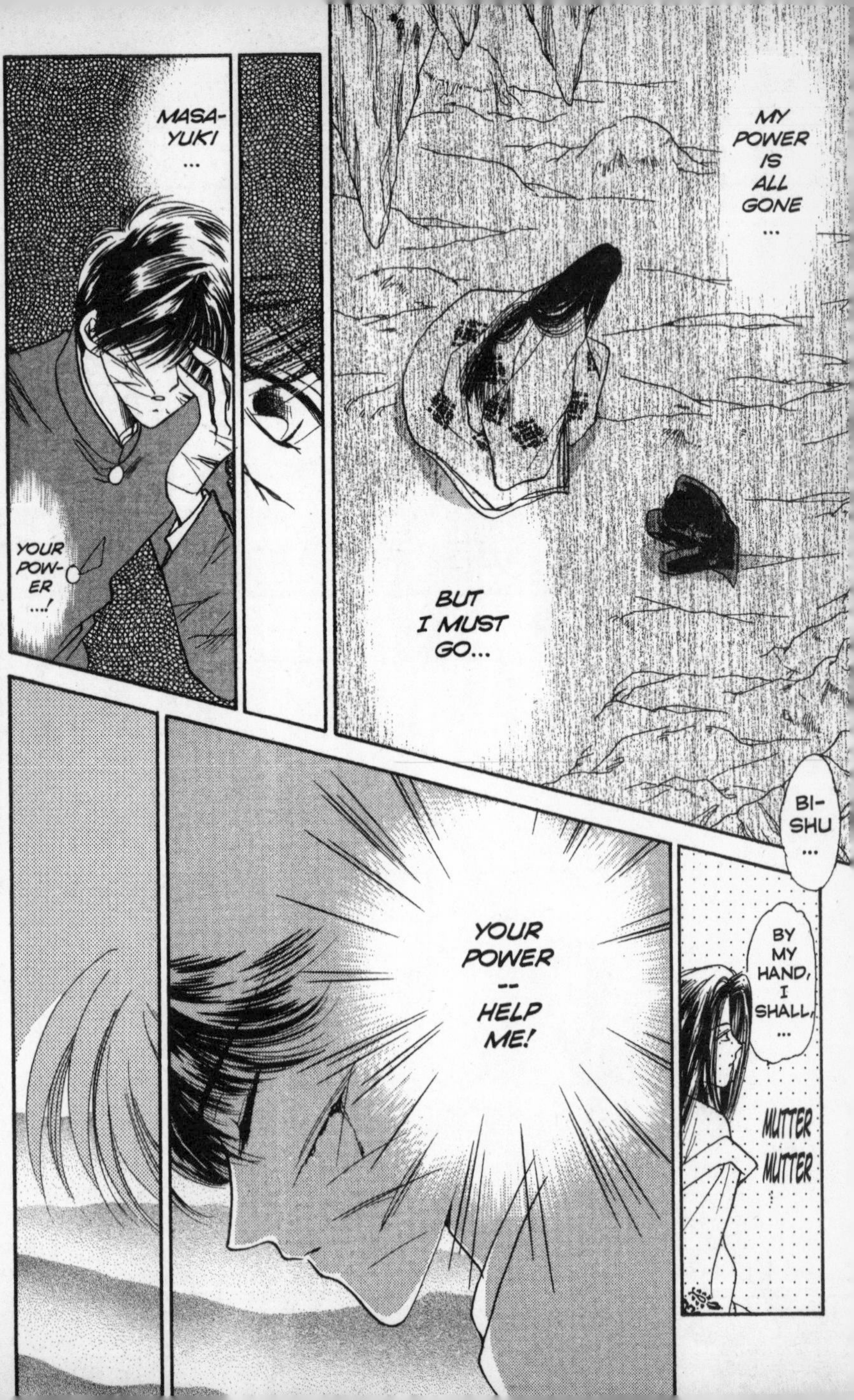
MY POWER IS ALL GONE ...
BUT I MUST GO...
MASA-YUKI ...
YOUR POW-ER ...!
BI-SHU ...
BY MY HAND, I SHALL, ...
MUTTER MUTTER
YOUR POWER -- HELP ME!

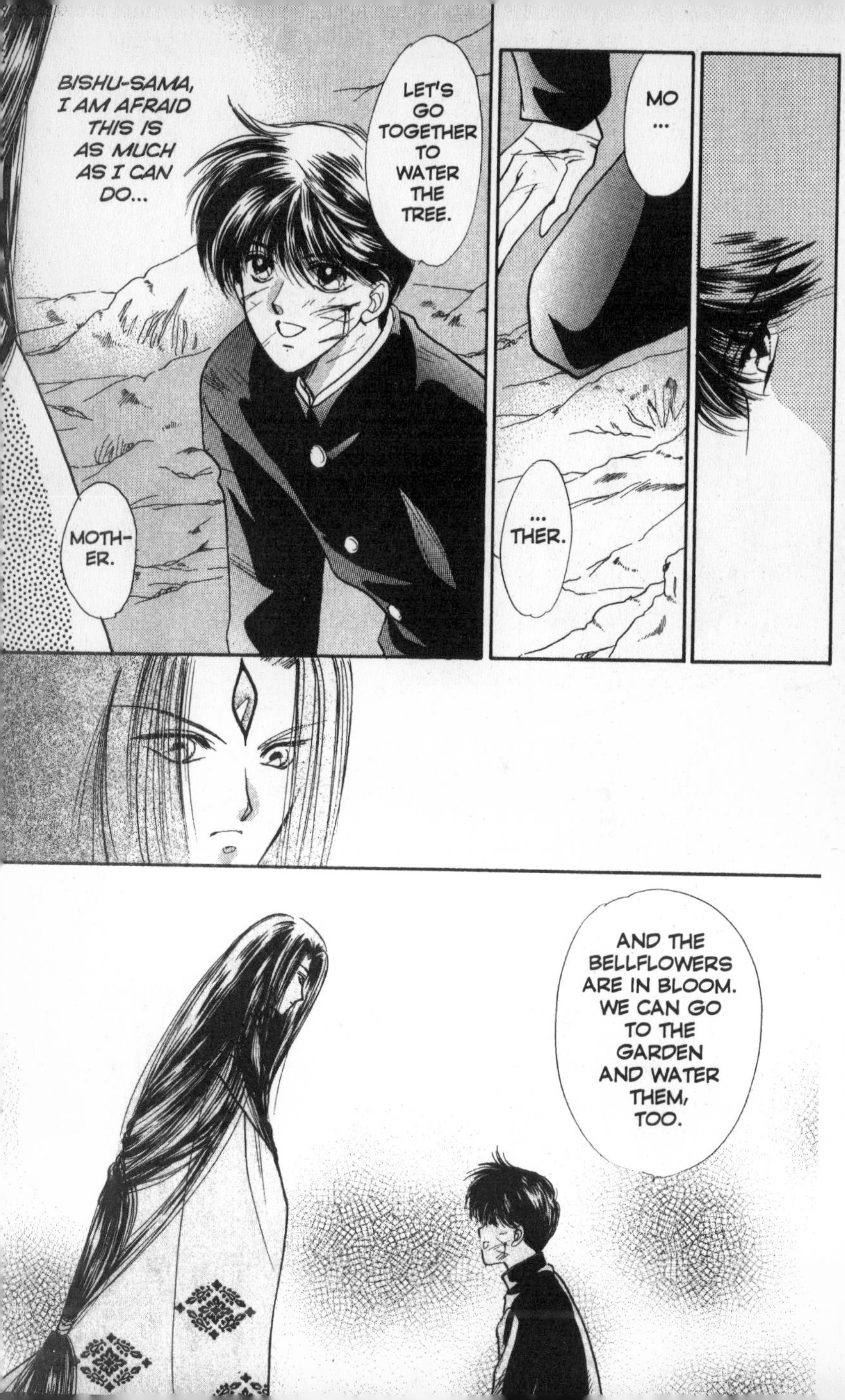
MO ...
... THER.
LET'S GO TOGETHER TO WATER THE TREE.
BISHU-SAMA, I AM AFRAID THIS IS AS MUCH AS I CAN DO...
MOTHER-ER.
AND THE BELLFLOWERS ARE IN BLOOM. WE CAN GO TO THE GARDEN AND WATER THEM, TOO.

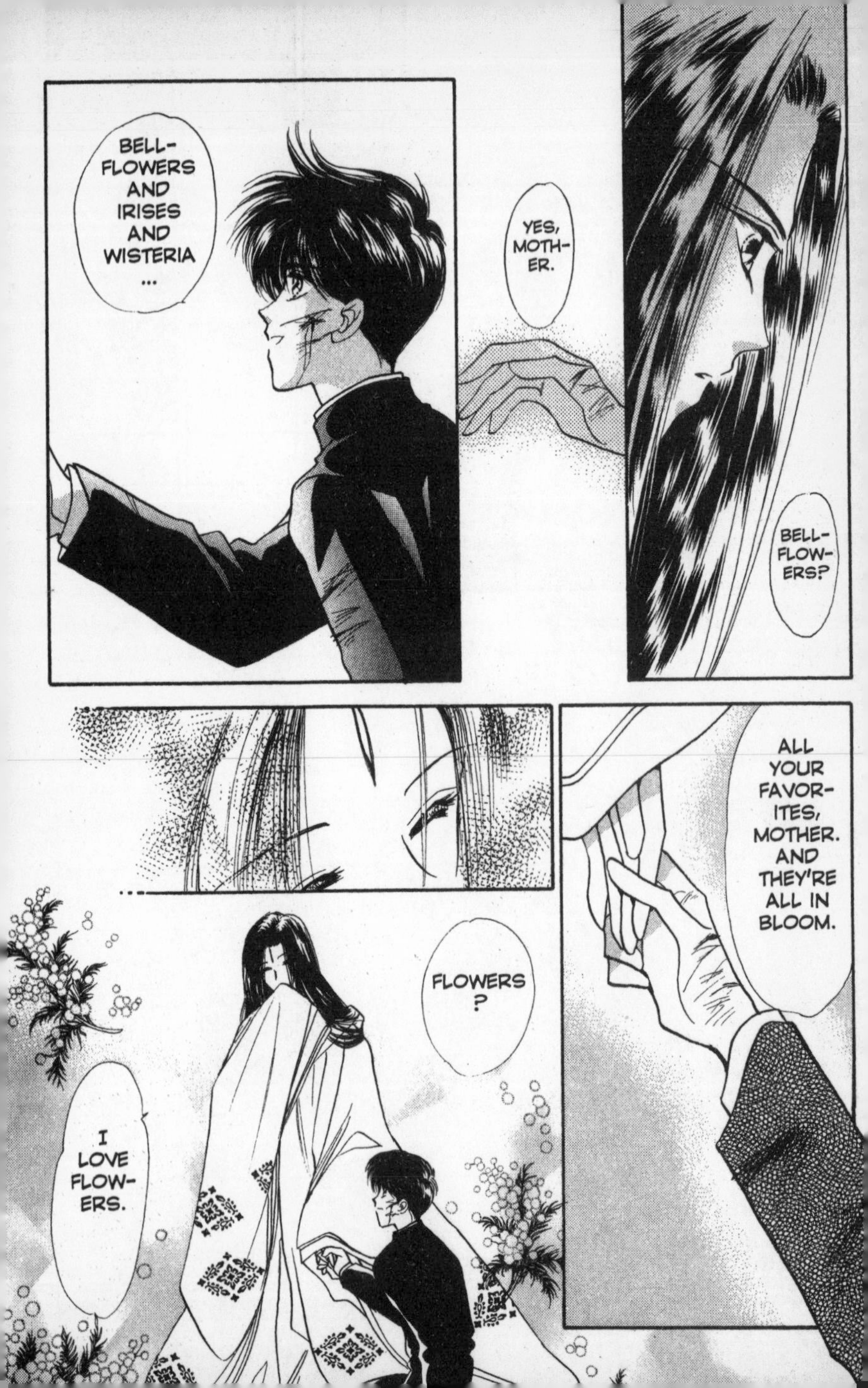
BELL-FLOW-ERS?
YES, MOTH-ER.
BELL-FLOWERS AND IRISES AND WISTERIA ...
ALL YOUR FAVOR-ITES, MOTHER. AND THEY'RE ALL IN BLOOM.
FLOWERS ?
I LOVE FLOW-ERS.

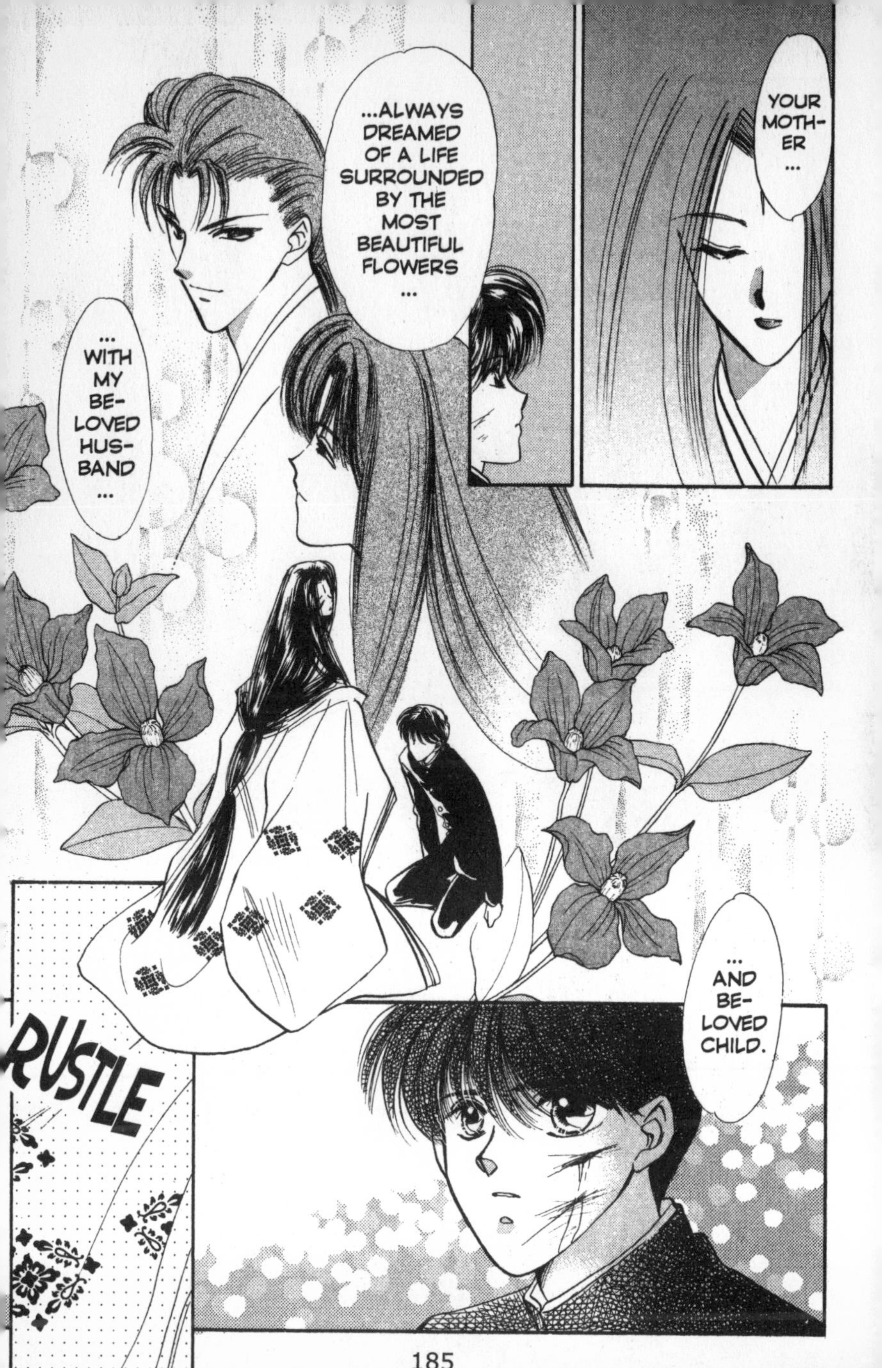
YOUR MOTH-ER ...
...ALWAYS DREAMED OF A LIFE SURROUNDED BY THE MOST BEAUTIFUL FLOWERS ...
... WITH MY BE-LOVED HUS-BAND ...
... AND BE-LOVED CHILD.
RUSTLE

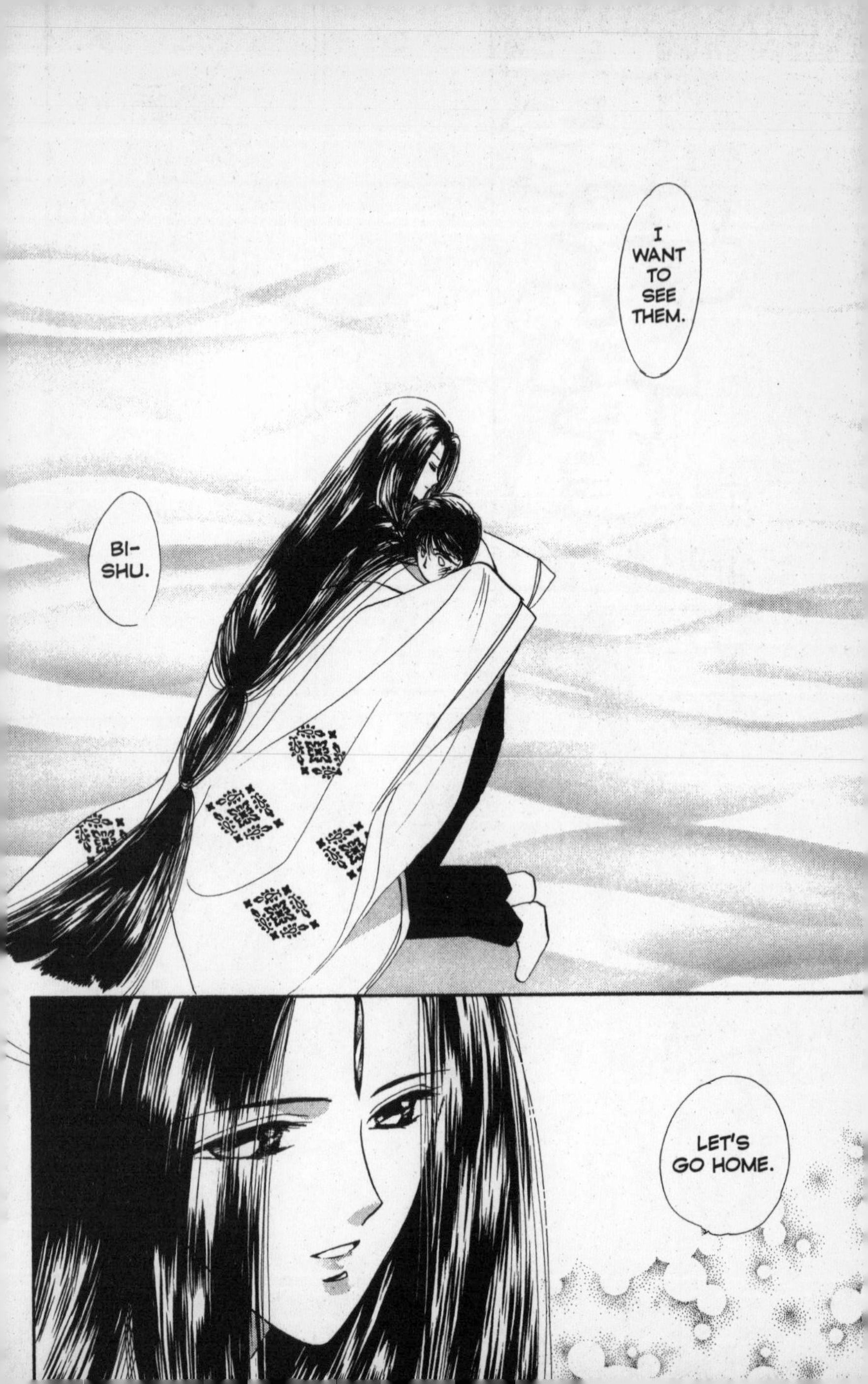
I WANT TO SEE THEM.
BI-SHU.
LET'S GO HOME.

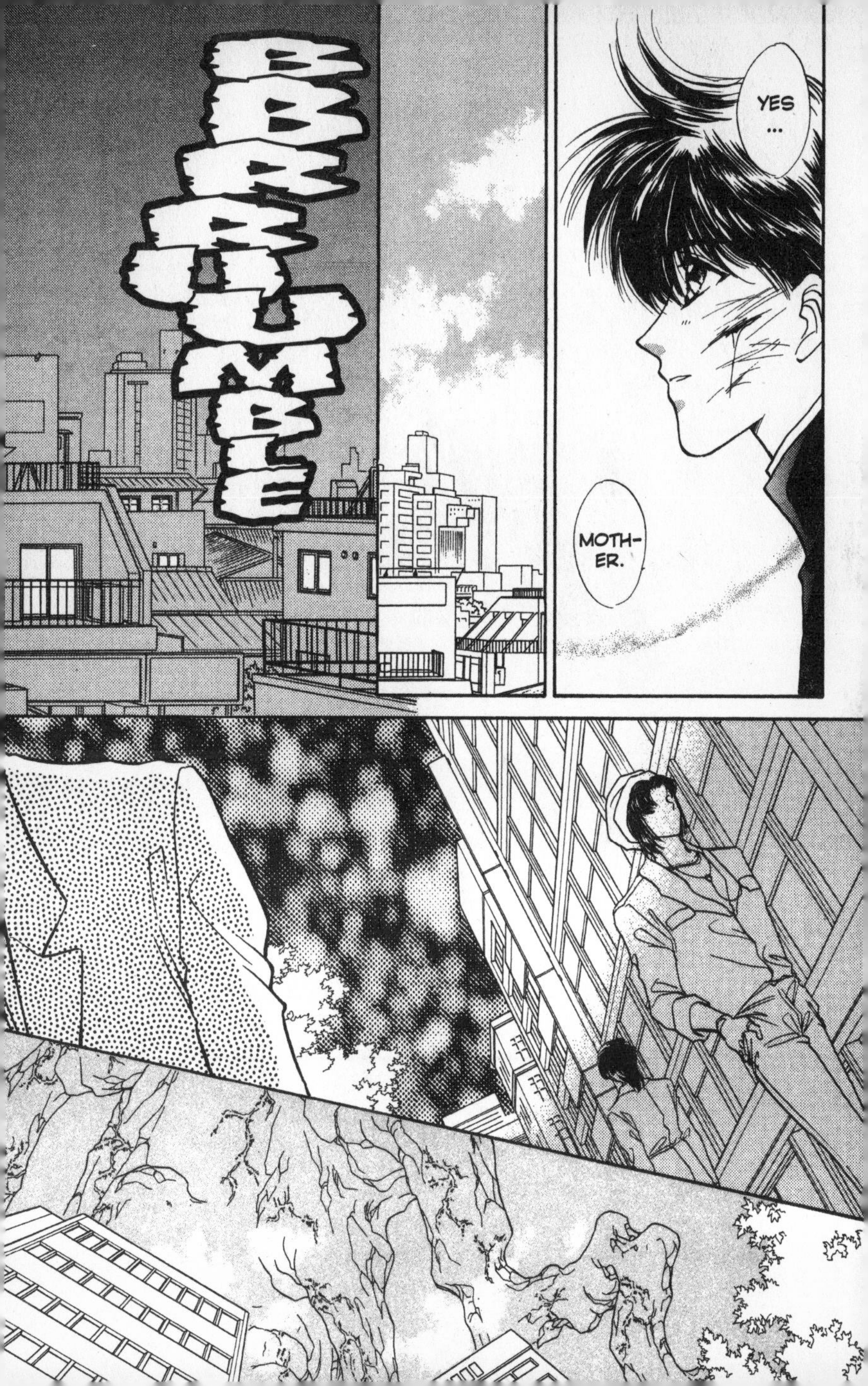
YES ...
MOTH-ER.
BBRRUUMBLE

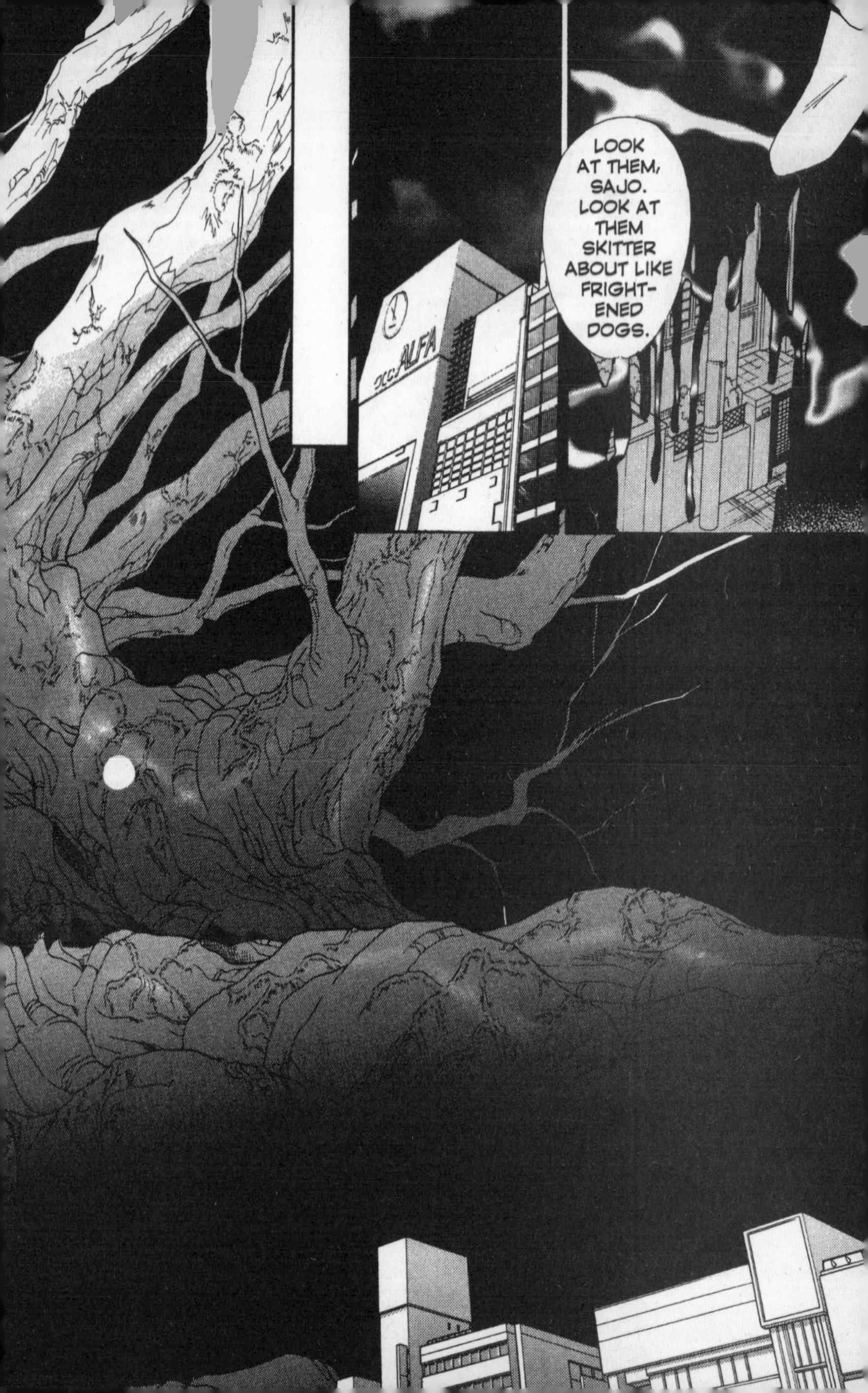
LOOK AT THEM, SAJO. LOOK AT THEM SKITTER ABOUT LIKE FRIGHT-ENED DOGS.

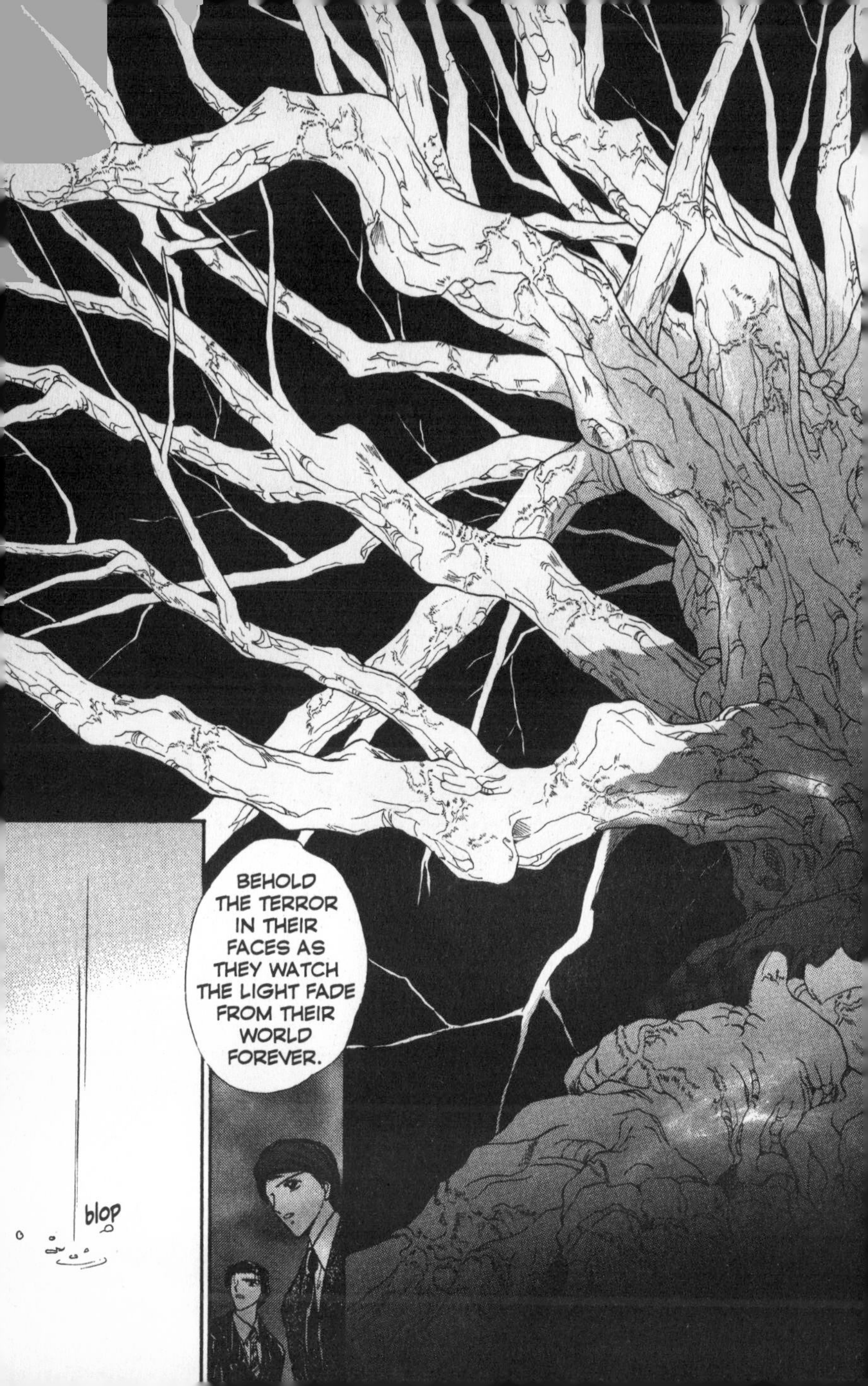
BEHOLD THE TERROR IN THEIR FACES AS THEY WATCH THE LIGHT FADE FROM THEIR WORLD FOREVER.
blop

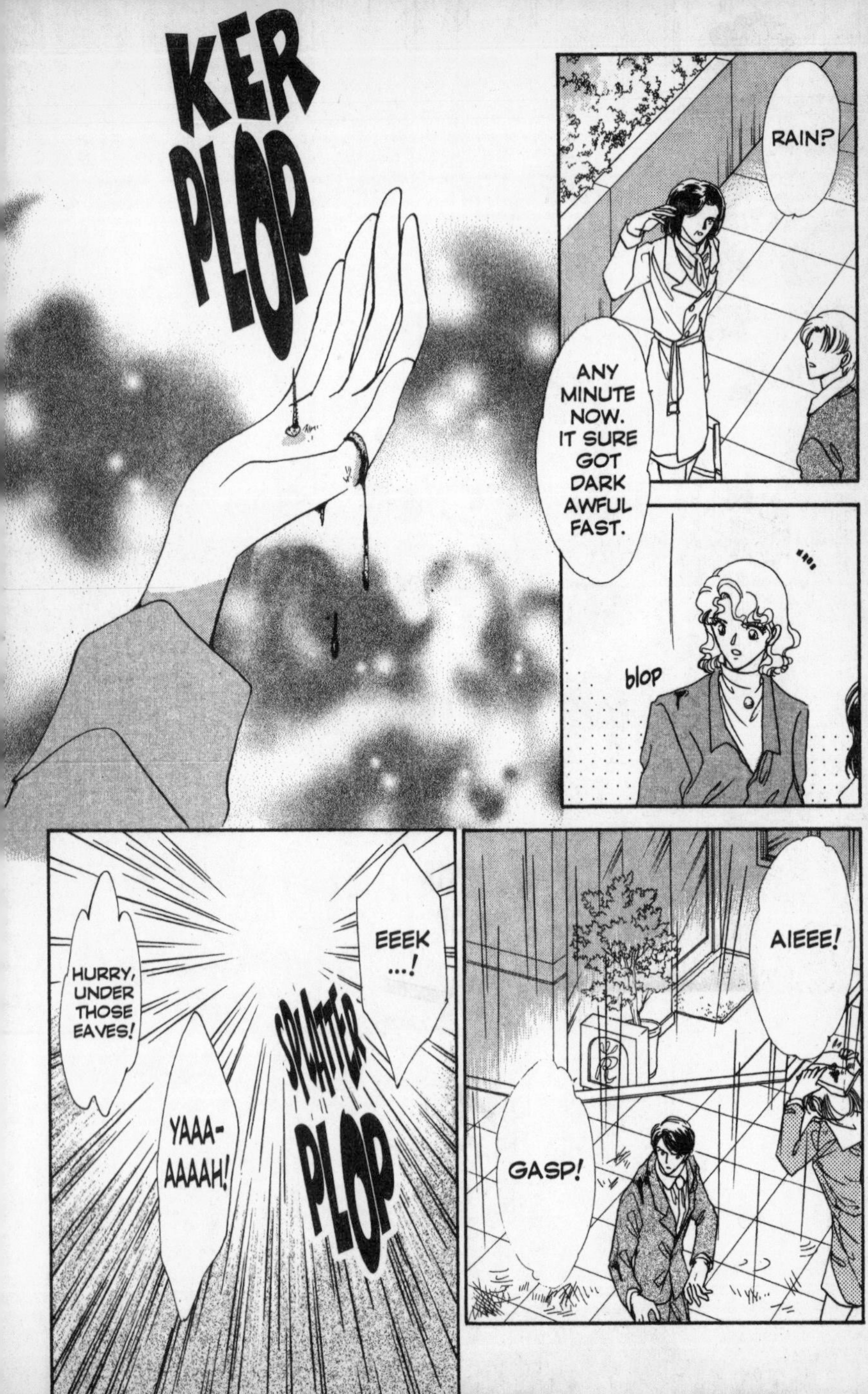
RAIN?
ANY MINUTE NOW. IT SURE GOT DARK AWFUL FAST.
blop
KER PLOP
AIEEE!
GASP!
EEEK ...!
SPLATTER PLOP
HURRY, UNDER THOSE EAVES!
YAAA-AAAAH!

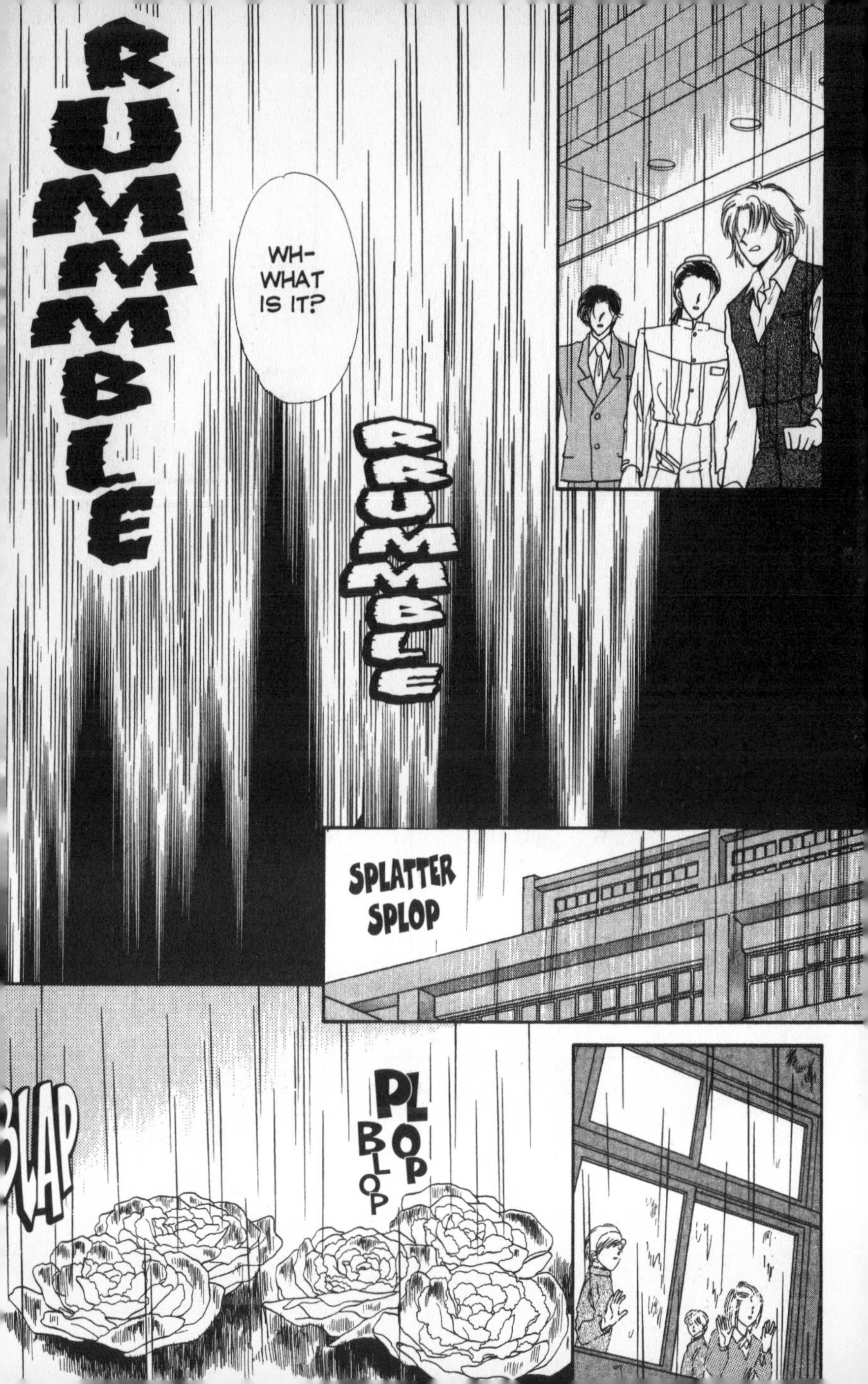
WH-
WHAT
IS IT?
RUMMMBLE
RRUMMBLE
SPLATTER
SPLOP
PLOP
BLOP
SLAP

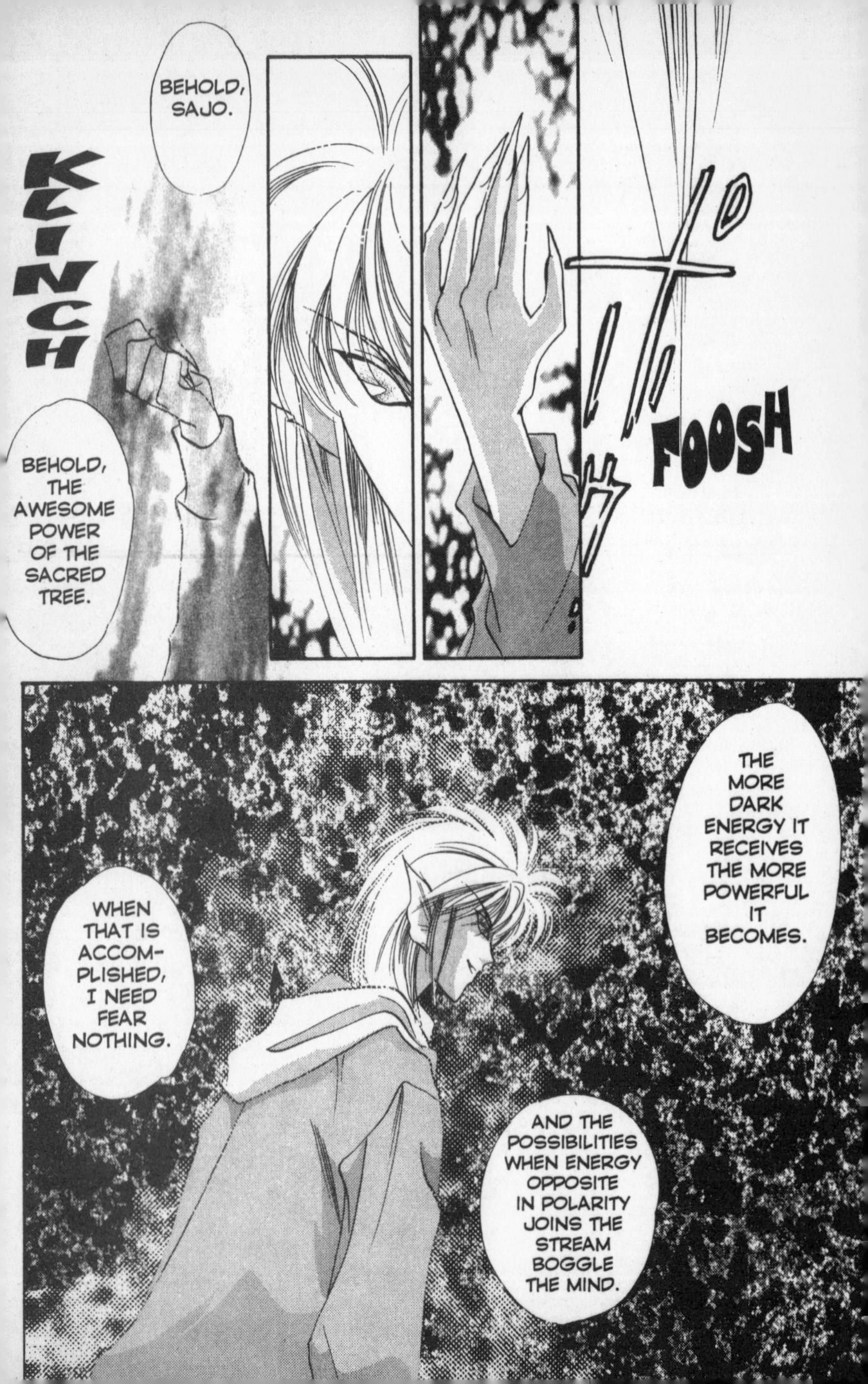
FOOSH
BEHOLD, SAJO.
KLINCH
BEHOLD, THE AWESOME POWER OF THE SACRED TREE.
THE MORE DARK ENERGY IT RECEIVES THE MORE POWERFUL IT BECOMES.
AND THE POSSIBILITIES WHEN ENERGY OPPOSITE IN POLARITY JOINS THE STREAM BOGGLE THE MIND.
WHEN THAT IS ACCOM-PLISHED, I NEED FEAR NOTHING.

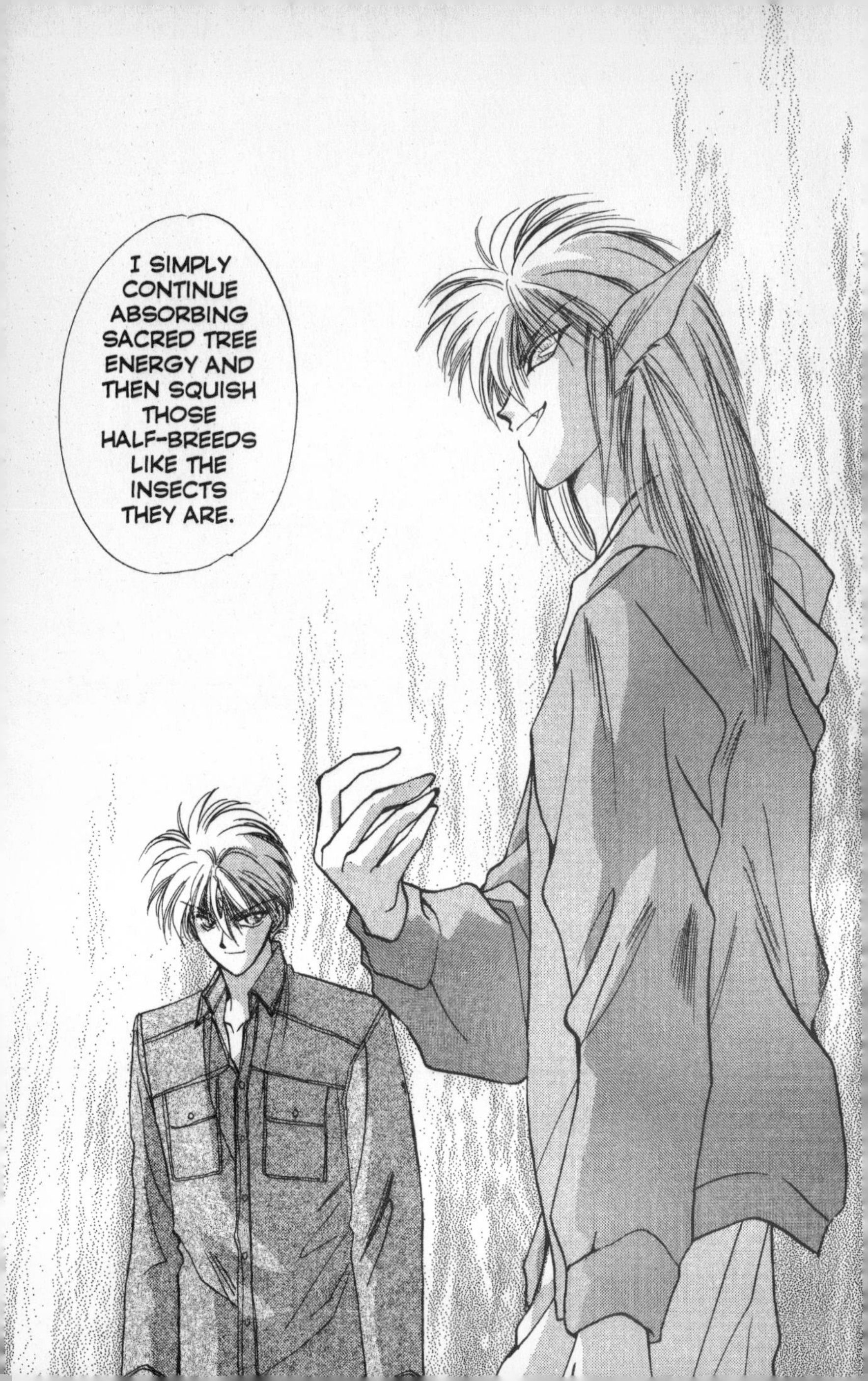
I SIMPLY CONTINUE ABSORBING SACRED TREE ENERGY AND THEN SQUISH THOSE HALF-BREEDS LIKE THE INSECTS THEY ARE.

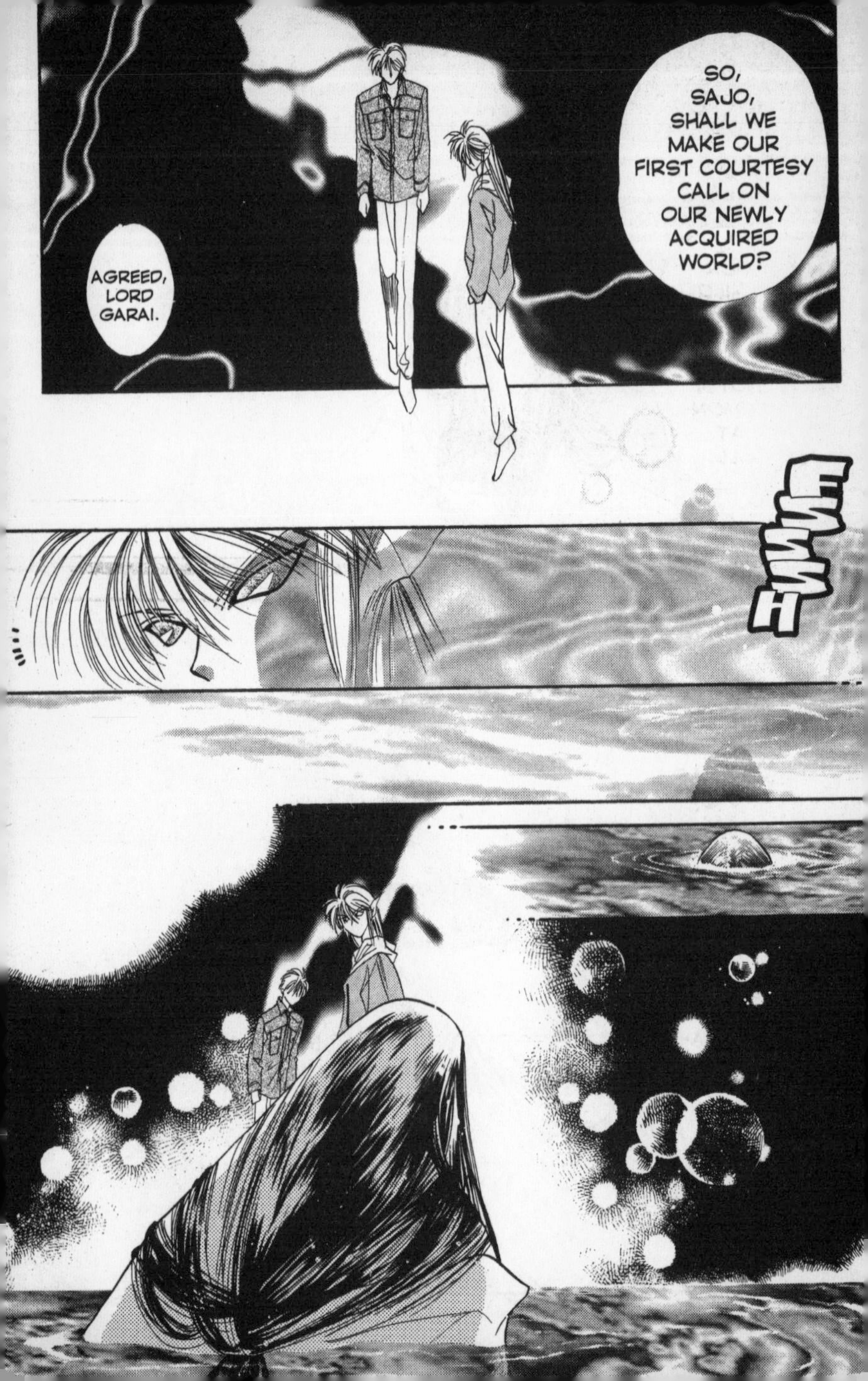
SO, SAJO, SHALL WE MAKE OUR FIRST COURTESY CALL ON OUR NEWLY ACQUIRED WORLD?
AGREED, LORD GARAI.
FSSSH

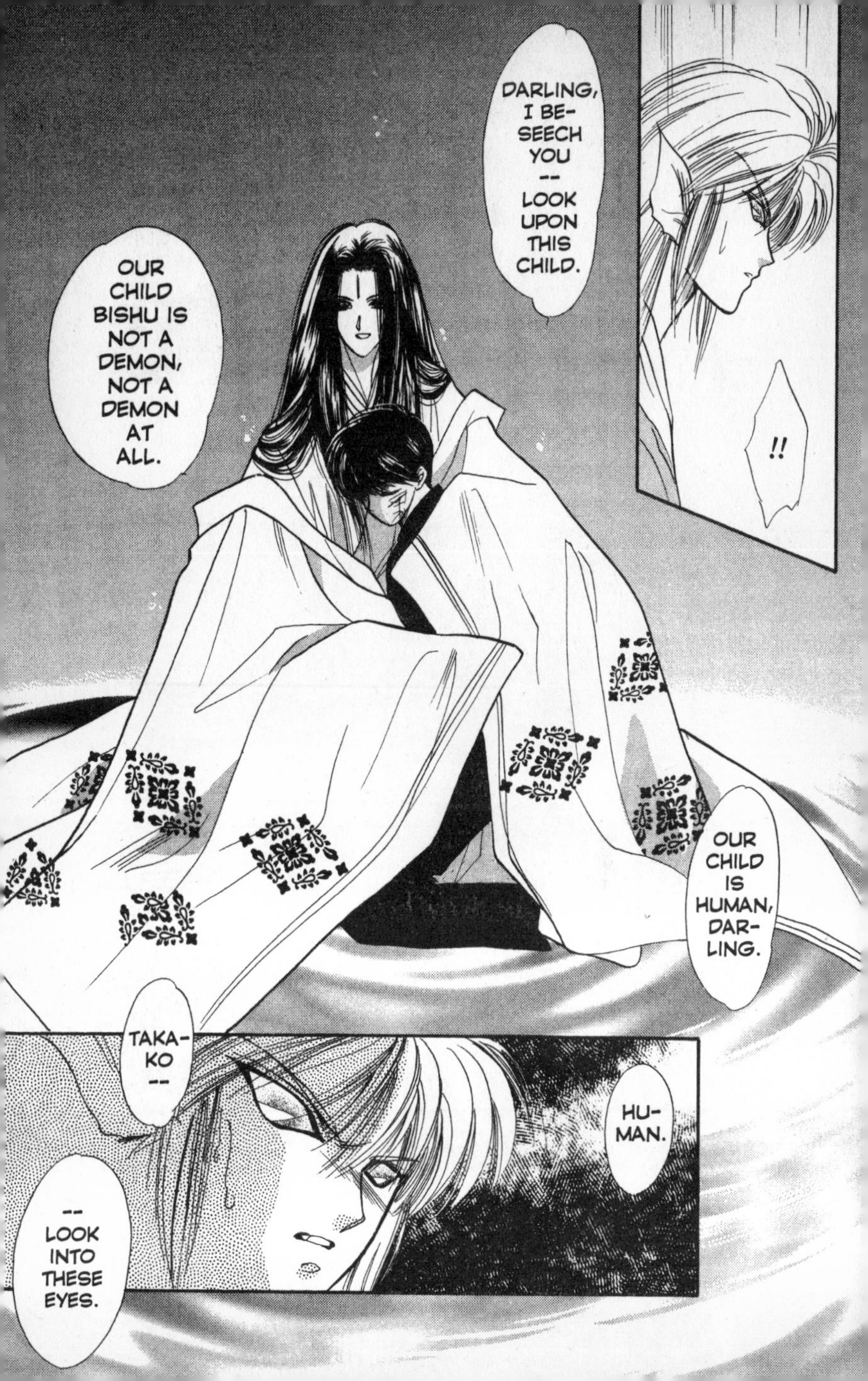
DARLING, I BESEECH YOU -- LOOK UPON THIS CHILD.
OUR CHILD BISHU IS NOT A DEMON, NOT A DEMON AT ALL.
!!
OUR CHILD IS HUMAN, DARLING.
HUMAN.
TAKAKO --
-- LOOK INTO THESE EYES.

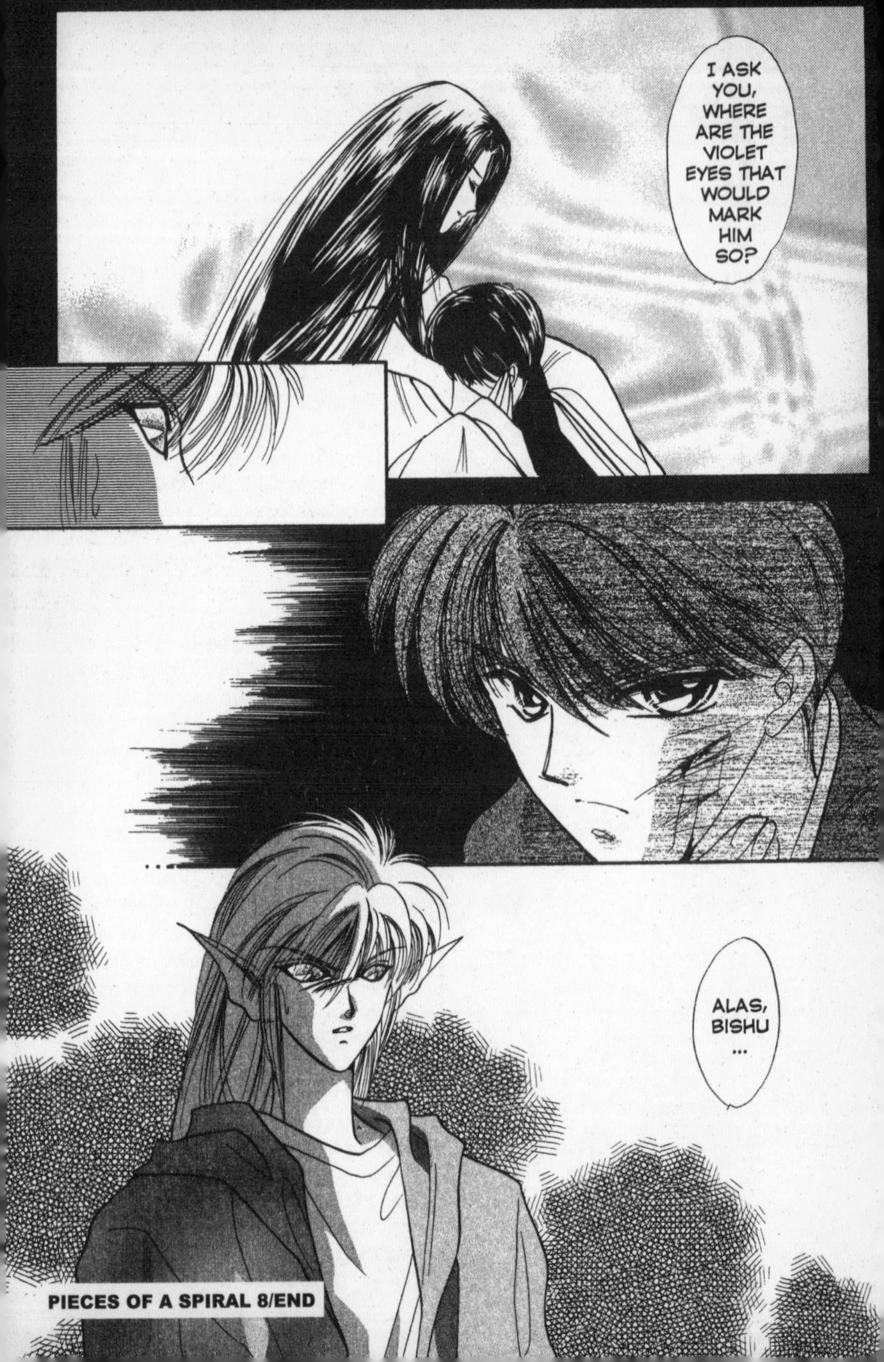
I ASK YOU, WHERE ARE THE VIOLET EYES THAT WOULD MARK HIM SO?
...
ALAS, BISHU ...
PIECES OF A SPIRAL 8/END

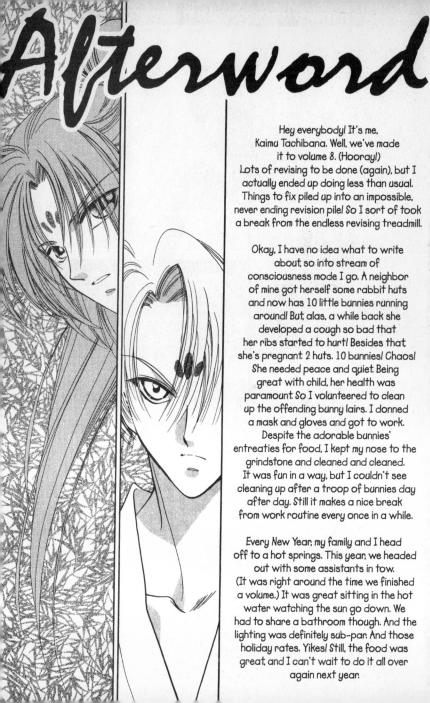

Afterword

Hey everybody! It's me,
Kaimu Tachibana. Well, we've made
it to volume 8. (Hooray!)
Lots of revising to be done (again), but I
actually ended up doing less than usual.
Things to fix piled up into an impossible,
never ending revision pile! So I sort of took
a break from the endless revising treadmill.

Okay, I have no idea what to write
about, so into stream of
consciousness mode I go. A neighbor
of mine got herself some rabbit huts
and now has 10 little bunnies running
around! But, alas, a while back she
developed a cough so bad that
her ribs started to hurt! Besides that,
she's pregnant. 2 huts. 10 bunnies! Chaos!
She needed peace and quiet. Being
great with child, her health was
paramount. So I volunteered to clean
up the offending bunny lairs. I donned
a mask and gloves and got to work.
Despite the adorable bunnies'
entreaties for food, I kept my nose to the
grindstone and cleaned and cleaned.
It was fun in a way, but I couldn't see
cleaning up after a troop of bunnies day
after day. Still it makes a nice break
from work routine every once in a while.

Every New Year, my family and I head
off to a hot springs. This year, we headed
out with some assistants in tow.
(It was right around the time we finished
a volume.) It was great sitting in the hot
water watching the sun go down. We
had to share a bathroom though. And the
lighting was definitely sub-par. And those
holiday rates. Yikes! Still, the food was
great, and I can't wait to do it all over
again next year.

I 'M ON TO YOU, MAN COMICS!

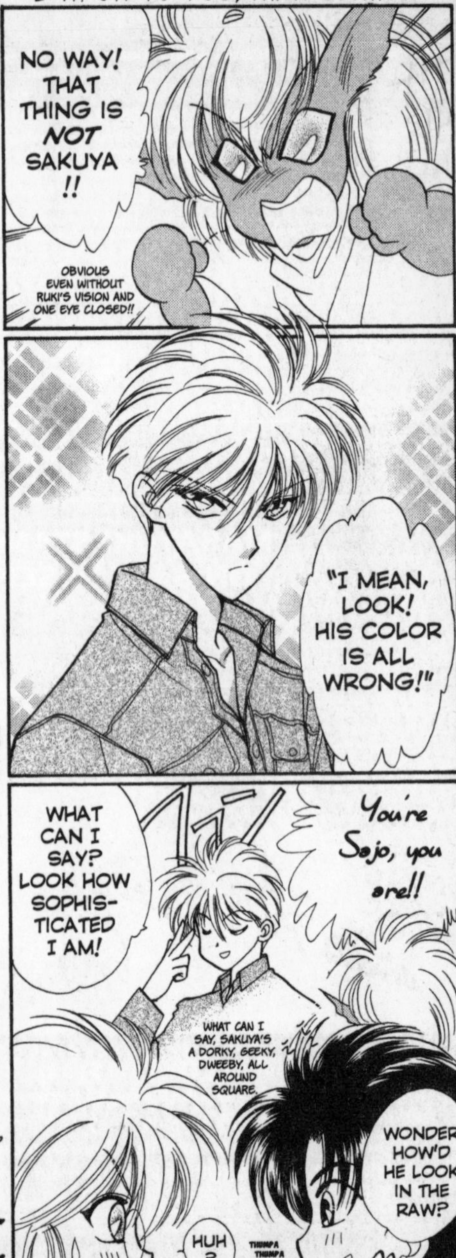
NO WAY! THAT THING IS *NOT* SAKUYA !!
OBVIOUS EVEN WITHOUT RUKI'S VISION AND ONE EYE CLOSED!!
"I MEAN, LOOK! HIS COLOR IS ALL WRONG!"
You're Sojo, you are!!
WHAT CAN I SAY? LOOK HOW SOPHIS-TICATED I AM!
WHAT CAN I SAY, SAKUYA'S A DORKY, GEEKY, DWEEBY, ALL AROUND SQUARE.
WONDER HOW'D HE LOOK IN THE RAW?
HUH ?
THUMPA THUMPA

Another year come and gone. And busy, busy, busy. Every year my stamina seems to ratchet another notch lower. I'm a little worried about that because next year's looking pretty busy, too. Kind fans tell me not to burn myself out. Burn myself out? No way! There's a few volumes in me yet. So, dear fans, don't give up on me! Volume 9 is on the way. I shall continue weaving tales of power and mad demons and the humans that despise them. As always, thank you so much for your letters. I can't answer them all, but I read every one --'cause they are balm for my manga writing soul. ♡

♡♡

Kaimu Tachibana
1996.12